DANISH LINERS
Around the World

Bruce Peter

Danish Liners Around the World
By Bruce Peter

1st edition, 2014
Copyright © 2014 Nautilus Forlag, Copenhagen

ISBN 978-87-90924-54-6

Layout: Ian Smith, Camrose Media
Editor: Pia Barnholdt Kristoffersen
Print: Ulma Press

Printed in Latvia 2014

Nautilus Forlag
Anker Engelunds Vej 1
DK-2800 Lyngby
forlag@polyteknisk.dk
www.nautilusforlag.dk

Nautilus

Contents

Front cover: The first of Maersk Line's epoch-making Triple-E class of container ships, the *Mærsk Mc-Kinney Møller*, passes southbound through the Dover Strait, well loaded with containers, in August 2013. (A.P. Møller-Maersk)

Title page: One of Maersk Line's smaller container ships, the 18,979gt, Odense Lindø-built *Clara Mærsk*, approaches the mouth of the River Tagus and Lisbon in September 2010. (Søren Lund Hviid)

Opposite: The *Mærsk Mc-Kinney Møller* passes beneath Denmark's Great Belt Bridge on her maiden voyage in August 2013. (Søren Lund Hviid)

Prologue

A Voyage on the *Selandia* in 1935

Recollected by Christian Høeg Povelsen (born 1917)

As a newly qualified baker and only 18 years old, like many other young men I had a great desire to go out and see the world. The only way to do this at that time was to go to sea in the Danish Merchant Navy and so I went to the East Asiatic Company's office and was given a job as a baker on board their passenger-cargo liner *Selandia*. As this was my first experience of life at sea, there was a great deal to learn. It was, though, a wonderful opportunity and, as things turned out, I was to spend five years working on board various EAC-owned cargo and passenger liners.

Although the *Selandia* had been in service for 23 years, when I boarded for the first time in February 1935 I felt there was still something special about her. It was also memorable to see the EAC's famous Chairman, H.N. Andersen, who came on board the ship before the departure to wish the Captain a good voyage to Australia. The crew numbered about forty but there were no passengers on board.

The first stage took us to Gothenburg and Oslo, then there was a long segment to Dakar in Senegal, where we enjoyed a few days in port. This was my first foreign encounter and I was taken to visit a nearby village consisting of huts. From Dakar, we continued to the Canary Islands, where the *Selandia* dropped anchor and local traders came on board to sell song birds in cages. From the Canaries, the voyage went direct to Australia via the Cape of Good Hope, taking around forty days. There were no serious problems – except that the Chief Officer had not taken quite enough food supplies on board and so, in the end, we were required to eat emergency rations which didn't taste very nice.

When we arrived in Sydney, we sailed under the newly completed Harbour Bridge, which was very memorable. In fact, the whole experience of arriving there was marvellous and we berthed at a quay just upstream of the bridge. Our stay in Sydney lasted around two weeks and there were a large number of receptions held on board, which meant extra work for the

Opposite: Fishermen on the inner harbour wall in Århus in the foreground of one of Maersk Line's giant container ships. (Søren Lund Hviid)

Below: The world's first ocean-going motor ship, the East Asiatic Company's *Selandia*. (Bruce Peter collection)

galley staff. There were also good sightseeing opportunities, including a visit to Sydney Zoo which was the only place in the world where one could see live sharks in an aquarium. I had a walk too across the Harbour Bridge. While in Sydney, we read in the newspapers that the Danish Kronprins Frederik and Kronprinsesse Ingrid had been married in Stockholm.

From Sydney, the voyage continued to Melbourne, again with a marvellous entry into port, and we stayed there for a little over a week. There were more receptions for guests and freight customers. We noted that one could only see Caucasians in Australian cities as it was forbidden for Aborigines to come within more than three kilometres of the city boundaries. Next we sailed via New Guinea to Hong Kong, where we docked for around five days and, after that, we had a short call in Manila. Then we continued to Cebu, where we lay at anchor for a week as there was no proper dock at which to berth. In Cebu, the locals were very welcoming and we were invited to watch a cock-fighting championship, which was one of the big local attractions. From there, we sailed to Upon, again with a week's stay. Both in Cebu and Upon, we loaded copra, which was delivered to the *Selandia* in barges and local sailing craft. The return journey to Copenhagen was via the Sunda Strait, from which we could see the volcano Krakatoa.

Off Port Elizabeth in South Africa, we experienced the only technical problem of the entire trip when the rudder was damaged. We hove to for three days in very heavy swells which caused the ship to roll alarmingly and made life on board most unpleasant. We got help from Port Elizabeth, the rudder problem was fixed and the voyage continued. The next call was at Dakar, where we took on bunkers and, after that, we continued to Saint Nazaire and Nantes in France. In Nantes, four crew members became sick with malaria. They were taken ashore where all of them died and so none saw Denmark again. When we arrived back in Copenhagen, it was necessary to drop anchor in The Sound for a few days of quarantine because there had been cases of malaria on board.

Even although the *Selandia* had served EAC for many years, by the time I voyaged on her she was still treated with special respect. Apart from the rudder problem, there were no technical difficulties whatsoever during the entire trip. The *Selandia* was a good ship with a pleasant atmosphere and comradeship amongst the crew. My career with EAC lasted until April 1940 when my last ship, the *Jutlandia*, was laid up in Nakskov Fjord because of the Second World War. Although my time at sea was over, I was greatly enriched by my experiences.

Introduction

Denmark is presently one of the world's leading maritime nations; its merchant fleet carries over 10 per cent of global sea trade, and Danish-owned vessels ship nearly a quarter of all goods in and out of Chinese ports. In August 2013, the Copenhagen-headquartered shipping conglomerate A.P. Møller-Maersk – the worlds's largest liner operator – introduced the *Mærsk Mc-Kinney Møller*, the first of a twenty-strong class of epoch-making 'Triple-E' container ships. The biggest and most sophisticated vessels of their type ever conceived, they carry more cargo using significantly less energy per ton shipped than hitherto between China and Europe. Ships such as these make possible our modern world of commerce, characterised by mass production, mass distribution, mass consumerism and globalised supply chains. Yet despite the shipping industry's prominent role in Denmark's economy – not to mention the great size of modern ships themselves – it can seem almost invisible to those not directly involved in its ongoing development and day-to-day operations.

This book will investigate how, since the nineteenth century, Denmark has become the foremost nation in liner shipping. This is perhaps surprising given that, unlike Britain, France and Germany, Denmark lacked the key raw materials of shipbuilding – coal and iron ore, both of which had to be imported. Furthermore, the country had a relatively small population (a little over 2.5 million in the first decade of the twentieth century and around 5.5 million today), meaning that there was a limited domestic market for imported goods. Additionally, as it had few colonial interests, there was no significant captive market for Danish-flagged ships engaged in worldwide trade. Instead, it was necessary to compete on cost and quality by designing, building and operating more efficient tonnage than Europe's Great Powers, who dominated deep-sea shipping until the mid-twentieth century. Therefore, the hypothesis is that a combination of advanced design and business innovation kept Danish liner companies ahead of their competitors.

The story of the development of Danish liner shipping began in the latter nineteenth century following the establishment in 1866 of a new and financially resilient national shipping line, Det Forenede Dampskibs-Selskab (in English, The United Steamship Company, but usually known as DFDS). Its founder, the wholesaler and financier Carl Frederik Tietgen, was a prominent liberal

DFDS was the first large Danish liner company. Its 1,236gt steamship *Christian IX* was built in 1875 by Burmeister & Wain for service between Königsberg, Copenhagen and London. In 1916, she was sold to an Icelandic owner.
(Bruce Peter collection)

DFDS' founder, the whole-saler, financier and business tycoon, C.F. Tietgen. (Bruce Peter collection)

who sought to help Denmark emulate Britain's success in the Industrial Revolution. At that time, the country was militarily and economically weak, having suffered a series of defeats. In the preceding half-century, it had lost control of Norway to Sweden and of the duchies of Slesvig and Holstein to the German Confederation.

At that time, Denmark's main export was livestock, much of which traditionally was exported to Britain via Slesvig. Once Germany annexed it in 1864, Denmark needed to develop its own port infrastructure and a financially resilient steamship company, able to match foreign competitors. C.F. Tietgen therefore used his position as a director of Privatbanken to force a merger between companies involved in the livestock export business belonging to the shipowner C.P.A. Koch and one providing domestic steamer services, run by H.P. Prior. Tietgen also financed the expansion of shipbuilding through his investments in Burmeister & Wain's yard in Copenhagen, the building of tramway and railway lines and the completion of a new port at Esbjerg in Southern Jutland in 1875-78. Indeed, he was a great Svengali figure, masterminding the expansion of Denmark's industrial base and national infrastructure. In so doing, he set the scene for the narrative of this book.

So far as international liner shipping was concerned, Copenhagen was Denmark's major hub, not only for the handling of cargo but also for shipping finance and management. In 1870 DFDS commenced a route from there to Bordeaux, extending this east to Italy in 1884. This was further expanded in 1887 to start and end in Russia, connecting St Petersburg in the Baltic via Copenhagen with Novorossisk, Sevastapol and Odessa on the Black Sea Coast. The opening in 1894 of a Free Harbour (Frihavn) in Copenhagen enabled the trans-shipment of goods without liability to taxation. In the following year, a trans-Atlantic service to New Orleans was inaugurated with calls en route at American East Coast ports, supplementing the existing Baltic, Mediterranean and Black Sea routes. Later, in 1907, a service to South American ports was added and so, by the time the First World War broke out in 1914, DFDS' liner network spanned from the Baltic across the Atlantic and to the Mediterranean. Through being the first major shipping line to be established in Denmark, by default DFDS became the national flag carrier and retained this status until the 1970s when, within a decade, nearly all of its international liner routes closed down and now, once again, the Company is a major player only in North European short-sea shipping.

In 1898, Østasiatisk Kompagni (the East Asiatic Company or EAC for short) began a liner route between Copenhagen, Colombo in Ceylon, Singapore, Bangkok and Hong Kong. EAC was founded in the previous year by Hans Niels Andersen, a former ship's captain whose business career had begun in Bangkok. As DFDS dominated the market for imports of raw materials to Denmark, it was necessary for EAC to develop a different business model, there being room for only one national flag carrier.

EAC's route was soon lengthened to serve Russia at both ends – extending from Copenhagen to St Petersburg and along the Chinese coast to Vladivostok. Calls were also introduced in Japanese ports. From the outset, Andersen's vision was that EAC should be an international conglomerate, controlling everything from the growing of tropical hardwood, palm trees, rice and soya to the manufacture of food and industrial goods. EAC's liner fleet shipped both raw materials and completed products around the world between EAC-owned plantations, factories and wholesalers and so EAC controlled all parts of the value chain.

By 1907, EAC's commercial interests in Siam were producing sufficient cargo that Bangkok required to be served by a separate line. Beforehand, in 1900, EAC began a liner service to South

Africa and in 1905 a route was opened to the West Indies. Next, in 1911, it began to serve the Pacific Coast of the Americas, via Cape Horn. Calls were made in Chile, Peru, Californian and Canadian ports. Once the Panama Canal opened in 1914, the route was split with two branches to serve respectively North and South America. Just before the outbreak of the First World War, EAC introduced a service from Copenhagen round Australia and home via Java. These routes typically were operated jointly with other leading Scandinavian liner companies, such as the Norwegian Wilh. Wilhelmsen, the Swedish East Asiatic Company and Rederi AB Transatlantic.

For EAC, shipping was just one integral component of a far greater industrial empire which spanned the globe from the Far East, via Europe and Southern Africa to the Americas. Notwithstanding relatively primitive communications between EAC's Copenhagen headquarters and subsidiaries located around the world, the conglomerate model worked well and, by the latter 1960s, it had become by far Denmark's largest publicly-quoted company. Thereafter, it expanded at an even greater pace, became burdened with debt and sold its liner shipping interests in 1993 to the A.P. Møller-owned Maersk Line – Denmark's third major liner operator and also arguably the most successful commercial shipping company the world has ever known.

Maersk Line expanded using a further different and distinctive business strategy from DFDS and EAC. Although the shipping entrepreneur Arnold Peter Møller founded the two owning companies, Dampskibsselskabet Svendborg (the Svendborg Steamship Company) and Dampskibsselskabet af 1912 (The Steamship Company of 1912), in 1904 and 1912 respectively, until 1928 these were involved only in tramp shipping. In the 1920s, A.P. Møller began negotiations with his cousin in New York, Hans J. Isbrandtsen, who was also a shipping entrepreneur, to commence a liner service from there via the Panama Canal to the Philippines, Japan and other destinations in the Far East.[1] This was a cross-trading service in which Danish-registered ships attempted to carry goods and some passengers more efficiently and therefore at lower cost than incumbent American, Japanese and British-owned tonnage. Such an initiative demanded very competitive vessels of high capacity and with low fuel consumption.

Furthermore, both EAC and Maersk Line undoubtedly benefited from their owners' international contacts in the Danish diaspora in the United States and the Far East. Hans Isbrandtsen was one such influential Dane living in America and another was Charles E. Sorensen, the Vice-Chairman of Ford which provided cargo in the form of export cars and motor components in the early days of the Maersk Line service.

In Denmark, DFDS, EAC and Maersk were known colloquially as 'Selskabet, Kompagniet og Rederiet.' 'Selskabet' implies an organisation orientated towards the business world, emphasising high finance, corporate take-overs and the prioritisation of shareholder value. By contrast, 'Kompagniet' suggests a version of the sorts of colonial trading company already established by imperial powers such as Britain – for example, the East India Company. 'Rederiet,' on the other hand, infers an organisation centred on shipowning. Of course, all three companies were

The East Asiatic Company's funnel-less motor ships were very distinctive and, between the end of the First World War and the 1960s, they were frequent sights in ports around the world. The *Asia* was built in 1918 by Burmeister & Wain in Copenhagen. After a lengthy career, she was scrapped in Japan in 1958. (Bruce Peter collection)

concerned with raising capital, serving markets and operating ships, yet the slight differences of emphasis implied by their colloquial names were indeed reflected in their managerial ethos and operational practices.

Of these three business models, that of DFDS, importing raw materials for the Danish home market and exporting manufactured goods, was most typical of liner shipping companies worldwide. The EAC and Maersk Line models were far less common, but by no means unique. For example, the British Vestey Group owned cattle ranches in South America and used its Blue Star refrigerated cargo liners to import beef to Britain. Similarly, Elders & Fyffes and the Geest Line brought bananas from their own plantations in the Caribbean. Other British companies, such as the British India Line and Alfred Holt's Blue Funnel Line, cross-traded, but mainly between British colonies around the world. With the end of empire, their services declined and they fell into oblivion. In contrast, EAC was an early example of a successful globalised business which was neither dependent on colonial authority nor on serving only a captive home market.

Liner shipping – the transportation of goods and passengers on regularly timetabled services between fixed ports of call – is a notoriously challenging maritime business sector in which to be involved. Unlike tramping cargo vessels, which sail wherever there is a lucrative enough cargo requiring shipment, liners depart on schedule whether or not they are fully laden. Liner shipping also demands serious investment in the development of related shore-based infrastructures, consisting of agencies to find cargo, warehousing and freight forwarding operations. In addition, less powerful flag nations, such as Denmark, and smaller shipping companies with fewer resources and peripheral influence on port and governmental authorities often suffered flag discrimination. (That is, either being banned from trading between ruling nations and their colonies, or being delayed in foreign ports where priority was given to loading and unloading vessels registered in the ruling nations, while being charged exorbitant port taxes.) Worse still for entrepreneurs wishing to break into the international liner trades, the major deep-sea routes tended to be operated as cartels (known as 'conferences') in which the dominant shipping companies clubbed together to set freight rates and to control port facilities – their strength in numbers theoretically reducing exposure to economic fluctuations and consequently varying amounts of cargo requiring to be shipped. (Here, a parallel may be drawn with pricing agreements among IATA member airlines during the early jet age.) The first liner conference was established in 1875 between London and Calcutta and the concept was subsequently replicated on the routes from Europe to China (1875), Australia (1884), West Africa, South Africa and Brazil (1895). As the Nordic nations were geographically outwith the conference systems' remit, it was possible for Scandinavian lines to supply their own limited home markets but not to call at other European ports regulated by the conferences to pick up or drop off cargo although, over time, that situation gradually changed. On trans-Atlantic and trans-Pacific routes to America, a more liberal conference system was agreed upon, whereby any operator could join so long as they maintained conference freight rates.[2]

As we shall see, Danish operators of cargo liners occasionally chose to work outwith the conference system, undercutting established operators and perhaps benefiting from their customers' frustration with the hegemony of such price-fixing cartels. Above all, the fact that Denmark was in the vanguard of developing and applying marine diesel technology to ocean-going merchant ships was surely of considerable benefit. Diesel engines were lighter, more compact and fuel-efficient than steam reciprocating or turbine machinery, enabling larger cargoes to be carried at lower unit costs.

In 1912 the maiden voyage took place of the pioneering ocean-going motor ship, EAC's passenger-cargo liner *Selandia*, built and engined by Burmeister & Wain in Copenhagen. Her completion and successful entry into service were not only important milestones in the development of modern shipping but also significant historical events which signalled the beginning of a profound shift in industrial culture and the experience of modernity. The first mechanical age, dominated by steam power and heavy engineering, was, arguably, Britain's golden era as the pre-eminent industrial nation. The second machine age was motorised through the parallel development of diesel and electric propulsion systems and these new sources of power heralded 'second wave' industrialisation and the mass manufacture and distribution of consumer goods. Thus, the *Selandia* was a vital symbol of modernity – and also, perhaps, of the

Opposite top: Maersk Line's **Anna Mærsk**, built in 1949 by Eriksberg Mekaniska Verkstads AB in Sweden, is seen receiving tugboat assistance off an American port in the early 1960s. (Bruce Peter collection)

Opposite bottom: The **Lica Mærsk** was a typical example of Maersk Line's cargo liners of the 1950s. Built in Bremen in 1956, she operated for the company until 1975. (Andrew Kilk)

beginning of the end of British industrial dominance and the increasing prominence of other countries, including Denmark.

British industrialisation was often characterised by a *laissez-faire* approach whereby entrepreneurs did only what was strictly necessary to make short-term profits. Thus, the British deep-sea merchant fleet was slow to convert from sail to steam in the second half of the nineteenth century, let alone from steam to diesel in the first half of the twentieth. Notwithstanding Britain's lead in developing and refining the steam engine – the world's first sea-going steam-powered ship, Henry Bell's *Comet*, had her maiden voyage on the River Clyde in 1812 – by the 1860s Britain still had 3.66 million gross tons of sailing ships and only 185,000gt of steamships. Almost all of the steam tonnage was, however, confined to coastal trips and to routes across the Irish Sea and North Sea.[3] This was, in large part, due to there not yet being reliable supplies of coal available in ports further afield.

Denmark's first steamer, the British-built *Caledonia*, was purchased in 1819 – but in the mid-1860s steam accounted for only 3 per cent of the Danish merchant fleet. Later, numbers of steamships increased rapidly and in 1897, for the first time, there were more steamers than sailing craft. Furthermore, there was an absolute geographical split between the two modes; steamers operated largely from Copenhagen and Esbjerg, where imported coal was readily available in bulk, whereas sailing ships were based predominantly in the provinces. Indeed, small ports such as Fanø, Marstal, Svendborg and Dragør remained loyal to sail well into the twentieth century. Yet, during the 1890s, the Danish merchant fleet experienced rapid modernisation, thanks in large

part to the expansion of Danish banking (most notably Privatbanken and Landmansbanken, both of which were significant investors in shipping). By the turn of the century, nearly 60 per cent of tonnage had been acquired in the five-year period since 1895 while, over the same span, 40 per cent of the old fleet had been sold.[4] Most sailing ships were tramps, whereas steamers tended to operate scheduled services across the North Sea and to Baltic ports – the largest of these vessels being operated in the emerging Mediterranean, trans-Atlantic and Far East liner trades. However, the majority of routes were of short duration and agricultural exports formed the most prevalent cargo from Denmark.[5]

Significantly, the 1890s saw the arrival in Danish shipping of a generation of enterprising and dedicated business entrepreneurs – merchants, brokers and Captains – whose accumulated practical experience and internationalist world view enabled them to spot new opportunities and make well-informed evidence-based decisions. H.N. Andersen exemplified this new spirit; from humble origins, in little more than a quarter of a century he had created a large and influential shipping business and was now owner of the most sophisticated and prophetic merchant ship in the world. Burmeister & Wain's engineers, led by Ivar Knudsen, displayed similar visionary ingenuity and entrepreneurship in overcoming significant technical hurdles to make the *Selandia* a successful reality.

It is also arguable that Danish (and Scandinavian) shippers actually benefited from economic downturns which weakened rival operators using less efficient tonnage and often paying higher labour rates to their officers and crews. As Maersk Line's founder A.P. Møller observed: 'I think that shipowners of whatever nationality must realise that they are running a business dependent on market trends and that nothing will be more damaging to that business than to try to suppress these trends. If that happened, everyone under the sun would go into shipping and it would not be lucrative for anyone. Thank Heaven for the bad times, I have always thought.'[6]

In making a success of cross-trading the Danes, and indeed Scandinavian liner operators as a whole, clearly required very cost-effective tonnage and their early adoption and subsequent development of motor ships was an important factor in their success. Furthermore, unlike Europe's major imperial powers, Britain and France, many of whose ships operated in a protected market in which flag discrimination kept foreign competitors out of routes between the colonisers and their colonies, Scandinavian ships operated without subsidy and competed as best they could in less regulated market niches. It is highly arguable, therefore, that in the post-colonial era from the latter 1950s onwards, the benefits of their established reputation for efficiency became increasingly apparent. Moreover, since the 1970s, for better or for worse, the market-led neo-liberal economic policies advocated by Professor Milton Friedman of Harvard Business School have become global orthodoxy and, in such a context, Maersk Line, in particular, has flourished.

It is worth noting, however, that while A.P. Møller-Maersk has benefited from globally-applied market deregulation, its parent companies were constituted in such a way as to keep the majority of shares with voting rights 'in house' (so-called 'A-shares') while external investors mainly buy and trade B-shares without voting rights. While both types are listed on the Copenhagen Stock Exchange, over 75 per cent of A-shares belong to three A.P. Møller funds, plus the private shareholding of the Møller family.[7] This has sheltered the business from profiteering by speculators and enabled a long-term business strategy to be developed. In 1939, A.P. Møller stated in Board minutes that he objected to the idea of the Company's assets, created through his own efforts, being embroiled in stock exchange speculation, which he found damaging and unfruitful. Quoting EAC's founder, H.N. Andersen, he observed that 'we cannot make a living by shaving one another.'[8]

The three major Danish liner companies each responded differently to the containerisation of liner services during the latter 1960s and early 1970s. The shift from general cargo liners to cellular container ships was a necessary one to reduce costs and it helped to bring about our modern global economy. As containers are inter-modal – meaning that trains, trucks, ships and aircraft can carry them – they allow valuable goods to be shipped securely. This, in turn, has enabled the manufacture of consumer goods to be outsourced and supply chains to be spread around the world. Thanks to container transport, goods are now manufactured where it is cheapest, meaning that production for the European and American markets increasingly is carried out in the Far East.

Half a century ago, a conventional general cargo liner spent about half of her time in port, while

Opposite: Maersk Line's E-class container ships marked the end of an era, being the final type to be built in Denmark. Subsequent large vessels for Maersk Line have been constructed at shipyards in South Korea. Here, the ***Estelle Maersk*** is seen leaving Århus. (Søren Lund Hviid)

the average crane could handle only between two and five tons. A nine-man gang of stevedores could shift around eight tons of cargo per hour with 20 per cent of their time spent resting. Therefore, harbour expenses accounted for 70 per cent of ships' operating costs. With the container revolution, time in port declined to 10 per cent and handling costs dropped to below 1 per cent of the cargo's value; the number of port workers employed, meanwhile, fell by 75 per cent. It is thanks to the container that nowadays we can buy seemingly anything anywhere and at any time of the year.[9]

DFDS did not significantly containerise its deep-sea liner routes and closed them one by one, instead concentrating resources on developing a North European ro-ro ferry network. EAC joined various container consortia – ScanStar, ScanDutch and ScanAustral – and contributed a couple of substantial vessels to each of these. Maersk Line, in contrast, came relatively late to full containerisation in the mid-1970s but made a large investment in its own fleet of nine very effective container ships, plus associated terminal infrastructure for operation on its Panama Line between American East Coast ports and the Far East, via the Panama Canal. By containerising late, but not too late, it is arguable that Maersk benefited from others' experiences with 'first generation' container ships and was thus able to improve upon existing designs when developing its own tonnage. Since the 1980s, Maersk Line has undergone thirty years of constant expansion and is nowadays the world's leading company in liner shipping with a fleet of around 600 owned and chartered vessels.

Today, the Danish merchant fleet includes the world's largest container ships. Although they operate between hermetically-sealed ports in out-of-town locations, mostly hidden from the public gaze, these vessels are vital enablers of our modern consumer culture. When the *Emma Mærsk* first docked in Felixstowe in November 2006 at the end of her maiden voyage from China to Europe, she was loaded with toys and other gifts to be sold in the weeks preceding Christmas. Among the cargo inventory of the 3,000 containers unloaded, there were 12,300 MP3 players, 101 leather sofas, 19,500 pairs of socks, 2,900 t-shirts and 17 containers each holding 14gt of Sudoku games, radio-controlled cars and other toys.[10]

The *Emma Mærsk* and her sisters also represent the final generation of liner to be built in Denmark. The more recent Triple-E class is also largely Danish-designed, but constructed in South Korea. We can now look back on more than a century of Danish liner shipping development from *Selandia* to the present day. We can also begin to investigate in more detail how shipping companies in Denmark used leading-edge ship design, technology and business strategies to arrive at their current pre-eminent position in the global liner trades.

Maersk Line's container ships operate liner services spanning the globe, shifting goods in unprecedented quantities and at low economic cost.
(Hanne Hansen)

Chapter 1

The origins and early development of the marine diesel engine

Although the *Selandia* is acknowledged as having been the world's first ocean-going motor ship, the story of the early development of marine diesel engines is necessarily complex. As we shall see, several brilliant engineers and entrepreneurs were involved in the process and a number of primitive experimental motor ships were constructed for use on inland waterways and coastal routes several years before the *Selandia* came to be designed and built. The consequences of her successful maiden voyage from Copenhagen to the Far East in 1912 were, however, profound.

Diesel power came increasingly to dominate the shipping world as the twentieth century progressed and the design of the internal combustion engine was refined to extract greater efficiencies in terms of power output and fuel economy. At the beginning of the 1920s, 95 per cent of all new vessels were fitted with steam propulsion units and only five per cent with diesel engines whereas, by the latter 1960s, the position was nearly reversed (in 1969, 989 new motor ships were completed but only 95 steamships).[11]

Rudolph Diesel, who has been credited with inventing the diesel engine, was born in Paris in 1858, the son of German-born immigrants. Diesel's father, Thomas, had moved there from Augsburg in Bavaria but, with the outbreak of the Franco-Prussian War in 1870, the family were forced to leave, emigrating to live in London. The young Diesel, however, was sent to Augsburg to be educated in German. There, he enrolled at the recently established Industrial School in 1873, meriting a scholarship for further study in engineering at the Royal Bavarian Polytechnic in Munich. Diesel then worked briefly for Sulzer Bros' Machine Works in Winterthur in Switzerland (later on, Sulzer became leading marine engine designers, licensed by Diesel). Thereafter, Professor Carl von Linde, who taught at the Royal Bavarian Polytechnic, employed him to work on the development of refrigeration equipment. This work gave Diesel a solid understanding of thermodynamics and, observing that a typical steam engine was only 15-19 per cent thermodynamically efficient, meaning that up to 90 per cent of energy was wasted, he began work to develop an engine with a far higher efficiency ratio.[12]

Rudolph Diesel, photographed around 1893. (MAN/Diesel House)

In his design, fuel was injected into the cylinder at the end of the compression and ignited by the high temperature resulting from this. Diesel patented his invention in 1892 and, in the same year, he published a paper entitled 'Theory and Design of an Economical Heat Engine to replace Steam Engines and Today's Internal Combustion Engines.' In the final paragraph, he hinted at the great possibilities he believed his design would offer:

> 'The advantages of this engine are obvious. It does not require a boiler, a funnel or open fires. Owing to its small size and simplicity, it is superior to other existing engines, and these factors alone would justify replacement of existing engines with the new one. Another factor is the saving of fuel... The more recent powerful marine propulsion plants occupy between four- and five-eighths of the space in a ship. The weight of machines, boilers and coal takes up the major part of the carrying capacity of the ship. It is hardly possible to assess what can be saved in this respect by smaller engines, a lower consumption of coal and the omission of boilers. Ships could be much smaller despite equally powerful engines, and yet carry a higher payload and be faster.'[13]

Diesel was severely criticised for his unorthodox theories regarding thermodynamics but, nonetheless, from 1893 until 1897 Heinrich von Buz, the Chairman of the Maschinenfabrik Augsburg (later known as MAN) gave him the opportunity to develop and test his ideas. Thereafter, the first diesel engine was demonstrated to the public in 1894 and discussions began about how it could be modified for use as a marine propulsion unit. The prototype was already twice as economical as a similarly dimensioned steam engine and one-and-a-half times as economical as the other internal combustion engines of its day.[14]

In the same year, Diesel and an American brewery magnate, Adolphus Busch, signed a licensing agreement to develop engines for static usage to power industrial plant. Diesel, however, wanted the entire engineering world to share his invention and so he granted further licences to reputable firms in Belgium, Denmark, France, Britain, Italy, Austria-Hungary, Russia, Sweden and Switzerland. Thus, he laid the foundation for the worldwide distribution of diesel engines for many diverse purposes. One consequence of this situation was that Diesel himself was forced to refrain personally from designing engines since licensing agreements had been signed with many competing companies and hence he was unable to render technical assistance to one firm without risking protests and legal action from the others.

In 1904, Diesel visited the United States for the first time. The diesel engine company founded by Adolphus Busch had, meanwhile, overcome initial teething troubles with their prototype engines and had even managed to build a number of reliable examples to power stationary plants. Although the United States Navy were interested in the engine – particularly for submarines – the design and construction of an effective marine diesel in America was yet to commence. Diesel was able to report to Busch, however, that some success had been achieved in their development in Europe.

In 1898-99, Diesel's French licensee, Frédéric Dyckhoff, a design engineer from Bar-le-Duc, had developed an experimental reversible 15 hp diesel engine. After further refinement, another example, produced jointly with Adrian Brochet, was installed in a boat named *Petit Pierre*, completed in 1903. This was a horizontal opposed-piston engine developing 25 hp. Later, MAN solved the problem of reversibility in a four-cylinder 300 hp design, examples of which were installed in two French submarines, the *Circé* and the *Calypso*. Later still, Sulzer made a reversible two-stroke engine and this was displayed at the 1906 World Exhibition in Milan.[15]

Until the *Selandia*, the engines of motor ships were designed around steam reciprocating technology and so their machinery spaces did not appear significantly different from those of steamships of their day. Arguably, the first commercial motor vessel was the *Vandal*, a triple-screw tanker built by Ludwig Nobel of St Petersburg in 1904 for use on the Volga River and Caspian Sea. Her engines were non-reversible and were coupled to an electric drive, giving an output of 300 kW. (The availability of appropriate oil distillates in the Caspian and Volga regions was, of course, a key reason for Nobel's initiative.)

In 1910, the Dutch-built tanker *Vulcanus* was constructed for coastal service and, therefore, is arguably a serious rival to the *Selandia*'s claim to be the ocean-going motor ship pioneer. She had two 6-cylinder 4-stroke Werkspoor engines which could develop 510 hp. The cylinders had a 40 cm bore and a 60 cm stroke and, running at 180 revolutions per minute, they could drive her at 8.4 knots. In common with the vessels cited above, however, her machinery was based upon steam reciprocating design precedents and she was even fitted with steam-driven auxiliaries. Because her main engines were direct-drive, two separate camshafts were fitted to enable them to supply a reverse thrust.

By 1911, there were twelve Russian-owned motor tankers on the River Volga and the Caspian Sea, four German tankers, one British and one American tanker (which sailed on the Great Lakes). Additionally, the Russians had 22 motor tugs, nine cargo vessels and, furthermore, a significant number of naval craft – particularly submarines – with primitive internal combustion machinery. All of these vessels were, however, unreliable and with limited sailing range as they were dependent on a fuel supply network which, so far as shipping was concerned, was still in its infancy. Therefore, they were unable to deviate from their regular routes.[16]

Unfortunately for Diesel, there were other claimants to the title of having invented what is now universally known as the diesel engine. One was an Englishman, Herbert Akroyd-Stuart (1864-

1927), who in 1886 had used paraffin to power a prototype engine similar to Diesel's. After further development work, he patented his design in 1890 and, thereafter, engines were manufactured by Richard Hornsby & Sons of Grantham. Rudolph Diesel's design was patented two years later, but it was Akroyd-Stuart's fuel injection system which initially came to be favoured by the majority of engine manufacturers. Furthermore, in 1892, Akroyd-Stuart and Hornsby had demonstrated a high-compression ignition system a full five years before Diesel built his high-compression prototype engine in Augsburg in 1897.[17]

Of course, Britain and Germany increasingly were industrial and military rivals. Rudolph Diesel appears to have benefited from his cosmopolitan background, being much better socially connected than his British rival, and so his status as the officially recognised inventor of the diesel engine came to dominate. The fact was that, from the outset, Diesel had acknowledged that his proposed engine design might have great potential for ship propulsion and this made him a hero for commentators on marine engineering and ship design innovation in Britain as well as on the Continent. In particular, A.P. Chalkley, the founding editor of *The Motor Ship* which subsequently became a leading shipping industry journal, was invariably loyal to Diesel, whom he knew as a personal acquaintance and whom he greatly admired.

On the night of 29-30 September 1913, Diesel died in suspicious circumstances while crossing from Amsterdam to Harwich on board the steamer *Dresden*, *en route* to a meeting in London, and his body was found ten days later in the North Sea by the crew of a Dutch coaster. Consequently, he never witnessed the part his engine played in the First World War. He was only 58 years old and, had he not either been killed or, more likely, committed suicide, it would have been quite possible for him to have lived long enough to witness his engine's conquest of the world's oceans.[18]

Towards the close of 1911, A.P. Chalkley completed his first book entitled 'Marine Diesel Engines.' The book was published in the spring of 1912 and, despite the fact that it thoroughly covered numerous projects for marine diesel propulsion, including detailed plans for installations in ships of all sizes, not one word was mentioned concerning the *Selandia*'s builder, Burmeister & Wain.[19] Most people in shipping and engine-building circles, however, were well aware that this firm, already established for three-quarters of a century in Copenhagen, had been one of

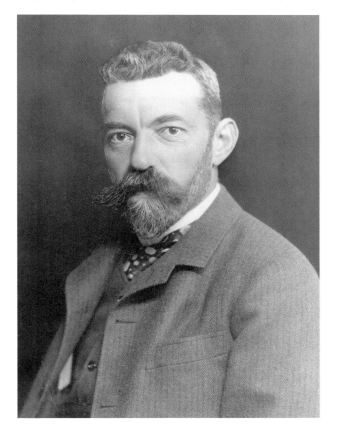

Ivar Knudsen, Burmeister & Wain's forward-looking Technical Director, whose effort helped make marine diesel propulsion viable. (MAN/Diesel House)

the earliest to co-operate with Diesel in the development of his engine. At the same time as Chalkley's book was on its way to the printer, the hull of what is generally regarded as being the world's first – and certainly by far the most technically sophisticated – ocean-going motor ship was being completed at B&W's yard. By the time the book was published, the *Selandia* had already started on her maiden voyage to the acclaim of virtually everyone involved in European merchant shipping.[20]

B&W's early interest in the diesel engine was thanks largely to David Halley. As with Carl Christian Burmeister's business partner, William Wain, Halley was of British origin. Born near Dunfermline in Scotland in 1852, he had studied engineering at The Andersonian University in Glasgow, thereafter joining the drawing office of Robert Napier's shipyard in Govan. Halley moved to Copenhagen in 1882 to work for B&W where he was was quickly promoted, becoming a director in 1887. In February 1894, he received a letter from Rudolph Diesel about the possibility of developing the diesel engine as a stationary prime mover. Although Halley's senior colleagues at B&W were sceptical due to the complexity of the technological development required to make Diesel's engine work reliably and profitably, he responded that B&W was indeed interested in Diesel's project. His caveat was that B&W would need to see a

completed engine being demonstrated in Augsburg before agreeing to co-operate. It was not until 1897, however, two years after Halley had died, that his former colleague, Ivar Knudsen, visited Augsburg to observe one- and two-cylinder test engines in operation.[21]

Ivar Knudsen was born in 1861 in a small village close to Kalø, to the north of Århus in Eastern Jutland. He learned his trade as a mechanical engineer in Caroc & Leth's Engine Company in Århus. Having studied at the Polyteknisk Læreanstalt in Copenhagen, he subsequently found employment with the municipal authority's Engineering Department. From there, he was head-hunted by B&W's Managing Director, G.A. Hagemann, who employed him as Chief Mechanical Engineer in 1895.[22] Only three years thereafter, he became Technical Director of B&W's engine works. On 28 January 1898, Knudsen and Diesel signed a contract licensing B&W to use Diesel's patent to develop engines of all sizes.[23] Between entering into a licensing agreement with Diesel and building a working marine diesel engine, Knudsen and Diesel kept in regular contact to discuss developments. Diesel characterised Knudsen as 'the one man in the whole world who not only understands my ideas best but also has the richest possibilities to bring them into reality.'[24]

As B&W was also involved in the construction of large stationary steam engines and, furthermore, the shipyard and engine works were being rebuilt and expanded, there was little opportunity to begin immediate development of a marine diesel engine in the main engine assembly shed. Another factor militating against Danish enthusiasm for diesel engines was that fuel oil was, at that time, very expensive in Denmark due to a high import duty. This notwithstanding, having completed the expansion of its premises B&W worked hard to develop a range of four-stroke diesel engines, initially for use on *terra firma* and subsequently to power ships. Such engines have four piston movements (or 'strokes') in each combustion

Above: The founder of the East Asiatic Company, H.N. Andersen, shown in a portrait from the 1930s, towards the end of his long and eventful life. (Bruce Peter collection)

Right:
In Siam (now Thailand), H.N. Andersen's EAC invested in forestry plantations which provided raw materials, such as copra and timber, for EAC's ships to transport to Europe. (Bruce Peter collection, from 'Udvikling')

cycle – an air intake stroke, a compression stroke, an ignition stroke and an exhaust stroke.

In 1907, discussions began between the directorates of the East Asiatic Company and Burmeister & Wain on the possibility of constructing a diesel-powered merchant ship. When B&W said that it was willing to build such a vessel measuring around 400gt, the EAC Chairman, Hans Niels Andersen, replied with a question: 'If 400gt, why not 1,000gt?'[25] When B&W accepted this challenge, EAC wanted to know whether it might be possible to build a 3,000gt ship and, within a short time, it was agreed that B&W should build one of approximately 5,000gt.[26] This would be powered by an engine installation consisting of two 8-cylinder 4-stroke diesels, generating 2,500 hp and driving twin screws to achieve a service speed of 11 knots. In quick succession, three such vessels were ordered by EAC – two to be built by B&W in Copenhagen and a third by Barclay, Curle & Co. in Glasgow – this shipyard having already completed a number of steamers for the EAC fleet. A leading force in taking EAC in this new and innovative direction was its ambitious Director of Shipping Christian Schmiegelow (1856-1949). He had been head-hunted by H.N. Andersen from the tramp shipping company Dampskibsselskabet Torm, which he had co-founded in 1888. Schmiegelow joined EAC's Board in 1909 and oversaw the *Selandia*'s design, construction and delivery. Thereafter, he remained a leading Board member for 29 years.

David Halley, Ivar Knudsen, H.N. Andersen and Christian Schmiegelow foresaw the future. The design, building and successful introduction of the *Selandia* would have a profound effect on the subsequent development of international shipping, helping to place Denmark in an increasingly advantageous position in the liner trades during the ensuing decades.

Bangkok, where Andersen began his business career, showing the Oriental Hotel and, on the right, Andersen & Co.'s original building. (Bruce Peter collection, from 'Tilbageblik')

Chapter 2

The development of Danish liner services and the impact of *Selandia*

The East Asiatic Company was a relatively young business at the time the *Selandia* was ordered. H.N. Andersen had founded the firm in 1897, his career until that point having involved the roles of Captain, merchant and diplomat for the Siamese Government. Born in 1852 in Nakskov, a harbour town in Lolland in Southern Denmark, from a young age he had shown a liking for the sea and a curiosity about ships – not surprising given that Nakskov's port became increasingly busy during his formative years in the 1860s. Having excelled at school, he briefly followed his elder brother's career path by becoming an apprentice shipbuilder, but he soon found this not to be sufficiently exciting and so, in 1872, he went to sea on a voyage to South America on the newly completed brig *Mars*, having previously been involved in her construction. More voyages followed – most significantly to the Far East in 1876 on the barque *Nicoline*. There he stayed, basing himself in Bangkok and crewing vessels trading mainly in the Straits of Malacca. In 1884, he gained his Master's Certificate.[27]

It was Andersen's vision to form a trading and shipping company, following the British model. The British colony Hong Kong was the centre of mercantilism in South East Asia at that time, but Andersen observed that the British controlled everything there, leaving no opportunities for a young Danish entrepreneur such as himself. In Bangkok, however, he found greater possibilities for business development as it was a relatively small and primitive place in comparison with Hong Kong but surrounded by rich natural resources which could be exploited – in particular, forests of hardwood. As an experiment, Andersen decided to charter the barque *Thoon Kramon*, on which he had previously served as First Officer, and to sail her to Europe with a cargo of teak, using a South East Asian crew. This voyage made a 93 per cent profit for Andersen and his backers and, upon the *Thoon Kramon*'s successful return to Bangkok in 1884, there was widespread delight that his local initiative had proven that a ship crewed and operated from Siam could trade successfully with Europe.[28]

Thereafter, King Chulalongkorn of Siam decided that the *Thoon Kramon* should become a sail training ship to prepare more Siamese crewmen for lives at sea. H.N. Andersen, meanwhile, shifted his activities to business development on *terra firma*. In Bangkok, he formed Andersen & Co to purchase the Oriental Hotel, surrounding jungle and swampland. Having secured a bank loan, he hired labour to clear this, enabling the construction of a new main street, Oriental Avenue, and on adjacent land he developed an estate of villas. He also built his new trading company's headquarters there, next to the hotel.

In 1887, the Oriental Hotel was rebuilt to attract tourists and businessmen – and King Chulalongkorn attended the re-opening ceremony. Next, in 1890, Andersen purchased his first ship, the small steamer *Crocodil*, to transport teak in local trade; Andersen was now a shipowner and soon he also possessed forestry rights covering 20,000 hectares north of Bangkok and also a sawmill. By 1890 his profit per annum was 26,000 dollars and, by 1896, this had risen to over 42,000 dollars.

In May 1892, Andersen was in Copenhagen during a European business trip and there he took the opportunity to make the acquaintance of Danish bankers as he sought to raise capital to fund a projected steamship line from Copenhagen to Far Eastern ports; this was a visionary project which would add a new dimension to Denmark's overseas trading possibilities. Both Carl Frederik Tietgen – the all-powerful Chairman of Privatbanken and the shipping line DFDS – and Isak Glückstadt – a director of Landmandsbanken – refused him funds, but Glückstadt was at least sufficiently curious about Andersen's activities in Bangkok to send an observer 'Out East' to gain a first-hand impression of the scale and robustness of his business interests there.

C.F. Tietgen's refusal to support Andersen's initiative was a cruel blow as Tietgen was the most powerful figure in Danish business in the second half of the nineteenth century. Born in Odense in 1829, as a young man he had worked for a Danish merchant in Manchester when the Industrial Revolution in Britain was at its height. Later, he entered the banking world as a founding director of Privatbanken, established in 1857, and thereafter he helped to create and finance several leading Danish businesses including engineering an amalgamation of shipping interests in 1866 to form Det Forenede Dampskibs-Selskab (DFDS); this grew into one of the world's largest shipping lines, controlling the largest proportion of Denmark's trade by sea. He was also involved in the financing and management of the Burmeister & Wain shipyard and marine engine builders, Det danske Spritfabrikker (Danish Distillers), De danske Sukkerfabrikker (Danish Sugar Factories), De Forenede Bryggerier (United Breweries) and, later, Københavns Telefon Aktieselskab (The Copenhagen Telephone Company). In short, he – more than anybody else – was the driving force behind Danish industrialisation.[29] Unfortunately, Tietgen also gained a reputation for being dictatorial and his fearsome demeanour, coupled with his unwillingness to compromise, gave Isak Glückstadt of Landmandsbanken an increasing influence over Danish business life as the century drew to a close. Born in Fredericia 1839 and the son of a merchant, Glückstadt, like Tietgen, had a keen eye for a lucrative business proposal.

Copenhagen Free Harbour

One such grand project was to establish a Free Harbour in Copenhagen to enable goods to be trans-shipped without liability to import tax. Since 1888, Hamburg had possessed such a facility and the subsequent opening of the Kiel Canal between the Baltic and North Seas would give the port significant advantages over Copenhagen. As Tietgen's shipping company, DFDS, operated from Copenhagen's historic Inner Harbour, he was strongly against the development of a free port. Moreover, the bulk of DFDS' network was focused on Danish domestic routes, North Sea agricultural exports services and the Baltic trades although in 1870 a cargo route had been opened to the Western Mediterranean. (Thereafter, in 1887, DFDS' Mediterranean services expanded East, with calls in Black Sea ports.[30]) As Tietgen showed neither interest in expanding DFDS' route network far beyond Europe nor in using a free port in Copenhagen, it was Glückstadt alone who carried the idea forward. In H.N. Andersen, he must have reasoned that he had a potentially useful ally and customer – hence his desire to find out more about Andersen's business activities in Bangkok.

During his 1892 visit to Copenhagen, H.N. Andersen also attended a reception at Amalienborg Palace, where he delivered a golden wedding anniversary gift to King Christian IX and Queen

Dampskibsselskabet Thingvalla was founded in 1880, when the company put the steamship *Thingvalla* in trans-Atlantic liner service from Copenhagen via Kristiania to New York. This marked the beginning of 'deep sea' liner services under the Danish flag. The *Thingvalla* linked Scandinavia and the USA until 1900.
(Museet for Søfart)

Louise. There, he met Prince Valdemar and his wife, Princess Marie – and they immediately became good friends. Thanks to Andersen's combination of natural charm and strong desire to be taken seriously, he consequently gained powerful allies in the Danish Royal Family, in addition to those he had already cultivated in Siam. Andersen had previously met other members of the Danish Royal House, however, as in 1890 Prince Nicolaj, the future Czar of Russia, and Prince Georg of Greece had visited Siam. Andersen joined the Royal Party at the invitation of King Chulalongkorn to thank him for helping the Siamese Navy to acquire new ships at a favourable price. (Subsequently, in 1893, Andersen travelled again to Europe, this time on a diplomatic mission on behalf of the Siamese Government who were worried about French aggression on the border with Indo-China; this clearly demonstrates the high regard in which he was held there.)

When the Copenhagen Free Harbour was opened in 1894, DFDS initially refused to use it and this led to King Christian IX remonstrating with Tietgen to the effect that it was his national duty to support an initiative which would have positive effects for Denmark as a whole; Tietgen had made the mistake of believing that his own business interests and Denmark's national interests were synonymous. This situation can only have further benefited H.N. Andersen who was an enthusiastic supporter of the new harbour development. With finance from Landmandsbanken, Andersen & Co's fleet of sailing ships grew and, in Copenhagen, they berthed in the Free Harbour, where the Company also established its Danish offices.

Meanwhile, as Tietgen and DFDS were apparently unwilling to cooperate, the Copenhagen Free Harbour Company began planning its own liner service to North America to help build traffic

Above: DFDS took over Dampskibsselskabet Thingvalla's activities in 1898, renaming the operation as the Scandinavia-America Line. The **Norge**, formerly owned by Thingvalla, is shown in DFDS' livery. Tragically, in 1904, she foundered in the Atlantic with considerable loss of life.
(Museet for Søfart)

Right: The DFDS cargo liner **Arkansas**; Burmeister & Wain-built in 1897, she remained in the fleet until 1933 when sold for scrapping.
(Museet for Søfart)

through the newly completed wharfs. Eventually, Tietgen was persuaded to engage by DFDS' agent in Russia, Konsul Bornholdt, who observed that America was beginning a period of exponential economic and population growth. Tietgen readily admitted that there would be no difficulty in finding enough eastbound cargo in the form of animal feed, but he feared that the American market was insufficiently developed to fill westbound sailings with European manufactured goods. Bornholdt, however, was most keen that DFDS should expand its network to serve America as, with mass migration from Europe underway, it appeared that the USA had the potential quickly to become the most important new source of revenue for the Company. By making use of Copenhagen Free Harbour, goods could be trans-shipped from one DFDS vessel to another and continue to ports in the Baltic and Mediterranean. Moreover, the United States was beginning to emerge as an economic power with which to be reckoned. In 1866, its trade surplus was 120 million dollars – but by 1900, this figure quadrupled.

The major diplomatic hurdle to be overcome was Tietgen's dislike and distrust of his main banking rival, Glückstadt. It was a Copenhagen broker called Thomas Schøller who was a business acquaintance of both Tietgen and Glückstadt who acted as diplomat to reach an acceptable agreement between the two financiers. Consequently, in September 1895, an understanding was reached. DFDS stated that it would order four steamers of approximately 3,000gt each for service between the Free Harbour and New Orleans. Until such time as these purpose-built vessels were completed, DFDS would charter sufficient suitable tonnage to enable a monthly trans-Atlantic service to be operated. Furthermore, DFDS promised the Copenhagen Free Harbour Company that it would ship goods to and from the Free Harbour for the same freight rates as from its existing berths in Copenhagen. If a minimum of half the freight capacity of a ship were available in the Free Harbour, the vessel would berth there and any additional cargo would be delivered by barge from DFDS' existing regular berths. If most cargo were at the existing berths, barges would move any waiting at the Free Harbour. The Copenhagen Free Harbour Company would pay for trans-shipment from the Free Harbour and DFDS would pay for moving there.[31]

This pioneering Danish trans-Atlantic liner service began in October 1895 with the chartered steamer *Malabar* and thereafter she was joined by DFDS-owned tonnage, switched from the

A pre-First World War view of the Clyde-built DFDS Scandinavia-America Line steamer **United States** leaving Copenhagen Free Harbour for Kristiania and New York.
(Museet for Søfart)

Company's Mediterranean and Black Sea routes. The service expanded quickly with the delivery of purpose-built steamers. These were the 3,648gt *Arkansas*, built by Burmeister & Wain and delivered in 1897, and the 4,401gt *Florida*, delivered from William Dobson's shipyard in Newcastle-upon-Tyne – the largest vessel in the DFDS fleet at that time. Soon additional calls were introduced at New York, Boston, Philadelphia and Baltimore and the service gradually became one of DFDS' most lucrative routes.[32]

DFDS quickly strengthened its presence on the North Atlantic through its take-over in 1898 of the loss-making Dampskibsselskabet Thingvalla which, since 1880, had operated four sail-assisted steamships carrying migrants and cargo from Stettin, Copenhagen and Kristiansand to New York. This was renamed the Scandinavia-America Line and, as its existing fleet was ageing, three substantial new 10,012gt passenger and cargo steamers were shortly ordered from Alexander Stephen & Sons of Glasgow – the *Oscar II*, the *Hellig Olav* and the *United States* – for delivery in 1902-03. Thus, notwithstanding initial reluctance, DFDS quickly established itself as Scandinavia's principal trans-Atlantic liner company.[33] Its management soon found out that running a trans-Atlantic passenger service required substantial resources; competition was tough

Above: The DFDS trans-Atlantic cargo vessel **Arkansas**.
(Museet for Søfart)

Right: Scandinavia-America Line's **United States**, delivered in 1903 by Alexander Stephen & Sons of Linthouse, Glasgow.
(Bruce Peter collection)

The ***Hellig Olav*** undergoing
sea trials on the 'measured
mile' off Arran on the Firth
of Clyde in March 1903.
(Bruce Peter collection)

and, as numbers of emigrants fluctuated from year to year, profitability was at best unpredictable. Worse still, on 28 June 1904, the ageing migant carrier *Norge*, inherited by DFDS from Thingvalla, sank rapidly after striking St Helens Reef, a ridge of stone protruding from the ocean floor near Rockall to the west of the Hebrides, in foggy weather while *en route* from Kristansand to New York.[34] Of her 727 passengers and 68 crew, 582 of the former and 45 of the latter drowned in what was the worst ever maritime disaster in Danish history.

The East Asiatic Company

By the mid-1890s, H.N. Andersen was married with three young children of school age and so, in 1896, he returned from Bangkok to Denmark, leaving a colleague, Emanuel Kinch, in charge of his firm's operations in South East Asia. In March 1897, Andersen founded the Østasiatiske Kompagni (East Asiatic Company, or EAC) in Copenhagen to inaugurate his long-planned steamship line to the Far East. At the same time, a rice mill was established in Gothenburg – and Landmandsbanken largely financed both the line and the mill. Andersen & Co's forestry plantation in Siam, plus the new rice mill, gave the new EAC two staple cargoes – hardwood and rice – to import in bulk to Scandinavia. Later, EAC established rubber and palm tree plantations on the Malayan Peninsula (the latter yielding copra – the white of coconut shells). In 1903, EAC invested in A/S Københavns Oliefabrik (The Copenhagen Oil Factory) which milled copra to produce palm oil. Later still, in 1908, A/S Dansk Sojakagefabrik (The Danish Soya Bean Cake Factory) began to process imported soya beans into oil and food. Unlike DFDS, which was entirely controlled from Copenhagen, Andersen's remarkable global vision for EAC was that it should be a multi-national conglomerate with business interests both in Denmark and in South East Asia, the various subsidiaries generating cargoes for the Company's liners to transport in both directions. To that end, Andersen & Co was absorbed into EAC upon the latter's foundation.

To operate EAC's new liner service, three new and relatively large steamers – the 3,875gt *Siam*,

The East Asiatic Company's first passenger- and cargo liner, the 3,875gt steamship *Siam* inaugurated EAC's liner service to the Far East. She served on the route until 1912 whereupon she was sold to Japan. Here, she is seen in Copenhagen Free Harbour at the beginning of her career under the Danish flag. (Bruce Peter collection)

the 4,847gt *Malaya* and the 4,075gt *Cathay* – were ordered respectively from Flensburger Schiffbau-Gesellschaft in Germany, William Hamilton & Co. of Glasgow and Ramage & Ferguson of Leith, both in Scotland, who additionally constructed a smaller coastal steamer, the 764gt *Natuna*. The *Siam* left Copenhagen on her first voyage 'Out East' on 2 March 1898 and thereafter EAC expanded rapidly. The Company was admitted to The Straits, China and Japan Conference, an alliance of liner companies monopolising trade between Europe and South-East Asian ports.

By controlling the production of raw materials, their shipment for processing and their subsequent use in manufacturing processes, it was possible both to reduce risk, avoid flag discrimination and – to an extent – cushion against the extremes of the economic cycle (as profits made by subsidiaries in one area could offset losses in another). Over time, EAC did indeed grow into a vast conglomerate with subsidiaries located all over the world. Managing such a business in the era before modern instant communications depended upon each subsidiary being largely self-sustaining with reliable leadership. Unfortunately, EAC's Bangkok representative, Emanuel Kinch, was found to have been increasingly exaggerating the value of the Company's assets and profitability in Siam in his accounts over a seven-year period between 1897 and 1904. When this finally came to light in Copenhagen, a scandal was only narrowly averted and serious embarrassment was caused to H.N. Andersen and EAC's directorate; there was even a suggestion that DFDS might take EAC over but this did not happen as, during the ensuing years, good profits were made in a new area of expansion – Russia – and these offset poorer results in the Far East. Kinch apologised for his dishonesty – but the affair did show the problems Andersen had in attempting to keep control over a global business in the early years of the twentieth century. In an era when business travel meant sea voyages lasting many weeks, it was necessary to give significant autonomy to the managements of overseas subsidiaries and to trust them to report their results to Head Office in an honest manner.[35]

In 1899 a new subsidiary, the Russian East Asiatic Company, had been founded, with EAC owning 50 per cent of the share capital, introducing services from Russian and other Baltic ports to the Far East. During the Russo-Japanese war of 1904-05, its steamers additionally acted as troop transports between St Petersburg and Vladivostok – a highly lucrative enterprise. Subsequently, there was an increase in emigration from the Eastern Baltic States to North America, and so the focus shifted to concentrate on a trans-Atlantic passenger and cargo service, operating under the Russian American Line banner in competition with DFDS' Scandinavia-America Line. This development meant that EAC-controlled liner services now spanned much of the globe from the East Coast of North America, via Northern Europe, to the Far East. By the time the EAC's pioneering motor ship *Selandia* was ordered, the Company had already operated 64 steamers and its current fleet (including the ships of subsidiary companies) consisted of 36 vessels. Although Denmark's total share of world tonnage increased from 1.3 per cent to 1.9 per cent during the 1890s, the merchant fleet was still only the eleventh largest (the leading fleets were those of Britain – owning almost half of the world's tonnage – followed by Germany, Norway, France, The Netherlands and the United States). Since Danes numbered only 0.2 per cent of the global population, in terms of tonnage per capita their fleet was surpassed only by Norway, The Netherlands and Britain.[36]

From steam to diesel

The *Selandia* was launched on 4 November 1911. Built for the transport of general cargo and passengers, the vessel measured 370 by 53 feet and had a conventional hull with a straight stem and a counter stern. Her superstructure was split into two sections with passengers and officers in a two-deck-high block located amidships and crew in a further deckhouse two-thirds aft with a cargo hatch between. Her accommodation for 20 First Class passengers was rather luxurious for a vessel of her type and era. Every two cabins had a shared toilet and bath and, adjacent, there were rooms for two servants (only wealthy travellers, such as aristocrats, financiers, merchants and diplomats, could afford a lengthy voyage 'Out East').

Carl Brummer, a distinguished Copenhagen-based architect, designed the *Selandia*'s interiors. His work on *terra firma* tended towards the neo-classical with only restrained baroque decorative flourishes. He was well-connected in the shipping world, having recently carried out design work for new offices at the Burmeister & Wain shipyard and, while drawing up *Selandia*'s interiors, he was simultaneously working on the passenger accommodation for DFDS' new trans-Atlantic passenger liner *Frederik VIII*, then under construction in Stettin for Scandinavia-America Line service. *The Shipping World* was impressed by Brummer's designs for the *Selandia*, reporting that:

> 'The whole of the midship erection, which is intended for passengers, is carried out in a specially fine yacht style… The large and bright cabins and rooms of the ship give one the feeling of being in a private home and not on a ship. The cabins are of exceptional size; each is fitted with a mechanical sofa which can be made up as a bed, a wash stand, writing table and chairs. There are also a large and elegant dining saloon and a ladies' saloon, all in white. The space aft of the dining saloon forms a hall, and a staircase gives access to the rooms above, where is found a smoking saloon and several specially equipped and furnished rooms, which combine sleeping-room and sitting-room. Moreover, there is a wireless telegraph on board and an extra smoking saloon is exclusively reserved for the ship's officers. On the whole, everything has been done to procure as fine, tasteful and convenient rooms as possible without attempting anything in the way of superfluous luxury.'[37]

Two cargo hatches were located ahead of the forward superstructure: one was amidships and the other aft of the crew deckhouse, hence except in one respect – her lack of a funnel – she looked very similar to other combined cargo and passenger liners of her era. Instead, diesel exhaust was carried up thin pipes attached to the mainmast, giving the vessel more the look of a sailing ship and rather suggesting that funnels might come to be viewed as a brief aberration in the wider history of shipping. Of course, the reverse was the case as, by 1912, funnels had come to be viewed as being of symbolic importance, signifying seaworthiness, strength and virility. (The fact that the *Titanic* had four funnels did not prevent her from sinking only two months after the funnel-less *Selandia* had been completed, however.)

The *Selandia* – and her subsequent near sisters – proved notably seaworthy vessels when fully laden but, as their engines were located aft of amidships, they tended to ride high at the bow when sailing without cargo and, consequently, gave an uncomfortable passage.

The *Selandia* ran trials in The Sound on 14 February 1912. As the water was iced over, she was unable to achieve her maximum potential – but the top recorded speed of 12.2 knots still exceeded the contracted 11-knot requirement and, moreover, she used only nine tons of fuel per day. Furthermore, it was claimed that her engine room could be manned by as few as eight men plus two boys, whereas a coal-fired steamer would additionally have employed dozens of stokers;

not only did this represent a significant cost saving but it also removed one of the dirtiest, most physically wearing and dangerous shipboard jobs.[38]

The East Asiatic Company was delighted with the *Selandia*'s initial performance and so she was handed over on 17 February 1912. After nearly a week spent taking on stores and initial cargo, on 22 February she departed on her maiden voyage to the Far East.[39] Joining EAC's Chairman, H.N. Andersen, on board for the initial leg through The Sound from Copenhagen to Helsingør were Kronprins Christian and Kronprinsesse Alexandrine. Thus, the European press paid closer attention to the ship than might otherwise have been the case without such prominent Royal patronage. Thereafter, the *Selandia* raised significant interest amongst the great imperial powers who, for the first time, began to take seriously the propulsion of both merchant and naval vessels using oil-fired diesel engines instead of coal-fired steam boilers. As B&W used considerable human and financial resources to develop and build *Selandia*'s engines, it was vital that her maiden voyage should be a success. A punctual and reliable performance had the potential not only to recoup the investment but also to place B&W in a prime position for further orders for similar vessels from other shipowners besides EAC.

The Royal Party and invited guests disembarked in Helsingør and the *Selandia* continued to Nørresundby on the Limfjord in Northern Jutland where she loaded a cargo of cement from EAC's factory there. *En route* East the *Selandia* called at London on 27 February, not to collect cargo but to enable British dignitaries to inspect her engine room. Her arrival on the Thames coincided with a miners' strike in Britain, leading to a great many steamships being temporarily laid up as there were no bunkers available. This situation only increased the attention paid to the *Selandia* as her departure was unaffected by a lack of coal.[40] On 1 March 1912, the First Sea Lord, Winston Churchill, was welcomed on board by H.N. Andersen and Ivar Knudsen. Churchill, who was at that time a Liberal politician and a keen supporter of free trade (so long as rival nations did not seriously threaten British hegemony), congratulated Denmark 'which has shown us the way and taken the lead in a venture that will form an epoch in the development of shipping. This new type of vessel is the most perfect maritime masterpiece of the century. Denmark, for many decades foremost in agriculture, has now also taken the lead on the seas.'[41]

Britain – at that time the world's leading nation in shipbuilding and with the largest naval and merchant fleets – would hardly have felt threatened by tiny Denmark having built a ship regarded by many as being an ingenious eccentricity. After all, Britain had substantial reserves of coal and there was apparently no great need to switch to running more technologically complex cargo vessels, powered by imported oil.

On 20 June 1912, B&W delivered the *Fionia* to EAC. A sister to *Selandia*, she began her maiden voyage to the Far East, sailing from Copenhagen to Hamburg via the Kiel Canal. In Kiel, H.N.

The 3,408gt steamer *Bandon* was Clyde-built in 1909 for EAC's route to Bangkok. Her career in the company's fleet was short, however, as she was sold to a Norwegian owner in 1916, displaced from the fleet by new motor ships.
(A. Ernest Glen)

Andersen welcomed Hamburg-America Line's powerful Chairman Albert Ballin on board and, later, even Kaiser Wilhelm himself paid a visit to the ship and experienced a short sail in the Kiel Fjord, during which the *Selandia* passed by at full speed on the return leg of her maiden voyage from Bangkok. Both Ballin and the Kaiser apparently were thoroughly impressed – so much so, in fact, that Hamburg-Amerika bought the *Fionia* from EAC there and then. As a tribute to her Danish origins, she was renamed *Christian X* in honour of the reigning Danish monarch and the Kaiser sent him a telegram stating that 'The Danish engineers have earned the right to consider themselves the creators of the first practical and successful example of a new direction; they are the master teachers of all us others.'[42] Albert Ballin was both ambitious and very well-connected in Government circles – indeed, Hamburg-Amerika was more or less a Government agency. Its immediate purchase of the *Fionia* was, therefore, highly politicised because the German authorities wanted access to diesel technology developed by B&W, especially as it appeared to have potential for adaptation to military applications.

On 26 June 1912, a flotilla of small craft and pleasure steamers sailed out of Copenhagen and nearby harbours to welcome the *Selandia* as she arrived back from the Far East. Tens of thousands lined the docks and large numbers visited her during the next days as her cargo of teak, pepper, copra and rubber was unloaded. Both the *Selandia* and her builder were now world-famous in the shipping industry and beyond. In the February 1937 issue of *The Motor Ship*, the *Selandia*'s Chief Engineer, K.F. Holm, gave an enthusiastic retrospective account of the maiden voyage:

> 'She arrived in Genoa on 16 March and sailed two days later for Colombo which was reached on April 6. Thereafter, she called at Penang and Singapore en route to Bangkok, where she berthed on 20 April. It was then that the first opportunity occurred to overhaul any of her machinery after 980 hours' running. All that was done was to clean and grind the fuel and exhaust valves and adjust some of the bearings. She left Bangkok on 1 May and thereafter maintained schedule throughout the return voyage to Copenhagen...'[43]

In fact, the *Selandia*'s maiden voyage had not been as problem-free as Holm's account suggests; outward-bound, she suffered two seized pistons and one of her lubricating oil pumps disintegrated *en route* from London to Antwerp. There, her Captain sent a telegram to B&W, who immediately dispatched a manager to her next port of call, Genoa, with a substantial inventory of spare parts.[44] Although she managed to maintain schedule, upon her return to Copenhagen her exhaust valves were replaced with new ones of improved design. Yet, notwithstanding her experimental nature, she acquitted herself remarkably well and, throughout her career, breakdowns were infrequent. Her engines were massively built, in the manner of steam reciprocating plant, and although they were subject to short stoppages for repairs to minor components, they generally managed to get the ship back to port under her own power.[45] *The Motor Ship* observed that:

> 'It is only necessary to realise what would have happened had she proved a failure to understand the responsibility shouldered by her owners and engineers. Had she broken down badly or even in the first year or two proved comparatively unsuccessful, the motor ship movement would undoubtedly have been set back by at least ten years. The shipping world as a whole was ready to condemn the motor ship. Hence, it could not be ignored and, after the *Selandia* proved her worth, it was not long before the more enterprising shipowners were investigating the question of adopting oil-engined tonnage.'[46]

While the *Selandia* and the first *Fionia* were being built in Copenhagen, a third EAC motor ship, the *Jutlandia*, had been contracted for construction on the Clyde in Glasgow by Barclay, Curle & Co. This yard, along with Swan, Hunter & Wigham Richardson on the Tyne, had been licensed by B&W to build diesel motors of the type fitted to the *Selandia*. Even so, several of the major components were actually manufactured in Copenhagen and shipped to the Clyde for installation. The *Jutlandia* was completed in May 1912 one month before the *Fionia*. *The Shipping World* reported that:

The **Selandia** undergoing builder's trials in February 1912.
(Det Kongelige Bibliotek)

'When Barclay, Curle & Co began to build the *Jutlandia* they did so in fear and trembling, but also in full confidence that the diesel engine… would commend itself to the public. During the official trials… a speed of 12.6 knots was attained… The *Jutlandia* could carry fuel to take her from the Clyde to South America and back without replenishing. It was estimated that on each round trip between Copenhagen and Bangkok £2,300 would be saved in the engine-room alone. This was quite apart from the profits to be obtained from the larger amount of additional cargo which she would carry.'[47]

In order to increase the market for B&W diesels, in 1911 the Company had set up a subsidiary called The Atlas Mercantile Company, which was jointly financed with B&W's existing British licensees. In March 1912, this was quickly renamed the Burmeister & Wain (Diesel System) Oil Engine Company, which was headquartered in Glasgow and, of course, the Clyde-built *Jutlandia* was a fine early advertisement for what B&W engines could achieve. During the First World War, Harland & Wolff took over this business from B&W and became responsible for licensing manufacture in the UK. Harland & Wolff's forthright Chairman, Lord Pirrie (William James Pirrie, 1847-1924) was an early British enthusiast for motor propulsion. Indeed, Pirrie had visited the first *Fionia* in Kiel on the same day as Albert Ballin and the German Kaiser. Pirrie was also a director of the White Star Line, for which Harland & Wolff built ships – not least, the unfortunate *Titanic*. By the 1920s, however, Harland & Wolff's shipyards and engine works in Glasgow and Belfast had become leading British users of B&W diesel engines and many notable passenger and cargo vessels were constructed.[48]

The success of the EAC diesel pioneers showed that motor propulsion certainly had a role to play in modern deep-sea shipping although some objected to the noise and vibration caused by diesel engines in relation to smooth, silent and fast steam turbines, which had been invented by the Newcastle engineer, Charles Parsons. In 1894, an experimental vessel called the *Turbinia* was completed to demonstrate Parsons' invention and, although only small in size, she was the fastest ship in the world, causing a sensation when she appeared at the 1897 Diamond Jubilee

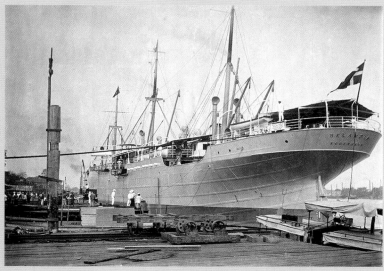

Above: Winston Churchill is welcomed aboard the *Selandia* in London on 1 March 1912. (Museet for Søfart)

Left: The *Selandia*, berthed in Bangkok at the end of her eastbound maiden voyage. (Bruce Peter)

Naval Review off Spithead. Consequently, many British lines held the view that noisy and relatively slow diesels were singularly unsuitable for crack passenger vessels – a position maintained, more or less, well into the 1960s, by which time most of the remainder of the world's merchant fleet had gone over to diesel power. There were, of course, exceptions such as Alfred Holt, White Star Line and the Royal Mail Group, all of which went over largely to diesel power between the two World Wars.

Other Scandinavian shipowners were as intrigued as EAC by the promised advantages of diesel propulsion and so, even while the *Selandia* was under construction, B&W began to receive orders for further similar vessels. The first was from Rederi AB Nordstjernan of Stockholm, which traded as the Johnson Line between North European and South American ports. It ordered two slightly smaller motor cargo liners, the *Suecia* and the *Pedro Christoffersen*, for delivery later in 1912 and early 1913. EAC followed with orders for the 6,700gt *Siam* and *Annam*, also completed in 1913 and with slightly more powerful engines generating 3,000 ihp each. These were the largest diesels B&W developed from the machinery first installed in the *Selandia* as subsequent designs that were more powerful still used an A-frame construction, a camshaft, more closely resembling that of a steam reciprocating engine and water, rather than oil, to cool the pistons.[49] Between October 1913 and May 1914, the *Siam* became the first motor ship to circumnavigate the world; this was a westbound voyage, via Cape Horn, South East Asia and the Suez Canal.[50]

When the *Selandia* returned to Copenhagen from her maiden voyage, DFDS' directorate decided immediately to order from B&W a motor cargo liner for their own trans-Atlantic liner service. At the same time, a similarly dimensioned vessel powered by a conventional steam reciprocating installation was ordered from the Joh. C. Tecklenburg Werft A.G. of Bremerhaven in order to conduct an objective comparative analysis of diesel versus steam power in long-distance liner service. The motor ship *California*, measuring 4,597gt, was delivered by B&W in October 1913 and the 5,136gt steamer *Maryland* followed from Tecklenburg's yard in January 1914. While the former was introduced on DFDS' North Atlantic route from Copenhagen to Boston, the latter made her maiden voyage on its more recent South Atlantic service to Buenos Aires and Montevideo, which had been inaugurated in 1907. As for the operational characteristics of the two vessels, DFDS' first observation was that, while the *California* had a greater cargo capacity due to the compactness and relative lightness of her diesel machinery and oil tanks in

Opposite top: The *Selandia*'s engine room, showing the control platform between her two engines. (Bruce Peter collection)

Opposite bottom: The *Selandia*'s lofty saloon, designed by the architect Carl Brummer. (Museet for Søfart)

Below: The *Selandia* off Frederikstad on St Croix in the Caribbean. (Museet for Søfart)

Left: The **Selandia**'s Clyde-built sistership, the **Jutlandia**. (Bruce Peter collection)

Centre: Building motor ships proved lucrative for B&W and soon export orders were received, such as the **Suecia**, delivered later in 1912 to Rederi AB Nordstjernan of Stockholm. (Bruce Peter collection)

Bottom: DFDS' first motor ship, the **California**, was delivered from B&W in 1914 and had similar dimensions to the **Maryland** (pictured opposite). Her career with the company was lengthy, lasting until 1958. Here, she is seen in post-World War 2 condition.
(Niels Krebs/Thomas N. Olesen collection)

comparison with the *Maryland*'s coal bunkers, the diesel ship had a limited range due to the lack of port facilities equipped to supply oil bunkers as an alternative to coal.

Unfortunately for DFDS, however, the *Maryland* became an early casualty of the First World War, sinking due to a mine or torpedo on 21 August 1914 after only seven months in service. The *California*, in contrast, enjoyed a lengthy career, surviving both world wars and remaining in the DFDS fleet until 1959. Although the First World War delayed progress, by the early 1920s numerous examples of this type of cargo liner had entered service with a variety of Scandinavian shipowners.

As for the pioneering *Selandia*, she completed 55 voyages for the East Asiatic Company before being sold in 1936 to Odd Godager of Oslo. He renamed her the *Norseman* and transferred her to the Panamanian flag. Upon her acquisition, he reported to *The Motor Ship* that 'my inspecting engineer found her to be in splendid condition as regards hull and machinery. It was unnecessary to do anything at all with her by way of modifications. She passed her last survey to the highest class of British Lloyd's.'[51]

In November 1938, General Franco's Navy seized the *Norseman* off the Spanish coast. Upon release, her ill-luck continued as, back in Oslo, her cargo of grain caught fire. She was repaired but, due to the outbreak of the Second World War, she was used initially in a static role as a grain store. She was sold in October 1940 to the Finnish-American Line but chartered to a Japanese company for coastal service in Japan. There, she grounded and was wrecked between Nagoya and Yokohama on 26 January 1942. She broke in two and sank on 30 January, exactly three decades after her first technical trial run when she revolutionised ship propulsion technology for ever.

Reviewing her career, *The Motor Ship* concluded that 'the record of the *Selandia* needs no elaboration. The name will ever be historic, and we have no doubt that the East Asiatic Co. and the Danish mercantile fleet will never be without their *Selandia* to recall to them the part which Denmark and the East Asiatic Co. have played in the history of shipping.'[52]

When DFDS decided experimentally to order the cargo liner **California**, it also purchased a similarly-dimensioned steamship, the German-built **Maryland**, shown here in New York. (Museet for Søfart)

Top: The East Asiatic Company's four-masted motor ship **Siam** was built by Burmeister & Wain in 1913. She was torpedoed and sunk in 1942 while in British war service. (Russell Priest collection)

Centre: The ship owner, Arnold Peter Møller, founder of Dampskibsselskabet Svendborg and Dampskibsselskab af 1912. (A.P. Møller-Maersk)

Bottom: DFDS' motor ship **Arizona** was built in 1920 by Nakskov Skibsværft for service between Copenhagen and South American ports. She remained in the fleet until 1958. (Museet for Søfart)

Chapter 3

The establishment of Dampskibsselskabet af 1912

The completion of the *Selandia* was only one of two momentous events in the annals of Danish shipping to have taken place in 1912; the other was the foundation of Dampskibsselskabet af 1912 (the Steamship Company of 1912), one of two firms behind what is today the foremost name in Danish shipping and, indeed, the world's largest transport logistics company – A.P. Møller-Maersk.

Denmark's third major player in liner shipping was a late entrant as it only began scheduled services in 1928, cross-trading over the Pacific Ocean between the United States and the Far East as Maersk Line. Until that point, its co-owner Arnold Peter Møller had been involved primarily in the tramping trade.

Maersk Line's antecedents were established in Svendborg, a major port in Southern Fyn. The founders were A.P. Møller, his father, Captain Peter Mærsk Møller, and a group of prominent local businessmen who together raised the initial share capital of 150,000 kroner. The Møller family originated from the island of Rømø, off Denmark's North Sea coast. A.P. Møller's mother, Anna Hans Jeppesen, however, came from a prominent ship-owning family from Dragør, to the south of Copenhagen. Following his marriage, Captain P.M. Møller also lived in Dragør when not at sea and his son, Arnold, was born there in 1876. When the Møllers failed to inherit the Jeppesens' shipping interests, losing out to Anna Hans Jeppesen's sisters and their husbands, Captain P.M. Møller moved his family to Svendborg in 1884. There, young A.P. Møller became an apprentice merchant, initially finding employment in a general store in Sorø.[53]

A.P. Møller had hoped to become an engineer, but his parents did not have the means to fund what would have been a relatively lengthy and expensive training. Instead, his father made use of British business contacts in Newcastle to find a work placement for young Møller in Harrison, Carr & Co's ship brokerage in 1895. At that time, Newcastle was a thriving industrial city, the River Tyne and nearby Tees entirely lined by shipyards and docks; Armstrong, Whitworth's Elswick Works on the Tyne's north bank stretched a mile along the river and could claim to be among the world's largest engineering enterprises. Yet, for all the wealth being generated, Newcastle and the coal mining towns surrounding it also were sites of great poverty and deprivation. Making do on a tight budget, life there would have been tough for young Møller who, not surprisingly, left in the summer of 1897. His spell in Britain taught him fluent English and this helped to secure his next job as an English language clerk with a hemp exporter in Königsberg in East Prussia. Thereafter, in 1899, he moved to St Petersburg in Russia, joining the chartering department of the shipbroker H.J. Pallisen. In addition, H.J. Pallisen owned two shipping companies – Dansk-Russisk Dampskibsselskab and The Northern Steamship Company.[54] After a slow start, H.J. Pallisen's Managing Director, Poul Mørch, took increasing notice of Møller's hard work and shrewd management skills. He was therefore given a three-year contract and placed in charge of the Company's book-keeping department. After only six months, he was promoted to lead its Shipping Department.

Although Møller was successful in operating the companies, which yielded enhanced profits under his management, he was irritated by office politics as older colleagues constantly questioned the extent of his authority, and so he longed to return to Denmark. Now fluent in English and German and with an outstanding practical knowledge of North Sea and Baltic tramp shipping, he would surely be a desirable employee for any Danish shipping company to hire. Indeed, in 1903 he was offered a directorship by DFDS – but he felt that this would be too much of a responsibility at so young an age.[55]

Instead, he became manager of the Chartering Department of C.K. Hansen, a respected ship brokerage and shipping company whose Rederiaktieselskab Dannebrog, founded in 1883, was one of Denmark's leading operators of tramping steamships. A clause in his contract allowed him to operate two steamers for his own account. Thus, in 1904, A.P. Møller co-founded Dampskibsselskabet Svendborg (The Svendborg Steamship Company) with investment from his father and from other prominent Svendborg businessmen. Captain P.M. Møller was the Managing Owner in Svendborg, while A.P. Møller was based in Copenhagen, working primarily for C.K. Hansen and additionally for Dampskibsselskabet Svendborg in such spare time as he could find.[56]

Given that Svendborg was home to a substantial fleet of sailing vessels, there was initially some opposition to making the transition from sail to steam. Yet, Dampskibsselskabet Svendborg's first vessels all yielded good profits, mainly by tramping around Baltic and North Sea ports with general cargo. These were the second-hand *Svendborg*, dating from 1902 and acquired in 1904, the *Peter Mærsk*, delivered new in 1906, the *Anna Mærsk* (1908) and the *Chassie Mærsk* (1910). The last of these was named in honour of A.P. Møller's wife, Chastine Mc-Kinney, a Scottish-American from Kentucky, whom he married in April 1910. Their first son and business heir, Arnold Mærsk Mc-Kinney Møller, was born in 1913.[57] As America emerged to become the world's leading economic and cultural power, the Møller family's American connections and cultural influences can only have been advantageous, particularly as Denmark was a small mainly agrarian nation and, in some respects, relatively parochial.

The young and ambitious A.P. Møller was frustrated by the procrastination of Dampskibsselskabet Svendborg's Board of Directors and so he founded a second shipping company – Dampskibsselskabet af 1912 (The Steamship Company of 1912 Ltd) – in which he held 80 per cent of the 50,000 kroner capital. This commenced operations with two small and ageing vessels acquired from C.K. Hansen, the 1889-vintage near sisters *Fredensborg* (later *Lexa Mærsk*) and *Rosenborg* (renamed *Hulda Mærsk*). Møller fixed lucrative charters for both vessels with Det Danske Kul Kompagni to transport light coke, and so Dampskibsselskabet af 1912 made a stable and profitable start.[58]

The statutes of Møller's new company gave him considerable personal authority to sell and mortgage ships, raise loans against bills of exchange and purchase new ships. With his energetic drive and his power to act immediately when he saw market conditions change and new opportunities emerge, Dampskibsselskabet af 1912 expanded at a quicker pace than the more conservative and traditionally-constituted Dampskibsselskabet Svendborg. By 1913, Dampskibsselskabet af 1912 had a total of six vessels and so Møller left C.K. Hansen on good terms to concentrate on their operation. By the outbreak of the First World War, the two Møller family-owned shipping companies controlled 11 steamers altogether – insignificant in comparison with Denmark's larger established firms, but nonetheless impressive given the short timespan within which their development had been achieved.

Dampskibsselskabet af 1912 commenced operations with two cargo steamers, bought second-hand from Rederiet Dannebrog (C.K. Hansen). The **Frederiksborg** was subsequently re-named **Lexa Mærsk**. She sailed for the company until 1917. (A.P. Møller-Maersk)

Chapter 4

The First World War and its aftermath

When Britain and Germany went to war in August 1914, Denmark made every effort to remain neutral while preserving normal contacts with the wider world as best possible. The two main combatants were also two of Denmark's nearest neighbours and biggest trading partners. Worse still, the country's position at the entrance to the Baltic particularly exposed shipping to damage in areas soon heavily mined and patrolled by naval craft. Having lost its southern duchies to Germany in 1864, Danish public opinion tended to favour Britain, France and Russia – although it was felt important not to anger Germany and risk attack from the south.

So far as the war at sea was concerned, the strategic perspective was that Germany – a very new country flexing industrial, cultural and political muscles – was a significant land-based power with pretensions to become a global imperial ruler while Britain was the supreme sea-based power. The German Naval Laws of 1898 and onwards demanded the building of a navy fleet way beyond German tactical requirements for the defence of its own coasts. This represented a strategic threat to Britain, whose response was to build its own enormous and very costly battle fleet to see off the German challenge. Thus, the Anglo-German naval race was brought into being.

At the start of the First World War, the British fleet, now termed the Grand Fleet, was massive and the German one about just over half its size but still the second largest in the world. All of this moved naval strategic focus to the North Sea as the arena where any clash would take place. All of the Grand Fleet was stationed there to contain the German High Seas Fleet and to prevent vessels 'escaping' to threaten British interests around the world. As part of this strategy of containment, the British constructed new naval bases at Scapa and Rosyth.

The vast majority of Danish liner routes passed through the North Sea, rendering ships particularly vulnerable to interference and assault by the combatants. Yet, particularly for DFDS, whose services provisioned the country with many of the basic commodities it required to function, it was absolutely necessary that they continued. During the war's early stages, Germany laid extensive minefields in the Southern Baltic and in the North Sea and so, even without coming under direct attack, merchantmen risked being sunk at random. Already on 21 August 1914, the first Danish steamer was struck by a mine; this was followed by another loss the following day.[59]

In September, the East Asiatic Company's well-connected Chairman, H.N. Andersen, was sent on a diplomatic mission to London on behalf of the Danish Government to establish how the Danish merchant fleet could continue to trade without falling victim to military action. More diplomatic travels followed in 1915 – on behalf of King Christian X to Russia for an audience with Czar Nicolas, then to Berlin to meet with the German Foreign Minister and Kaiser Wilhelm. While

The **Hulda Mærsk** started out as the **Rosenborg**. She was operated by Dampskibsselskabet af 1912 from its establishment until 1918, when she was sunk by a German submarine. Notwithstanding their prominent neutrality markings, Danish ships frequently came under attack, particularly during the war's final stages. (A.P. Møller-Maersk)

Andersen failed to broker any kind of peace deal to bring the war to a quicker end, eventually he came to be viewed in Denmark as something of a hero for at least trying to exert some influence.[60] Andersen was, of course, driven primarily by the need to earn money and he believed that what was good for EAC and what was good for Denmark were inextricably linked.

On 2 November 1914, the British Admiralty declared the North Sea a war zone, stating that all eastbound ships from America crossing a line between the Outer Hebrides and Iceland would do so at their own risk. The Admiralty stated that shipping bound from America to Scandinavia should instead sail via the Dover Strait, thus making it easier for the British authorities to control vessels' cargoes as they passed close by the country's East Coast. Danish shipowners, however, knew only too well that sailing through the Dover Strait brought with it a much higher risk of succumbing to German minefields and so it was decided to continue to use the existing route around Northern Scotland. After all, as the British would risk a diplomatic uproar by deliberately sinking neutral tonnage, the worst they could do was to use warships to stop vessels and inspect their cargoes.[61]

In October, the British strengthened their blockade against Germany by insisting that all Europe-bound vessels from North America should be diverted through British ports where detailed inspections would take place while at the quayside and any suspect goods would be offloaded. The fact that supposedly 'neutral' ships were being interfered with in this way by the British, of course, only raised German suspicions that cargo bound for non-combatant nations was being 'stolen' to aid the British war machine. By January 1915, a formal agreement was reached between the British and Danish Governments whereby vessels in trans-Atlantic service would be searched eastbound in either Stornoway or Kirkwall and, if the British authorities found goods they did not want forwarded, these items would be impounded by their Danish counterparts in Copenhagen; from there, they would be sent to Britain on other ships.

From the Danish Government's point of view, maintaining routes importing basic commodities was of the utmost priority and, as DFDS operated the majority of the most strategically important liner services, its operations were central to Denmark's survival. The crucial issue was how to insure tonnage against the greatly increased risk of damage or loss due to mines, torpedoes or being seized and sunk by German warships on the suspicion of carrying cargoes beneficial to Britain and her allies. The immediate solution was for the Danish Government, insurance companies, shipowners and the major commercial banks to work together to create a special

The EAC's *Fiona*, built in 1914, is seen underway at Melbourne. In 1955, she passed to Hong Kong owners.
(Russell Priest collection)

wartime insurance fund. Of its initial capital amounting to 13.5 million kroner, the Government guaranteed just over a third while the insurance industry provided a further 20 per cent. DFDS, The East Asiatic Company, Handelsbanken, Landmands-banken and Privatbanken supplied the remainder, each contributing a million kroner. The fund existed for the duration of the war and, as the situation for Danish shipping deteriorated, its capital was increased commenurately.[62]

In February 1915, Germany began to deploy its new fleet of submarines and so the British responded by strengthening its

Above: The **Asia**, delivered by Burmeister & Wain in 1918, is seen underway at Melbourne in the early 1950s.
(Russell Priest collection)

Below: A stern view of the **Asia** alongside at Hobart.
(D.E.Kirby, Russell Priest collection)

North Sea blockade with the primary intention of stymieing as best possible any further development of new military hardware. Consequently, Danish ships experienced even stricter controls by the British authorities to prevent goods of any kind from America reaching Germany via Denmark. Freight manifests were sent by telegraph to the UK for approval before ships were loaded and any materials found unacceptable by the British were not carried at all. Unsurprisingly, the Americans greatly disliked this and so they threatened to prevent ships from leaving without loading fully all of the cargo stated on the initial manifest. The Danes' counter-argument was that, as such cargo would be impounded in Copenhagen anyway, there would be no point because the British would not allow it to reach Germany. With some reluctance, America accepted this argument.[63]

The British blockade of trade with Germany was effective and led to shortages there. It also caused those determined still to trade with Germany to falsify paperwork with regard to the destinations for American exports and so the British further intensified their checking of ships' manifests. Trans-Atlantic vessels were thus diverted to Halifax in Nova Scotia for searching, which in the context of Germany's increasing use of submarines was at least safer than Scotland's Northern Isles as it was out of their range. During 1915, DFDS, frustrated by Danish and British bureaucracy restricting its trade, began to investigate the possibility of beginning an American-flagged trans-Atlantic service in conjunction with the New York shipping agent P. Brown & Co. The principal advantage of the American flag was that the United States was a large and strong neutral nation and so its ships were less likely to be threatened or interfered with by the main combatants; to do so would risk causing America to enter the war on the opposing side.[64]

Right: The EAC's *India*, built by Burmeister & Wain in 1920.
(Bruce Peter collection)

Below: A further view of the *India*; in 1937, the vessel was sold to Odd Godager of Oslo, who also bought the *Selandia*.
(Bruce Peter collection)

In the autumn of 1915, H.N. Andersen co-founded a new insurance company called Baltica in Copenhagen. The rationale behind its creation long pre-dated the war, however. Because there was no existing insurer in Denmark willing or able to take responsibility for the largest and most valuable EAC and DFDS ships, they were insured in London. During the war, both companies understandably were keen that all of their vessels should be insured in Denmark. So, along with Landmandsbanken and other leading Danish shipping companies, a starting capital of 6 million kroner was raised.[65] Interest in Baltica's war insurance proved so great, however, that its capital quickly expanded four-fold. The cost of this insurance was passed on to users of liner services through higher freight rates. Ships' officers and crews also were paid additional sums to compensate them for the increased dangers they faced. Meanwhile, the Danish Government used a variety of strategies to ensure that preference was given by shipping lines to carrying what it considered as vital commodities – such as coal, corn, animal feed and fertilizer.[66]

As the war progressed, Britain and Germany became more desperate and each placed more draconian restrictions on neutral nations' merchant fleets. For example, from 1916 onwards, the

British Government mandated that all foreign-flagged vessels docking in UK ports to coal would be required to carry out compulsory voyages at flat charter rates. What with forced inspections, submarine warfare and extensive minefields hindering its Merchant Navy, Denmark was, to an extent, boxed in. The Danish Government responded in May 1916 by establishing Fragtnævnet (The Chartering Committee) to ensure that imports of goods deemed vital to the national interest would be maintained – and this gave shipping companies steady employment.[67] It also enacted legislation to prevent ships being sold overseas without approval. Although freight rates were fixed at well below commercial levels, Danish shipping companies made steady profits for the remainder of the First World War's duration and thereafter.

When the United States entered the war in April 1917, there was a new emphasis on trans-Atlantic supply routes. In June 1917, Denmark entered into an agreement whereby a quarter of its merchant fleet was given over for Allied use. Later, in September 1918, it agreed to make available a further third of its tonnage to the United States. While war risk insurance was an additional cost which all shipping companies had to bear, vessels were fully employed and profits

Above: The *Java*, introduced in 1921, was EAC's first large motor cargo liner built at the company's own shipyard at Nakskov. She was scrapped in Japan in 1958.
(Bruce Peter collection)

Left: The *Java*, tied up alongside.
(Bruce Peter collection)

Right: Unusually, DFDS decided to order the 1927-built motor ship **Louisiana** from The Ardrossan Drydock Co. Ltd on the Firth of Clyde in Scotland. She served her owner until 1959.
(Bruce Peter collection)

Below: DFDS' trans-Atlantic steamer **Tennessee**, built in 1933 by Jönköping Mekaniska Verkstads AB, was torpedoed in the North Atlantic in 1942.
(Museet for Søfart)

were good. Yet, it was very difficult to order new tonnage due to materials shortages and to naval craft taking precedence in most shipyards; additionally, the main combatants prioritised the building of merchantmen to sail under their own flags. Thus, the more prudent Danish shipowners were able to build up substantial financial reserves for investment come the Armistice.[68]

During the war, freight rates increased ten-fold and the gross freight income of the Danish merchant fleet increased from 100 million kroner per annum to 500 million while the average value of shares in shipping companies increased by more than 300 per cent.[69] Not only was Copenhagen's financial world delighted but the Danish public also had reason to be pleased with the Merchant Navy's achievements under duress. Merchantmen had worked hard to keep the country supplied for the duration of the conflict; a famous incident garnering good publicity was the arrival in Copenhagen of the pioneering EAC motor vessel *Selandia* just before Christmas 1917 loaded with rice, coffee, figs, spices, dates and oranges – all key ingredients for Christmas dinner.[70]

By the First World War's end, roughly one-third of the Danish merchant fleet – totalling 165 vessels – had been lost to mines, torpedoes and shelling. With only two losses due to acts of war, one forced sale and one vessel foundering, the A.P. Møller companies came out of the war in a relatively strong position. EAC, meanwhile, recorded three war losses. In contrast, DFDS was among the least fortunate with 26 losses in the 1914-1918 period due to acts of war plus a further five vessels foundering for other reasons (of course, the DFDS fleet was far larger overall and an important part of its business involved sailing through dangerous North Sea waters).[71] Having come out of the war with the biggest loss of tonnage, DFDS compounded its difficulties by squandering its reserves to pay shareholders large dividends, buying ageing replacement tonnage at over-inflated prices and taking out loans at high interest rates. DFDS, therefore, entered the turbulent inter-war years in a weakened position. This was largely the fault of an overly optimistic management and greed on the part of institutional investors, most notably Landmandsbanken, which aggressively demanded big dividends.[72]

The First World War brought radical changes to the map and politics of Europe. Revolutions in Russia and Germany saw feudal monarchies being respectively superseded by a Communist regime and a Social-Democratic republic. Following the Treaty of Versailles, many independent nation states were created from the collapsed Russian, German and Austro-Hungarian empires. In the Baltic region, Finland, Estonia, Latvia, Lithuania and Poland all now were self-governing. The Treaty of Versailles was particularly harsh towards Germany, insisting on its demilitarisation, its surrendering large tracts of territory and its making swingeing reparations payments to the war's victors, money which the virtually bankrupt nation could ill afford. Besides, as Germany itself had deposed Kaiser Wilhelm and created its own new constitution, it could fairly argue that the regime which caused the war no longer existed. Largely as a result of the Treaty's arguably unreasonable demands, in the post-war years Germany struggled to reinvigorate itself, suffering high unemployment, hyper-inflation and, increasingly, sharply divisive political tensions.

Before the war, Germany was mainland Europe's industrial powerhouse, generating a great deal of cargo for indigenous and foreign-flag liner operators, but as it stagnated there was less sea trade and freight rates were low. The problem of over-capacity and insufficient cargo was compounded by large numbers of new American-built cargo steamers suddenly coming on stream. In 1916, the United States Shipping Board had been established to commission a large cargo fleet to supply American forces in Europe. The Armistice came too quickly, however, and most of the 1,770 vessels constructed were, in fact, delivered in the 1918-1922 period, making the United States a serious mercantile power for the first time – indeed, taking into account British war losses, the American fleet was the world's second biggest by the early 1920s. The sudden introduction of this vast new flotilla into civilian service permanently altered the balance of power in international shipping, Europe's established maritime nations generally losing out to a newly confident and asset-rich United States fleet.[73]

More generally, the world's merchant fleet increased four-fold between 1914 and 1939 but the growth in demand could not keep pace with this increased supply and so less efficient ships were laid up while shipping company failures were not infrequent occurrences. In his history of the Far Eastern Freight Conference, Eric Jennings observes:

> 'As a result of diversion of a large part of the British merchant marine to war duties and substantial losses by belligerent and neutral merchant fleets there was a general scarcity of tonnage during the war. The British and Americans had launched great shipbuilding programmes. Neutrals had expanded their fleets to make them self-sufficient in their sea-borne trade. Apart from a short period immediately after the war, the next two decades witnessed declining world trade and an excess supply of shipping space. By 1922 about 11 million tons were idle for want of employment. The depression hit both the tramp and liner trades.'[74]

DFDS, for instance, had 30 steamships laid up in 1921 – but even it was not too badly affected as short-duration coastal routes and overseas liner services were less exposed to market fluctuations than fleets consisting entirely of itinerant tramping vessels.[75] Shipowners discussed whether joint action would make shipping more profitable, but few plans came to fruition and usually only with limited success. Instead, overseas governments preferred protectionism in the form of subsidies and flag discrimination against foreign ships.[76]

Britain's ultimate victory in the First World War came at a great cost in terms of human lives and a generation of young men were either killed or written off as invalids. This – and the

The ***Chastine Mærsk***, built at Odense in 1923. (A.P. Møller-Maersk)

economic cost of waging such a modern war of attrition – caused Britain to lose significant momentum, not least in naval architecture, shipbuilding and operational practices. Indeed, Britain's victory appeared to cement the pre-war *status quo* and so replacements for war losses tended to be little different from their pre-war predecessors; British coal-fired steamers with reciprocating machinery completed in 1920 were much the same as those delivered in 1910. In contrast, in the Scandinavian countries – particularly Denmark and Norway – diesel propulsion was embraced and fleets hitherto dominated by steamships went over largely to diesel during the 1920s. Even A.P. Møller began to build motor vessels – an innovative move for an operator of tramps as the initial cost of diesel machinery was much greater than steam reciprocating plant. Thereafter, A.P. Møller deployed subsequent examples in liner service. EAC never built another steamer and, instead, took delivery of a succession of passenger and cargo motor ships, each one representing a refinement over the previous example (between 1918 and 1939, EAC added 21 such vessels to its fleet).[77]

During 1920, the Danish merchant fleet reached its pre-war tonnage level and then continued to expand until the beginning of the 1930s. Thereafter, growth stagnated as the Wall Street Crash led to an intractable depression. The large-scale renewal of the Danish merchant fleet ensured that it became increasingly competitive. Motor vessels made rapid inroads displacing sail and steam and, by 1939, accounted for 54 per cent of Danish merchant tonnage, a figure exceeded only by Norway.[78]

Other emerging industrial and maritime powers – for example Italy – likewise became convinced of the benefits of diesel propulsion. There, Swiss-designed Sulzer diesels were manufactured under licence for fitment especially to new passenger liners; like Denmark, Italy lacked a significant indigenous coal supply.

One means by which shipowners could ensure a supply of suitable tonnage at favourable prices was by controlling shipbuilding. In a Danish context, DFDS was the first liner company to acquire a shipyard when in 1913 it financed the expansion and modernisation of Frederikshavns Værft & Flydedok A/S in Northern Jutland, saving it from being taken over by the German shipbuilder Howaldtswerke. (From 1872 until 1898, DFDS' founder, C.F. Tietgen, had chaired Burmeister & Wain's Board of Directors, although the two Companies otherwise remained entirely

EAC's motor ship ***Danmark*** was delivered by B&W in 1925. She was sunk in 1942 by a German submarine while under British wartime management.
(Bruce Peter collection)

separate.) In 1913, DFDS purchased from B&W a substantial shareholding in its subsidiary Helsingørs Jernskibs- og Maskinbyggeri, thereafter buying more shares to gain a majority interest in 1916. This proved to be a canny investment; subsequently, the yard built over ninety vessels for the DFDS fleet.[79]

In the wake of the First World War, the major shipbuilding nations, Britain and Germany, had full order books as they battled to make good their own war losses and Scandinavian yards also were exceptionally busy. Moreover, steel was in short supply (Scandinavian shipowners frequently had to source their own and supply it to yards in Denmark and Sweden before construction could commence) and currency fluctuations – including the kroner – added to the risk of placing new orders.[80] For these reasons, during the 1914-1918 period shipbuilding costs nearly doubled. This situation strained long-standing relationships between shipping lines and particular yards. For example, EAC had hitherto commissioned numerous motor ships from B&W – but now found the yard giving preference to other shipowners who were prepared to pay more for newbuildings than its directors thought was prudent to invest. This meant that, rather than being the yard's favoured customer as in the recent past, EAC now had to take its place in the queue, delaying expansion and modernisation plans. Consequently, its Chairman, H.N. Andersen, decided to open a new yard in his home town, Nakskov, specifically to build vessels for the EAC fleet. Nakskov had a long tradition of building sailing ships and fishing cutters but to build ocean-going liners would be a significant step in a new direction.[81]

Nakskov Skibsværft opened in October 1916 and, henceforth, contributed a significant number of vessels to EAC – and to other shipping companies as well. Having decided to focus solely on diesel-powered liners, EAC transferred its last seven steamers to a subsidiary called Dampskibsselskabet Orient (The Orient Steamship Company) where they acted as a reserve fleet, time-chartered as back-up vessels to operate the Company's liner routes.[82] Thereafter, a succession of larger and faster motor vessels was built, some at Nakskov and others at B&W. With the delivery from Nakskov of the 3,013gt motor tanker *Mexico* in 1920, EAC additionally entered the oil transport business. This was becoming very lucrative, not only due to the requirements of an increasingly oil-fired Danish Merchant Navy but also as a result of the onset

The ***Meonia***, completed at Nakskov in 1927, is seen departing from Helsingør; she survived until 1961 when she was scrapped in Hong Kong.
(Det Kongelige Bibliotek)

The **Alsia** leaves the shipyard in Nakskov in 1929; a decade later, she burned out near Ceylon. (Bruce Peter collection)

of 'second wave' industrialisation in general, bringing with it an exponential growth in the use of internal combustion engines on *terra firma*.[83]

Not only did H.N. Andersen appreciate the benefits of taking shipbuilding 'in house,' but also A.P. Møller realised that there would be advantageous synergies in expanding into building cargo ships as well as operating them. During his stay in Newcastle in 1895-97, the youthful Møller had observed the operations of the West Hartlepool shipbuilding and shipping company Robert Ropner & Co, which successfully combined the construction and operation of tramping cargo steamers. At first, he considered taking over the ailing Baltica Yard in Copenhagen's South Harbour but rejected this in favour of a new site in Odense, Denmark's third largest city. There, Møller rented 15 acres of land next to a bend in the Odense Canal in 1918. With additional land acquisitions on which to build workers' housing and the construction of two building berths, his total investment was two million kroner – representing the majority of revenues earned by his shipping companies during the First World War.

Møller proposed that the new shipyard's two launchways should be occupied by newbuilding contracts for Dampskibsselskabet Svendborg and Dampskibsselskabet af 1912 respectively, but the ever-cautious Svendborg Board protested about investing in the yard as Svendborg was already a shipbuilding town and so they did not want to support the establishment of a rival business elsewhere. Nonetheless, A.P. Møller prevailed and by April 1919 the Odense Staalskibsværft was complete. Thus, the keels could be laid for the first newbuildings – the tramp steamers *Robert Mærsk* for Dampskibsselskabet Svendborg and the *Lifland* for another Danish shipping company, Dansk-Fransk; both were delivered in 1920. In the following year, the first A.P. Møller motor ship, the 2,295gt *Leise Mærsk*, was completed, also for Dampskibsselskabet Svendborg.

Back in 1912, A.P. Møller had been an invited guest on the *Selandia*'s demonstration voyage in The Sound from Copenhagen to Helsingør. Finding that the Chief Engineer was an old acquaintance, he spent his time in the engine room, familiarising himself with the layout and characteristics of her B&W diesel engines. Shortly thereafter, Møller wrote to B&W's Technical Director Ivar Knudsen asking him for a quotation to build a similar vessel – but did not receive a reply because Knudsen clearly did not believe he was a man of substance. Nearly a decade later, Møller was in a position to build such a ship in his own yard instead. For this purpose, he purchased from B&W the first of a new type of long-stroke 6-cylinder 1,500 hp B&W diesel engine. The *Leise Mærsk* was, therefore, the first single-screw motor cargo ship and her 10.5-knot service speed was about a knot faster than similarly dimensioned steamers joining the Dampskibssel-skabet Svendborg and Dampskibsselskabet af 1912 fleets in the same period – and with even better fuel economy than her owners had expected. She was also the first motor ship built for tramping rather than liner operation but, later in the decade, she inaugurated the first Maersk

Line service.[84] Diesel engines were much more expensive than steam reciprocating machinery and boilers (the *Leise Mærsk*'s engine cost 1,150,000 kroner – meaning that the ship was 80 per cent more costly to build than a similarly dimensioned steamer). Yet, as diesel ships could carry much more cargo, lifetime costs were lower. Moreover, a diesel ship burned only 0.35 pounds of oil per horsepower per hour, whereas an oil-burning turbine steamer used one pound (or almost three times as much).[85]

This differential in operational costs between diesel and steam propulsion was significant because in 1921 there was a dramatic fall in average freight rates while the price of coal grew markedly. So great was the post-war shipbuilding boom that the world's merchant fleet was three times as big as when the war began. In Denmark, the repayment of war insurance and a reduction in the wages paid to certain categories of seamen also helped to offset low profitability and, besides, in the 1922-24 period there was also some welcome economic growth.[86]

A.P. Møller was convinced that for larger cargo ships diesel represented the best way forward, while steamships still were better for local Baltic and North Sea routes.[87] As the 1920s progressed, further motor vessels were built in Odense for Dampskibsselskabet af 1912's tramping operations;

Above: The ***Amerika*** represented a departure for EAC and B&W from their hitherto typical funnel-less design to a silhouette similar to the latest British and Italian diesel passenger liners.
(Bruce Peter collection)

Right: The ***Amerika***'s remarkably compact but powerful double-acting, two-stroke diesel engine.
(MAN/Diesel House)

these were the *Sally Mærsk* and *Chastine Mærsk* (both 1923), the *Emma Mærsk* (1924) and the *Nicoline Mærsk* (1925).[88]

In time, Odense Staalskibsværft became one of Denmark's largest and most efficient shipbuilding enterprises. Having moved to a larger site at Lindø in 1959, since the latter 1960s the yard has built some of the world's biggest and most technologically advanced oil tankers and container ships.

In 1925, there was a new economic downturn which was harder on Danish shipping than on other nations' merchant fleets. The Danish Government re-valued the kroner to its 1914 level, causing money paid out in kroner to outstrip revenue from cargo paid in by foreign customers in other suddenly less valuable currencies. This situation was particularly tough on larger ships operating in the international market.[89] The following May, Britain experienced a ten-day General Strike, during which coal mining ground to a halt, and this gave Danish shipping a chance to recover, partly by carrying coal to Britain and partly by filling in for temporarily laid-up British tonnage. Of course, every miners' strike in Britain strengthened the case for oil-burning motor ships and Denmark was already a proven leader in this area.

Perhaps with this in mind, in 1926 A.P. Møller entered the oil tanker business, signing charter agreements with the Anglo-Saxon Petroleum Company, the transport division of Shell, and with the Standard Oil Company of New Jersey. Five tankers were ordered for the purpose – two from Københavns Flydedok and three from Odense – for delivery during 1928. His following EAC's lead in entering the tanker trade would have significant positive implications for his shipping companies' future development. As increasingly enthusiastic users of oil-fired motor ships, it was advantageous for EAC and A.P. Møller to be involved also in oil transport and distribution.

Meanwhile, significant developments were taking place with regard to marine diesel engine design. After a period of comparative calm in engine development during the period of the First World War and its immediate aftermath, competition began once more in the 1920s between the various leading marine engine builders –B&W, MAN and Sulzer – to achieve greater reliability, fuel

The EAC's motor ship *Amerika*, photographed passing beneath a splendid Gothic-style suspension bridge at Vancouver. (Museet for Søfart)

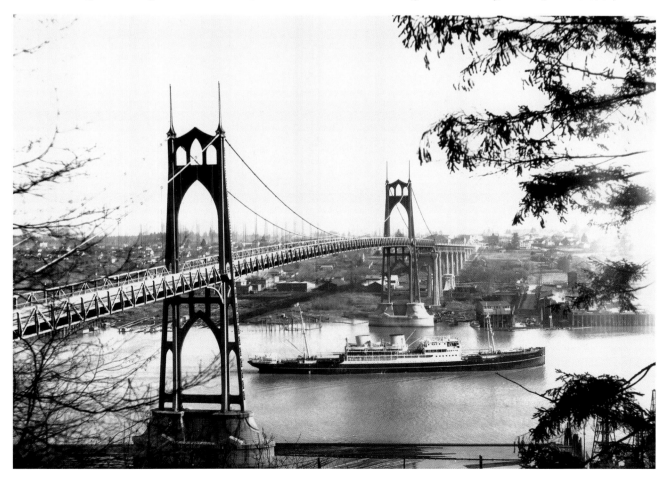

economy and power output while at the same time endeavouring to design engines that would require less maintenance and take up less space inside ships' hulls.

In 1919, B&W's Technical Director Ivar Knudsen retired from the Company but continued to work on its behalf in an independent consulting role. In March 1920, he died in Bombay, India, while on a business trip. Responsibility for B&W's marine diesel development then fell to his replacement, Hans Henrik Blache (1874-1952). Blache was the son of a distinguished maritime painter and academic, Professor Christian Blache of Copenhagen's Royal Academy. He regularly accompanied his father to look at ships in Copenhagen Harbour and, when visiting the 1888 Nordic Exhibition in Copenhagen as a teenager, he was greatly taken by a Møller & Jochumsen steam engine in a display case; seeing this gave him his ambition to become an engine builder. After a three-month spell working for Nielsen & Winther's engine works, he joined the Polyteknisk Læreanstalt to study engineering. Upon graduation, he joined the Danish Royal Naval shipyard Orlogsværft for a year, then moved to B&W in 1898. There, he was one of only three employees who had an academic qualification (the others were Engineer Ove Munch and Technical Director Ivar Knudsen). In 1900, Blache began a year's travel around Europe to study design developments in engine works elsewhere – such as G. Kuhn of Stuttgart and Babcock & Wilcox in London. Thereafter, he returned to B&W, where initially he was mainly concerned with the design of steam engines as Knudsen was in charge of diesel development.[90]

During the inter-war era, Blache became one of the best-known figures in European shipbuilding and shipping circles – and also a distinguished and widely travelled writer and lecturer on the subject of diesel engine design. In 1929, the Polyteknisk Læreanstalt gave him an Honorary Doctorate in recognition of his outstanding work in diesel engine research, development and promotion during the preceding decade.[91] His career trajectory also reflected the growing importance of academic input in Denmark's continued development of diesel technology and ship design. On the occasion of his 60th Birthday in 1934, *The Motor Ship* stated that 'it is doubtful whether any man has had more influence on diesel engine and motor ship progress than Dr Blache.'[92]

In 1921, the first B&W trunk-piston engines for marine usage appeared; 'trunk piston' refers to the piston skirt (or trunk) taking the thrust caused by connecting-rod angularity and transmitting it to the side of the cylinder liner. They were, for their time, very economical units.

In the 1920s, single-screw motor ships began to appear in large numbers and to obtain higher efficiency it was necessary to build engines which would give a very low propeller speed. For this purpose, B&W produced a crosshead engine with a very long stroke that gave an output of only 85 revolutions per minute. It was during this period that increasing numbers of shipping lines began to show an interest in diesel propulsion for their ocean-going passenger liners. To meet the requirements for powering this type of vessel, B&W started large-scale experiments with an

The *Europa* was the second of the series of three near-sisters built for EAC in the 1930s for liner service between Scandinavia and the West Coast of North America. (Museet for Søfart)

The *Europa*'s forward deck and superstructure. (Thomas N. Olesen collection)

experimental 4-stroke double-acting engine. ('Double-acting' means that each cylinder has an ignition at either end so that the power output is doubled without an appreciable gain in either size or weight.) Following several years of research, culminating with an endurance test during which a prototype engine ran non-stop for a month, two 6-cylinder units were built and installed on the Swedish American liner *Gripsholm* which was built by Armstrong, Whitworth & Co. in Newcastle and delivered in 1925. These engines had a combined output of 13,500 bhp.[93]

Until the latter 1920s, all marine diesel engines had been built with compressed air fuel injection (known as blast injection) but, as the result of successful experiments, B&W decided instead to favour solid fuel injection for most of its engines. The main advantage was the elimination of the drain of power from the main engine to drive the blast air compressor (this could amount to as much as 10 per cent of the total power output). Throughout the decade, there had been interest in the supercharging of marine diesel engines as this promised an increased power yield of up to 30 per cent and so, in 1922, B&W started to equip some of its engine installations with electrically-driven blowers. The next major development in this field was the adoption of exhaust gas-driven blowers and in 1929 two British Blue Funnel Line motor ships, the *Agamemnon* and the *Menesteus*, were fitted with B&W engines supercharged in this way. B&W became best known for its large-bore, slow-speed marine diesels, rather than for medium-speed engines which were developed principally by other manufacturers (for example MAN and Sulzer).[94]

While the first half of the 1920s was characterised by stagnation, the decade's latter years saw renewed growth. In 1926, Britain reintroduced the Gold Standard, which had been suspended since 1914 due to deflationary pressures caused by the First World War. Its re-establishment ensured that the value of one pound sterling was equivalent to that of a pound of gold and, early in 1927, Denmark followed suit with the kroner. Another, arguably even more significant, initiative came from America, which was concerned that Germany's lack of growth and run-away inflation, due largely to the terms of the Treaty of Versailles, were holding back development throughout the Western World and might even be threatening European stability. In August 1924, the American lawyer, politician and eventual Vice-President Charles Dawes presented the so-called Dawes Plan to make Germany attractive once more to international investors. This proposed a loan to Germany of 800 million dollars from American investment banks, a reorganisation of the Reichsbank under Allied supervision and a rescheduling of German reparations payments to a sustainable level. For this work, Dawes received the Nobel Peace Prize and, as expected, American financiers thereafter became major investors in Germany, their money underwriting much of its economy. Consequently, trade picked up very satisfactorily in the 1926-1929 period.

The second half of the 1920s was thus a lucrative period for Danish shipping, during which the leading liner operators added significant numbers of new vessels. In 1925 EAC took delivery from B&W of the 8,391gt *Danmark* – at that time the largest cargo vessel in the Danish merchant fleet and fitted with two 6-cylinder 4-stroke engines, generating 5,400 ihp and giving a 12.75-knot service speed. From Nakskov came the 5,145gt *Lalandia* (1927), followed by the similarly dimensioned and powered *Meonia* and *Alsia* (both 1929). The substantially larger 9,549gt *India* was completed in 1930 also in Nakskov while the 5,821gt *Boringia* came from B&W.[95] DFDS continued to order steamers for liner services but switched to motor ships for North Sea and Scandinavian overnight routes.

In early 1928 EAC's Chairman, H.N. Andersen, called B&W's Technical Director, H.H. Blache, to a meeting. Andersen told him how satisfied he was with the motor ships B&W had built so far, but that he thought the Company would not remain the market leader in engine design and manufacture for much longer unless it made serious attempts to develop 2-stroke engine designs, rather than its favoured 4-stroke varieties. Andersen explained that he had sent his Inspector to visit Sulzer in Winterthur in Switzerland to report on the design development of double-acting 2-stroke engines for single-screw ships and that he had received very positive feedback. He made clear to Blache that, in future, he would be seeking to order single-screw motor ships and that B&W therefore had better set to work designing a suitable engine to power them. Blache, who had hitherto stoutly defended what he considered to be the advantages of 4-stroke engines in terms of superior combustion and B&W's dominant market share, could only agree with Andersen and so he diligently set his engineers to work on the project.[96] Two-stroke engines are mechanically more straightforward than 4-stroke varieties as scavenging air intake and exhaust removal take place as the piston moves up and down, rather than being enacted by separate piston strokes. Already, B&W's rivals, Sulzer and MAN, had a lengthy lead in 2-stroke engine development but, thanks to Blache's prioritising of development work to fulfil Andersen's demand, B&W caught up quickly.

The saloon on the **Europa**. (Thomas N. Olesen collection)

Shortly after Andersen and Blache's meeting, EAC placed an order for a new passenger and cargo liner to be powered by the first B&W-designed and -built double-acting 2-stroke engine, a 6-cylinder unit developing 6,450 bhp on a single shaft. The 10,218gt *Amerika* in which this was installed entered service in the spring of 1930; at that time she was the largest ship yet constructed in Denmark. (In the Danish merchant fleet, only DFDS' 1913-vintage Scandinavia-America trans-Atlantic liner *Frederik VIII* was bigger at 11,850gt – but this steamer had been built in Stettin in Pomerania.)

The *Amerika* was the first of a trio of passenger-cargo liners built for a new EAC liner route from Northern Europe to ports in California on America's West Coast, via the Panama Canal. A key aspect of EAC's rationale for opening its 'Californian Service' was to bring fresh fruit to Denmark and so the *Amerika* and her subsequent near sisters were each equipped with a large refrigerated hold.[97] Fruit was a lucrative cargo as the expanding and increasingly health-conscious middle classes were becoming avid consumers. *The Motor Ship* observed:

> 'In developing a motor cargo and passenger service to the Californian ports, the East Asiatic Co. are following several other well-known shipping lines, practically all of whom have adopted motor propulsion of these craft exclusively. In fact, the trade represents one which is nearly ideal for the motor ship, first because the price of diesel oil is low (about 30 shillings per ton) and, secondly, because the voyages involved are very long.'[98]

The *Amerika* was also the highest-powered single-screw ship built to date but subsequently versions of the type of diesel engine installed in her were fitted in large numbers of single-screw vessels of all types. Her fuel consumption was remarkably low, however – only 24 tons per day when maintaining a steady speed of 14.5 knots. The double-acting engine design enabled a considerable weight saving per brake horsepower generated and so made available extra deadweight capacity for cargo. *The Motor Ship* reported that the *Selandia*'s engine weighed over 400 pounds per bhp while a standard single-acting 4-stroke B&W diesel weighed around 300 pounds per bhp. In contrast, the double-acting 2-stroke engine installed on the *Amerika* weighed a mere 360 tons in total – meaning that the weight was only around 115 pounds per bhp.[99]

In terms of appearance, the *Amerika* followed the latest Italian and British motor ship design trends, being fitted with two short and wide funnels, the forward of which concealed the exhaust uptake while the aft funnel contained water tanks. Key precedents were the Italian Cosulich Line sisters *Saturnia* and *Vulcania*, delivered in 1927 from the Cantiere Navale

A passenger cabin on the
Europa. (Thomas N. Olesen
collection)

Triestino at Monfalcone; these were fitted with 8-cylinder B&W diesels manufactured by the Macchine Sant'Andrea of Trieste. In Britain, meanwhile, the Harland & Wolff shipyards in Belfast and Glasgow, whose Chairman was Lord Pirrie, constructed a succession of B&W-engined liners, mainly for the yard's owning company, the Royal Mail Group, of which Pirrie was also a director. Royal Mail's *Asturias* (1926) – measuring 22,500gt and the largest motor ship in the world at the time of her completion – was followed by her sister, the *Alcantara*, and Union-Castle Line's *Carnarvon Castle* later the same year. Next, the Nelson Line's *Highland Chieftain* was completed in 1928, the first of five sister ships delivered between then and 1932. Simultaneously, White Star's *Britannic* (1930) and *Georgic* (1932) plus Huddart, Parker's *Wanganella* (1931) were also completed, as were a further four motor liners for Union-Castle. Externally, all were of very distinctive – but generic – appearance with vertical stems, flat-fronted superstructures and short, broad, flat-topped funnels.[100] This design solution had a practical purpose as these motor ships' funnel casings contained exhaust silencers and so needed to be spacious in comparison with the slender stacks of steamships. Meanwhile, the prestigious German Blue Riband-winning *Bremen* and *Europa* of 1929 were steam turbine-powered, but they too had similar low and wide funnels when delivered and so perhaps EAC and B&W also felt that this aesthetic was appropriate for a flagship vessel engaged in trans-Atlantic service – even if only of intermediate size.

The *Amerika*'s passenger accommodation represented a new approach to the trans-Atlantic passenger liner trade as she was designed as an all First Class ship, carrying only 52 passengers in considerable luxury and with four additional berths for their personal servants. *The Motor Ship* observed:

> 'The number of passengers carried is larger than in most of the mixed cargo and passenger ships that have recently been built. The principle in furnishing the passenger quarters and saloons has evidently been to provide extremely comfortable but not lavishly decorated rooms and to give that sense of space which is usually absent, at any rate, in a greater part of the cabins of the typical very large liner. On the Bridge Deck are twelve cabins on each side and two more on the Promenade Deck. All are extremely large and have 'dry' electric heaters and the punkah-louvre system of ventilation. Six have bathrooms adjoining and eighteen have one bed and one sofa which, whilst in such use, gives no indication of the possibility of converting into a bed; this can, however, be effected very rapidly.
>
> On the Promenade Deck, forward, is the smoking room panelled in dark mahogany, the chairs and settees being upholstered in green. The lounge, on the opposite side of the entrance hall, is in cherry wood and has exceptionally large windows. The chairs and settees are covered in hand-woven tapestry and both of these rooms, as well as the dining saloon on the deck below, are light and airy compartments, particularly attractive in a ship which will experience a good deal of hot weather. The dining saloon is furnished in polished birch, which is much favoured by Danish shipowners, and on the walls are a series of paintings. The entrance hall is also finished in polished birch and includes a bar. This leads to the hall above between the lounge and smoking room by means of a broad stairway, again in polished birch.'[101]

Having observed the extensive use of polished birch veneers on the interior bulkheads, *The Motor Ship*'s correspondent turned his attention to the details of the builder's trials:

> 'Before leaving the berth at 9 am on January 21st, the engine had been running for a time with the ship tied up, but within a comparatively few minutes after casting off the vessel was proceeding with the propelling motor turning at 90 rpm and shortly after at 100 rpm without any preliminary running in. Throughout the day the behaviour was faultless. There was not a trace of main engine vibration even at the maximum speed of 110 rpm, and throughout the whole ship movement could scarcely be felt, although the vessel was light. The noise from the main engine was less… than might naturally be imagined and such noise as there was came mainly from blowers and auxiliaries in the

engine room… With merely two levers to control, one engineer handled the 7,000 bhp plant with the utmost ease and certainty. As for the ship, the day was perfect and no opportunity occurred of demonstrating her seaworthy capacity.

There were about 50 people on board, practically all technical men who showed great interest in the new machinery. Among those… were the technical directors or superintendent engineers of many prominent companies, including Blue Funnel Line, the Bergen S.S. Co, DFDS, the Swedish-American Line, the Norwegian America Line and the Linea Sud America. Several of the licensees of Burmeister & Wain were also represented.'[102]

The *Amerika* attained a top speed of 16.55 knots, making her the fastest single-screw motor ship yet built. She was followed a year later by the 10,224gt *Europa*, also built by B&W. A third near sister, the 11,108gt *Canada*, delivered in 1935 from Nakskov, differed from her elder sisters in having a cruiser stern, rather than the earlier vessels' counter design. Unfortunately, all three were lost during the Second World War.

These vessels made their debut at around the same time as DFDS was winding down its own Scandinavia-America Line passenger operation, which closed in 1935 but was briefly re-established in 1939 using cargo liners. (In this mode, it re-commenced after the Second World War, continuing until 1970.) During the 1920s, there was a steep decline in emigration from Europe to the USA as migrant quotas were first introduced in 1921, then tightened in 1930. This meant that liners built in the Edwardian era of the type used by DFDS, the majority of whose passenger capacity consisted of Third Class 'steerage' accommodation, required replacement.[103] Moreover, these vessels were coming to the end of their natural lives and were now seriously outmoded in comparison with their more recent steam turbine and diesel-powered competitors.

New generation trans-Atlantic passenger liners aimed to attract increasingly prosperous American tourists, often the descendents of migrants, to visit Europe, rather than migrants sailing cheaply *en masse* in the opposite direction. Famous 1920s tourist-oriented liners were the French CGT's *Ile de France*, Swedish-American's *Kungsholm* and the German near sisters *Bremen* and *Europa*. In terms of comfort, hospitality, technology and aesthetics, these ships set new trends and were much admired and emulated – not least by EAC's *Amerika*, *Europa* and *Canada*.

The *Canada*, which differed in outward appearance from her two elder sisters by having a cruiser stern. (Thomas N. Olesen collection)

Chapter 5

The advent of Maersk Line

A.P. Møller's entry into liner shipping in 1928 had been a decade in the planning. In the immediate aftermath of the First World War, he had considered establishing a service from Hamburg to Mediterranean ports as Germany then had a severe shortage of tonnage – but this was only a short-term problem, hardly worthy of a major long-term investment in dedicated tonnage.

Later, in 1922, Møller was contacted by his cousin in New York, Hans J. Isbrandtsen, who attempted to persuade him to co-operate in running a cross-trading liner service from ports on America's industrialised Eastern Seaboard. Isbrandtsen was born in Dragør in 1891, the son of A.P. Møller's aunt and uncle, Nicoline and Captain Jacob Isbrandtsen. As a young man, Møller had found him his first job with C.K. Hansen. Next, he was employed as a charterer by Albert Jensen, a Copenhagen shipowner and coal merchant. During the First World War, the British Government blacklisted Jensen's fleet of ten steamers as it was discovered that he was supplying contraband copper to Germany and so Jensen was forced to sell them. As no Danish shipowners wanted to risk further British wrath by buying or chartering the vessels from Jensen, thus rewarding him for his complicity in supporting Germany in the war, he sold them instead to a New York-based company, American Transatlantic Inc, and Hans Isbrandtsen was sent to New York to manage them. Later, Isbrandtsen established his own shipping company in Delaware, Hans Isbrandtsen Inc.[104]

In 1919, A.P. Møller visited the United States, meeting Isbrandtsen in New York and forming a new joint venture, The Isbrandtsen-Moller Company Inc (ISMOLCO). Although Isbrandtsen was unable to finance his own allotted shareholding (for which Møller himself borrowed the necessary capital), Isbrandsten was named President and placed in charge of the joint firm's day-to-day New York-based operations. Møller clearly admired his young cousin – but soon found him to be rather wayward and with an unfortunate tendency to take unilateral business decisions, such as a failed attempt to buy the steamer *Eastbreeze* from the United States Shipping Board in 1920 without any prior consultation.[105]

Both men were strong-willed but it was Isbrandtsen who was the prime mover at first in establishing scheduled liner services. While Møller exuded a gentlemanly but conservative demeanour – a classic shipowner – Isbrandtsen evidently was aggressively 'go-getting' and preferred to circumvent niceties when he thought there was money to be made. Reputedly, he kept in the desk drawer of his New York office a Colt revolver and a bottle of amphetamine pills. The former he held in reserve in case it became necessary forcibly to remove unwelcome visitors and the latter were dished out to his subordinates when he felt they required a little 'pick-me-up' to maintain the work rate he expected of them.[106]

Having invested heavily in expensive projects in Denmark – such as Odense Staalskibsværft – A.P. Møller was initially more cautious about opening a liner service from America. Yet, Møller also was aware that liners were taking over increasing chunks of the global general cargo trades, marginalising tramp ship operators. At first Isbrandtsen favoured services from New York and Delaware to Central and South America, a sphere of operation in which he had prior expertise from his time spent managing Albert Jensen's steamers during the First World War. Møller, however, thought that a cross-Pacific service between the USA and the Far East had the potential to be much more lucrative.[107] In 1914, the Panama Canal had opened and so there was a good business opportunity to carry manufactured goods from ports near America's industrial heartland in the North Eastern states as well as raw materials from South East Asia via the Canal. Already, Dampskibsselskabet Svendborg and Dampskibsselskabet af 1912 vessels had occasionally called at American and Far East ports, either under charter to other liner companies or when collecting cargos as part of their tramping operations. The first call in an American port was in 1913; the first to pass through the Panama Canal was in 1917 and the first to reach China and Japan was in 1924.[108] To operate a fully-fledged liner service so far away from Denmark would be altogether more ambitious, requiring substantial investment in vessels and shore-based infrastructure.

To drum up custom for their proposed liner service, A.P. Møller encouraged Isbrandtsen to arrange a meeting with the head of the Ford Motor Company, Henry Ford, and his right-hand man, the Danish-born Charles E. Sorensen. Their plan was to secure a contract with Ford to carry cars and spare parts to the Far East, providing the guaranteed revenue needed to make a cross-Pacific liner route a sufficiently low-risk investment. In 1928 Isbrandtsen concluded an agreement and so, on 12 July, the motor vessel *Leise Mærsk* left Baltimore and sailed via the Panama Canal to Yokohama, Kobe and Moji in Japan on the first voyage of the new Maersk Line, as the service was named. Another important early customer in America to sign a long-term contract was the Dow Chemical Company.

In 1929, Isbrandtsen came to Copenhagen properly to conclude agreements with A.P. Møller and with the Boards of Dampskibsselskabet Svendborg and Dampskibsselskabet af 1912 regarding Maersk Line's day-to-day management and future expansion. Isbrandtsen, as President of ISMOLCO, was given control of westbound services from the USA to the Far East, while A.P. Møller managed the eastbound legs. As the two men also had differences regarding the merits of joining the Pacific Liner Conference, this was a pragmatic solution. Isbrandtsen – and his main client, Henry Ford – disliked conferences, whereas Møller was keen to join in order to reduce the Maersk Line service's exposure to risk. Maersk Line's initial chartered steamers (and the motor ship *Leise Mærsk*) were slower than many of their

The *Gertrude Mærsk* of 1930 was the first of the fleet purpose built for liner service. An up-to-date and effective vessel, she and her subsequent sisters established Maersk Line as a significant liner operator in the trans-Pacific trade. The *Gertrude Mærsk* continued in service until 1955. (A.P. Møller-Maersk)

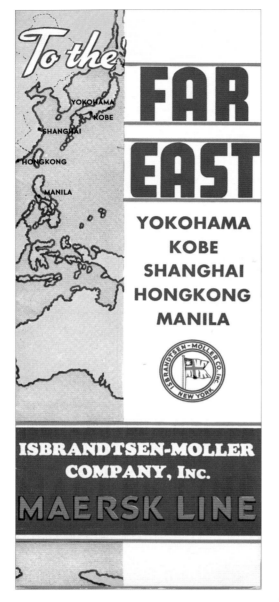

competitors but, as they slightly undercut the conference rates, they attracted custom – and also incurred the wrath of established operators who, particularly in the wake of the Wall Street Crash, blamed them for their poor results.[109]

Thereafter, a new class of motor vessels was ordered from Odense Staalskibsværft specifically for the Maersk Line service. The first of these, the 5,038gt *Gertrude Mærsk*, was delivered in May 1930. A twin-screw vessel, powered by two 6-cylinder B&W diesels which provided a 13.5-knot service speed, she was the largest and fastest cargo liner yet delivered to A.P. Møller; only his oil tankers were slightly bigger. Between January 1931 and May 1932, her four near sisters – the *Niel Mærsk*, *Peter Mærsk*, *Anna Mærsk* and *Nora Mærsk* – joined the fleet. In all respects, these were very progressively-designed vessels with generously-proportioned hulls, able to carry substantial volumes of cargo – indeed, similar shelter deck cargo liners continued to be built for A.P. Møller's liner services until the early 1950s. *The Motor Ship*'s correspondent wrote glowingly of the *Nora Mærsk*'s luxuriously-appointed accommodation for eight passengers:

> 'The passenger accommodation includes four two-berth cabins in the forward deckhouse on the shelter deck... Each has an adjoining bathroom and is also fitted with hot and cold water. The dining room is panelled in polished birch and the smoke room in oak. In order to improve the passenger amenities, there is a swimming bath and a sports deck, together with good promenade space.'[110]

In 1932, A.P. Møller visited the United States, then the Far East, for a total of six months to drum up new business for Maersk Line, establishing a lucrative agreement to transport sugar from the Philippines on behalf of the Spanish-owned Tabacalera sugar mill in Manila. Roughly half of the shipments from the USA to the Far East consisted of Ford cars and parts, with cotton, tobacco and coal accounting for much of the remainder. On the return leg, hemp, silk, pineapples, sugar, tea and tinned fruit were carried. With the new ships, A.P. Møller felt he was in a strong enough position to join the Pacific Conference on the 'homebound' leg from the Far East to the USA, but Hans Isbrandtsen remained adamant that Maersk Line would not join in the opposite direction (even though this position was marginalising the Line's profitability). This was one of a number of points of disagreement between Møller and Isbrandtsen, whose relationship became increasingly strained as the 1930s progressed; other points of conflict were a dispute regarding rights to use the Maersk Line name, disagreements over the chartering of ships and Isbrandtsen's unilateral decision to open a new line between the USA and India, for which he chartered tonnage without deigning to consult A.P. Møller.[111]

The rapid and continuing expansion of A.P. Møller's shipping activities was achieved largely through the re-investing of profits rather than by borrowing money. In 1920, a conservative estimate of the assets of Dampskibsselskabet Svendborg and Dampskibsselskabet af 1912 was 16.4 million kroner and 20.9 million kroner respectively. By 1939, they were estimated to be worth 33.7 and 42.8 million kroner respectively. The capital account of the ships dominated the assets and debt accounted for a mere 3 per cent of the total. To avoid speculation, the Companies were run with a relatively small external share capital. The expansion and renewal of the fleet was, therefore, almost entirely financed from profits.[112]

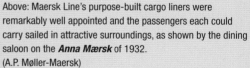
M. S. NORA MAERSK

FRIENDLY ATMOSPHERE

● Good solid accommodation for freighter passengers! Large lounge on M.V "Nora Maersk", the newest ship in the Far East Service. Four single and four double state-rooms provide quarters for twelve passengers.

WELL PATRONIZED

● Dining salon on M.V "Nora Maersk". Substantial comfort and good catering are appreciated features carefully studied for the few passengers accepted for the Far East freighter service in which the M.V "Nora Maersk" has entered.

SMOKING ROOM

● This feature is identical on both the Motorships "Peter Maersk" and "Anna Maersk". A den for men. Upholstered in dark tone leather. In one corner is a cozy fireplace (electric) for cold weather

THE LOUNGE HALL

● Both the M.V "Peter Maersk" and M.V "Anna Maersk" have the same make-up. Note stairway to dining salon at left. Glass topped round tables and cushioned armchairs. The rendezvous spot.

Above: Maersk Line's purpose-built cargo liners were remarkably well appointed and the passengers each could carry sailed in attractive surroundings, as shown by the dining saloon on the *Anna Mærsk* of 1932.
(A.P. Møller-Maersk)

Left and opposite top left: A mid-1930s brochure for Maersk Line's service from the USA to the Far East, emphasising the high quality of passenger accommodation on the *Nora Mærsk*. (Bruce Peter collection)

Below: A passenger cabin on the *Anna Mærsk*.
(A.P. Møller-Maersk)

Above: A deck scene on the **Gertrude Mærsk**, *en route* across the Pacific in 1935, during a fire drill – hence the crew members assembled on deck around the funnel casing. (Kurt Røll)

Below: The **Gertrude Mærsk** at Shanghai in July 1935. (Kurt Røll)

Above: The **Gertrude Mærsk**
alongside in Baltimore. (Kurt Røll)

Below: The **Anna Mærsk**, which entered
service in 1932. (A.P. Møller-Maersk)

ANNA MÆRSK

Chapter 6

After the Wall Street Crash

On 29 October 1929, share prices on the New York Stock Exchange collapsed. Their value continued to fall for a whole month afterwards. In the weeks leading up to the crash, the market had been unstable with waves of stock being sold, followed by waves of rallying share prices and renewed purchasing. By Christmas, there was a partial recovery, followed by a second, more severe decline and a new crash on 8 July 1932, from which the Dow Jones Industrial Average of shares did not fully recover for over twenty years.[113]

During the five years preceding the initial 1929 crash, the value of shares had increased five-fold but, on the day of the initial crash, 17 per cent was wiped off their value, equating to $14 billion. Playing the stock market had become a popular pastime during the 1920s and many of the speculators who lost out were private individuals who had themselves borrowed the money they invested. As the value of shares had grown, an increasing disparity between publicly-quoted businesses' assets and their share value had appeared. The Wall Street Crash led to a widespread and catastrophic loss of confidence in the market which left many destitute and brought about a Great Depression. This situation had a disastrous effect on the shipping world – particularly less efficient companies, many of which were forced to lay up their fleets of steamers and some of which declared bankruptcy.

From 1930 onwards, there was a breakdown in international trade, worsening the depression's negative effects, especially in countries whose economies depended on exports. Businesses and individuals consequently defaulted on their loans and this caused banks to collapse, further compounding the problem.

In order to try to induce recovery, some governments intervened with subsidies to the private sector and also substantial public works projects; leading among these were totalitarian Italy and Germany, where massive construction and military armament programmes were initiated to create employment. (Germany had been particularly badly hit by collapses in share values in America as the modernisation of its industrial base in the wake of the First World War had been financed to a large extent by American loans.) Britain – the world's leading imperial and maritime power – also suffered terribly, unemployment reaching 2.5 million by the end of 1930 (around 20 per cent of the working population). Northern industrial cities engaged in shipbuilding were severely affected as yards' order books were suddenly empty and their employees were laid off. In these circumstances, Government intervention to alleviate suffering was welcome – and a loan to Cunard-White Star Line enabling the completion of their moth-balled trans-Atlantic flagship liner *Queen Mary* by John Brown & Co. at Clydebank was a very prominent manifestation of this policy.[114]

The Danish Government was likewise forced to intervene to stabilise the Burmeister & Wain shipyard and engine works. During the 1920s, B&W developed rapidly – in terms of diesel engine design, market share and the expanse of its shipyard and marine engine works infrastructure. By the latter 1920s, 45 per cent of the world's diesel-driven merchant fleet was powered by B&W engines, mainly built in Copenhagen. In 1929, B&W delivered engines with a total power output of 195,000 ihp, but orders fulfilled in 1930 saw this drop to 181,000 ihp and in 1931 it was down to 111,000 ihp. While these figures suggest that, even in the worst of the recession, motor ships were being built in fairly substantial numbers, B&W had been preparing for growth rather than retraction. In the shipyard, a new launchway was under construction and simultaneously new construction halls were being built to manufacture engines at a greater rate than hitherto, while a new administration building was also nearing completion. These initiatives had required substantial investment. In 1932, B&W's senior management approached the Danish Government to ask for a moratorium on loan repayments to be imposed in order to secure the Company's future; this was passed in February 1933 – it stipulated that B&W's less lucrative divisions should be wound down and that the Company should concentrate solely on shipbuilding, engine design and manufacture.[115] The fact that the Government was concerned to assist B&W through its short-term difficulties indicated the firm's importance to the Danish economy and to Denmark's international prestige as an industrial nation.

Denmark's larger shipping companies – most notably EAC and A.P. Møller – continued to build new tonnage during the depression years. The latter 1920s had been a profitable period for Danish shipping, meaning that, come the Wall Street Crash, these operators – and even smaller companies – had money in the bank. As shipyards now had empty order books, these firms could potentially commission newbuildings at very low cost, enabling fleet modernisation to occur at the very moment when operational efficiency was to prove most crucial to survival.

Britain's withdrawal from the Gold Standard in September 1931 prompted a 30 per cent fall in the value of sterling. Denmark and the other Nordic nations followed suit, the Danish kroner's value falling 12 per cent below its previous position relative to the pound. As a result, Danish ships gained a significant advantage as it became cheaper to ship goods under the Dannebrog than other flags (concurrently, German and Dutch vessels were laid up in large numbers for this reason).[116]

Above all, the Scandinavian countries' large proportion of motor ships now came into their own, their greater economy giving their owners a decisive advantage at a point when freight rates were depressed and profit margins slim. Indeed, it is arguable that Scandinavian shipowners operating motor vessels actually benefited from the shakeout of weaker companies which the Wall Street Crash precipitated. In May 1931, the editorial in *The Motor Ship* was entitled 'Psychology in Depression in Shipbuilding.' The editor observed:

> 'During the past year, of the ships launched 62 per cent have been motor vessels and 38 per cent steamers. In the same period the vessels commenced have comprised 64 per cent motor ships and 36 per cent steamers. These figures do not include Russian tonnage, which is almost wholly motor vessels. Depression turns owners thoughts to economy, and during the past year the motor ship has shown to special advantage. Thus we shall probably see an increase in motor tonnage contracts relative to steamers in the future, just as we did in the last depression. A few weeks ago a shipowner operating four large motor liners and about eight big cargo motor ships, in addition to a similar number of steam-driven passenger liners and about 20 cargo steamers, stated

With its fleet of modern and economical motor ships, EAC was in a relatively strong position when the Great Depression caused a collapse in freight rates. Furthermore, its conglomerate structure and investments in the food industry protected it from the Depression's worst effects. The *India*, built at Nakskov and delivered in 1930, was a capacious vessel, her largest hold able to accommodate no less than 5,000 tons of cargo, around a third of her total capacity. (Thomas N. Olesen collection)

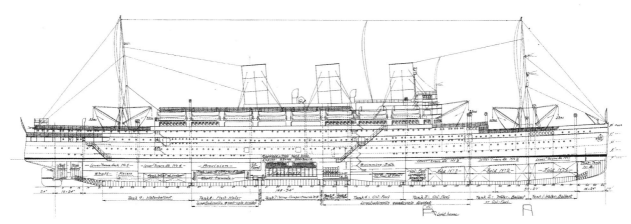

that whereas the motor cargo ships were just able to make a profit the steamers were being operated at a loss. This is notoriously common experience in many trades, and it has to be remembered that as the future orders will be largely for cargo ships, since passenger vessels have continued to be constructed since the depression, the progress of the motor ship should be advanced in the future.'[117]

This proved to be highly prophetic, especially so far as the development of the Scandinavian merchant fleet was concerned. Looking back at the depression years from 1937, *The Motor Ship* observed:

'Early participation in the motor ship movement has changed the whole aspect of shipbuilding in the three Northern countries. If we consider the new era to have commenced in earnest at the end of the war, say, in 1919, the Scandinavian mercantile fleet has increased since 1919 from 3,500,000 tons gross to over 8,700,000 tons gross, and has grown from 7½ per cent of the world's total fleet to 10½ per cent. Although owning only 10½ per cent of the total merchant fleet of the world, more than 27 per cent of the tonnage of motor ships afloat sails under the Norwegian, Swedish or Danish flag… The Scandinavian merchant fleet is the most modern, since 39 per cent is under 10 years old, compared with a world figure of 25 per cent, and of 34½ per cent for the United Kingdom. About 12½ per cent of Norway's ships are under five years old (about equal to Japan) compared with 11 per cent in Denmark and 9½ per cent in the United Kingdom.

Norway, with a population about one-third that of London, is the third shipping country in the world and is the first to have more motor ships than steamers, the former representing 53 per cent of the total tonnage, the corresponding figures in Denmark and Sweden being 49.9 per cent and 37.5 per cent, whereas for the rest of the world it is only 37.5 per cent. In Scandinavia, therefore, the oil-engined vessel has been adopted

Above: By the latter 1920s, DFDS was well aware that its existing trans-Atlantic passenger liner fleet needed replacement. The company's technical staff produced a new design, employing up-to-date diesel technology. Although three funnels were specified, the two forward and aft were dummies, included only to make the silhouette more impressive. (Thomas N. Olesen collection)

Below: A model of DFDS' proposed new liner, a project which never came to fruition due to a lack of support from the Danish Government and opposition from other ship owners. (Bruce Peter collection)

to at least three times the extent, relatively, as compared with other countries, and there is a larger tonnage of motor ships owned in Norway, Sweden and Denmark combined than in the United Kingdom... Shipowners in the three countries, practically without exception, after taking delivery of their first motor vessel, have ordered ships exclusively of this type. Several now have no others. The East Asiatic Co., for instance, owns 26 motor ships, the Nordstjernan Rederi AB, Stockholm, 18 motor ships... and neither of these owners has a single steamer... One might go through the whole gamut of Scandinavian owners in the same way and with similar results. The case of Messrs. Wilh. Wilhelmsen may be specially emphasised, since in 15 years these owners have built up the largest singly owned fleet of motor vessels in the world, totalling some 300,000 tons. They have continued to order motor ships throughout the whole of the depression and have added 13 new vessels since 1930.'[118]

The Motor Ship concluded:

'The correctness of the policy of Scandinavian shipowners in adoping oil-engined vessels from the first has been confirmed in two ways. There are now far larger numbers

Right: J. Lauritzen's route from New York to the West Coast of South America was operated by, amongst others, the steamer **Marna**, built at Helsingør in 1936. (Thomas N. Olesen collection)

Centre: The motor vessel **Argentinean Reefer**, built at Aalborg and delivered in 1941, was a state-of-the-art refrigerated cargo carrier. (Museet for Søfart)

Bottom: The J. Lauritzen diesel cargo liner **Nora**, also Aalborg-built and completed in 1941, was intended to serve on the New York-South America service. Her career was short because, while requisitioned for American war service, she was torpedoed off Halifax, Nova Scotia, in 1943. (Museet for Søfart)

of shipowners in other countries who are now adopting motor vessels than when they were first employed in the three Northern countries and, secondly, it will readily be agreed that Scandinavian shipowners have weathered the recent years of the severest depression as well as, if not better than, their competitors; and this is without any subsidy, a circumstance on which it is only fair to lay stress.'[119]

During the Great Depression, it was operators of older tramp steamers who suffered most. In April 1932, 129 Danish tramp steamers were laid up in ports and fjords around the country and

many were sold for scrap shortly thereafter. This clear out of old tonnage, however, arguably had longer-term benefits. In other leading shipping nations, the situation was repeated and so when the first signs of a tentative and patchy recovery began to be seen in 1933-34, the size of the world's merchant fleet had declined by 6 per cent (pre-war tonnage being largely removed from the market in the process). This led to improved freight rates and the generally modern Scandinavian fleets were well positioned to benefit from this upswing.[120] For operators of coal-fired steamers who survived the worst depression years, the 1930s continued to prove tough going. Port taxes became higher for vessels requiring coaling and the infrastructure in place to supply these became increasingly worn – not least in British ports where coal was still used much more than in Scandinavia.

In 1938, the East Asiatic Company became Denmark's largest shipping company, pushing DFDS into second place, while A.P. Møller was third, but undergoing rapid expansion. Both EAC and A.P. Møller's Maersk Line were involved in the Far East trade; the Great Depression affected this less than DFDS' North European and trans-Atlantic services. Furthermore, these companies were the greatest enthusiasts for motor ships, whereas DFDS continued to run a larger proportion of steamers on its liner routes. Neither EAC nor Maersk Line at any point laid up motor cargo liners and EAC's share price remained more buoyant throughout the crisis than that of DFDS.[121]

It appeared also that EAC's conglomerate status protected it from the worst effects of the Great Depression. Although 30 per cent of share value was lost overall, some subsidiaries – such as Dansk Sojakagefabrik – enjoyed steady profitability throughout. EAC's increasing involvement in transporting foodstuffs on its liners was also lucrative and so most of its newbuildings were fitted with some refrigerated capacity to enable high-value cargo of this kind to be carried on a regular basis. Meanwhile, the Company's forestry plantations in Siam also made money and employed 1,400 lumberjacks plus 265 elephants.[122]

The subject of protectionism was, however, worrying for Scandinavian shipowners. Already, most were used to facing flag discrimination and the banning of their vessels from trading between mainland Europe's imperial powers – particularly The Netherlands, Belgium and France – and their colonies. Britain was more liberal with strong established political and economic traditions arguing in favour of free trade. In such circumstances, the majority of Scandinavian shipowners were keen to avoid even accusations that any of their ships were either built or operated with the benefit of subsidies.

In the early 1930s, DFDS understandably wanted to replace its existing trans-Atlantic passenger liner fleet, which dated from the 1902-1913 period, with at least one new flagship, the building of which would require a Government subsidy of 18 million kroner (DFDS proposed to invest only 3 million in the project).[123] In Denmark, this provoked a heated debate among leading

Dampskibsselskabet Torm's motor ship **Thyra S**. was built in 1936 by Nakskov Skibsværft.
(Museet for Søfart)

shipowners, who feared that if Danish ships were built and operated with subsidies, this would lead to greater flag discrimination against their vessels by powerful foreign governments who might regard Danish state intervention as unfair competition. In this debate, A.P. Møller was the most vocal in arguing against the subsidised construction of new tonnage. Instead, he reasoned that the Danish merchant fleet benefited from market-led liberal practices, based upon operational efficiency and freedom to trade without restrictions. When DFDS failed to win the argument in favour of subsidy and instead decided to withdraw its final Scandinavia-America passenger liner, the *Frederik VIII*, in 1935, A.P. Møller observed that 'to operate ships merely for prestige gives no meaning.'[124] The implication was that there were only two basic principles underpinning best practice in the Merchant Navy – market need and profitability. In the context of the 1930s, when European and other powers subsidised what they considered to be their most important liners and liner routes, this position was unorthodox – but today it has become the understood and accepted approach throughout the world.

Yet, in public discourses on the plight of shipping in rival nations, the suspicion persisted that Scandinavian success in liner shipping was due to unfair economic advantages rather than to superior technology and business practices. One correspondent wrote as follows to *The Scotsman* newspaper in November 1938, using the pseudonym 'Economist':

'In 1914 it was our proud boast that Great Britain possessed more than half of the shipping of the world. Today it has about 30 per cent. Our shipping, compared with 1914, is down by 2,500,000gt and 1,600 ships. What are the causes of this decline? The answer is to be found in subsidies, State control, frozen credits, and standard of living… The value of merchant shipping under construction in British yards for foreign owners is about £3,500,000, whereas more than £5,000,000 worth of shipping is being built to British order in Scandinavian, Dutch and German yards. With the Scandinavian and Dutch yards, it is all a question of price…

There is a growing feeling of resentment among the workers on the Clyde and in other British shipbuilding centres at this unfair competition. It is even suggested in some quarters that shipyard workers should make an active protest by refusing to buy Danish butter, eggs and bacon. It is no good being squeamish about our measures to remedy this situation. Our very existence as an Empire is at stake.'[125]

This drew a swift response from Erik Schacke of the Royal Danish Consulate in Edinburgh who replied:

'With reference to Economist's letter in your issue of 24th, allow me to point out that in Denmark neither shipping nor shipbuilding is subsidised in any way whatsoever. On the contrary, Danish industry is handicapped, Denmark not possessing any minerals and having to import all its requirements of coal, iron, steel &c… Today the tonnage of Danish motor ships exceeds that of steamers. The world's total motor tonnage is 15 million tons gross, of which 41 ½ per cent are provided with Danish B&W diesel engines, built either by Burmeister & Wain, Copenhagen, or by its licensees.

As regards trade between Great Britain and Denmark, an agreement between the two countries was entered into some years ago and Denmark, in spite of it being only half the size of Scotland, is Great Britain's third largest European customer. Calculated per head of population, it is the best customer.'[126]

One way to mitigate the worst effects of the Great Depression was to become involved in emerging specialist shipping markets, preferably transporting delicate high-value goods and, better still, carrying items without which Europe's burgeoning urban populations could not survive. Such a niche in which certain Danish shipping lines came to excel was refrigerated food transport, specifically the trades in frozen meat and refrigerated fruit.

British and French shipping lines first pioneered refrigerated cargo ships. The impetus for their development was finding a way to link the large cattle ranches in Australia, New Zealand and Argentina to the enormous consumer markets in Britain and Europe. Hitherto, only canned mutton and beef products could be shipped over such long distances and so finding a better solution became a challenge for engineers and scientists alike. An early French experiment in 1876, using the former Elder Dempster vessel *Eboe*, was successful. The engineer Charles Teillier converted the ship by fitting methyl ether machinery and insulating the cargo holds with layers of cork. Renamed *Frigorifique*, she sailed from Rouen to Buenos Aires with a small meat cargo as an experiment, returning to France with 25 tons of chilled meat in good condition. The carriage of bananas – a particularly delicate fruit – developed somewhat later as shipboard refrigeration plant required to be capable of precise calibration to maintain a fairly constant

temperature of 12 degrees celsius with a controlled atmosphere, no matter how hot or cold conditions were outside or how fast the ship was sailing.

Reefer ships operate either as tramps or liners, depending upon whether they are engaged in seasonal work (such as carrying fruit from the Eastern Mediterranean lands and North Africa to Northern Europe) or regular year-round service (transporting deep-frozen meat from New Zealand and South America or bananas from the Caribbean and Central America to Europe). In shipping industry jargon, tramping reefers are known as 'wild reefers,' whereas reefers in scheduled liner service are referred to as 'non-wild reefers.'[127]

From the latter 1930s onwards, J. Lauritzen – the operating arm of Dampskibs-selskabet Vesterhavet, a shipping company founded in Esbjerg by Ditlev Lauritzen in 1895 and hitherto mainly involved in the tramping trades – became particularly successful as a specialist operator of refrigerated cargo ships and also became increasingly involved in cross-trading liner services. The development of these particular aspects of cargo shipping coincided with Ditlev Lauritzen being succeeded by his two sons, Ivar and Knud, in 1932. By then, Lauritzen senior was aged 73

and reaching the end of his remarkably vigorous business career. Not only did Ivar and Knud Lauritzen continue to develop J. Lauritzen's business interests, but they also set about introducing much more modern ship designs.[128] Whereas before, J. Lauritzen had competed on price, in future, ships would also be designed to be as efficient and modern-looking as naval architecture and marine engineering would allow. During the mid-1930s, this meant for the Company a belated (but rapid) shift away from steam to diesel propulsion in the context of its growing involvement in the shipping of fruit. Diesel propulsion was ideal for reefers as the engines could supply power to electric generators running the refrigeration plant.

Ditlev Lauritzen had first attempted to compete with the established Associated Liners Conference between Northern Europe and the Mediterranean in 1927. At the invitation of the Sicilian fruit exporter, Agenzia Generale Trasporti, he began to divert his tramp steamers via Palermo on the return leg of their voyages to North African ports, having delivered their cargoes of coal from Poland and timber from Finland. Agenzia Generale Transporti were frustrated by Associated Liners' decision unilaterally to increase freight rates by 25 per cent and hoped that J. Lauritzen's vessels could carry fruit to Northern Europe at a rate undercutting the Conference. (Associated Liners consisted of five companies: the Nordenfjeldske Dampskips-selskap, Wilson Line, Adria Line, Ocean & General and Deutsche Levante.) The initiative was only marginally profitable due to the seasonal nature of the orange and lemon harvest. As vessels otherwise sailed northbound in ballast, in the wake of the Wall Street Crash, the operation was temporarily suspended. In 1931, however, Ditlev Lauritzen decided to resume his offensive against Associated Liners. Freight rates were further reduced for fruit as well as general cargo and calls were introduced *en route* at Naples, Genoa and Marseilles. Although the service still was hardly profitable, its withdrawal in 1935 was primarily due to Danish Government sanctions against Italy resulting from the Fascist dictator Mussolini's brutal invasion of Abyssinia, rather than any desire by J. Lauritzen to capitulate to Associated Liners.[129]

Meanwhile, Ditlev Lauritzen shifted his attention to America, sending his son Knud to New York in 1933 to built contacts there with the intention of developing both the refrigerated fruit trade and liner services – perhaps taking inspiration from A.P. Møller's Maersk Line. This resulted in agreements with La Frutera Sudamericana and La Fruta Chilena, which were followed up in 1934 by

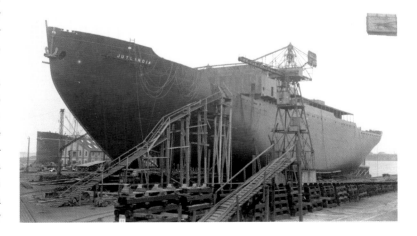

The **Jutlandia**, as she appeared when completed. For the duration of the Second World War, she was laid up in Denmark, thereafter re-entering service for EAC. (Museet for Søfart)

one of J. Lauritzen's dynamic young managers, Tage Nielsen, a key figure in the expansion into liner shipping and subsequently a long-serving director of the Company.[130]

During 1934, liner services were established between Canada and South Africa (operated jointly with the Liverpool-based Elder Dempster Lines) and from Chile to New York via the Panama Canal with calls in Cuba, Ecuador and Peru. Known as the West Coast Line, the route soon proved to be a good initiative. The 1,517gt Nakskov-built steamer *Jonna*, delivered the previous year, inaugurated it and soon three vessels were involved, bringing general cargo southbound while fruit, potassium nitrate and sugar were carried northbound. The American freight market grew significantly in the second half of the 1930s in the wake of President Roosevelt's 'New Deal,' whereby the Government intervened in the economy with large public works programmes to boost growth, and the outlook in Britain also improved. The Italian Fascist regime's military adventures in Africa and the advent of the German National Socialist regime in 1933, however, caused increasing political instability in Europe, meaning that cross-trading activities centred on American ports were a relatively lucrative and politically stable area in which to be involved. Therefore, J. Lauritzen's West Coast Line managed to achieve highly satisfactory financial results in the years preceding the Second World War.[131]

Meanwhile, in Denmark, unemployment remained high in the wake of the Wall Street Crash and the Danish Government was keen to boost shipbuilding. Consequently, Lauritzen negotiated a low-interest 70 per cent Government loan to build new reefers. Of eight vessels subsequently ordered from various Danish shipyards, two built by Burmeister & Wain in Copenhagen were the first motor ships in the Lauritzen fleet and their design proved to be highly influential. This situation reflected the ongoing power-shift from Ditlev Lauritzen, who wanted only steamers, to Ivar and Knud, the young generation, who believed that motor ships were better on all counts.[132] (Incidentally, Ivar Lauritzen's wife, Lillian Kirkebye, was the daughter of the Danish fruit importer A.W. Kirkebye and so his involvement with reefer shipping was on a personal as well as a business level.[133])

The Danish Shipowners' Association (Danmarks Rederiforening) protested at the subsidies enjoyed by Lauritzen, which its other members probably assumed were the result of Ditlev Lauritzen's close association with the Social Democratic Shipping Minister, C.N. Hauge. It pointed out that such subsidies might lead to Danish ships suffering increased flag discrimination in foreign ports, as they might be seen to have an unfair market advantage (besides, A.P. Møller, a leading protester against subsidies, was also peripherally engaged in the fruit trade at that time). This notwithstanding, with a somewhat reduced subsidy, the first

Lauritzen motor reefer, the 1,794gt *Asta*, was launched at Burmeister & Wain in June 1934.

The *Asta* was the prototype vessel of a more-or-less standard design of medium-sized cargo ship also subsequently built with slight variations for DFDS, Dampskibsselskabet Torm and several other Danish and Scandinavian shipping companies during the ensuing decade. In contrast to the steamers and the majority of existing motor ships, which typically had straight stems and counter sterns, these 'new generation' motor vessels had spoon-shaped sterns and bows with rounded stems. The superstructure was amidships with two cargo holds forward and two aft and a prominent monkey island between each pair of holds; the large size of the monkey islands reflected the fact that they were insulated and contained parts of the refrigeration plant. Eleven passengers could be carried and the passengers and officers' cabins, lounges and dining room were amidships, with crew accommodation in a deckhouse at the stern. Capping the silhouette was a broad, almost vertical, motor ship funnel. Below this, in the engine room, there was, of course, a Burmeister & Wain diesel engine and, to starboard, an auxiliary engine to power the refrigeration plant.[134]

The *Asta*'s engine was the first of a new 6-cylinder 2-stroke single-acting B&W design which used poppet valves rather than sleeve valves for the exhaust. This generated 2,270 bhp and enabled the *Asta* to achieve a speed of 15 knots on trials. In addition, a new type of reversal system was fitted, capable of changing the engine's direction in only a few seconds. Three 2-stroke single-acting auxiliary diesels were installed to power the refrigeration plant with sufficient back-up in case of a failure. Thus, the *Asta* was not only thoroughly modern in appearance but also mechanically state-of-the-art.[135]

A couple of months after she entered service, *The Motor Ship* reported: 'There are an increasing number of fruit ships calling at Cape Town. The new Lauritzen motor ship *Asta* [called] at Cape Town on March 6 on her maiden voyage to South Africa to load the first citrus fruit of the season for Scandinavia. She aroused much interest in port on account of her yacht-like lines.'[136] The stylish appearance of the latest generation of Danish cargo liners can only have helped to boost the image of its merchant fleet – in contrast with the more conservative designs favoured by many ships in the merchant fleets of the major imperial powers, not least Britain. *The Motor Ship* continued: 'With her in dock on the same day was the [British-built and -flagged] *Wairangi*, also on her first voyage to South Africa and Australia' – but the journal refrained from commenting in any way upon the latter's design.

A second Danish tramping company to enter the fruit trade with similarly designed vessels was Dampskibsselskabet Torm. This had been founded in 1889 by two former ships' officers, Captain Ditlev Emanuel Torm and Christian Schmiegelow, the latter an ambitious former First Officer who was only aged 32 at that time. (Schmiegelow subsequently joined the EAC Board in

A port-side view of the ***Jutlandia*** underway. (Russell Priest collection)

The East Asiatic Company's second *Selandia*. (Thomas N. Olesen collection)

1909, where, as Director of Shipping, he oversaw the Company's switch to motor ships and the inauguration of *Selandia*.)

Initially, Torm operated tramp steamers in the Baltic and North Sea areas (Captain Torm's mantra was 'Riga-Ghent-Burntisland-Kiel, you know here you are with them!').[137] In the 1920s, using larger steamers, Torm began to sail trans-Atlantic too. Thanks to a lucrative ongoing contract with the Soviet Union to transport timber to Britain, Torm's fleet was well employed during the worst years of the Great Depression (1930-32).

In the latter 1920s Torm, like J. Lauritzen, had entered the fruit trade, and it too found that this was profitable. Two lines were established in 1930 – one linking Hamburg and Antwerp with Tenerife and Las Palmas de Gran Canaria (but also making occasional calls in Spanish ports) and the other between Hamburg/Antwerp and the Eastern Mediterranean, calling at Alexandria, Port Said, Jaffa, Haifa, Beirut and Tripoli. Ten new ships were purchased between 1933 and 1938, mainly to serve these routes. The first was the Nakskov-built *Almena*, Torm's initial motor vessel. Strangely, its next three newbuildings were steamers, including its first refrigerated cargo ship, the Helsingør-built *Estrid* of 1933. Newbuilding five was the 1,738gt *Thyra S.*, a motor ship delivered from Nakskov in 1936 and similar in design to Lauritzen's *Asta*. (The *Thyra S.* was fitted with fruit decks but, unlike the *Asta*, there was no refrigeration equipment.) Come the mid-1930s, Torm was well established in the Mediterranean fruit trade and even accepted into the British-dominated liner conference serving the Eastern Mediterranean. Reflecting this new status, a series of four 2,252gt, 14-knot refrigerated cargo liners was built in Helsingør for delivery in 1937-39: these were the *Helvig*, *Olga S.*, *Ragnhild* and *Gertrud*; each could carry five passengers.[138]

A similar design to Lauritzen's *Asta* and Torm's *Thyra S.* was used for a series of four 1,690gt cargo liners for DFDS' Mediterranean routes. The *Tunis*, *Marocco*, *Algier* and *Sicilien* were completed in Helsingør between 1936 and 1938. Between ordering and taking delivery, Mussolini's Italy invaded Abyssinia as part of his military strategy to create a new Roman Empire by annexing the nations around the Mediterranean. This cruel aggression drew sharp condemnation from Europe's remaining democratic governments – not least in Scandinavia – and so sanctions against Italy were proposed as a protest. For DFDS and other shipowners trading to the Mediterranean, instability and trade restrictions caused loadings to decline and so DFDS gave thought to redeploying its new vessels. As its trans-Atlantic liner services to North and South America were particularly buoyant, carrying to Denmark large quantities of corn, animal feed and general cargo, the four Mediterranean route motor ships were moved in 1939 to the

Copenhagen-New York service. This enabled a cascade of tonnage, helping also to provide for the growing trade with South America. The fact that these vessels each had accommodation for 12 passengers enabled DFDS briefly to revive the Scandinavia-America Line, albeit on a much smaller scale than before 1935.[139]

In 1936, A.P. Møller too very briefly owned a single purpose-built refrigerated cargo liner, the 3,159gt *Francine*. She was initially ordered from Odense Staalskibsværft by a French firm, Compagnie de Navigation de Transport, for the shipment of bananas between Cameroon and France. The *Francine* had a novel machinery-aft arrangement with the superstructure arranged much like an oil tanker; the officers' accommodation and wheelhouse were amidships and the crew were domiciled at the stern, around the base of the funnel. With a stern-located engine room and consequently a short propeller shaft, space and weight were saved but it was not until the 1950s that this layout became commonplace in cargo liner design.

Due to currency exchange restrictions, the *Francine* was never delivered to her French owner and instead Dampskibsselskabet Svendborg and Dampskibsselskabet af 1912 jointly took her over. Their intention was to operate her between Cameroon and France for their own account.[140] Unfortunately, French union-inspired flag discrimination coupled with low demand for bananas in France meant that the *Francine* never entered service. Following five months in lay up in Copenhagen, she was sold to J. Lauritzen in 1937, becoming the *Egyptian Reefer*.

In the 1937-38 period, J. Lauritzen expanded its American cross-trading liner services, adding a route from Gulf of Mexico ports via the Panama Canal to ports on the west coast of South America, marketed as the Gulf Line, and one from US east coast ports to Rio de Janeiro, Santos, Montevideo and Buenos Aires, known as the East Coast Line. On this route, four new state-of-the-art reefers were deployed.[141] These were the 2,308gt Nakskov-built *American Reefer* and *Australian Reefer*, both of which entered service in 1937, the 2,815gt *Indian Reefer*, delivered in 1939 from Helsingørs Jernskibs- og Maskinbyggeri, plus her near-sister, the *Argentinean Reefer*, completed by Aalborg Værft in 1941. All three were B&W-engined twin-screw vessels capable of a 15.5-knot service speed.[142] Their naval architect was Knud E. Hansen, a very progressive and skilful practitioner who, until 1937, was employed by the Helsingør yard. He then established an independent consultancy that soon became world-famous in shipping circles. The *Argentinean Reefer* was built in Aalborg because in 1938 J. Lauritzen took over the former Aalborg Maskin- og Skibsbyggeri, renaming it as Aalborg Værft and instituting a major programme of investment and modernisation. Thereafter, it became a prime supplier of new tonnage for the Company.

Another important aspect of J. Lauritzen's approach to shipping was its provision of exceptionally good crew accommodation as well as social and cultural activities to encourage its employees' personal development. Even before the First World War, loans were provided to

With the motor ships **Kina** and **Korea** of 1939, EAC introduced a more conventional design approach with a single large funnel. The **Kina**, shown here, sank in a typhoon in the Philippines in 1947 but soon a very similar replacement was ordered. (Thomas N. Olesen collection)

The EAC's **Korea**, photographed in Copenhagen in the latter 1950s, had spent the Second World War laid up in Denmark.
(Niels Krebs/Nautilus Forlag archive)

seamen who wanted to further their education and a training ship was bought in 1930. J. Lauritzen's late-1930s newbuildings had individual cabins for each crew member with comfortable furnishings and even radios to listen to while off duty. All other shipping companies restricted such refinements to their senior officers and initially they railed against J. Lauritzen's 'softness,' but eventually followed suit with similar enhancements during the 1950s-60s period.[143] Undoubtedly, a forward-thinking attitude to employees' working conditions encouraged loyalty, efficiency and good labour relations.

In the longer term, only Torm and Lauritzen made a success of reefer shipping under the Danish flag. In the post-war era, the latter specialised mainly in 'wild' tramping reefers, rather than in liner shipping. Their mid-1930s newbuildings, however, demonstrated the advantages of investing in the most up-to-date and competitive tonnage and of how becoming an acknowledged leader in a particular market niche could be an effective way of prospering in the aftermath of a severe economic downturn.

During the second half of the 1930s, Torm decided to change its focus from tramp to liner shipping. Already established in the Eastern Mediterranean, its next project was a trans-Atlantic service from there, plus a linking route between North and South American ports. By the outbreak of the Second World War, Torm's fleet consisted of 24 ships.[144]

Both EAC and A.P. Møller also added further new motor ship tonnage to their liner routes as the global economy began to pick up in the latter 1930s. EAC's 8,457gt Nakskov-built passenger and cargo liner *Jutlandia*, delivered in 1934, and Maersk Line's 8,494gt Bremer Vulkan-built sisters *Grete Mærsk* and *Marchen Mærsk* of 1937 were significant in that all three were fitted experimentally with Maier-form bows. The design had first been developed by an Austrian-born naval architect, Fritz F. Maier (1844-1926), who had studied engineering in Vienna and who worked in Norddeutcher Lloyd's Research Department in Bremen. Following his death, his son Erich Maier (1901-1981) continued development work during the 1930s. Maier-form bows featured V-shaped framing and a curved stem above and below the waterline supposedly to improve hydrodynamic efficiency while increasing a hull's internal volume.

When the *Grete Mærsk* was handed over by her builder and registered under the Danish flag, for the first time the Danish merchant fleet contained more motor ship tonnage than steamers.[145] The Maier bow design cannot have been found as advantageous as expected because, after *Marchen Mærsk*, all subsequent newbuildings for EAC and A.P. Møller were designed with conventional stems, but their experimental early adoption of the Maier design nonetheless shows how open-minded Danish liner operators were to trying out new ideas which might lead to further efficiency gains.

In 1938 EAC took delivery from Nakskov of its second *Selandia*, an 8,482gt passenger and cargo motor ship, and this was followed in 1939 by the 9,823gt K-class sisters *Kina* and *Korea*, vessels of an entirely new design for the Company and rather similar in appearance to typical A.P. Møller cargo liners of the period. On trials, however, the *Kina* attained a speed of 18 knots, making her one of the fastest examples of her kind. The K-class sisters were each fitted with an 8-cylinder 2-stroke double-acting B&W diesel generating 10,400 ihp.[146]

The Danish liberal and *laissez-faire* approach to shipping in the 1930s contrasted markedly with the massive Government intervention to bolster the American merchant fleet as part of President Roosevelt's New Deal, announced in 1933. By the mid-1930s, the numerous vessels commissioned by the United States Shipping Board between 1918 and 1922 were becoming obsolescent. Thus, in 1936 the Merchant Marine Act was passed, leading to the formation of the United States Maritime Commission as a successor to the Shipping Board, with responsibility for designing a series of standard ship types to upgrade the American fleet. The Commission created nine categories of vessel signified by a letter (P for passenger, C for cargo, T for tanker and so on) and a numeral – the higher, the bigger the vessel type's dimensions. Thus a C2 was a moderately-sized cargo vessel, while a C4 was a large one. The C2 cargo liner and the T2 tanker were to be the most successful (and ubiquitous) of the new American merchant armada. The first C2, the *Donald McKay* completed in 1939, was diesel-powered, but most subsequent examples were steam turbine vessels – as were the T2 tankers.[147] America's ability to mobilise vast resources of manpower and industry to mass-produce standard ship designs would have a significant impact upon the outcome of the Second World War and the subsequent development of merchant shipping in the post-war era.

The *Korea* alongside at Hobart in Tasmania in the late-1950s; in 1967, she was sold to Hong Kong breakers. (L.D.Rex, Russell Priest collection)

Chapter 7

The Second World War and its aftermath

Germany, still feeling injured national pride from capitulating in the First World War and having suffered draconian post-war settlement terms, went on to experience economic turmoil in the wake of the Wall Street Crash then turned Fascist in 1933 with the election of the National Socialist Party, led by Adolf Hitler. A command economy was instituted, prestigious national infrastructure projects commenced and Germany re-militarised. Invading and plundering neighbouring countries would recoup the cost of funding these initiatives. The vision was to create a 'Greater Germany,' spread across most of mainland Europe. Notwithstanding the 1938 Munich Agreement's promise of 'peace in our time,' on 1 September 1939 Germany attacked and invaded Poland, resulting only two days later in a declaration of war by Britain and France.

Prior to the war's commencement, a committee of the Danish Shipowners' Association had worked out a proposal for war insurance of Danish ships, resulting in legislation being passed in May 1939. Next, the Danish Government reconstituted Fragtnævnet (The Chartering Committee) as they were understandably keen to maintain essential overseas supplies – coal, coke and animal feed – using Danish-flag tonnage. During the first months of the conflict, Denmark hoped that, as in the First World War, by remaining neutral, it could obtain some protection for its merchant fleet. In March 1940, a delegation of three leading Danish shipping company directors, consisting of DFDS' Managing Director J.A. Kørbing, EAC's Chairman Prince Axel – who had succeeded H.N. Andersen upon the latter's death in December 1937 – and A.P. Møller, visited London for talks at the Ministry of Shipping to negotiate the rights of Danish ships to continue trading with Britain as before the war. This soon proved a naïve hope. In anticipation of a German invasion of Scandinavia and to prevent acts of sabotage by their crews, on 30 March 1940 the US Coast Guard seized all German, Italian and Danish ships in American ports.

When Denmark was invaded by Germany on 9 April 1940, the Danish merchant fleet was cut in two. Vessels in Scandinavian waters were locked in and could only trade in this area for the war's five-year duration (such vessels became known as the 'home fleet'). The remainder, in neutral or Allied ports outside the German blockade (or seized by the Allies) formed the so-called 'overseas fleet.' Officially, the 'home fleet' only carried supplies to Denmark from its near neighbours, but the Germans insisted that it also transport agricultural goods, timber and, from Sweden to Germany, iron ore to assist with the German war effort.[148]

Upon Germany's invasion of Denmark, DFDS lost control of 31 ships, of which 21 were requisitioned by the British authorities and re-flagged in the United Kingdom (while often retaining partly-Danish crews). Three cargo ships in Brazilian ports were sold under duress to the Brazilian Government. Of DFDS' home fleet, most of the motor ships were laid up due to a lack of fuel.[149] EAC, meanwhile, lost 17 vessels to Allied control and a further six were laid up in Danish ports. A.P. Møller's Dampskibsselskabet Svendborg and Dampskibsselskabet af 1912 together contributed ten steamers to the home fleet, but the vast majority of their ships, like those of DFDS and EAC, were in foreign ports and 36 subsequently entered Allied service.[150]

Fearing that either the German authorities – or the Danes acting on their behalf – would seize his ships, on the eve of Germany's invasion of Denmark A.P. Møller handed powers of attorney over the Dampskibsselskabet Svendborg and Dampskibsselskabet af 1912 fleets to his cousin and New York-based partner in ISMOLCO and Maersk Line, Hans Isbrandtsen. That evening, he sent his trusted associate, Thorkil Høst, by ferry to Sweden, from which he sailed to Finland, initially hoping to reach New York via Russia and Siberia. When that proved impossible, he bought instead a trans-Atlantic passage on a freighter named *Mathilda Thordén* from Petsamo.[151] Hans Isbrandtsen meanwhile used his authority to transfer the Mærsk fleet to ISMOLCO so that they could continue to trade under the US-registered company – but the Allies refused to recognise this arrangement, much to Isbrandtsen's frustration and fury.[152] Thereafter, on 31 May, A.P. Møller sent his son, Mærsk Mc-Kinney Møller (born 1913), to New York to take care of the Møller Companies' interests there; this happened only a week after Møller junior was made a partner in his father's firm and nine days after his marriage to his former school sweetheart, Emma Neergaard Rasmussen. He sailed from Genoa on United States Lines' *Manhattan*, arriving in New York in June 1940.

Mærsk Mc-Kinney Møller had a great deal to prove. Like his father, he had begun his business career with C.K. Hansen in 1930. After two years, he began an itinerant phase working for various shipping-related businesses in Germany, France and Britain, to hone his business skills – again, much like his father had done, but in rather more dangerous political and economic times. In terms of physique, Mærsk Mc-Kinney Møller was very different from his father, being tall and slender, whereas his father was thick-set and therefore physically commanding; both men were, however, similar in terms of character, combining steely determination with considerable charm. Moreover, the young Møller was determined to live up to his father's expectations by displaying good business acumen and through hard work.

A.P. Møller gave his son his half of the shares in ISMOLCO but Hans Isbrandtsen refused to accept his influence in what appears to have been a clear attempt to seize all of ISMOLCO for himself. As a result, A.P. Møller withdrew Isbrandtsen's powers of attorney and gave them instead to his son. Isbrandtsen refused to accept this and so he set up a new company, Isbrandtsen Steamship Co Inc. In light of this development, A.P. Møller's American lawyers recommended termination of all co-operation with Isbrandtsen. In response, Mærsk Mc-Kinney Møller too set up new US-registered companies with a view to replacing ISMOLCO as Maersk Line's American agent once the war was over.[153]

On 7 December 1941, Japanese warplanes attacked the US Naval fleet in Pearl Harbor, Hawaii, and this unprovoked act of aggression brought the United States into the war. America's existing merchant shipbuilding programme, begun in the wake of the 1936 Merchant Marine Act, was redoubled. Fordist mass-production techniques were instituted to churn out vast numbers of standard cargo ships and tankers at a faster rate than the German and Japanese Navies could sink them. As the existing C2 and C3 standard cargo liner types were of typically American solid construction and high specification, they were too slow to build and too valuable to be expendable in this time of emergency. Thus, a much less sophisticated – even old-fashioned – type of cargo vessel was developed instead, based upon a British-built tramp steamer prototype. For propaganda purposes, the new American wartime standard cargo vessels were dubbed 'Liberty' ships. Measuring just over 7,000gt, they were powered by a triple-expansion steam engine, giving a speed of around 10 knots. The most innovative (and controversial) aspect of their

Above: The ship owner Mærsk Mc-Kinney Møller as a young man.
(A.P. Møller-Maersk)

Left: A wartime view of the **Peter Mærsk** in Philadelphia with neutrality markings painted on her topsides.
(Bruce Peter collection)

design was the adoption of all-welded construction to save steel by avoiding the need to lap plates and to speed up their assembly. Early examples were prone to metal fatigue, but the majority were long-lived and notably successful both in wartime and post-war civilian service. Existing shipyards were expanded and new yards established to build the Liberty fleet and altogether 2,751 such vessels were constructed – the fastest building time being around seven weeks from keel-laying to handing-over a completed ship. In addition, 534 'Victory' ships – a more sophisticated 7,700gt steam turbine-powered cargo liner design – were also constructed. The majority of these vessels went on to form the backbone of the post-war merchant fleet.[154]

Meanwhile, Mærsk Mc-Kinney Møller gained permission from the War Shipping Administration to establish a joint company with other Danish shipowners' representatives in New York called the Danish Ship Operating Corporation with Thorkil Høst as President and representatives of J. Lauritzen and EAC on the Board; together, they controlled 14 ships and they aimed to use this tonnage to assist America and the Allies to win the war against Germany and Japan. Because of the Danish shipowners' intimate knowledge of diesel propulsion systems, they were given the responsibility to manage requisitioned and seized motor vessels

Above: The **Grete Mærsk** as an American troopship in 1942. (A.P. Møller-Maersk)

Right: The **Marchen Mærsk** in Allied wartime service; note the additional inflatable life rafts attached to the sides of her superstructure. (A.P. Møller-Maersk)

of other nationalities as well.[155] Writing in A.P. Møller's house magazine *Mærsk Post* in 1976, Høst recalled:

> 'It was an unforgettable experience to work with the Americans in those years. The war needed to be won and so everyone worked long hours. There were meetings with the War Shipping Administration at 7 in the morning and 11 at night. Time passed quickly – especially when one had to cope with sinkings and seamen losing their lives.'[156]

More than two years after the Allied victory, in November 1947 Mærsk Mc-Kinney Møller returned to Copenhagen. During his time in New York, he had made numerous influential acquaintances in the shipping community, in the business world in general and even in the emerging worlds of computing and information technology (he had become a close personal friend of the IBM chief, Tom Watson). These American links would serve the A.P. Møller shipping companies' interests well in the post-war era.[157]

In 1948, A.P. Møller's wife, Chastine, died after an illness and Møller's own health began to decline due to the stresses of the war, business responsibilities and his wife's illness. Therefore, Mærsk Mc-Kinney Møller was given greater responsibility for the day-to-day management of the A.P. Møller companies. While A.P. Møller retained overall responsibility for the Ship Owning Department (which managed tramp vessels), the Tanker Division, the Newbuilding Department, and financial matters, Mærsk Mc-Kinney Møller took charge of the technical organisation, chartering, insurance and liner services (the Panama Line had re-opened in April 1946). In the latter role, A.P. Møller's nephew, Georg Andersen, assisted him.[158]

The business dispute between A.P. Møller and Hans Isbrandtsen was finally settled in 1949 following more legal action; Isbrandtsen dropped all actions against Møller in exchange for the annulment of Møller's shares in ISMOLCO. Isbrandtsen's confrontational temperament evidently did not do his health any good, however. In 1953 he died of a heart attack and his body was carried back to Denmark for burial aboard EAC's *Falstria*. His will had been adjusted to ensure that his remains were not taken on an A.P. Møller-owned vessel.[159]

The DFDS cargo liner *Tunis* in American service during the Second World War, renamed as the *Aquila*. Returned to DFDS and renovated, she served the company until 1966. (Museet for Søfart)

The *Laura Mærsk* at Shanghai in 1947, showing the grey hull livery which was standard for A.P. Møller's cargo liners until the 1950s. (Bruce Peter collection)

Top: The DFDS cargo liner **Bolivia** was built by Frederikshavn Værft og Flydedok and delivered in 1943, when she was laid up in Holbæk Fjord. Here, she is seen at Langelinie in Copenhagen with a Maersk tanker behind. DFDS sold her in 1964. (Bruce Peter collection)

Centre: The **Colombia** was built by Burmeister & Wain under instruction from Germany as a Hansa C-type cargo vessel. DFDS acquired her in 1947 and thereafter she served the company for 18 years. (Bruce Peter collection)

Bottom left: Three new DFDS cargo liners – the **Uruguay**, the **Bolivia** and the **Argentina** – wait to enter service to South America after the end of the Second World War. (Museet for Søfart)

Bottom right: The **Maine**, built by Frederikshavn Værft og Flydedok, entered DFDS trans-Atlantic service in 1945, lasting 21 years in the fleet. (Bruce Peter collection)

Top: The EAC cargo liner *Manchuria* was completed by Burmeister & Wain in 1942, then laid up until 1945. (Bruce Peter collection)

Centre: The new *Kina*, built by Burmeister & Wain in 1948, was very similar to her lost 1939 namesake. Here, she is seen in the English Channel in the mid-1950s. (Bruce Peter collection)

Left: The *Jeppesen Mærsk* was delivered by Burmeister & Wain in 1951 for Maersk Line's USA-Far East service. (Bruce Peter collection)

Chapter 8

Re-establishing liner services in the 1950s

The ending of hostilities in 1945 brought an urgent requirement to replace the many vessels lost during the conflict. The Danish merchant fleet had suffered badly with about half of the tonnage from 1939 destroyed or damaged beyond repair by war actions. In 1939, it had amounted to 558 ships, whereas by 1945 it was reduced to only 226. DFDS and A.P. Møller lost 24 and 25 ships respectively while EAC suffered 13 casualties; smaller companies suffered too – Dannebrog lost eight vessels and Torm 12. Altogether nearly 1,600 Danish seafarers lost their lives.[160] For all the Danish liner companies, the challenge was to restart operations before competitors took away their market share. This was made difficult by the severe shortage of available tonnage, compounded by a lack of building materials – especially steel and non-ferrous metals – leading to relatively long delivery times for new vessels. The commissioning of a new steelworks at Frederiksværk in 1949 alleviated this situation and all the Danish shipyards struggled to cope with full order books.[161]

A number of ships delayed during construction in the years of occupation were completed and entered service quickly once hostilities ended – DFDS had seven in this situation, including a new flagship passenger liner for the Esbjerg-Harwich route, the *Kronprins Frederik*. Between 1945 and 1950, the Company introduced no less than 20 new ships, commencing with the Helsingør-built *Argentina*, *Uruguay*, *Paraguay*, *Florida* and *Maine*, plus the *Bolivia* from Frederikshavn, all for deployment on trans-Atlantic services to North and South America.[162] For EAC, Nakskov completed the elegant all-white four-mast passenger-cargo liner *Falstria* plus the cargo vessel *Malacca*, while B&W finished off the *Mongolia*, *Manchuria* and *Kambodia*. A.P. Møller, meanwhile, received from Odense Staalskibsværft the cargo liners *Chastine Mærsk*, *Sally Mærsk*, *Leise Mærsk* and *Trein Mærsk*. Not surprisingly, the majority of these vessels were little different from their pre-war counterparts. Further examples of the type included the *Peter Mærsk*, *Anna Mærsk*, *Olga Mærsk*, *Nicoline Mærsk* and *Jeppesen Mærsk*, built in various shipyards and delivered between 1949 and 1951, by which time their basic design was over twenty years old. In addition, A.P. Møller commissioned three new tankers from Odense which also had been laid up during the latter war years.[163]

America with its vast numbers of war-built standard cargo vessels was in a strong position, its fleet having tripled in size during the conflict, and decided to become a leading maritime power in the post-war era. During the implementation of the Marshall Plan – whereby America bankrolled the rebuilding of Europe, particularly Germany and Italy – it was stipulated that half of the aid carried across the Atlantic must be transported on US-flag vessels, a continuation of 1930s protectionist practices. Unfortunately for Scandinavian liner operators, this inspired other nations to become increasingly brazen in carrying out flag discrimination during the 1950s and 60s.

In the 1945-50 period, America sold two-thirds of its wartime fleet to Europe, favouring smaller and less powerful nations over established maritime powers – particularly, Britain. Thus, Greece acquired a substantial fleet of 'Liberty' ships at relatively low cost and consequently emerged in the 1950s as a leading nation in tramp shipping, undercutting existing companies specialising in the tramping trades. As a temporary measure, Denmark's leading shipping companies augmented their surviving pre-war tonnage and new Danish-built vessels left incomplete for the war's duration with Liberty and Victory ships. EAC acquired three of each type while DFDS took two Liberty ships and A.P. Møller one Liberty plus four C1 cargo liners – the latter acquired by Mærsk Mc-Kinney Møller who had become well-connected in American diplomatic and business circles and adept at charming those in authority to assist his cause (that he was himself half-American by parentage can only have helped).[164] While these vessels undoubtedly filled a gap at a desperate time of need for tonnage, they represented several steps backwards from typical Danish liner tonnage of the 1930s, much of which had been lost in the

Opposite top: DFDS' Burmeister & Wain-built Hansa C-type cargo liner ***Venezuela*** is seen on the River Thames in the early 1960s. She was sold out of the fleet in 1965. (Mick Lindsay collection)

Opposite centre: The ***Paraguay*** was built at Helsingør in 1944 and operated for DFDS for 20 years. She too is pictured on the Thames. (Mick Lindsay collection)

Opposite bottom: The ***Florida***, also delivered from Helsingør in 1944, is seen tied up in Philadelphia in the late 1950s. (Bruce Peter collection)

war. In Denmark, where shipping companies had relatively high operational costs, it was necessary to move back 'upmarket' as quickly as possible, leaving the tramping trade to cheaper operators using primitive 'Liberty' tonnage.

Maersk Line's service from the US East Coast via the Panama Canal to the Far East re-opened in 1946 with monthly departures in each direction, the first of several lines to be opened by the Company in the post-war era. This time, as Isbrandtsen was not involved, Maersk Line joined the Pacific Conference in both the westbound and eastbound directions. Next, in 1947, a trans-Atlantic route was added, connecting US East Coast ports with Le Havre, Antwerp and Rotterdam, but this was discontinued in 1954 as American imports to rebuild Europe dwindled and increasing protectionism marginalised cross-traders such as Maersk Line. In contrast, cross-Pacific services were lucrative for Scandinavian companies, especially as the powerful German and Japanese lines, which with Britain had hitherto dominated this trade, were temporarily handicapped by the loss of their fleets during the war. Maersk Line clearly benefited from this situation – the latter's Panama Line being increased in frequency to two departures monthly each way. Certain sailings were extended to serve Southern India and Red Sea ports, returning to the USA via the Suez Canal and a trans-Atlantic passage. Once there was sufficient new tonnage, this service was formalised in 1949 as the Suez Line: the first Danish-owned round-the-world liner route. Meanwhile, there were significant compensation claims against the Allied authorities to be settled for use and loss of tonnage during the conflict. The Danish Shipowners' Association quickly agreed terms of compensation with the British Government, amounting to £10 million. America offered $50 million – but only if Danish shipping companies were willing to forego their demand to have all seized vessels returned. There followed protracted negotiations and it was not until 1958 that America finally settled in full.[165]

In 1948 A.P. Møller procured three ships from the Japanese Mitsui Zonen shipyard at Tamao – the first time that a Danish shipping line had placed an order in the Far East and a sure sign that American Marshall Plan aid was enabling Japan to build new and competitive shipbuilding capacity while also benefiting from cheaper labour rates than in Europe and America. As Maersk Line intended to use the vessels on a new line between Japan and the Persian Gulf, this initiative made good sense and, moreover, Europe's shipyards were full to capacity and could cope with no further additional orders (in consequence, prices were also high). The 4,689gt *Else Mærsk*, *Ellen Mærsk* and *Kirsten Mærsk* entered service in the spring of 1950; all were powered by 7-cylinder B&W diesels, manufactured in Japan under licence by the builder.[166] Being of entirely riveted construction, their hulls were rather heavy in comparison with welded wartime standard freighters and this somewhat reduced their available deadweight capacity for cargo (riveted plates are lapped, whereas welded plates are butted together).

The next series, commencing with the Odense-built 6,462gt *Chastine Mærsk* of 1953, followed by the *Maren Mærsk* and *Johannes Mærsk* from Howaldtswerke of Kiel, were more progressive-looking – and relatively speedy too, each having a 10-cylinder B&W diesel capable of 17.5 knots. Indeed, they were typical examples of 'superstructure amidships' shelter deck cargo liners of their era. Furthermore, unlike the Japanese newbuildings, they were of partially welded construction, their hull plates being welded together but riveted to the transverse framing; this saved 12-13 per cent of the hull weight. Five further examples followed between 1954 and 1956: the *Susan Mærsk* and *Rita Mærsk* from Nakskov plus the *Sally Mærsk*, *Effie Mærsk* and *Marit Mærsk* from Odense. Yet another series of five appeared after that: the *Lica-*, *Luna-* and *Lexa Mærsk* from A.G. Weser of Bremerhaven and the *Leda-* and *Laust Mærsk* from Odense. These thirteen vessels operated a large proportion of Maersk Line's services until the advent of containerisation.[167] They also introduced a new and distinctive livery for the A.P. Møller fleets. Hitherto, the Company's vessels had been painted with either black or slate grey hulls but now it was decided to try a light blue colour (a lighter shade than the funnel band of the existing livery). After various experiments in 1955, the shade now known as 'Maersk blue' was selected and the new livery soon became iconic in ports all over the world.

In the early 1950s, EAC expanded its business empire into the African continent – particularly South Africa, where it had first invested in the South African Trading Company as long ago as 1900. In 1949, it acquired the Old East Africa Trading Company Ltd. in Mombasa, exporting animal skins, coffee, copra, coconut oil and pyrethrum, used in the manufacture of the pesticide DDT. Next, in 1950, EAC purchased R.T. Briscoe Ltd in Ghana in West Africa (the former British colony Gold Coast), owner of 190,000 hectares of forestry plantation. This company also imported German and Italian cars and had a licence to assemble Mercedes bus bodies, imported as kits. These activities in West and South Africa provided more cargoes for liners *en route* to and from the Far East via Cape Town and Durban.[168]

EAC's most newsworthy activity, however, was its providing the 1934-vintage passenger-cargo liner *Jutlandia* for use as a United Nations hospital ship during the Korean War between 1951 and 1954. The vessel had been laid up in Nakskov Fjord for the duration of the war, being damaged in a mistaken attack by Allied aircraft during the conflict's dying days. She was converted to carry 101 medical staff and 300 patients. After the Korean War, she was converted back to a passenger-cargo liner and continued in the EAC fleet until 1965.[169]

In terms of external appearance, EAC's initial post-war liner newbuildings, like those of Maersk Line, followed directly from the standards set by its latter 1930s tonnage. Yet, following the precedent of the first *Selandia*, EAC liners continued to be technologically

Above: The **Chastine Mærsk** was launched at Odense in 1943 but first completed in 1945, when the order to paint neutrality markings was not yet rescinded. In 1946, the vessel commenced the first post-war Maersk Line sailing from the USA to the Far East.
(A.P. Møller-Maersk)

Below: DFDS' 'Liberty' wartime standard cargo ship **Nevada** was initially built by the California Shipbuilding Corporation in Los Angeles as the **Amy Lowell**. EAC and Maersk also operated examples of the type in the immediate post-war years.
(Museet for Søfart)

innovative and were usually the first to be fitted with the latest and most efficient B&W diesel engine designs.

In 1950 EAC took delivery from B&W of the *Mombasa*; she was the first vessel fitted with a new type of long-stroke single-acting 6-cylinder diesel and, from then onwards, EAC only specified single-acting engines developed from this prototype. The long-stroke design, combined with a larger cylinder diameter (740 mm) produced the same torque as an engine with a shorter stroke and a larger number of smaller cylinders. The advantage of fewer cylinders for the same power yield was that the engine block was 1.3 metres shorter (but only one metre taller) and this freed up more of the hull's volume and deadweight capacity for cargo.[170]

During the war, B&W was compelled temporarily to suspend co-operation with its overseas licensees, yet a great deal of research was, nonetheless, carried out with the aim of improving supercharging. During the latter 1920s, B&W had introduced electric fans to force air into the cylinders of 4-stroke engined ships – but these could only supply air at low pressure. To produce air at high enough pressure to optimise the efficiency of a large 2-stroke engine while avoiding the excess weight and fuel cost of a mechanical system, a different solution was required.

It was found that exhaust gases could be used to power a turbine, driving a centrifugal air compressor – a technology first developed by Brown Boveri in Switzerland. This was of relatively light weight in comparison with mechanically-driven blowers and would require no additional fuel to be used. The benefits of the research work leading to this solution were made apparent when the tanker *Dorthe Mærsk* was completed in 1952. She had a 6-cylinder turbocharged engine, capable of developing 7,500 bhp at 115 revolutions per minute – about 35 per cent above that which could have been developed by an engine of similar size equipped with mechanically-driven blowers. The fuel consumption was three per cent below that which would have been possible without turbocharging. After further uprating, units of corresponding size and speed were capable of developing 9,000 bhp in continuous service.

EAC's B&W-built 8,627gt, 16.8-knot *Songkhla*, completed in 1953, was the first of a series of eight S-class cargo liners to be equipped with an engine of this type (the others were the *Samoa*, *Sibonga*, *Sumbawa*, *Siena*, *Simba*, *Sargodha* and *Sinaloa*).[171] *The Motor Ship* observed:

'The seven-cylinder supercharged engine in the *Songkhla* is capable of developing 8,750 bhp, representing a 35 per cent increase in output over a non-turbocharged engine. If compared with a non-turbocharged engine of almost equivalent output – a nine-cylinder unit developing 8,300 bhp – there is a weight saving of about 30 per cent while the overall length of the engine is reduced by 20 per cent. This reduction in length is equal to a saving in the engine room length of three frame spaces. It will be apparent that other substantial savings are to be gained in the weight, capacity and cost of the starting air receivers, main engine service pumps and other auxiliary units.'[172]

As B&W wanted control over the whole turbocharging process, it developed its own design of turbine and compressor, the first of which was fitted to EAC's *Sargodha*, delivered in 1956. DFDS' initial vessels with turbocharged engines were a pair of passenger and cargo liners delivered later in 1956 for trans-Atlantic service, the 2,806gt

Helsingør-built *Oklahoma* and *Ohio*, each equipped with a 6-cylinder B&W engine.

During the ensuing decade, a B&W engine with an 84 cm cylinder bore became arguably the most popular diesel engine for deep-sea merchant ships. This had a 10,000 bhp output and made its debut with a test bed run in the summer of 1959. It was one of a number of essentially similar large bore marine diesels being developed at that time by the rival leading marine engine designers and builders but, as B&W completed its first, it was assured a prime market position and rivals were forced to try to catch up as best they could. As so often in the past, the first such engine was fitted to an East Asiatic Company vessel, the tanker *Java*. The next six engines of this type were installed in tankers ordered by Sigval Bergesen, but these had a higher degree of turbocharging than the prototype. By 1970, more than 2,600 engines of the type had been constructed by B&W and its licensees, meaning that they powered a large proportion of the world's merchant fleet.[173]

Apart from speed, another way of signifying a superior quality of liner service was through the progressive appearance of the vessels operating it. In the 1950s, general cargo ports were most often located in city centres, overlooked by the offices of merchants, agents and charterers. In a shipping world then dominated by old-fashioned-looking (and frequently rusty) Liberty vessels, a modern streamlined cargo liner would attract positive notice from potential customers.

During the 1930s, Danish passenger ships had been amongst the earliest to incorporate streamlined forms into their superstructures. This aesthetic was first applied to the DFDS Copenhagen-Oslo passenger vessel *Kronprins Olav* of 1937. Later, in 1940, the North Sea

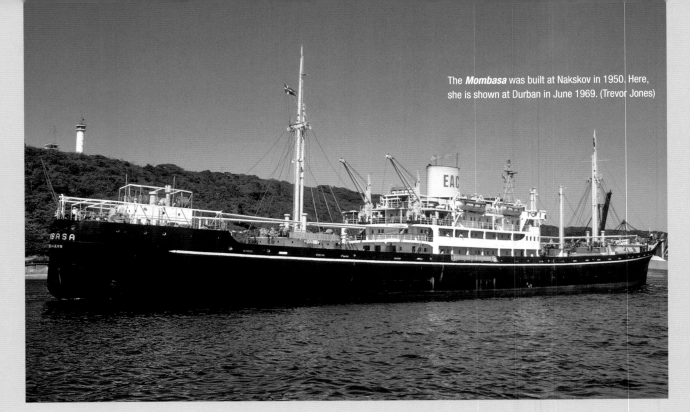

The *Mombasa* was built at Nakskov in 1950. Here, she is shown at Durban in June 1969. (Trevor Jones)

Above: The *Mombasa* alongside at Hobart in 1958 (D.E.Kirby, Russell Priest collection)

Left: The *Jutlandia* when serving as a hospital ship during the Korean War in the early 1950s; when sold for scrapping in 1964, she brought to an end the era of funnel-less motor ships in the EAC fleet. (Russell Priest collection)

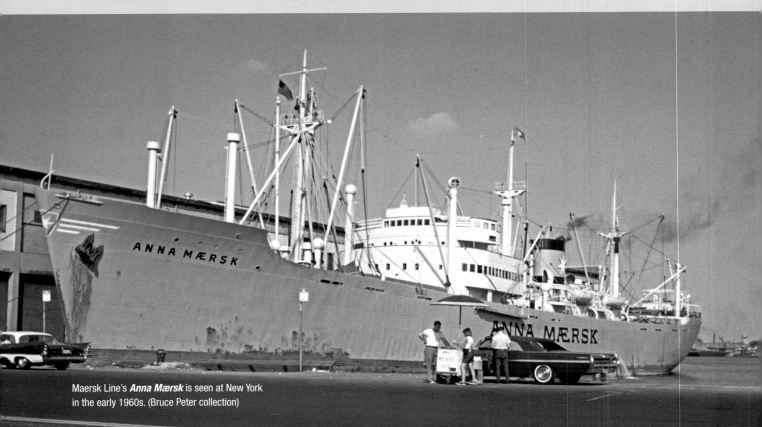

Maersk Line's *Anna Mærsk* is seen at New York in the early 1960s. (Bruce Peter collection)

Onlookers gaze towards the **Olga Mærsk** arriving at San Francisco in the latter 1950s. (Bruce Peter collection)

The EAC's veteran cargo liner **Meonia** at Cape Town in the late 1960s. (Ian Schiffman)

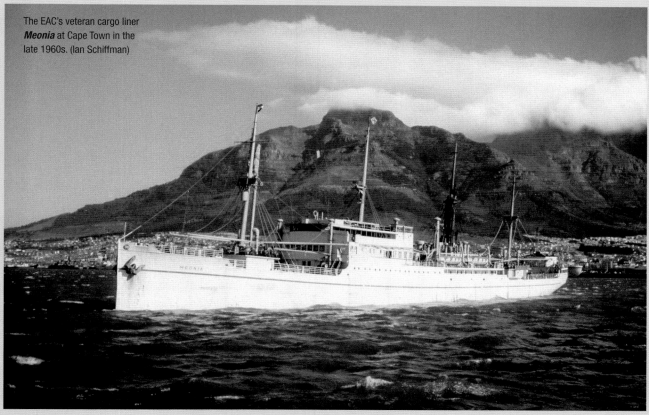

Right: The **Peter Mærsk** in
the process of being loaded
with bales of silk.
(A.P. Møller-Maersk)

Below: The EAC's **Jutlandia**
is shown in heavily-laden
condition in the early 1960s.
(Bruce Peter collection)

passenger ship *Kronprins Frederik*, again with a streamlined forward superstructure, was largely completed, but laid up for the duration of the war. This was because her propellers were lost due to the sinking of the vessel delivering them to her builder in Helsingør. In 1941, the Danish State Railways, DSB, published proposals for new streamlined train ferries to link Denmark and Germany – but these were not built.[174]

The British, usually rather conservative with regard to ship aesthetics, were also among the earliest to streamline cargo liners, the South American Saint Line's *St Essylt*, built by J.L. Thompson & Sons in Sunderland and delivered in 1947, being one of the first to display this new look. At the same time, Sweden's Johnson Line (Rederi AB Nordstjernan), trading between Scandinavian and South American ports, took delivery of the *Seattle*, the first of a class of six from Kockums Mekaniska Verkstad; these vessels were also significant in their being fitted with

electric cranes rather than cargo derricks. Thereafter, in terms of styling, Port Line's refrigerated combination passenger-cargo liners *Port Auckland* and *Port Brisbane* of 1949 were similarly adventurous.[175]

In a Danish context, the parallel moves from tramp to liner shipping and towards the streamlining of cargo liners could be seen in the post-war fleets of Ove Skou, Dansk-Fransk and Torm. Ove Skou, a coal merchant from Copenhagen, founded his shipping company in 1930 when aged only 24. He bought one

small cargo vessel from his former employer, Theophilus Hansen, who was also engaged in the coal trade. Skou was famously a very hard worker, running his coal importing business by day and developing his tramp shipping company by night. By the Second World War, he had six steamers trading in the Baltic and North Sea areas – but it was only after the war that his Company became a force in international shipping.[176] In 1945, Skou finally took delivery of his first newbuilding, the motor vessel *Benny Skou* from B&W which had been ordered in 1943 but severely delayed by the war. As with US Liberty ships, she was largely of welded construction and, as the hull plates therefore did not require to be lapped for riveting together, a weight saving of 6-7 per cent was achieved. All deck gear was electrically powered and the bow had a rounded forepeak which improved motion in head-on seas.[177]

The *Benny Skou* had well-appointed accommodation for 12 passengers in double cabins, a smoking saloon and restaurant, connected by an elegant Y-formed staircase. She was relatively fast too, her 8-cylinder B&W diesel giving a 16-knot maximum speed. Indeed, in the spring of 1946, she reached Montreal from Copenhagen in only 8 ¼ days. During a previous return crossing from Copenhagen to Baltimore, she managed to maintain an average speed of 15.7 knots – a record for a Danish cargo ship in trans-Atlantic service. Although Ove Skou was an operator only of tramp ships, his plan was to build further vessels improving on the *Benny Skou*'s high standards so that these could be chartered to liner companies. A modern appearance, high-quality passenger and crew accommodation, efficient cargo handling gear and – above all – speed were of the essence; Skou was determined that his ships should be on average three knots faster than standard for cargo liners of their era. Skou's next B&W newbuilding, the *Jytte Skou* (1949), further

Cabin plans

M V "OHIO"

12 Passengers

Smoking Saloon on Top Deck.

M V "ALABAMA"

12 Passengers

Hot and cold running fresh water
in all cabins.
Air-conditioning provided for hot
and cold air.
Plugs in all cabins for 110 volt A.C.
Bedside lamps at all berths.
Radio set and gramophone in Smoking
Saloons.

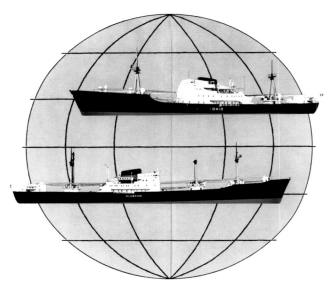

A voyage across the Atlantic in a D.F.D.S. cargo liner is an enchanting experience. Freed from compulsions of any kind you relax completely in an atmosphere of comfort and luxury where good food vies with clean air and sunlight. You are at peace with the world. It is being increasingly recognised that for men and women leading busy lives, travel by sea presents an opportunity of getting away from the strains and stresses of life today. A D.F.D.S. cargo liner, because of its limited passenger accommodation enables you to enjoy this experience to the full.

D.F.D.S.
THE UNITED STEAMSHIP COMPANY LTD. · COPENHAGEN

From the 1950s onwards, Danish shipping companies provided liner services spanning the globe and although their main purpose was to transport general cargo, passengers were also carried in limited numbers, but in comfortable accommodation. Here, we see brochures for Maersk Line (USA-Far East), DFDS (Scandinavia-USA) and the East Asiatic Company (Europe-Far East). (Bruce Peter collection)

MAERSK line

PASSENGER SERVICE

An Experience

On board the MAERSK LINER you are not obliged to go through the strenuous and fashionable routine of the big passenger liner. We offer you an interesting experience, a carefree and restful time with the opportunity of becoming acquainted with life on the seven seas and with the population at the many out-of-the-way-places we touch on our way.

You will find a world unknown and fascinating, richly faceted. New ways of life, strange and appealing will present themselves, and meanwhile you may enjoy the comfort and untiring care with which we make it a point to surround the passengers.

MAERSK LINE · FA

Travelling on a Maersk Liner gives you a chance to see many interesting places which you may miss going by the big liners.

Because the **Maersk Line** for more than a quarter of a century has symbolized service, comfort, and security, the name of **Maersk** is the guarantee that YOU will receive the full benefit from a voyage by our big, modern cargo liners. **Maersk Line** maintains a fortnightly service from U. S. Atlantic and Pacific ports to the Far East: Philippine Islands, Formosa, Hongkong, Saigon and Bangkok. The vessels on this line return to the U. S. from Bangkok via the Philippines, Hongkong, Formosa and Japan. The vessels are equipped with up-to-date passenger accommodations in light, agreeable colours. The cabins - single or double - are provided with private baths and will comply with

Passenger Accommodation

The plan shows the typical passenger accommodation in a Maersk Liner serving U.S.A. and the Far East. For accommodation-plan of the individual Maersk Liner apply to the agent.

Rest and Relax - Go by Sea

Sun Deck, m.s. "Alabama"

View towards Sun Deck from Hall, m.s. "Alabama"

In their North American and South American Services the modern cargo liners of D.F.D.S. have accommodation for twelve passengers in spacious single or double-berthed cabins, certain of which have their own private bath and toilet. Apart from the excellence of the cabins, the passenger accommodation offers an attractive dining room where can be found

Dining Saloon, m.s. "Alabama"

Smoking Saloon, m.s. "Alabama"

all the delights of the world-famous Danish table. And when one is replete there is the elegantly-furnished lounge or the sun-deck to which to adjourn - perhaps for a hand of Bridge or a drink and a chat or possibly with no other object than to do nothing more than exult in the goodness of life. On the Service to and from the U.S.A. there are sailings several times monthly in each direction principally between Copenhagen and New York, the voyage being of an average duration of 11-12 days. On the South American Service there are frequent sailings

the whole year round between Denmark and Brazilian and Argentinian ports, the duration of the voyage varying between 18-21 days or a week or two more if intermediate ports are visited. Further information with regard to sailing dates and booking arrangements can be obtained from Travel Bureaux, from the Company's Agents in North and South America or from D.F.D.S.'s Passenger Office in Copenhagen. Current fares as well as the addresses of D.F.D.S. Offices and Agents in North and South America are given in this brochure.

Smoking Saloon, m.s. "Oklahoma"

Single Cabin, m.s. "Oklahoma"

Double Cabin, m.s. "Alabama"

EAST SERVICE

Maren Maersk Sally Maersk Susan Maersk	...sengers in 3 double cabins
Anna Maersk Jeppesen Maersk Laura Maersk Nicoline Maersk Olga Maersk Peter Maersk Trein Maersk	12 passengers in 4 double and 4 single cabins
Hulda Maersk Lexa Maersk	12 passengers in 6 double cabins

...e food is outstanding - the Danish ...is world-famous. There is a special ...charm to this way of travelling so ...ent from the ordinary life on a pas-...m the very moment you step over ...u are part of the ship's little com-...on board from captain to messboy ...you feel at home. Another Maersk ...fortnightly, takes you from East-...Atlantic and Pacific ports to Japan, ...ng, Saigon and Bangkok. These ...e United States via the Suez-Canal, ...y from Bangkok at Straits Settlement ...lombo, Malabar Coast, Red Sea ...enoa.

You will always find a Maersk Liner ready to serve you on your trip to the East or U.S.A.

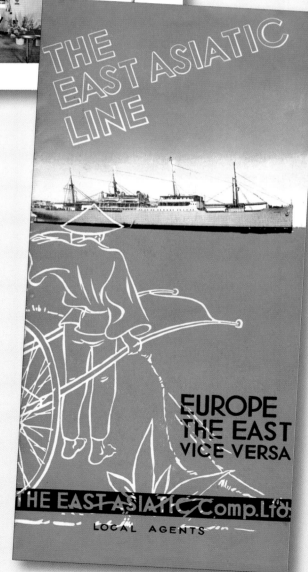

THE EAST ASIATIC LINE

EUROPE THE EAST VICE VERSA

THE EAST ASIATIC Comp. Ltd.

LOCAL AGENTS

Opposite: The turbocharged main engine on the EAC's **Sargodha**. (MAN/Diesel House)

Left: DFDS' **Ohio**, built in 1956, saw service from Copenhagen to the USA and on the Nordana Line route from the Gulf of Mexico to the Mediterranean. Here, she is seen in Copenhagen in the latter 1950s. (Niels Krebs/Nautilus Forlag archive)

Below: The EAC's **Siena** passing under the suspension bridge at Vancouver. (Russell Priest collection)

developed the principles established with the *Benny Skou*, which was sold as early as 1951 to Polish Ocean Lines of Gdynia with three other Danish ships for more than double her original cost in a deal brokered by the Danish Government in exchange for Polish coal. Already, Ove Skou had a new and improved *Benny Skou* under construction at B&W. Next, the similar *Lotte Skou* was delivered in 1952 by Howaldtswerke of Kiel and, thereafter, Skou ordered a large number of cargo liners for tramp service and charter to liner companies.[178] The majority of these were built in Helsingør, which after the frantic initial post-war years of rebuilding the DFDS fleet was now very glad of orders. Indeed, the yard was prepared to build such vessels with only a small profit margin. One reason was that Skou was a supplier of coal for use in its furnaces and so had good connections with the management.

Ove Skou's numerous Helsingør-built cargo liners were characterised by exaggerated streamlining of the superstructure and funnel and by sleek hull lines. In all, the yard built 21 vessels for Skou between 1953 and 1974. These graceful ships, painted in an all-white livery with blue boot topping and funnel, became known around the world as 'Skou's white swans.'

Helsingør's reputation for designing elegantly streamlined ships began in the mid-1930s when

The *Samoa* in the St
Lawrence River.
(Russell Priest collection)

The *Songkhla* and *Basra* in
London Docks. (Mick
Lindsay collection)

The *Sibonga* at Cape Town. (Ian Schiffman)

the naval architect Knud E. Hansen designed the DFDS Copenhagen-Oslo passenger ship *Kronprins Olav*, which was delivered in 1937. When Hansen left the yard to set up his own independent naval architecture consultancy, the Chief Naval Architect, K.E. Olsen, perpetuated the streamlining of ships' superstructures. During the latter 1950s and throughout the 1960s, Helge Andersen and Poul Jørgensen co-ordinated the design of most of the vessels built there. According to Hans Henrik Petersen who also worked in the drawing office, Andersen had a gift for designing aesthetically striking ships while Jørgensen had a central co-ordinating role, drawing most of the general arrangements, which consisted of the profiles and deck layouts.[179]

Dampskibsselskabet Torm was a second up-and-coming Danish shipping company to construct new streamlined cargo liners in the post-war period, commencing with the 4,153gt *Estrid Torm*, built in Nakskov and delivered in 1951, followed by the similar *Birgitte Torm*, completed at Odense in 1952 and the 4,137gt *Freya Torm* from Helsingør, delivered in April 1953 for use on Torm Lines' trans-Atlantic service between Mediterranean ports, North and Central America.[180]

Only seven months later, in December 1953, Dansk-Fransk became a further Danish shipping company to take delivery of a streamlined cargo liner, the 3,654gt *Belgien*, a slightly shorter version of the *Freya Torm* and likewise built in Helsingør. This was the first of four sisters constructed there between 1953 and 1958 for Dansk-Fransk's liner service from Copenhagen and other North European ports to the Belgian Congo.[181]

Dansk-Fransk was established in 1902 through an amalgamation of French and Danish shipping interests to operate tramp steamers between France, the UK and Baltic ports. The joint management was unsuccessful and so the Company became solely Danish-owned in 1912, managed by a former Torm Captain, A.N. Petersen. While profitable, it remained a relatively minor player in the Danish merchant fleet until the 1950s. At this point, Dansk-Fransk grew rapidly, adding oil and bulk shipping to its tramping activities, which provided additional profits. Ships began to operate between Copenhagen, other North European ports and West Africa – particularly the Congo – bringing hardwood as the return cargo to Copenhagen. In 1946 the first such load was carried by the 1930-vintage motor ship *Bornholm*. She sailed northbound not only with her holds filled but also with some 700 cubic metres stacked up on her decks. This surprised the Belgian port authorities in Boma and Matadi as they were not used to the Baltic tradition of carrying so much timber as deck cargo and believed that the vessel might capsize, but Dansk-

The **Songkhla** and the **Kambodia** in London Docks in the early 1960s. (Mick Lindsay collection)

The ***Leise Mærsk***, berthed
at the pier in Philadelphia.
(Bruce Peter collection)

The ***Leise Mærsk***, berthed
at the pier in Philadelphia.
(Bruce Peter collection)

Fransk's officers and crews had previous expertise, having shifted cargos of this type for many years around Northern Europe. The *Bornholm* was one of a trio of vessels ordered from B&W at the worst point in the Great Depression when the yard was glad to receive any order it could find (her sisters were the *Ireland* and the *Bretagne*). Designed specifically for the Baltic timber trade, she had a generous hull volume and good stability.[182]

As a result, in 1951 Dansk-Fransk established a regular liner service between North European ports and the Congo, marketed as Dafra Line. Competition was tough with Dutch, German, Portuguese and especially Belgian shipping companies dominating the trade, but even so Dafra Line became part of the recently-formed Central West Africa Lines Conference and four new cargo liners were ordered from Helsingør specifically to operate the route. The *Belgien* and her three sisters, the *Congo*, *Mayumbe* and *Africa*, were elegant and well-equipped multi-purpose ships. Each was fitted with a refrigerated hold to carry fruit and vegetables from the Canary Islands, where they called *en route*, as well as tanks for vegetable oil. In addition, there was stylish accommodation for 12 passengers. Hardwood was the principal homeward cargo; exotic veneers such as African wengé were becoming fashionable in modern Danish furniture design and manufacture, which was a very successful industry, as well as for the finishing of the bulkheads in Danish-built passenger ships of the era. By the early 1960s, Dansk-Fransk had grown to be Denmark's sixth largest shipping company – but the good years were not to last.[183]

During the 1960s, Dansk-Fransk established further liner services. In 1960, Union West Africa Line commenced services from Europe to West and South Africa; this was a joint operation with the East Asiatic Company and Britain's General Steam Navigation Company. Later, in 1969, Medgulf and Gulwa Lines were opened, linking American Gulf ports with Mediterranean and West African ports respectively – the latter service importing equipment for the Nigerian oil industry.[184]

Unlike other Danish shipping companies involved in the liner trades, Dansk-Fransk's services were tied up with the fortunes of the Congo and of other West African countries which, during the 1960s and '70s, began to experience the traumas of the ending of the colonial era. The Congo had a sad history of cruelty and exploitation by Belgium and, when it gained independence in 1960, it began to suffer serious post-colonial angst in the form of corruption, criminality and civil war, making it difficult and dangerous successfully to do business there. Waiting times for berths in Boma and Matadi became unacceptably long and, having invested in expensive new tonnage for Dafra Line in the early 1970s, Dansk-Fransk's problems were compounded by the effects of the 1973 Oil Crisis. It became insolvent in 1979 and the remaining vessels and liner routes were sold.[185] Its fate mirrored the experience of several smaller liner companies headquartered in Europe's former colonial powers, but it was unique in a Danish context. The Europe-West Africa route was sold to Dannebrog and the lines to the USA were sold to Torm.[186]

The design of Torm's *Freya Torm* and Dansk-Fransk's *Belgien* and her sisters formed the template for DFDS' next eight cargo liners from Helsingør for services from Denmark to North and South America, although its version was slightly longer (137.2 metres versus *Belgien*'s 125.5). DFDS' series measured approximately 5,500gt, and was outfitted only to handle dry cargo. This class consisted of the *Brasilien* (1954), *Ecuador* (1955), *Alabama* (1957), *Virginia* (1957), *Colorado* (1958), *Minnesota* and *Arizona* (both 1960).[187]

In December 1957, DFDS became a cross-trading liner company for the first time when, jointly with Fearnley & Eger of Oslo, it established the Nordana Line, linking Gulf of Mexico ports in Mexico, Venezuela and the West Indies with Morocco, Algeria, Tunisia, Libya, Egypt, Syria, Greece, Italy, France and Spain. (Hitherto, all DFDS services had called in

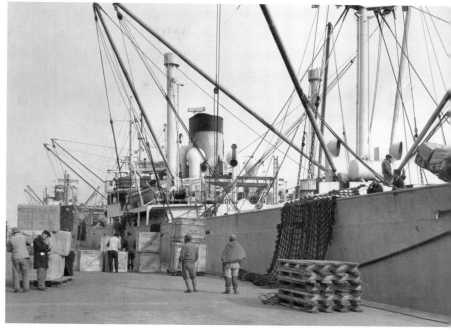

Danish ports.) The collaboration with the Norwegians continued until 1964, after which DFDS continued to operate the route alone.[188] In the 1980s, civil war in Lebanon, US sanctions against Libya and general instability in the Middle East reduced revenues and so DFDS sold Nordana Line to another Danish company, Dannebrog, in 1984. By that time, it was DFDS' final long-haul liner service.[189]

Above: Crates are loaded on board the ***Chastine Mærsk*** at Yokahama in 1948. (A.P. Møller-Maersk)

Below: The ***Nicoline Mærsk*** off San Francisco in the early 1960s. (Andrew Kilk)

In the post-war era, J. Lauritzen operated only one liner service – the West Coast Line from New York, via the Panama Canal to Peru, Ecuador and Chile – which was re-established in 1950. Its final new vessel was received in 1955: the 5,543gt *Tilda Dan*, built by Aalborg Værft and of very similar appearance to Lauritzen's streamlined Aalborg-built tramping reefer ships of the same era, such as the *Mexican Reefer* (1952), *Brazilian Reefer* (1953), *Peruvian Reefer* (1954) and *Arabian Reefer* (1957). While the reefers prospered, the West Coast Line became increasingly marginalised in the early 1960s due to the South American nations it served imposing regulations limiting cross-traders to only 20 per cent of sailings calling there. The remaining 80 per cent was split evenly between these nations, the idea being to encourage the development of their merchant fleets rather than allowing outsiders to inhibit it. Consequently, J. Lauritzen closed the West Coast Line in 1963 and sold its remaining vessels employed on the route.[190] The so-called '40:40:20' rule also negatively affected DFDS' liner service to South America, forcing it to enter

Above: The EAC's *Sinaloa* at sea in the latter 1950s. (Russell Priest collection)

Left: The *Sargodha* at Vancouver. (Russell Priest collection)

Below: The *Sibonga* at Durban. (Trevor Jones)

an agreement in 1969 with other shipping companies in Scandinavia and Brazil to share the trade. Thereafter, cargoes were split 50/50 between Scandinavian and Brazilian ships and in 1980 DFDS withdrew altogether.[191] Following South America's lead, in 1974 the United Nations drafted legislation known as the 'Code of Conduct for Liner Conferences' to apply similar restrictions worldwide. This was backed by the Soviet Union and so faced strong opposition from traditional shipping nations in the West, not least Denmark. Due to vehement protesting by the European Economic Community, which viewed it as iniquitous to free trade, it was never fully ratified.[192]

In the early 1950s, all of the leading Danish shipping lines except DFDS expanded in the oil tanker market. EAC and Maersk had been involved in this trade since the 1920s, but now J. Lauritzen, Dannebrog, Torm and Dansk-Fransk entered as well for the first time, building medium-sized motor tankers with aft-located machinery and the officers' accommodation and wheelhouse amidships. Indeed, J. Lauritzen placed a joint order with Dannebrog and Torm at Lindholmens shipyard in Gothenburg for five 16,000gt tankers – three for Lauritzen and one for each of the others, paid for with American reparations money to compensate for war losses in Allied service.[193] While utilising a similar layout, EAC and Maersk tankers tended to be somewhat larger and this made them more competitive as charterers came to favour more capacious – and therefore more efficient – tonnage.

The experience of operating these tankers possibly inspired the layout of the next generation of cargo liners for EAC which, like the tankers, had machinery aft and accommodation split between two deckhouses, one amidships and the other at the stern, around the base of the funnel. A.P. Møller's experimental refrigerated cargo vessel *Francine* of 1936 was another obvious precedent.

Foreign-flag cargo liners of the post-war era arranged this way included the American C4 standard cargo ship of the latter 1940s, evolved from a 1941 blueprint for American Hawaii Lines. Later on, the Italian Lloyd Triestino *Adige* and her three sisters, completed in 1950-51, and the West German Hansa Line's 1950s heavy-lift ships perpetuated this solution (the lead ship of the series was the *Lichtenfels* of 1954). The key advantage was that a very short propeller shaft could be installed, freeing up more of the mid- and aftbody for cargo stowage.[194]

Between the mid-1950s and early 1970s, EAC's Newbuilding Department was headed by its Shipping Department Deputy Director, Torben Bille. Bille's entire career had been with the Company, where he started in the 1930s as a controller of movements in Copenhagen Free Port. Early on, his managers spotted his potential and so they recommended him for an EAC-funded scholarship to study naval architecture at the Technical University of Denmark (formerly the Polyteknisk Læreanstalt) in Copenhagen. During the latter 1950s and throughout the 1960s, Bille advocated incorporating the latest and best technology in successive new EAC cargo liners.[195]

The lead member of EAC's six-strong B-class, the 8,797gt *Bogota*, was delivered by

Below: The Ove Skou cargo vessel **Benny Skou** in London Docks in the early 1950s.
(Mick Lindsay collection)

Bottom left: The **Lotte Skou**, heavily loaded in the New Waterway in the latter 1960s.
(Mick Lindsay collection)

Bottom right: The **Susanne Skou** at sea.
(Bruce Peter collection)

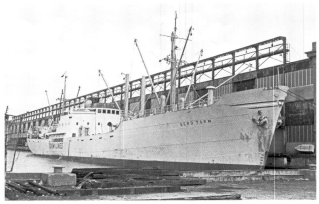

B&W in 1956 and, as with the previous S-class liners, she was fitted with an 8-cylinder turbocharged B&W diesel. The *Busuanga* and *Boma* followed from Nakskov, while B&W delivered the *Beira*, *Basra* and *Boribana*.[196] EAC's next series, the A-class, followed from 1960 onwards and its initial members, the Nakskov-built *Ayuthia*, *Asmara* and *Andorra* (measuring between 10,083gt and 10, 465gt) also featured an aft-located engine room with the bridge amidships.[197] Each of these embodied slight improvements and innovations over previous examples of the type. For example, the *Asmara* was designed without coamings around her 'tween deck hatch covers to enable forklift trucks to move without hindrance as stowing cargo using forklift trucks was faster and more efficient than using teams of stevedores to manhandle it into position. Subsequently this system was also briefly adopted by Maersk Line and DFDS on their liner tonnage in the years immediately before the advent of full containerisation, as well as on numerous foreign-flagged vessels commissioned in the latter 1960s.

The *Andorra*, built in 1964 by Nakskov Skibsværft, was the first single-screw cargo liner ever to be fitted with a KaMeWa controllable pitch propeller. Developed in Sweden by Karlstads Mekaniska Werkstad (hence KaMeWa), these used a system of gears to enable the blades to be rotated, their changeable angle enabling the ship's speed to be finely altered, whereas previously speed alterations could only be made by adjusting the engine to slow, half or full.[198] The first ocean-going merchant ship ever fitted with KaMeWa propellers was the Swedish Johnson Line (Rederi AB Nordstjernan) twin-screw refrigerated cargo vessel *Los Angeles*, built by Kockums of Malmö and delivered in 1948. Another feature of the *Los Angeles* and her sisters adopted on the *Andorra* and subsequent EAC cargo liners was the installation of electric cranes to handle cargo as these were easier to rig and faster to operate than traditional masts, derricks and booms (although these were retained in addition on the *Andorra* to handle heavier goods).

In addition, the *Andorra* was the first cargo liner in which the machinery space could be left unattended, monitoring being carried out from an adjacent control room. Furthermore, the engine was operated directly from the bridge rather than by the engineer on duty acting upon instructions received via telegraph signals from the bridge officers. This latter innovation was developed by Søren T. Lyngsø, a mechanical engineer by training whose expertise was in engine balancing and control and who worked closely with the engineers in the Engine Department at the B&W shipyard.[199] The first instance of its application was on Torm's 7,999gt *Thyra Torm* of 1963 which, like the *Andorra*, was built in Nakskov.[200] These technological advances enabled the *Andorra*'s crew size to be slightly reduced from 45 to 42, leading to cost savings while also improving the working conditions of engineering staff as manning a diesel engine in tropical heat was neither a comfortable nor a healthy task.

Top left: Torm Lines' **Grete Torm**.
(Bruce Peter collection)

Top right: The **Gerd Torm** is seen at Philadelphia in the early 1960s.
(Bruce Peter collection)

The logical next step was to move the entire superstructure aft, completely freeing up the midbody for cargo stowage. This solution was first seen on A.P. Møller's 3,218gt *Ras Mærsk* and 3,646gt *Hartvig Mærsk*, designed by Knud E. Hansen and delivered in 1957 by Frederikshavn Værft and B&W respectively.[201] Later, EAC followed suit, its *Ancona*, *Azuma*, *Aranya*, *Arosia*, *Alameda* and *Atrevida* (measuring between 10,768gt and 12,935gt) all featuring aft-located superstructures and mid-bodies without sheer, signalling the way ahead towards the development of the Company's first fully-cellular container ships.[202] The idea of moving the entire superstructure aft did not meet with approval from many of EAC's Captains who were concerned that their view ahead would be seriously impaired by having to overlook nearly an entire hull's length stacked with cargo, cranes and derricks; thus it took several years to implement this development.[203] In the end, engineering logic and economic reality won the argument in favour of aft location.

Without a superstructure amidships to add rigidity, relatively fast open deck cargo liners were potentially prone to torsional forces causing hull deflection, especially when taking seas from their bow and stern quarters. This twisting concentrated strain at the corners of hatch openings and so, on the *Alameda* and *Atrevida*, additional strength and rigidity were gained from a box girder running along the centreline at upper deck level, the cargo hatches being arranged on either side of this longitudinal division, rather than a sequence of centrally-located hatches as fitted to previous vessels with midships superstructures.[204] This helped to reduce the absolute magnitude of the distortions due to hull girder warping and also had some beneficial effect in

The ***Freya Torm*** under construction at Helsingør early in 1953.
(Kenn Eilersen collection)

The **Birgitte Torm** at New York with the bow of **Olga Mærsk** on the left.
(Bruce Peter collection)

Above: The **Freya Torm** undergoing sea trials in The Sound in July 1953.
(Kenn Eilersen collection)

Right: The **Alice Torm**, which was built at Nakskov in 1958, is pictured at Valetta, Malta in the early 1960s.
(Bruce Peter collection)

Above: The Burmeister & Wain-built **Gunhild Torm**, delivered in 1958, is seen at Cape Town in the early 1970s. (Ian Schiffman)

Below: The **Torm Gunhild**, ex **Gunhild Torm**, at Philadelphia in the mid-1970s; she was sold out of the fleet in 1978. (Bruce Peter collection)

Above: Dansk-Fransk's **Belgien** is shown undergoing builder's trials off Helsingør in December 1953.
(Kenn Eilersen collection)

Right: The **Afrika**, also pictured during her trials off Helsingør, in June 1958.
(Kenn Eilersen collection)

Left: One of Dansk-Fransk's latter generation of cargo liner, the **Kinshasa**, built by Fujinigata at Osaka in Japan in 1967, is seen in the company's final curry yellow livery. (Museet for Søfart)

Right: Dansk-Fransk, in common with many liner companies, frequently supplemented the vessels it owned with chartered tonnage, such as the **Dafra Merchant**, ex **Rhein**, built in 1961 and owned by Hansa Line. She is shown here in 1976. (Bruce Peter collection)

Left: The Odense-built **Sally Mærsk** of 1954 was a typical Maersk Line cargo vessel of a type built from the mid-1950s onwards. Vessels of this generation were replaced in the 1970s by container ships. (A.P. Møller-Maersk)

Centre: The **Jesper Mærsk**, ex **Chastine Mærsk**, built at Odense in 1953, is seen arriving at Durban in the late 1960s. She was sold in 1973. (Trevor Jones)

Bottom: The **Sally Mærsk** passes the Swedish Rederi AB Transatlantic cargo liner **Kirribilli** in the Panama Canal. (A.P. Møller-Maersk)

Above: The German-built **Lexa Mærsk** of 1957 was one of five sister ships built by Odense Staalskibsværft and A.G. Weser of Bremen between 1956 and 1958. (Bruce Peter collection)

Right: A stern view of the **Leda Mærsk**, built in 1957 by Odense Staalskibsværft. (A.P. Møller-Maersk)

absorbing longitudinal bending moments. On the *Atrevida*, electric cranes were mounted on moveable gantries spanning the cargo holds; these ran on tracks located on either side. In addition to general cargo and bottom tanks for liquids, two of her holds were refrigerated for the carriage of foodstuffs and all were equipped with cell-guides, meaning that she could carry a total of 354 20-foot containers. She was, therefore, a semi-container ship and her design pointed the way ahead for EAC's first fully-cellular container vessels designed shortly after her delivery and with the benefit of experience gained from operating her in liner service.[205]

As deliveries of the A-series progressed, each new vessel completed was more powerful and speedy than the previous example, and this factor also increased stresses on their hulls, especially in stormy weather. The *Andorra*'s 8-cylinder B&W diesel mustered 13,300 ihp and drove her at 18.4 knots, whereas the 1966-built *Aranya*'s had 10 cylinders, producing 16,600 ihp and giving a 20.8-knot speed. Finally, the 1968 *Atrevida*'s 12-cylinder engine enabled her to sail at up to 22 knots.[206] There was a reckoning, however, as the latter became notorious for pronounced cavitation and vibration due to so much power being applied to a single four-bladed propeller beneath a fuller aftbody configured to accommodate the additional two cylinders of her main engine. In subsequent newbuilds, this problem was solved by fitting instead a six-bladed propeller and modifying the form of the aftbody above to a more slender profile.[207]

Maersk Line's cargo vessels of the 1960s followed a similar 'machinery aft' layout to those of EAC. In 1957 Captain Troels Dilling, a former Master of Maersk Line tankers and cargo vessels, joined A.P. Møller's Technical Department, where Mærsk Mc-Kinney Møller gave him responsibility for technical aspects of liner operation, such as the optimisation of cargo capacity, loading procedures and safety matters.[208] During ensuing years, however, Dilling's role grew and increasingly he became involved in the development of new Maersk Line tonnage.

A.P. Møller was particularly fortunate to be a leading established operator of liner services between what were two politically stable and economically expansive market areas – North America and the growing industrial economies of South East Asia. In contrast, many of Europe's established liner shipping companies, which hitherto had transported goods to and from colonies in Africa or what was once French Indo-China, suffered as these gained independence and, in some cases, descended into post-colonial civil war and chaos. (The Vietnam War also boosted Maersk Line as some of its vessels were diverted to carry American military supplies to Saigon.) Crises in the Middle East, involving the closure of the Suez Canal between 1967 and 1975, were a cruel blow to many European liner companies but Maersk Line's trans-Pacific services were far removed from such problems and thus the advantages of being a cross-trading company in this market became increasingly obvious.

Outwith the operation of ships, in the latter 1950s and early 1960s A.P. Møller undertook two vital initiatives which in the long term bore fruit and ensured his Companies' future success after

DFDS' *Colorado*, delivered in 1958, one of eight near-sisters built in the 1950s at Helsingør for trans-Atlantic service to North and South America, is seen at Copenhagen. She was sold only a decade later.
(Niels Krebs/Nautilus Forlag archive)

The **Virginia**, during her
trials off Helsingør in
December 1957.
(Kenn Eilersen collection)

his own passing in 1965. Firstly, he oversaw the building of a new, large and modern shipyard near Odense and, secondly, he invested in the exploration for oil and gas in Danish territorial waters in the North Sea.

A.P. Møller's existing shipyard in Odense occupied a constricted site and the width and depth of water adjacent severely limited the sizes of ships that could be built there. This was particularly problematic when it came to building oil tankers, a type of vessel already growing markedly in scale and forecast to become larger still. Therefore, in 1956 the yard's Managing Director, Erik Ringsted, developed an outline plan for a new and large out-of-town shipyard at Lindø, twelve kilometres to the north-east of the Company's existing facility. There, it would be possible to build a dock in which ships could be constructed then floated out, rather than building on slipways and launching them into the Odense Canal as was the traditional method. To construct the new Odense Lindø shipyard, Dkr 50 million would be required in the first instance and, within a year, the two A.P. Møller shipping companies had agreed to make this investment. Shortly afterwards, Odense Staalskibsværft managed to secure an order for five new oil tankers from Standard Oil's California Transport Corporation in the United States to be built at the new yard. By the autumn of 1959, two vast building docks had been completed and a large hall covering an acre-and-a-half in which to assemble ship sections had also been erected. That September, the keel for the first newbuilding, the tanker *T.S. Petersen*, was laid, but due to labour difficulties and contractual disputes with Standard Oil she was not finished for delivery until October 1962. For the new shipyard, this was an inauspicious start. With employment high in Denmark, it was difficult to find enough skilled workers and an attempt to bring Scottish platers and welders from the declining Clydeside shipyards around Glasgow was a failure due to cultural differences.[209]

The **Arizona** was the last of
DFDS' series of eight ships
for American services and is
shown undergoing trials in
March 1960. Her DFDS
career lasted for only seven
years.
(Kenn Eilersen collection)

At this point, the first of three new T-class cargo liners, the *Trein Mærsk*, was under construction at Odense Lindø for Mærsk's Panama Line service. A substantial 9,050gt vessel with slender hull lines but generous capacity, she was also relatively fast, her 9-cylinder B&W diesel generating 20,800 ihp to give an impressive 23-knot speed. Unfortunately, her construction was delayed by a series of strikes at the yard, leading A.P. Møller to order that she be towed to Burmeister & Wain in Copenhagen to be completed there as he was fed up with the slow progress being made at Lindø (she was delivered in April 1962).[210] Her sisters, the *Thomas Mærsk* and *Tobias Mærsk*, were both constructed by B&W with delivery in August 1962 and September 1963 respectively. All three were highly successful, serving Maersk Line until the early 1980s.

Simultaneously, A.P. Møller ordered a series of three comparable (though not identical) cargo liners in the 6,000gt range, two from Helsingør (the *Henriette Mærsk* and the *Torben Mærsk*) and one from Mitsui Zonen in Japan (the *Anette Mærsk*). All of these six vessels had superstructures located towards the stern. The Odense- and B&W-built trio had no sheer amidships and a hull configuration with appropriately slender bow and stern lines, flaring out to rather full lines at main deck level, meaning that there was relatively generous space to load containers atop and around the cargo hatches – at least in comparison with other cargo liners of their generation.[211]

Industrial relations at the Odense Lindø yard continued to be poor with nine strikes halting work in 1962 – a situation which led A.P. Møller to intervene again, this time with a strongly-worded message to all employees to the effect that without their full co-operation and a radical improvement in productivity, the yard would be closed.[212] The Odense Lindø yard's teething troubles were compounded by a weak market for orders in the early 1960s and so to try to give it the best possible chance to prosper A.P. Møller persuaded the Boards of Dampskibsselskabet Svendborg and Dampskibsselskabet af 1912 to order two large tankers. A.P. Møller warned the yard that this would be the last time he would sanction interventions to give it a chance to succeed. Fortunately, the appointments in 1964 of a new Managing Director, Iver Hoppe, and a new Technical Director, Carl-Erik Carlsson, helped to transform the situation and the Odense Lindø shipyard soon became a model of modern efficiency, accounting for around 40 per cent of Danish shipbuilding output by the second half of the 1960s. At this point, of course, numerous British yards were closing, unable to compete with more modern Japanese and Scandinavian shipbuilders, and in 1965 the old Odense Staalskibsværft was also closed with all work transferring to Lindø.[213] Thereafter, the Lindø yard became increasingly prosperous. During the latter 1960s and throughout the 1970s, mainly large turbine-powered oil tankers were built there but, come the 1980s, vessels for Maersk Line's routes came to be constructed as well.

J. Lauritzen's Helsingør-built ***Tilda Dan***, delivered in 1954, was the company's final new building for its West Coast Line service; it withdrew from liner shipping in 1963 when faced with flag discrimination in South American ports.
(Museet for Søfart)

118

The EAC's **Boribana**, built in 1961 by Burmeister & Wain, in the Thames Estuary; she was sold to Indonesian owners in 1977. (Mick Lindsay collection)

Right: The **Boma**, pictured shortly before launching at Nakskov Skibsværft in 1957. (Thomas N. Olesen collection)

Below: The **Boma** arriving at Hobart in 1958. (L.D.Rex, Russell Priest collection)

Bottom: A stern-quarter view of the **Busuanga** at sea; built at Nakskov in 1957, she sailed for the EAC until 1976. (Nautilus Forlag collection)

Left: The **Busuanga** undergoes final adjustments before leaving on her builder's trials. (Thomas N. Olesen collection)

Bottom left: The crew's mess room on the **Bogota**, built in 1956 by Burmeister & Wain. (Bruce Peter collection)

Bottom right: The captain's day room on the **Bogota**. (Bruce Peter collection)

Above: The **Busuanga** in the River Thames. (Bruce Peter collection)

Below: The Burmeister & Wain-built **Beira**, which EAC owned from 1958 until 1978. (Thomas N. Olesen collection)

Top: Maersk Line's cargo liner **Robert Mærsk**, built by Frederikshavn Værft og Flydedok in 1958, with the superstructure entirely aft-located. (A.P. Møller-Maersk)

Centre: The newly-completed **Hartvig Mærsk** is pictured off the Danish coast; built by Burmeister & Wain and delivered in 1957, she operated for Maersk Line until 1978. (A.P. Møller-Maersk)

Bottom: The Frederikshavn-built **Ras Mærsk**, dating from 1957, was another with the superstructure at the stern. (A.P. Møller-Maersk)

Above: Torm Lines' **Thyra Torm**, delivered by Nakskov Skibsværft in 1963, is seen at Valetta in Malta. (Thomas N. Olesen collection)

Below: The **Thyra Torm** was a very modern cargo liner and the first with an engine controlled directly from the wheelhouse. (Bruce Peter collection)

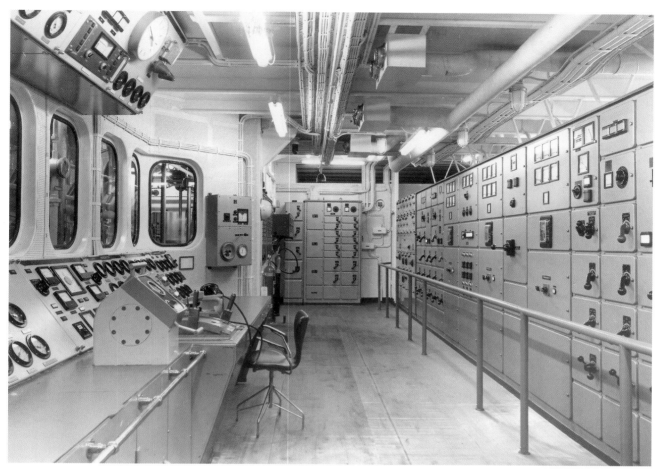

A.P. Møller's other great initiative was to invest in oil exploration. In September 1957, a German company, Deutsche Erdöl, announced that oil had been found near to the border with Denmark and so it approached the Danish Government to gain permission to make test bores on the Danish side. When A.P. Møller discovered this, he was greatly disturbed as he did not like the idea of such natural resources as Denmark had being tapped by Germans – especially with the Second World War and Denmark's occupation such recent and painful memories. Møller was advised that, if he objected so much, then he too should formulate a plan to find and exploit Denmark's possible oil resources himself. By this point, some experimental holes had already been drilled in Denmark, but as no oil had been found potential partners such as Shell and Esso declined to be involved. Fortunately, Gulf Oil was persuaded to collaborate with A.P. Møller, bringing much-needed expertise to bear, and so a 50-year concession was signed in July 1962. Shortly thereafter, Shell's senior management changed their minds and decided that it too should join the group, which was named Dansk Undergrunds Consortium. In 1963, the concession was extended to cover Danish territorial waters, including the Danish sector of the North Sea where oil was soon discovered in quantity.[214]

By this stage, A.P. Møller was an elderly man whose health was in decline. His son, Mærsk Mc-Kinney Møller, was doubtless worried about the stress which the new shipyard and oil exploration initiatives were causing him and so he was not initially enthusiastic about the Company's involvement in the latter activity. For A.P. Møller, however, national pride was at stake and so positive actions were required, come what may.[215] Once North Sea oil was found later in the 1960s and production began in earnest, the substantial and reliable profits yielded greatly strengthened the A.P. Møller Group, making it almost invincible. With North Sea oil money flowing in, it was possible to weather the peaks and troughs of the economic cycle to which the liner and oil tanker divisions were more directly exposed. Indeed, it is arguable that A.P. Møller's exploitation of North Sea oil, more than anything else, gave Maersk Line a unique advantage in maintaining and developing its liner services during the ensuing decades.

A.P. Møller died in June 1965, aged 88. His was truly a remarkable life and his legacy was a

The engine control room on the **Arosia**, completed at Nakskov in 1967; with extensive automation and direct operation from the bridge, the majority of engine room staff could work in an air-conditioned environment, away from the heat and noise of the main and auxiliary engines. She passed to an Indian owner in 1979.
(Thomas N. Olesen collection)

The first of EAC's A-class cargo liners, the Nakskov-Ayuthia of 1960, was very obviously a direct development from the B-class. She operated for EAC until 1978, after which her subsequent owner chartered her to Torm Lines. (Kristian Kielsholm Madsen)

Above: The second A-class, the **Andorra**, built at Nakskov in 1964, had a great deal of automation to enhance economy and efficiency. Here, she is seen during builder's trials, flying the flag of Nakskov Skibsværft.
(Thomas N. Olesen collection)

Left: The **Andorra** is shown in the Thames in the early 1970s.
(Mick Lindsay collection)

Above: Delivered in 1965 by Nakskov Skibsværft, the *Ancona* was the EAC's first cargo liner with an aft-located superstructure. Here, she is shown shortly after delivery in the New Waterway, near Rotterdam. In 1977, EAC sold her to a different Danish owner. (Russell Priest collection)

Left: The EAC's Nakskov-built cargo liner *Aranya*, the design of which was developed from that of the *Ancona*. (Thomas N. Olesen collection)

The *Aranya* is seen while undergoing builder's trials; note the significant use of electric cranes in addition to booms and the single row of hatches along her centerline, as per most traditional cargo liners. (Thomas N. Olesen collection)

Nakskov Skibsværft, seen here in a mid-1960s aerial photograph, was owned by the East Asiatic Company and so EAC cargo liners dominate the scene. At the outfitting quay, a new A-class cargo liner is undergoing construction while, to the left, a pair of older vessels are being overhauled. In the middle of the image, however, is a ship owned by Ove Skou. While A.P. Møller realized that the original shipyard in Odense was too small for the new generation of larger specialized tonnage and so opened a new yard at Lindø, EAC failed to make a similar move, notwithstanding the limitation on the size of vessels that could be built in Nakskov due to the narrowness of the fjord there. (Thomas N. Olesen collection)

Right: The *Alameda* with a
tug in attendance.
(Bruce Peter collection)

Above: The *Azuma*, built by
Mitsui Zosen at Tamano in
Japan in 1966, is seen in
the Panama Canal in the
early 1970s.
(Bruce Peter collection)

Left: The Nakskov-built
Atrevida of 1968, anchored
at Melbourne in 1969.
(Mick Lindsay collection)

Left: The two final members of the A-class, the **Alameda** and **Atrevida**, had two rows of hatches with more space to stack containers. Between these, the hull was stiffened along the centerline by a box girder. Here, we see the **Alameda**'s deck, also showing her electric cranes.
(Niels Krebs/Nautilus Forlag archive)

Below: With the **Atrevida**, the A-class had developed into a semi-containership. Her two rows of hatches are clearly visible.
(Thomas N. Olesen collection)

large and financially strong shipping and shipbuilding group with lucrative interests in other sectors too. His son and heir, Mærsk Mc-Kinney Møller, would prove equally dynamic and, under his leadership, the A.P. Møller Group and Maersk Line continued to develop successfully.

From 1962 until 1967, A.P. Møller's Head of Newbuilding was S.A. Paulsen, a ship's Chief Engineer before coming ashore to work at the Company's headquarters. Paulsen was, therefore, responsible for Maersk Line's final generation of break-bulk cargo liners, delivered in the latter 1960s: the seven-strong C-class. A young Norwegian naval architect and entrepreneur called Eric Heirung, who had gained a reputation for advising German and Norwegian liner companies

Above: The 1962-delivered **Trein Mærsk** with New York's imposing skyline in the background. (A.P. Møller-Maersk)

Right: In Hong Kong, cargo liners rarely came to quays, but instead dropped anchor in the harbour, where goods were loaded and unloaded into barges, sampans and junks. (A.P. Møller-Maersk)

Top right: Maersk Line ran the Burmeister & Wain-built *Tobias Mærsk* until 1981 when the company's final general cargo ships were withdrawn. (A.P. Møller-Maersk)

Right: The *Torben Mærsk* of 1963 was a sister ship of the *Anette Mærsk* and *Henriette Mærsk*. (A.P. Møller-Maersk)

Below: The *Thomas Mærsk* is shown undergoing outfitting at Burmeister & Wain's shipyard in 1962. (A.P. Møller-Maersk)

Above: The **Thomas Mærsk** as she appeared in the latter
1960s; she is equipped with hatches in the hull's topsides to
enable goods to be loaded and unloaded by forklift truck.
(Bruce Peter collection)

Below: The **Henriette Mærsk**, built at Helsingør and delivered
in 1962, is shown shortly after entering service at Hong Kong.
(A.P. Møller-Maersk)

in building more effective tonnage, assisted him. During Heirung's student years, he read 'Cheaper by the Dozen,' an autobiographical account of the lives and work of the American developers of time and motion study, Frank Bunker Gilbreth Jnr and Ernestine Gilbreth Carey. In line with their theories, he believed that making vessels more profitable would involve the introduction of more effective cargo handling systems to reduce dwell times in port.[216] From 1957, Heirung worked in the drawing office at Stord Værft, where he helped to design oil tankers. There, he argued for the acquisition of forklift trucks to move parts and inventory from storage areas to the hulls under construction and, although the yard's management was at first sceptical, they proved significantly faster than cranes. Heirung thought that forklift trucks could also be used to speed up the loading and unloading of general cargo liners, but this would require hatches to be cut in the shell plating, something disliked by the classification societies who argued that cutting through the stringers would reduce hulls' structural integrity. Nonetheless, Heirung produced a prototype design for a Norwegian coaster called the *Verma* and this worked

The 1968-built *Chastine Mærsk* was a product of Bergens Mekaniske Verksteder. One of Maersk Line's seven C-class of cargo liners, she was designed to carry loads on palettes and also containers in appreciable numbers. (A.P. Møller-Maersk)

The C-class vessel *Christian Mærsk*, also built in Bergen, in the English Channel. (Bruce Peter collection)

Opposite: A dramatic view of the Kockums of Malmö-built *Charlotte Mærsk* at speed; not only does it illustrate the C-class vessels' power but also the causes of their stability problems – fine hull lines and heavy cargo-handling gear.
(A.P. Møller-Maersk)

Left: A stern-quarter view of the *Clara Mærsk*, built by Kockums in Malmø.
(Bruce Peter collection)

Below: The Kockums-built *Cecilie Mærsk* passes beneath the Golden Gate Bridge in San Francisco Bay.
(A.P. Møller-Maersk)

so well, shifting cargo with half the crew in a fraction of the time required by previous ships of the type, that he soon found himself in demand as a consultant to various liner shipping companies hoping to achieve similar efficiency gains.[217]

From 1962 until 1964, Heirung worked for the Meyer Line, converting its Hamburg-Rotterdam-New York-Baltimore route to carry general cargo loaded on pallets using forklift trucks and thus reducing the hitherto standard eight-week return schedule to only five due to faster turnarounds at each port. Next, he was hired by A.P. Møller to advise on designing its seven new 11,000gt C-class cargo liners for trans-Pacific service so that they could operate in a similar manner.[218] These

were built by Kockums Mekaniska Verskstad in Malmö (three vessels) and Bergens Mekaniske Verksteder (four vessels) in the 1967-69 period. Popularly known as the 'Seven 'C's,' the vessels had a very high speed potential, thanks to their 9-cylinder B&W engines. Indeed, on trials, the Bergen-built *Cornelia Mærsk*, which was ship number two in the series, managed to reach over 26 knots. Their hulls were fine-lined, but there was no sheer amidships, where the hull was 81 feet wide, meaning that up to 330 containers could be carried, a proportion of which were double-stacked, two abreast on either side of the steel hatch covers. A bulbous bow was fitted to enhance hydrodynamic efficiency by changing the amplitude of the waves ahead of the hull, enabling it to cut through more ideal conditions.[219]

These ships also boasted substantial superstructures and an extensive and weighty array of cargo-handling equipment, consisting of kingposts, heavy-lift derricks and electric cranes. This meant that the centre of gravity was higher than would have been ideal and so, to maintain stability, they needed to carry extra ballast in holds 1 and 3. Notwithstanding this deficiency, the 'Seven 'C's' were very flexible and handsome ships. As well as being able to load cargo in the conventional way, palletised freight could be loaded and unloaded through side hatches by means of forklift trucks. Marketed by Maersk Line as the 'Unit Load Concept,' this was a brief but important step on the road to full containerisation.

The first two examples of the series were deployed on the Panama Line from America's Eastern Seaboard to the Far East, via the Panama Canal. Ships three and four, the *Charlotte Mærsk* (built by Kockums) and the *Christian Mærsk* (from Bergen), were placed on a new liner route from Europe to the Far East, operated jointly by Maersk Line and the third largest Japanese shipping line, Kawasaki Kisen Kaisha, and inaugurated in 1968. The first sailing was outwith the conference system but, after lengthy discussions with other lines engaged in this trade, Maersk Line and Kawasaki joined, initially with monthly sailings in each direction and, from 1970 onwards, operating eighteen each way per annum. With scheduled departures from Copenhagen and Århus, Maersk Line thus commenced liner services from Denmark for the first time in its history.

The *Chastine Mærsk* with cargo on pallets being handled by a fleet of forklift trucks; this was a brief but important development in liner shipping before the advent of fully cellular container ships.
(A.P. Møller-Maersk)

Chapter 9

Containerisation and EAC's response

Although developments in the design of cargo liners between the end of the Second World War and the mid-1960s improved efficiency through more productive cargo handling – for example, the use of electric cranes or forklift trucks to speed up loading and unloading – and in terms of the performance of diesel engines and the introduction of automation, the cargo liner remained an inefficient ship type. One reason was that they carried goods of all kinds, from bulk cargoes like grain to pieces of heavy engineering as well as smaller items, manhandled by teams of stevedores. Merely unloading and loading such vessels meant spending more than half the time in port – and this was costly in terms of taxes and both ship- and shore-based labour (cargo liners had big crews and ports employed stevedores in large numbers to heave and haul). A further disadvantage was that goods were prone to damage and more valuable cargoes suffered pilferage. Therefore, faster and more secure ways of shipping general cargo were sought, while bulk cargoes – such as grain or iron ore – increasingly were carried on dedicated vessels, offering high capacity and using specialised port facilities.

In liner shipping, containerisation provided a welcome solution to the problems of security, speed of loading and inter-modal transfer of general cargo. Rather than being shipped loose, or in crates and boxes of various shapes and sizes, stacked by hand in the 'tween decks, the introduction of metal boxes of standard sizes which could be transferred quickly from factory to rail or road modes and directly onto ships proved highly advantageous. Indeed, it is arguable that what we call 'globalisation' – the worldwide transfer of the production and consumption of consumer goods and services – is in fact a direct result of containerisation as the manufacture of high-value goods could be outsourced and businesses could more cheaply and efficiently bring their products securely to wider markets than ever before.

The American truck owner Malcom P. McLean (1913-2001), whose business was based in North Carolina, is credited with inventing the modern shipping container. In the latter 1930s, McLean had observed the inefficiencies of break-bulk cargo handling in the port of New Jersey as he waited for a consignment to be shifted by stevedores from his truck to a cargo liner. During the ensuing decade as America boomed, McLean's business grew, and in January 1955 he purchased the Pan-Atlantic Steamship Company, based in Mobile, Alabama. Three months later, using Pan-Atlantic as collateral, he bought its parent company, the Waterman Steamship Corporation (this is what we would nowadays term a 'leveraged buyout'). Founded in 1933, Pan-Atlantic operated coastwise cargo services under the provisions of the Jones Act, a law passed in 1920 intended to stabilise America's merchant marine in the wake of the First World War, ensuring that only US-built and -flagged tonnage could operate between American ports. Having acquired Pan-Atlantic, McLean bought two standard T2 tankers, which were sent to Bethlehem Steel for conversion so as to be able to carry containers on raised spar decks, installed above the existing tanks, forward and aft of their midships officers' accommodation and wheelhouse. The two were named *Ideal X* and *Almena*. Meanwhile, McLean worked with the Brown Trailer Company of Toledo, Ohio, to design flatbed trailers and detachable trailer bodies.[220]

McLean's converted tankers entered service in the spring of 1956, the *Ideal X* being the first to sail from Port Newark, New Jersey, on 26 April bound for Houston in Texas. Each could carry 58 containers, all attached directly to the spar deck (they were never stacked). The service was marketed as Sea-Land.

Two further T2 tankers were converted and then a series of C2 freighters was rebuilt. Whereas the T2s made use of shore-based cranes, the C2s were fitted with their own gantry cranes and there were large sponsons on the hull sides to increase buoyancy and maximise the deck area on which containers could be loaded. Furthermore, the plan was that these conversions should carry stacked containers and so a new design was required. Firstly, the containers would require

Above: In 1974, Maersk Line began painting the company name, rather than ships' names, on the hull topsides. Here, the **Tobias Mærsk** is shown in the mid-1970s, carrying several dozen containers as deck cargo. (Bruce Peter collection)

Right: Although Maersk Line's fleet was generally modern, a few older cargo liners survived into the 1970s, such as the **Clementine** (ex **Anna Mærsk**), shown here at Cape Town. (Ian Schiffman)

Below: The **Leda Mærsk** in the revised Maersk Line livery. (Bruce Peter collection)

EAC's *Samoa* at Vancouver; in 1976, she was sold to Singaporean owners. (Russell Priest collection)

Left: The ***Maren Mærsk***, built by Howalswerke Deutsche Werft in Kiel in 1953, rolls in swells off Durban in the mid-1970s. From 1973 until 1977, Maersk Line operated her under the Liberian flag. (Trevor Jones)

Below: The ***Panama***, constructed in 1950 by Naka Nippon of Kobe in Japan, is seen in the Thames Estuary in the late 1960s. She was sold to Somalia in 1972. (Mick Lindsay collection)

EAC's *Sargodha* off Vancouver in the latter 1960s. (Bruce Peter collection)

The *Boribana* underway. (Russell Priest collection)

The 1951-built *Magdala* off Hobart in 1969. Somali interests acquired her in 1972. (D.E.Kirby, Russell Priest collection)

sufficient structural integrity to support others loaded above and, secondly, they would need to be locked together to prevent movement, even in moderate seas. Thus, McLean developed and patented cube-shaped corner castings with 'eyes' on the three outward-facing sides, into which twist-locks could be inserted, enabling stacks to be unified into solid vertical structures. The containers were 35 feet long – the maximum length of lorry trailer permitted in the state of Pennsylvania. Thereafter, Sea-Land standardised on this unit size, but the American Standards Association decided in 1958 that containers should be built to lengths of up to 40 feet, divisible by ten. Thus, all subsequent container operators used 20- and 40-foot containers, known as TEUs (Twenty-foot Equivalent Units) and FEUs (Forty-foot Equivalent Units). Sea-Land grew throughout the 1960s into America's pre-eminent container business, but its equipment remained non-standard until the early 1970s when it too switched to using only TEUs.[221] No doubt, Sea-Land subsequently suffered for being the pioneer of deep-sea container shipping (much as Britain had when it invented the railway a century previously but chose too small a loading gauge; in developing new transportation modes, it seems to have been better *not* to be the initiator). Yet, as with the diesel engine half a century before, the origins

of the sea-going shipping container are not so straightforward as the above narrative appears to suggest – and Denmark has a good claim to have been an early adaptor of the concept.

The earliest known record of inter-modal cargo movement involving ship and rail modes actually dates from the height of the Railway Age in mid-nineteenth century Britain. In 1841, the great railway engineer and inventor Isambard Kingdom Brunel devised a special system for trans-shipping coal from the Vale

Above: In 1950, DFDS introduced a form of containerisation on its Danish domestic cargo routes, a full six years before Malcom P. McLean's Sea-Land began to sail with containers. DFDS' containers were relatively small and they could not be stacked. The coasters *Axelhus* and *Riberhus* were fitted with electric cranes to handle them, but otherwise were not specially adapted for containers. As can be seen, much of the vessels' cargo consisted of boxes of beer and other items in crates and on pallets. (Museet for Søfart)

Left: Containerisation involved switching all liner cargo to standard-sized steel boxes which could be moved inter-modally between various forms of transport. The American truck-owner Malcom P. McLean is generally credited with bringing the innovation to fruition with his Sea-Land shipping company. At first, it used converted general cargo ships, such as the rebuilt C2-type shown here, which could carry 230 35-foot containers. The vessel's original slim bow- and stern lines have been retained but, amidships, her hull has been fitted with sponsons to increase capacity. (Bruce Peter collection)

of Neath Railway in South Wales to ships in Swansea Docks in boxes which were lifted by crane from railway wagons and lowered into the ships' holds, where the coal was tipped out; each box could carry 2 ½ tons of coal. Much later on, in the mid-1920s, Britain's four railway companies introduced steel-framed wooden containers for general goods on railway wagons and lorries, and it is from these that the term 'container' most likely originates. The design was a success but for two factors: the containers already weighed 3.5gt when empty (accounting for 50 per cent of the total weight allowed when filled) and their roofs were cambered like railway carriages, meaning that they could not be stacked.[222]

In 1950, DFDS first introduced a 'door to door' principle for transporting cargo in square wooden containers using the 471gt coastal cargo vessels *Riberhus* and *Axelhus*, delivered that year from Helsingør. Although DFDS claimed that these ships were of innovative design, they were in fact conventional small motor cargo ships of the 'shelter deck' type, the only distinction being that their hatch openings were larger than would otherwise have been normal on vessels of their size. As they were highly successful, DFDS subsequently commissioned two further ships of a similar type, the *Koldinghus* (1959) and the *Bergenhus* (1964). Soon after, in 1966, DFDS introduced its first roll-on, roll-off cargo vessels on the North Sea – the 999gt *Suffolk* and *Sussex* – which carried beer and agricultural exports destined for the British and Belgian markets. DFDS subsequently became a leading ro-ro operator – indeed, the Company is now among the biggest names in this sector with a fleet of over eighty ships and a route network covering much of Northern Europe.

Strangely, given DFDS' early development of a primitive form of container shipping for Danish coastal routes, it did not containerise international liner services in the 1960s. Instead, a new generation of eight approximately 4,500gt, 22-knot general cargo liners was ordered from Helsingør and Burmeister & Wain for delivery between 1966 and 1967; these were the *Nebraska*, *Missouri*, *Michigan*, *Alberta*, *Wisconsin*, *Manitoba*, *Ontario* and *Labrador*.[223] Developed by DFDS' English-born Technical Manager, Brian P.C. Walker, as their names suggested these vessels were intended primarily for trans-Atlantic service. In line with recent trends, their superstructures were aft-located and they were fitted with side hatches and flush 'tween deck hatch covers to enable forklift trucks to move around with ease but, otherwise, their design concept was obsolescent as they were too small and fine-lined to carry containers in appreciable quantities.[224]

By the time that the first of the class had been completed, the J. Lauritzen shipping company, run by the brothers Ivar and Knud Lauritzen, had secured a majority of shares in DFDS and Knud Lauritzen was elected to its Board of Directors in 1964. Only the previous year, J. Lauritzen had abandoned its sole remaining liner route, the West Coast Line from New York via the Panama Canal to Chile, and so the Lauritzen brothers must have realised that profit margins in traditional

cargo liner operation were becoming increasingly marginal.[225] Thereafter, J. Lauritzen concentrated instead on operating tramping reefers, polar ships and bulk cargo vessels and on the development of DFDS' services.

On 18 March 1966, three months prior to the maiden trans-Atlantic voyage of the first of DFDS' new cargo liners, the first container-carrying liner in North Atlantic service, United States Lines' C4-type vessel *American Racer*, departed New York for Europe. United States Lines, like DFDS, had initially been sceptical about the value of containerisation, not least because it had no wish to incur the wrath of New York's dock workers whom it feared might go on strike if asked to handle container ships as there would be far less need for manual labour. When the senior management discovered that Trans World Airlines was advertising the shipment of 435-pound packages from Chicago to Zurich in 15 hours at a price of $208, as opposed to 20 days at $267 by sea, they changed their minds. (In other words, by the early-1960s the cost of shipping cargo on a traditional cargo liner was so high that it would be cheaper to use airmail.)[226]

Just over a month later, Sea-Land's *Fairland*, a converted C2-type cargo liner, left Elizabethport bound for Rotterdam carrying 226 containers – the first pure container ship in trans-Atlantic

Above: DFDS failed to begin containerising its liner routes in the 1960s and instead built a class of new vessels for trans-Atlantic service that was obsolete in that trade almost as soon as it appeared. Here, the 1966-built *Michigan* is seen on the River Thames in the late 1960s.
(Mick Lindsay collection)

Below: The *Virginia*, one of DFDS' earlier 1950s-built cargo liner series, in London Docks in the latter 1960s.
(Mick Lindsay collection)

The DFDS trans-Atlantic cargo liner **Nebraska**, built at Helsingør in 1966, is shown with only a single container lashed to the deck. (Bruce Peter collection)

Above: The earlier members of EAC's A-class could carry only smaller numbers of containers, most of which were lashed on deck beside the hatches, as shown by the ***Arosia***. (Bruce Peter collection)

Below: In 1968, three of EAC's older S-class cargo liners, the ***Simba***, ***Sargodha*** and ***Sinaloa***, were rebuilt so that no. 2 hold was able to carry containers with more on deck. This was one of the first developments in the company's switch to container shipping. (Bruce Peter collection)

service.[227] Meanwhile, several of Europe's leading trans-Atlantic liner companies worked on a joint response to the United States Lines and Sea-Land initiatives. Their discussions resulted in the establishment of Atlantic Container Line (ACL) – a consortium eventually numbering six leading operators: Cunard, Holland-America, Compagnie Générale Transatlantique, Swedish American, Wallenius and Rederi AB Transatlantic.

The plan was to develop a combined container and ro-ro service, with each constituent contributing a single vessel. (The involvement of three Swedish lines is significant, given Sweden's enthusiastic role in the development of ro-ro ferry services in Scandinavia during the 1960s.) ACL's service commenced in the autumn of 1967, its first vessel being the *Atlantic Span*. European shipowners later continued to develop the consortium model to develop their container services using purpose-built rather than converted tonnage. This was a markedly different approach from that of the American container shipping pioneers, each of which operated independently and initially made use of ingeniously converted standard cargo liner and tanker designs. The requirement for consortia reflected the high costs involved in designing and building

The top of the engine on EAC's first pure container ship, the *Falstria*. (Nakskov Local History Collection)

Top: The *Falstria* on trials; note the separation of the
hatches along her centre line.
(Nakskov Local History Collection)

Above: The *Falstria* ready for launching at Nakskov
Skibsværft, showing her six-bladed propeller.
(Niels Krebs/Thomas N. Olesen collection)

Right: In contrast with the A-class vessels, the *Falstria*
had no cargo-handling equipment and was dependent on
shore-based container cranes. (Bruce Peter collection)

Left: The *Falstria*'s sister, the *Meonia*, at Hobart. (K. Barr, Russell Priest collection)

container ships, typical examples each costing on average ten times as much as a conventional cargo liner.[228] Another significant difference was that American lines generally specified steam turbine propulsion because, to qualify for Government shipbuilding subsidies, it was necessary to specify US-designed and -built machinery and America had little expertise in the field of marine diesels. Although the first generation of European-owned container ships likewise were steam-driven, by the mid-1970s, on account of rising fuel costs and the parallel development of more powerful diesels, European lines had largely switched to diesel, either by converting their existing vessels or by building anew.[229]

The establishment of Atlantic Container Line was a severe blow to DFDS' trans-Atlantic cargo liner operation and so the service was closed down in 1970. Although not a member of ACL, DFDS became its agent in Denmark and so Danish cargo bound for North America was sent instead on British, French, Swedish and Dutch-flagged container ships, rather than on Danish ones. In ordering so many general cargo vessels in the mid-1960s, DFDS had badly miscalculated at a time of rapid change in the shipping world. Some of its nearly new vessels were briefly redeployed on the route to South America, while others joined the Nordana Line, cross-trading between Mediterranean and Gulf of Mexico ports, areas in which containerisation was yet to make an impact; three of the class were sold already in 1972.[230]

Next, the container revolution spread to routes from Europe to the Far East and Australia through the formation of two significant British consortia – Overseas Containers Ltd (OCL) and Associated Container Transport (ACT). The former consortium, serving the Far East, consisted of British & Commonwealth, Furness Withy and P&O whereas the latter, operating to Australia, comprised Ellerman, Blue Star, Ben Line, Harrison Line and Port Line. As with ACL, both consortia built standard classes of steam turbine-powered vessels able to maintain a high service speed. Furthermore, they were large for their era – OCL's first delivery, the *Encounter Bay* completed in 1969, being one of the earliest container ships to carry over 1,000 TEU.[231]

In the Far East, meanwhile, a new generation of enterprising shipowner was emerging, benefiting from lower

Below: A cellular hold on the *Falstria*. (Nakskov Local History Collection)

Above: The smoking saloon on the *Falstria*.
(Nakskov Local History Collection)

Right: The *Falstria*'s crew mess.
(Nakskov Local History Collection)

Below: A crew cabin on the *Falstria*.
(Nakskov Local History Collection)

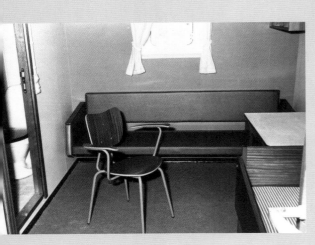

labour costs than American and European lines and from the beginnings of the South East Asian industrial boom. Firstly, in 1960, Japan's deep-sea shipping lines were re-organised into only six powerful companies – Nippon Yusen Kaisha, Kawasaki Kisen Kaisha, Mitsui O.S.K. Lines, Yamashita-Shinnihon, Showa Line and Japan Line – which jointly introduced a Japan-Australia container service in 1961. (In the same year, China's Communist Government collectivised all of the nation's shipping to form the China Ocean Shipping Company (COSCO) although this did not become a potent force in container shipping until China embraced capitalism in the 1990s.) Later on, in 1968, there were two new Asian shipping initiatives which subsequently had a profound influence on the development of container shipping. In Singapore, Neptune Orient Line was established with investment from the Singaporean Government, while in Taiwan the entrepreneurial Captain Chang Yung-Fa founded Evergreen.[232] At first, these firms operated second-hand traditional cargo liners, but at rates undercutting established European and American lines. To compete in future with these and other Asian upstarts, it would therefore be necessary for established operators, such as the East Asiatic Company, to cut costs by greatly enhancing efficiency – and this meant embracing containerisation.

In common with most European lines trading with the Far East, EAC continued to build conventional cargo liners until the latter 1960s. The routes on which they operated were containerised slightly later than the trans-Atlantic services between the advanced and relatively technologically sophisticated nations of Northern Europe and North America. Furthermore, rather than finding itself locked out of investing in container ships, as DFDS had done by spending available money on a suddenly obsolescent ship type, EAC was fully involved in the development of key container ship-operating consortia.

EAC's final generation of general cargo liners was bigger than those recently delivered to DFDS, each measuring just over 10,000gt, and so they gave greater economies of scale and operational flexibility as they were fitted with a mix of derricks and electric cranes. Additionally, due to their more generous dimensions, it was possible to stack fairly large numbers of containers

Above: With a speed of over 31 knots, the **Selandia** and **Jutlandia** were among the fastest ever Danish merchant ships. Here, the **Jutlandia** is shown at sea. (Museet for Søfart)

The **Selandia** under construction at B&W,
clearly showing the three-way division of
the holds across her beam and the two box
girders running along her length between.
(Museet for Søfart)

on deck around and atop the cargo hatches. Indeed, EAC's final cargo liner, the *Atrevida*, was a semi-container ship.

EAC's senior management were enthusiastic about the possibilities offered by containerisation. With many industrial interests spread around the world, its directors would have been only too aware of the limitations of traditional means of handling cargo. In 1968, the 39-year-old Henning Sparsø joined EAC's Board to manage the containerisation of liner services. Sparsø had first

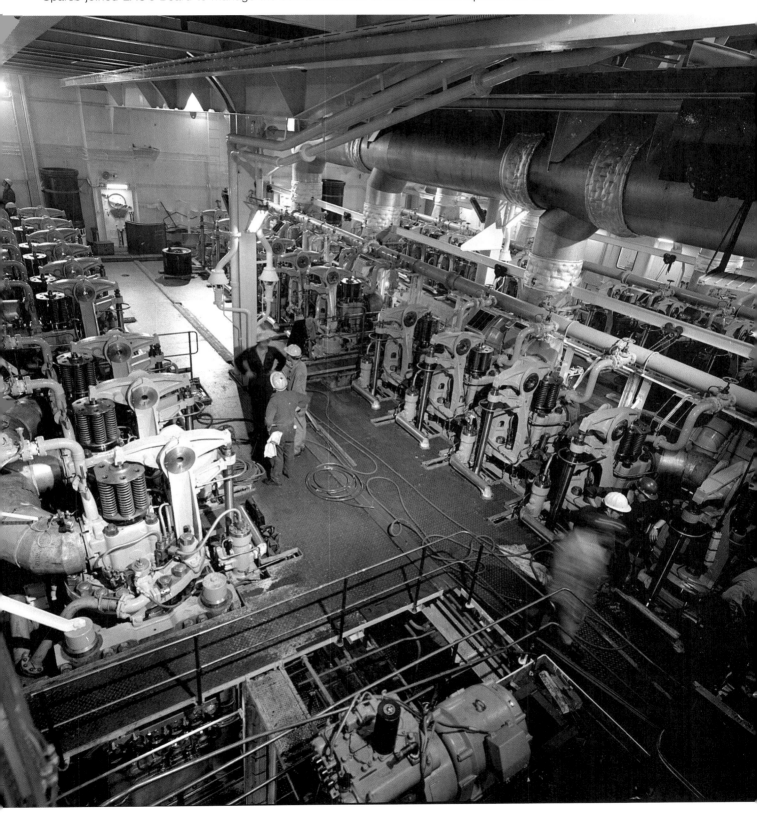

The engine room on the EAC container ship *Selandia*, showing the tops of two of her three main engines. (MAN/Diesel House)

joined EAC in 1951, initially being employed in London at its United Baltic Corporation subsidiary. After that, he spent time working for EAC companies in the Far East before being summoned to join the senior management at its Copenhagen headquarters.

The crucial problem for all liner companies suddenly faced with containerisation – including EAC – was the vast investment required to build new tonnage. Cargo liners of the type EAC built immediately after the Second World War cost 5 million kroner each; by the mid-1960s, they cost 25 million kroner, whereas the forthcoming container carriers each cost more than 70 million kroner for the first generation and 160 million for the second generation.[233] The most obvious solution was to join forces with old rivals or fellow members of established liner conferences to form consortia.

From 1969 onwards, EAC therefore joined a series of consortia to introduce container ships on key liner routes. As we have seen, liner traffic traditionally was dominated by conference agreements to set schedules and freight rates – and container consortia merely took the process a stage further. Being much larger, often faster and considerably more structurally complex than conventional cargo liners, container ships were costly investments. Moreover, one container ship of the type EAC proposed to build could do the work of a handful of traditional cargo liners thanks to having more than double the hull volume and much shorter dwell times in port. Therefore, rationalisation and co-operation between shipping companies were felt by most established liner operators to provide the best way to develop the container business.

Initially, EAC joined three consortia. The first to be established was ScanService, set up jointly with the Svenska Ostasiatiske Kompagniet (Swedish East Asiatic Company, a part of the Gothenburg-based Broströms Rederi AB) and the Norwegian Wilh. Wilhelmsen of Oslo to prepare for containerisation between Northern Europe and the Far East.[234] Between this original agreement and fully-containerised services actually commencing, the Royal Netherlands Lloyd, which traded as Nedlloyd, joined the consortium and so it was renamed ScanDutch. Next, in July 1970, EAC joined a second consortium – Scan Australia Carriers Ltd, known as ScanAustral – to containerise the service from Northern Europe to Australia; at first, this consisted of Wilh. Wilhelmsen and Sweden's Rederi AB Transatlantic. Initially, fleets of conventional cargo liners operated for these consortia, albeit additionally carrying containers on deck as necessary; Scan Austral involved the use of 16 vessels and there were no less than 51 employed on the ScanDutch route (out of which 17 belonged to EAC) – but the plan was to introduce dedicated container ships as soon as practicable.[235]

The third consortium began as a collaboration between EAC and Britain's Blue Star Line, which was a member of the Vestey shipping and cattle-ranching conglomerate. Soon, Sweden's Johnson Line (Rederi AB Nordstjernan) joined and, together, the three companies jointly marketed their service as Johnson ScanStar. This inaugurated a container line from Northern Europe via the Panama Canal to US and Canadian West Coast ports in May 1972, using a combined fleet of nine container ships – two belonging to EAC, two to Blue Star and five to Johnson Line.

EAC's vessels for the route were ordered from Nakskov Skibsværft in 1969. These were the 20,187gt *Falstria* and *Meonia*, which were delivered in September 1971 and April 1972 respectively; the *Falstria* was, therefore, Denmark's first large ocean-going container ship and could carry 918 TEU with two layers on deck when fully loaded. Most of the design drawings for the pair were produced by Nakskov Skibsværft's drawing office, headed by Chief Naval Architect Henrik Fogh, following instructions from EAC's five-man Newbuilding Department, headed by Torben Bille.[236]

The engine room was located fully aft with the superstructure slightly ahead of this, much as on the recent cargo liner *Atrevida*. Power was provided by a single 2-stroke 10-cylinder B&W diesel, generating 27,300 ihp and enabling a 22.25-knot service speed. As with EAC's most recent cargo liners, the *Falstria* and her sister were designed and outfitted to a very high specification. So as to improve manoeuvrability in port, a bow thrust propeller was fitted while, on deck, there were automatic mooring winches rather than capstans. On the fantail, there was a single hatch through which spare parts and ship's stores were loaded. [237] The crew numbered 29 and their accommodation was spacious and comfortable.

The hull lines were largely devised by H. Ditlev-Jørgensen, a young naval architect who had

Opposite top: The *Selandia* at the container terminal in Hong Kong with the New Territories under construction in the background. (Bruce Peter collection)

Opposite bottom: The magnificent *Selandia* at speed during her builder's trials. (Bruce Peter collection)

joined EAC's Newbuilding Department in 1968 having previously been employed at the Hydro and Aerodynamics Laboratory (HyA) in Lyngby, to the north of Copenhagen. Ditlev-Jørgensen worked closely with Preben Søgaard from the Design Department of Nakskov Skibsværft and a series of hull tests was carried out in the tank at the HyA Laboratory. The lower speed-to-length ratio of the design they developed in comparison with the A-class allowed for a fuller hull form enabling easier container stowage while still maintaining a service speed of over 22 knots. (Moreover, in following seas, the most recent EAC A-class cargo liners – such as the *Atrevida* – rolled alarmingly with heeling angles of up to 40 degrees due to their fine-lined hulls.) Compensating for the *Falstria*'s fuller – and therefore potentially less sleek and fast – hull, a bulbous bow was specified, the first ever on a Nakskov-built ship. In addition, to avoid the serious cavitation and vibration experienced on the *Atrevida*, a new stern configuration was devised with adequate clearance above and forward of the fixed six-bladed propeller, producing a more even wash and obtaining a lower thrust per blade, despite the bigger engine.[238] Thus, EAC abandoned the concept of using controllable pitch propellers coupled to two-stroke engines on single-screw ships. [239]

A problem for the designers of such large container ships was how best to control hull deflection when taking seas from the bow and stern quarters due to their straight lines and the size and span of their holds. To control this problem, a double hull with side tanks and box girders below main deck level, through which cabling was routed, created a robust U-shaped structure. As with the cargo liners *Alameda* and *Atrevida* and the majority of other 'first generation' fully-cellular container ships of the latter 1960s, a third longitudinal box girder was installed along the centreline at upper deck level, the hatches and cellular holds being arranged on either side of this.[240] As the *Falstria* and *Meonia* were designed to make use of shore-based container handling equipment, no cranes were fitted and this saved weight.

The *Falstria* was delivered in September 1971, the *Meonia* following in April 1972. While they were under construction, EAC entered into an agreement with the Danish State Railways, DSB, to develop and operate container terminals, allowing the efficient inter-modal transfer of containers from ship to rail and road modes. In addition, in 1967 EAC established a new information technology subsidiary, ØK Data, to operate computer systems managing the accounts of its various subsidiary businesses. Once container services began, ØK Data became an important component in enabling their smooth operation.[241]

The *Falstria* and *Meonia*'s British-owned Blue Star Line counterparts were the West German-built *California Star* and *Columbia Star*. Measuring 188.71 metres in length, these were slightly shorter than their Danish fleetmates, carrying up to 871 20-foot containers each, as opposed to the Danes' 918. Furthermore, they were deeper drafted, operating at 10 metres when loaded in comparison with the 8.84 metre maximum draft of the EAC sisters. The British sisters were undoubtedly excellent vessels for their time and served between Europe and South America until well into the 1990s, but the *Falstria* and *Meonia* clearly had a slight economic advantage due to their relatively low draft when fully laden, coupled with their greater capacity. Rederi AB Nordstjernan's five-strong container fleet was built in Finland by the Wärtsilä shipyard in Helsinki to a different design again, featuring three hatches across the width of their hulls and two box girders between to brace the hull structure (thereby lowering the density of the container cells). They were each fitted with four Wärtsilä-Pielstick medium-speed diesels and gantry cranes to handle containers independently of port facilities.[242] Of the three types of vessel used by Johnson ScanStar, however, the EAC's were overall slightly the more efficient in terms of capacity, hull form and propulsion. Yet, a consortium service involving a variety of different vessel designs would inevitably have higher operational costs than one operating with a uniform type.

The ScanDutch service from Europe to the Far East required larger, faster and, therefore, more technologically complex vessels than Johnson ScanStar. This would compete with the established and financially powerful British container consortium Overseas Containers Ltd (OCL), established in 1965.[243] To achieve a commercial advantage, it was necessary for ScanDutch to sail faster than OCL and to offset the extra cost with larger vessels offering superior economies of scale.

Opposite: The **Selandia** sails straight towards the picture plane, making a bold impression of modern mercantile power at sea. (Bruce Peter collection)

The *Jutlandia*, passing
through the Strait of
Malacca.
(Bruce Peter collection)

As the route operated from the Far East to Europe via the Panama Canal because of the Suez
Canal's closure between 1967 and 1975 due to war between Egypt and Israel, their size was
restricted by the dimensions of the Canal's locks. (Large container ships – as well as tankers,
bulk and vehicle carriers – of the maximum size capable of squeezing through these locks are
described as 'Panamax' vessels.) The three initial consortium members – EAC, Wilh. Wilhelmsen
and Swedish East Asiatic – agreed at an early meeting in Gothenburg that the best solution would
be to order triple-screw diesel-engined container ships. The decisive reason for this was that
EAC's Torben Bille had been shown an intriguing paper found in *Shipbuilding and Shipping
Record* by his younger colleague in the Newbuilding Department, H. Ditlev-Jørgensen.[244] Written
by Sinclair and Emerson of the British propeller suppliers Stone-Manganese, this demonstrated
that three propellers would result in a saving of 5,000 horsepower on a Panamax container ship
averaging a 28-knot service speed, meaning that only 75,000 hp would be required of the
propulsion plant rather than the 80,000 necessary from a twin-screw example.[245] A consequence
of this was that smaller engines could be used than in a twin-screw vessel as the EAC's Chief
Mechanical Engineer, Ejler Kongsted, worried that bigger units might cause unacceptable
vibration in hulls with such slender aftbody configurations. Furthermore, a single rudder could
be fitted behind the centre propeller to give superior steering characteristics in comparison with
a twin-screw ship with a single rudder.[246]

EAC, Wilh. Wilhelmsen and Swedish East Asiatic all agreed that, for reasons of economy, a
triple-screw solution would be best. Wilhelmsen had, however, already decided to order its single
contribution to the consortium, the *Toyama*, from Mitsui Zonen at Tamano in Japan due to the
lower cost of building there. The only trouble was that the Japanese had never previously
constructed a triple-screw diesel container vessel, preferring instead twin-screw steam turbine
propulsion. Already, the yard was planning to build a Panamax twin-screw turbine container ship
to be named *Elbe Maru* for the Company's Mitsui O.S.K. Line subsidiary and, in order to be sure
of winning and delivering a prestigious export order to Wilhelmsen, this was re-designed as a
triple-screw ship to gain experience.[247] Already, Mitsui was the world's largest licensed builder of
B&W diesel engines and so assembling and installing these to fulfil the Wilhelmsen order would

not be a problem.[248] The *Toyama* was a near-sister to the *Elbe Maru* and both vessels followed the then-standard approach to hull structure, having a deep and heavy longitudinal structural member running along the centreline with hatches on either side.[249]

EAC, represented mainly by Poul Damkjær Nielsen, Torben Bille's most experienced naval architect, and Swedish East Asiatic technical staff worked closely on the overall design specifications for their contributions to the consortium, although each company would place orders respectively in Danish and Swedish shipyards and it would be the builders who independently carried out the detailed design work. The Swedes ordered the 50,000gt, 2,204 TEU *Nihon* from AB Öresundsvarvet in Landskrona. This striking all-white vessel was propelled by three Götaverken diesel engines, driving three propellers at a service speed of 26 knots.[250]

EAC's two-vessel contribution, meanwhile, was ordered from Burmeister & Wain. Given their record-breaking size, speed and novel construction, appropriately they were named *Selandia* and *Jutlandia*, reviving memories of B&W and EAC's collaboration sixty years previously on the pioneering ocean-going motor ships of these names. Each was to measure 49,890gt and would have a 2,272 TEU capacity. Most unfortunately, shortly after winning the contract to build them, B&W had a brief but severe financial crisis. This situation alarmed EAC's senior management who were understandably concerned that the yard might not be able to complete and deliver the vessels on schedule. To boost confidence that the work would indeed be carried out within the required timescale, EAC persuaded B&W's Board of Directors to appoint Torben Bille as Managing Director. Bille was already a long-standing friend of B&W's Chief Naval Architect, Johannes Petersen, as the two had studied together at the Technical University of Denmark. Thereafter, Bille's place in EAC's Newbuilding Department was taken by his colleague Ejler Kongsted and this meant that EAC had sympathetic and knowledgeable people in key positions both in its own organisation and at the yard. Tragically, however, Bille did not live to see the first of the new container ships, the *Selandia*, enter service in September 1972 as, that March, he was killed in a plane crash in the United Arab Emirates while flying home from a holiday in Ceylon (Sri Lanka).[251]

In the interests of cost saving, from the latter 1960s onwards B&W preferred to build hulls entirely of single curved plates. This technique had been developed by Leif Sidenius who worked in the yard's Steel Department and so the hull design chosen for the *Selandia* and *Jutlandia* followed this methodology with flat topsides and neither concave nor convex forms in the bow profile. The stern was a flat transom. Indeed, the only significant element in the entire hull structure with a double curvature was the very pronounced bulbous bow. (Subsequently, B&W even managed to eliminate the need for double curves in bulbs, as seen in the bulk carriers it designed and built between the latter 1970s and mid-1990s.) In contrast, the otherwise broadly similar *Nihon* had considerable flare and pronounced knucklejoints fore and aft.

Structurally, the *Selandia*, *Jutlandia* and *Nihon* were very progressive. As each measured 290.85 metres in length by 32.25 metres breadth (whereas the *Falstria* and *Meonia* were only 201.85 by 25.91 metres), controlling hull twisting was an even greater challenge for their designers. Unlike a similarly dimensioned oil tanker, on which the deck is an unbroken expanse of strength-giving steel with stiffening members welded to its underside, such container ships were open-deck vessels with only two to three metres' width of plating around the hatch openings. Thus, much of the hull's strength was derived from the bottom and side structures and the transverse bulkheads which accordingly were thickly plated, particularly in the hull's upper region. The placement of the superstructure two-thirds aft rather than fully astern also helped to brace the structure. On most large container ships in their size bracket – such as the *Elbe Maru* and *Toyama*, described above – a big and heavy centreline girder stiffened the hull. In contrast, the design solution for the *Selandia* and *Jutlandia* (and the *Nihon*) gained extra strength from two far smaller longitudinal box girders of a similar size and type to those fitted on the *Falstria* and *Meonia*. On the *Selandia* and *Jutlandia*, these ran in parallel for most of the hull's length between centre and side hatches, much as on Johnson Line's Finnish-built container vessels also described above. *The Motor Ship* observed that:

> '…An extensive R.I.N.A. paper presented earlier this year on the design of the [OCL]

Above: A stern-quarter view of EAC's roll-on, roll-off container (con-ro)
vessel *Lalandia* at Melbourne. (R.Verhoeven, Russell Priest collection)

Below: The *Lalandia* arrives at Melbourne.
(R.Verhoeven, Russell Priest collection)

Liverpool Bay class of steam turbine vessels… pointed out that hull deflections of as much as 100 mm as well as other problems have been recorded on the earlier *Encounter Bay* class ships. As a result, a number of rival designs have been evolved for the third-generation ship; and thus the *Selandia*… is based on a light arrangement strongly braced, which has resulted in a considerable reduction in the light ship weight.'[252]

Indeed, the weight saving on the *Selandia*, *Jutlandia* and *Nihon* was no less than 2,000 tons in comparison with the *Toyama* and so their structural solution became the standard for larger container ships built during the ensuing decades as this enabled more deadweight capacity to be released for revenue-earning cargo. The calculations were carried out at B&W by one of its naval architects, Bjarne Moth-Poulsen.

Having produced the most effective design, extensive model testing took place at the Danish Maritime Institute to prove that the design could maintain the required 28-knot service speed in nearly all conditions. The propeller suppliers, Stone-Manganese, suggested that the centre propeller should have fixed blades with controllable pitch propellers mounted on the wing shafts and twin rudders. This was the arrangement favoured by the British Dover Strait car ferry operator Townsend for its most recent 'Free Enterprise'-type ferries, but it was rejected by EAC as the *Selandia* and *Jutlandia* were intended to operate as single-screw vessels during short voyages between ports in Northern Europe and in triple-screw configuration for long deep-sea passages to and from the Far East. Specifying a single rudder and fitting a four-bladed controllable pitch propeller to the centre shaft would, therefore, be the most effective solution to ensure good steering and speed control during short legs, while propellers with six fixed blades were attached to the wing shafts. Power to the centre shaft was provided by a 30,000 bhp 12-cylinder B&W engine with two 22,500 bhp 9-cylinder units driving the wing propellers. One further potential advantage of this solution was that engine maintenance could take place on the side units while the vessels were underway – an important consideration given container ships' short spells in port.[253]

The *Selandia* was the biggest vessel yet constructed by B&W, so much so that there was insufficient space to build her hull as a single unit, and so her bow was added as a prefabricated section only once her hull had been partially floated out towards the end of the construction process. She sailed for Hamburg without her bulbous bow, which was added there in Howaldtswerke Deutsche Werft's drydock. A few months later, the *Jutlandia* went through the same convoluted but ingenious process.

The *Selandia* was completed in September 1972, running trials in the Kattegat during which she reached a remarkable maximum speed of 31.5 knots. For ScanDutch's Commercial Department, this made excellent copy to attact customers and it delighted all those involved in the ship's design and construction. She was then the fastest and most sophisticated vessel in the history of the Danish Merchant Navy; she was also magnificent-looking with a striking profile, topped off by twin tapering funnels, and immaculately painted in the very smart EAC livery. Her sister, the *Jutlandia*, was completed in December 1972. Notwithstanding their great speed, however, the *Selandia* and *Jutlandia* were more efficient by a third in terms of fuel consumption than steam turbine container ships of their size and generation. Typically, they burned around 300 tons of fuel per day, whereas similarly dimensioned turbine powered examples used 400 tons to achieve a similar speed.[254] Of sophisticated design and superb appearance, these state-of-the-art vessels attracted great interest from industry technical journals.

Nedlloyd, meanwhile, ordered from Bremer-Vulkan in West Germany its own slightly larger pair of twin-screw turbine vessels for ScanDutch service, the 58,716gt 2,952 TEU *Nedlloyd Dejima* and *Nedlloyd Delft*. When delivered in April 1973, *Nedlloyd Dejima* was the world's most capacious container ship, but her presence in the consortium resulted in a fleet that was uniform neither in terms of capacity, propulsion nor fuel consumption (whereas the rival British OCL operation used six nearly identical ships). Shortly thereafter, in July 1973, Messageries Maritimes joined ScanDutch, contributing the 2,900 TEU *Korrigan* which was different again.[255] While this would not have mattered so much in the break-bulk era, as container shipping grew

increasingly competitive rigorous standardisation became ever more important in generating efficiency savings and optimising capacity. Add to that variations in union-negotiated wage rates and crew sizes between the vessels of the different flag members and further complications arose. Nevertheless, these six container ships, with a total deadweight capacity of 106,040 tons, could do the job of a much larger conventional cargo liner fleet with 245,955 tons of capacity, largely thanks to the container ships' shorter turnaround times in port and significantly faster service speeds.[256]

The ScanDutch container service was at first highly successful. Vessels loaded at the Gothenburg, Hamburg and Rotterdam container terminals before sailing to the Far East. In 1973, unfortunately, there was a sudden and exponential rise in the cost of oil which caused the world economy to fall into recession. Since the Second World War, oil prices had remained more or less stable at around ten dollars a barrel, but in 1973 the cost more than quadrupled. The reason was that Arab oil-producing countries who together formed the Organisation of Petroleum Exporting Countries (OPEC) were infuriated by American support for Israel in the Yom Kippur War and, in protest, they slashed oil production. As shipping companies were amongst the heaviest commercial oil users, they were particularly badly affected.[257] As a result, the ScanDutch container fleet was slowed down from its record-breaking 28-knot performance to the more traditional liner speed of 21 knots. (The practice of 'slow steaming' was in fact introduced out of necessity by all operators on the Europe-Far East route in the mid-1970s and, in the recent 2009-2011 recession, it returned again.)

In 1973, EAC took delivery of a single ro-ro container ship, the 13,874gt *Lalandia*, built by Eriksbergs Mekaniska Verkstad in Gothenburg, as its contribution to the ScanAustral consortium. This vessel was designed by the technical staff of Rederi AB Transatlantic, the consortium's Swedish member.

The consequences of the Oil Crisis were deeply felt throughout the shipbuilding world, which suffered a steep decline in ship and engine orders being placed. This led Burmeister & Wain to experience a second financial trauma in 1979, the result of which was that in 1980 it decided to sell its Engine Division to an old rival, MAN in West Germany; after this sale, the division was renamed B&W Diesel. It was not only the poor state of the shipping industry that caused B&W serious problems, however. Unlike most Danish shipyards, which generally enjoyed good labour relations and high productivity, B&W's Shipbuilding Division had come to be plagued by strikes, low productivity and pilfering – problems which hastened the demise of shipbuilding in Britain at the same time.[258] (The B&W shipyard survived and continued to build mainly tankers and bulk carriers until the mid-1990s.)

When MAN took over B&W's Engine Division, several leading members of its technical staff withdrew in protest and so there was a significant intake of new staff. The market for ships grew in the early 1980s and so B&W Diesel was well placed to benefit from this welcome upswing. Oil remained expensive and so its flexible and economical engine designs were very attractive to shipowners who were forced more carefully to consider the lifetime costs of their vessels. Whereas in the 1960s 'voyage costs' accounted for only 20 per cent of the total average bill for operating a ship, by the 1980s they amounted to 50 per cent.[259] By 1981, B&W Diesel had gained over 50 per cent of the worldwide market for slow-speed marine diesel engines.[260] The manufacture of B&W Diesel marine engines in the Christianshavn works in Copenhagen continued only until October 1987. From then onwards, production in Denmark was maintained in Frederikshavn until 2010. Today, such engines are assembled by MAN Diesel's licensees all over the world – but Copenhagen is still where they are designed and where prototypes are tested.

Opposite: The *Lalandia* at Sydney, with the Opera House and Harbour Bridge in the background. (Museet for Søfart)

Chapter 10

The decline of EAC

While B&W struggled to stem losses in the wake of the Oil Crisis, its long-standing patron for innovative ships and engines, the East Asiatic Company, also became financially troubled. Unlike B&W, EAC's problems were almost entirely self-inflicted through a combination of arrogant management and poor corporate governance. EAC underwent a period of rapid expansion during the 1970s, financed mainly with borrowed money at a time when the world economy was sluggish and moderate investment was generally considered a wiser course by other big businesses. EAC's Managing Director, Mogens Pagh, was attempting to make it into a giant international conglomerate through the purchase of numerous diverse businesses around the world ranging from the manufacture of tobacco products, food and drink, medicine, finance and insurance, information technology – and even a licence to manufacture Vespa scooters in the Far East. EAC employed 40,000 people worldwide in 1971, making it Denmark's biggest and most successful business. (At that time, Denmark's second largest was A.P. Møller with 10,000 employees.) In 1971, EAC's share capital was 280 million kroner; in 1973 it had shot up to 500 million kroner and in 1978 it was 765 million kroner – but thereafter things took a severe turn for the worse.[261]

To replace its remaining general cargo liner fleet, EAC ordered a series of relatively small and slow multi-purpose freighters with some container capacity called 'Liner Replacement Vessels' (LRV). At first, it was thought that no less than twenty ships of this type would be needed to replace existing vessels on all EAC secondary routes (in other words, the entire liner fleet, bar the container ships). During the design phase, the hull was lengthened by one hold, tanks for liquid cargo were added and cell-guides were specified in the cargo holds (whereas initially containers were only intended to be carried on deck).[262]

The newly-completed *Sargodha* in Nakskov Fjord in 1978. (Nakskov Local History Collection)

Top: The **Samoa**, built by
Nakskov Skibsværft and
delivered in 1978.
(Russell Priest collection)

Above: The **Simba** at anchor
off Singapore in 1980.
(Russell Priest)

Left: The **Siena**, delivered
from Nakskov Skibsværft in
1979, is seen at Fremantle.
(E. Drake, Russell Priest
Collection)

A stern-quarter view of the *Siena* at Fremantle. (E. Drake, Russell Priest collection)

They were 16,149gt single-screw motor ships capable of only 16.2 knots maximum and with fairly bluff hull lines rather more akin to smallish bulk carriers than recent pure container vessels or indeed the cargo liners they were intended to replace. The idea was that they should be able to handle not only containers and bulk cargoes – such as heavy engineering exports, forestry products, ore and grain – but also general cargo. Their slow speed was a reflection of the high cost of fuel and the expectation that the price would not decrease in the foreseeable future, while the multi-purpose design reflected EAC's particular business model which required liners to transport a variety of raw materials and manufactured goods between the Company's various plantations and factories around the world. Yet, carrying freight for external customers, especially in containers, was increasingly important for the profitability of its liner shipping operations, a factor which the LRV ships proved ill-suited to cope with due to their low speed and constricted dimensions.

Topsides, each was fitted with six electric cranes to handle cargo independently of shore-based facilities; these not only added weight but also limited the deck space available for containers. They were expensive and complex ships with full engine room automation from bridge controls, but they failed to do any one job properly in a shipping context in which increasing specialisation had been taking place for at least the past decade. (Other operators – such as Britain's Ocean Group subsidiaries Blue Funnel Line and Palm Line – took delivery of similar ships in the mid-1970s, apparently finding little more success than EAC.)

Six LRV vessels were built at Nakskov Skibsværft. Of these, only five were delivered to EAC – the *Samoa*, *Sargodha*, *Sinaloa*, *Simba* and *Siena* – while the sixth was cancelled while under construction and instead completed for Pakistan. (This contract was taken over by the Danish Government and completed as a gift to aid development there; named the *Makran*, the vessel was delivered in 1979 to the Pakistan National Shipping Corporation.)[263] Two further examples, the *Sumbawa* and *Songkhla*, came from Mitsui at Tamano in Japan. The Japanese-built examples cost 85 million kroner each, whereas those constructed at Nakskov each cost 115 million; this meant an overall additional cost of 150 million kroner which could almost have purchased a further two ships but, as EAC owned the Nakskov shipyard, it was apparently willing to pay this difference.[264] The initial idea was to use the vessels on secondary routes to ports in Africa and

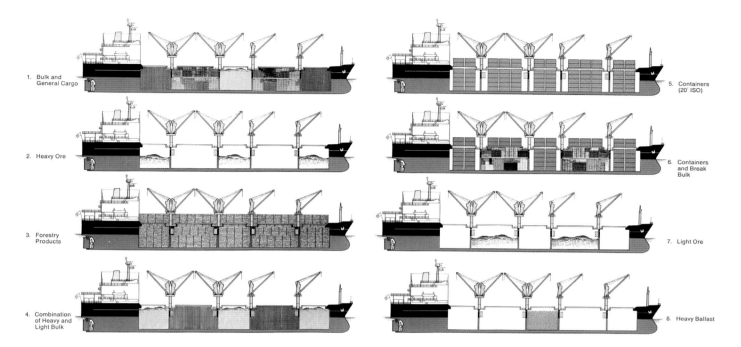

1. Bulk and General Cargo

2. Heavy Ore

3. Forestry Products

4. Combination of Heavy and Light Bulk

5. Containers (20' ISO)

6. Containers and Break Bulk

7. Light Ore

8. Heavy Ballast

India where speed was less important than the flexibility to transport mixed cargo – but early on in the procurement process there was a very unwise change of plan.

With established container services from Northern Europe to America's West Coast, via the Panama Canal, and with a service from Europe to the Far East, EAC decided to fill the gap between by launching a Trans-Pacific Line, which was scheduled to open in May 1977. It was on this new route that EAC decided to concentrate the new highly unsuitable Liner Replacement Vessels. The Pacific was among the first areas of international shipping to have been containerised and competition was tough between the various American and Far East-owned lines operating large and fast vessels – as well as numerous cross-trading liner operators. Among the most efficient in the latter category was Maersk Line, which had cross-traded there since the 1920s.

Apart from EAC's Liner Replacement Vessels being too slow (and therefore unreliable as they could not catch up for delays due to adverse weather), they lacked capacity as their hatch covers provided mainly stowage space for small 20-foot containers, rather than the larger 40-foot units that were becoming increasingly popular. EAC's customers quite reasonably expected their containers to be delivered on time – something that could not be guaranteed using the LRV type of ships – and so they took their business elsewhere. Furthermore, the route served numerous ports and was therefore more like a traditional general cargo service than a point-to-point container line. (One reason for this was to include calls in harbours close to EAC's forestry plantations in Washington State and Canada.) Consequently, even when operating according to schedule, voyages were lengthy while freight rates were low due to there being intense competition.[265] At first, EAC blamed this factor rather than the unsuitability of the ships for the losses being incurred.

For EAC, the LRV vessels proved to be a costly miscalculation. Already in 1978 EAC's Trans-Pacific Line had lost 120 million kroner.[266] Even then, its directorate had begun to discuss whether it might be more prudent to close down the route while the order for the seventh LRV ship was cancelled, even as the hull was taking shape in Nakskov. Notwithstanding the losses being incurred, Henning Sparsø was strongly against closure of the Trans-Pacific Line, arguing that it played a vital part in EAC's operations.

Meanwhile, over the decade from 1971 to 1981, EAC's overall debt burden grew from 3.8 billion kroner to 11.2 billion. In April 1980, Mogens Pagh retired as EAC's Managing Director, to be replaced by Henning Sparsø. For EAC, the 1980s proved to be a difficult decade as its management struggled to make sense of the vast portfolio of business interests bequeathed from

The LRV ships should have been able to fulfill a number of diverse requirements, ranging from the transport of containers, to general and bulk cargoes. In reality, they were not designed to carry out any task properly and so, when placed in trans-Pacific service, the result for EAC was catastrophic. (Bruce Peter collection)

Above: So far as interior design was concerned, little expense was spared on the LRV
ships. The bar on the **Samoa** features Werner Panton 'System' furniture. EAC's belief was that
the ships could act as 'ambassadors' for Danish design and that visitors would be impressed.
(Nakskov Local History Collection)

Below: The lounge on the **Samoa** was in a typically
1970s idiom. (Nakskov Local History Collection)

Right: The **Sumbawa** with EAC-Knutsen Line hull markings during a brief liason between the Danish and Norwegian companies to run the trans-Pacific service in the early 1980s; EAC provided six LRV ships while Knutsen ran two chartered vessels. (Bruce Peter collection)

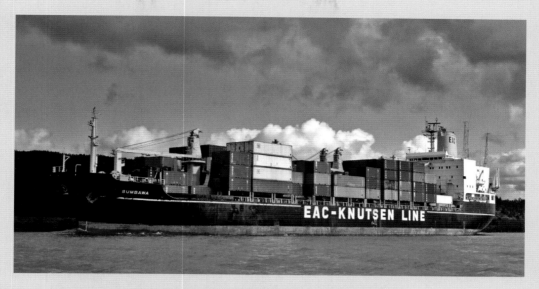

Left: A stern-quarter view of the **Sargodha**. (Russell Priest collection)

Below: The **Siena** is shown leaving Vancouver in 1982. The following year, EAC chartered her to a Mexican company. (Bruce Peter collection)

the Pagh era – and to control the mounting losses and debt.[267] In these circumstances, EAC was in no fit condition to order further significant container tonnage. Indeed, the Newbuilding Department was slimmed down from five employees to two in 1983.

Perhaps EAC's greatest mistake was the failure of its management to distinguish between the particular characteristics of container shipping and the shipping of general and bulk cargo. Although the Company had been Denmark's international container shipping pioneer, its subsequent policy continued to focus instead on its motley collection of subsidiary businesses as the key source of revenue for liner operations. This ignored profound changes in the dominant ideology and structure of the world economy as they affected the ongoing development of liner shipping.

Since Roosevelt's 'New Deal,' economic policy in the Western industrialised world had been dominated by theories propounded by John Maynard Keynes, who believed that a mixture of private entrepreneurship and state intervention was the best way to secure stability and steady growth. The idea was that, during downturns, government intervention would create jobs and thus stimulate the economy, enabling debt to be recouped during the ensuing upswing.

With the growth of industries in South East Asia, coupled with the ongoing negative effects of the Oil Crisis, Keynes' ideas were challenged by Western problems of increasing debt, inflation and unemployment, especially in Britain and the USA. Rather than being short-term measures to maintain stability, many now saw government intervention and protectionism as fundamental reasons for Western industrial decline. Furthermore, the ongoing Cold War led to a polarisation of ideologies between an emerging American 'free market' ethos and the Soviet Union's strictly-controlled command economy. Sceptics of governmental intervention found their hero in Milton Friedman, Professor of Economics at Harvard Business School, who believed in small government and in regulating growth only through the adjustment of interest rates. Come the 1980s, his theories were first practised by Margaret Thatcher's Conservative Government in Britain and by Ronald Reagan's Republican administration in the United States. A decade later, they were introduced in Eastern Europe and Asia in the wake of the Soviet Union's collapse and nowadays they are mainstream orthodoxy almost everywhere. The spread of market deregulation was followed by a significant increase in global trade and, thanks to container shipping, it became possible to transport items of relatively high value more quickly, cheaply and securely than ever before.

As the container market grew, the development of fast and reliable services allowed American and European retailers to outsource manufacture to South East Asia and so time-critical cargoes of consumer goods, such as fashion clothing and footwear, became a lucrative source of income for operators. Before a new fashion line is launched, however, the market is prepared by advertising campaigns, celebrity endorsements and product placement in the movies and on television. Therefore, the goods must arrive on schedule and it is estimated that even a two-day delay can lose an American clothing retailer up to 15 per cent of the sales of a specific collection.[268] Set against this new reality, EAC's multi-purpose LRV vessels were very retrograde indeed, representing a reversion to 1930s standards in terms of speed and schedule keeping. How could they ever attract profitable container cargoes of high-value consumer goods while also spending several days in relatively remote Canadian ports loading low-value timber logs from EAC-owned plantations? In 1983, the route lost 150 million kroner and was being dubbed the 'Trans-Panic Line' by some of Henning Sparsø's increasingly sceptical – but apparently powerless – fellow directors.[269]

In the same year, a World Bank study of liner routes between Europe and West Africa showed that a semi-container ship took between seven and eight weeks to make a single voyage, whereas full container ships required only between three and four, and that lines operating semi-container vessels were already phasing them out. Fortunately, EAC's Africa service was by this point operated by a pair of Nakskov-built container ships, the 20,295gt *Fionia* and *Boringia*, delivered in 1977 but of similar design to the pioneering *Falstria* and *Meonia* completed six years previously. EAC threatened to swap these for LRV ships from the loss-making Pacific route, but the managers of the African service strongly resisted this request. Instead, EAC withdrew the troublesome LRVs from the Pacific, replacing them with chartered container vessels, but still the route failed to yield

Opposite top: The **Boringia** was one of two Nakskov-built container ships successfully deployed by EAC on the route to West Africa from 1977-78 onwards. Unlike the earlier **Falstria** and **Meonia**, they were fitted with cranes. (Bruce Peter collection)

Opposite bottom: The **Boringia** operating for the Compagnie Maritime Belge; during the 1980s, EAC entered several joint arrangements with other lines with varying degrees of success. (Bruce Peter collection)

Left: Henning K. Sparsø, photographed here at the launching of the LRV **Siena** with the vessel's godmother, Lise Kongsted, was one of the driving forces behind EAC's initial switch to containerised tonnage. Later, he was responsible for the slow LRV ships continuing in trans-Pacific service with heavy financial losses. (Nakskov Local History Collection)

Below: In 1984, the **Selandia** and **Jutlandia** were lengthened by 15 metres. Here, the **Selandia** has just been cut in two sections enabling the new hull section to be inserted. (Museet for Søfart)

In 1991, EAC took over the Norwegian and Swedish ScanDutch partners' large container ships **Toyama** and **Nihon**, the latter of which is seen in the Solent wearing EAC's funnel logo. (Mick Lindsay)

profits. It finally closed in 1992, having lost over a billion kroner.[270]

For a while, business was better on the Europe-Far East ScanDutch service, but it too suffered from increasing competition by newer and more efficient vessels, forcing down freight rates and squeezing profit margins. In a bid to enhance their economies of scale, the *Selandia* and *Jutlandia* were lengthened in 1984 (as were the *Nihon* and *Toyama*), increasing their capacities to 2,821 containers each. At the same time, their engines were down-rated to operate at a service speed of only 21 knots (24 maximum) as a fuel-saving measure. Come the early 1990s, relations between the leading ScanDutch members EAC and Nedlloyd deteriorated, while their Swedish and Norwegian partners also decided to withdraw from the consortium. Therefore, EAC purchased the *Nihon* and *Toyama* in 1991 and at the start of the following year entered into a joint agreement with the ailing British company Ben Line; this was marketed as Ben-EAC and headquartered in Sevenoaks in England. For many years they were keen competitors in the Europe-Far East trade, but since the latter 1970s they had been partners of EAC in the bulk shipping business in which both Companies had invested heavily. Ben owned three ageing container ships of a similar type and size to the existing ScanDutch vessels: the 2,804 TEU *Ben Alder*, *Ben Avon* and *Ben Arty* (ex *City of Edinburgh*). These twin-screw sisters had been constructed with steam turbine plants but were subsequently rebuilt as motor ships. Thereafter, EAC only ever ordered two further container ships for the route, the 49,874gt, 4,000 TEU Mitsui-built *Arosia* and *Alsia*, delivered in 1990, but it was too little, too late.[271]

Outwith shipping, EAC made further losses through unwise acquisitions and closure costs and 1992 ended with a loss of over 1 billion kroner, of which Ben-EAC accounted for 260 million while bulk shipping lost 103 million.[272] As a consequence of these major losses, EAC contacted A.P. Møller to find out whether it might consider acquiring EAC's container routes to integrate them into an expanded Maersk Line network. Finance Director Michael Fiorini led A.P. Møller's negotiating team. Despite EAC's crisis, its management was unimpressed by Fiorini's offer and so negotiations were terminated. In September 1992, however, Henning Sparsø was forced to

The **Australia** was another formerly Broström-owned container ship to join EAC at the same time. Here, she is seen at Singapore. (K.Barr, Russell Priest collection)

EAC's Japanese-built container ship **Arosia** in the Solent in the early 1990s. (Mick Lindsay)

resign and thereafter a new Board of Directors was appointed. Between them, Sparsø and his predecessor, Mogens Pagh, had ruined EAC by incurring debt when expanding the Company seemingly randomly in many directions and through over-estimating the profit potential of the various disparate subsidiaries. Following his departure, Sparsø has never explained his actions and refuses to speak with the media, but in 1993 a former fellow director, Chresten A. Bjerrum, published a book about EAC's catastrophic decline. In it, he characterises Sparsø as having become an egotistical man who ran EAC as his own personal fiefdom.[273] Due to the Company's constitution, there were insufficient checks upon the power of the directors and, unlike A.P. Møller which also had a managerial structure built around the cult of the Chairman and Managing Director, there was no controlling family interest with a strong desire to achieve success rather than play internal power politics. Besides, EAC, with its many diverse subsidiaries, was a much

more complicated business than A.P. Møller and, therefore, it was harder for private and institutional investors to analyse what was actually happening until it was too late. Most probably, they assumed that the Company was competently led.

EAC urgently needed a new Managing Director and decided that, rather than making an internal promotion, as was Company tradition, a candidate would be head-hunted from outside. The man EAC opted to appoint was none other than Michael Fiorini from A.P. Møller. It was certainly a most unusual occurrence for a top manager to leave this firm other than to retire as loyalty was considered sacrosanct – and even less usual when the appointment was to another shipping company. Yet, it may be that A.P. Møller made Fiorini available to try to salvage EAC before it collapsed altogether.

When Fiorini joined EAC, it was involved in negotiations to sell parts of its container services

Opposite: A dramatic aerial view of the *Arosia*, well loaded with containers. (Thomas N. Olesen collection)

Left: In 1991, EAC negotiated a joint agreement with the long-established British shipping company Ben Line to work together to provide weekly departures between Europe and the Far East. The two companies had a longer history of co-operation, however, and in 1989 EAC's *Meonia* operated under charter as the *Bencairn*. (Mick Lindsay)

Below: The *Jutlandia* in the New Waterway in 1986. (Chris Howell collection)

to American President Lines. The plan was to use income from these sales to purchase jointly with APL a new fleet of ten so-called post-panamax container ships (that is, container ships with bigger dimensions than the Panama Canal's locks could accommodate). EAC and APL would jointly acquire these vessels and Howaldswerke Deutsche Werft in West Germany and Daewoo in South Korea would build them. The plan was forward-looking and, to see it through, EAC employed an engineer called Jens J. Kappel, who from the early-1970s until the mid-1980s had been responsible for overseeing the design and successful introduction of Maersk Line's initial classes of container ship (described below). Between planning the new EAC/APL ships and placing orders, disagreements broke out between the two companies. Besides, as EAC was severely burdened with debt, its bankers insisted that this be reduced before any such new investments could be contemplated.

When EAC's discussions with APL broke down in March 1993, Michael Fiorini decided to contact his former boss, Mærsk Mc-Kinney Møller, to ask him whether A.P. Møller would again consider purchasing the entire EAC liner business. In the ensuing brief negotiations, A.P. Møller was represented by its recently appointed Managing Director Jess Søderberg. As Søderberg and Fiorini were former colleagues and as they could use documentation prepared for previous discussions, a deal was quickly struck, giving Maersk Line the Europe-Far East service with nine container ships, a large number of containers plus four feeder lines between South East Asia and Australia.[274] The *Selandia* and *Jutlandia* were not included in this deal and instead they were sold to the United States Sealift Command.[275] From being Denmark's foremost liner company in the early 1970s, only two decades later EAC had lost so much that they no longer even featured. The future belonged to Maersk Line – and it went about containerisation very differently from EAC.

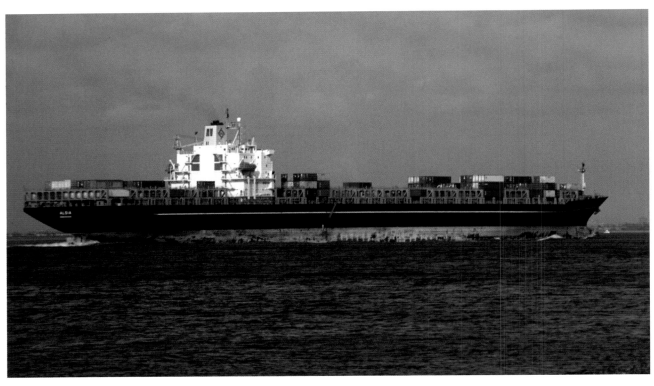

Above: The **Alsia** heading out to sea from Southampton in the early 1990s. (Mick Lindsay)

Right: After the sale of its liner operations, EAC continued to run a small number of vessels in the tramping trades. The final **Selandia** was a Polish-built bulk carrier, delivered in 1996, and is seen arriving at Melbourne in 1998. An order for a sister ship, to have been named the **Jutlandia**, was cancelled and the **Selandia** was sold already in 1999. Thereafter, EAC ceased to be involved in shipping. (Russell Priest)

Chapter 11

The containerisation of Maersk Line's services

Today, Maersk Line is not only the world's biggest operator of container ships but also presently the owner of the twenty largest container ships ever constructed: the Triple-E class. Nowadays, Maersk Line's containers are a familiar sight on highways and in railway yards all over the world – so much so, in fact, that it is difficult to imagine that the Company nearly did not enter the container shipping business at all. During the 1960s, while other liner shipping companies were joining the container trade, Mærsk Mc-Kinney Møller summoned a group of senior managers and analysts from his Company's offices around the world and, with external advice from management consultants, sought their opinion on whether Maersk Line should build dedicated container ships and associated port facilities. The answer was negative as such an investment was deemed to constitute too great a risk and, besides, Maersk Line had only recently invested heavily in building seven fairly advanced C-class cargo liners. Fortunately, Møller's instinct was that the majority of his colleagues and the consultants were wrong and so, after further consideration, he concluded that containerisation represented the future of liner shipping and that Maersk Line could not afford to stay out of the container business.[276] (He had personal experience of a container ship as, during a visit to the United States in 1965, he had closely examined a Sea-Land vessel but was apparently unconvinced of the need to act immediately.) His instinct was correct and Maersk Line arguably benefited from coming slightly late – but not too late – into the container business. Thus, the Company learned from the successes and failures of its rivals and was able to construct superior container ships which, over time, were able to beat competitors in terms of cost-effective transportation, speed and reliability.

In contrast, Denmark's two existing 'flag carriers' were far less successful in making the transition from break-bulk to containerised liner services. On the one hand, DFDS failed to containerise its international liner services and, instead, closed down one route after another so that, by the latter 1970s, only the Nordana Line remained; this was belatedly containerised in 1979 with four combined ro-ro and container vessels. On the other hand, while the East Asiatic

Following the sale of its liner business to A.P. Møller in 1993 and its incorporation into Maersk Line, a couple of the former EAC ships appeared in Maersk's light blue livery. The **Nihon** became the **Ladby Mærsk**, as shown here, but was quickly sold out of the fleet. (Bruce Peter collection)

Top: DFDS' Nordana Line from the Gulf of Mexico to the Mediterranean continued to use a few general cargo ships until the late 1970s, such as the *Michigan*, a vessel originally built for trans-Atlantic service. (Bruce Peter collection)

Above: A lack of quay space in North African ports caused a switch to roll-on, roll-off container (con-ro) vessels, which could berth stern-in, saving time and space. The *Dana America* was one of four built in Japan by Nippon Kokan at Shimizu and chartered to DFDS by the shipyard.
(Bruce Peter collection)

Centre right: The *Dana Caribia* at Valetta in Malta in the early 1980s. (Bruce Peter collection)

Right: Offloading a container from one of Nordana Line's con-ro vessels. (Bruce Peter collection)

Company's 'first generation' container ships were relatively efficient for their time, the 1973 Oil Crisis so drastically changed the economics of shipping that they were far less competitive thereafter. EAC's second generation of multi-purpose LRV ships represented a foolishly retrograde step, being too small and too slow ever to make a profit. Thus, amongst Denmark's leading liner companies, Maersk Line alone made a very great success of container shipping. It is also worth noting that, in containerising their Panama Line across the Pacific, Maersk followed the American model of building its own fleet rather than the European one of contributing a few ships to a larger consortium.

As a first tentative step, it was decided that the jointly-operated Maersk Line and Kawasaki Kisen Kaisha route from Denmark to Japan should be the first to have fully-cellular container ships – a prime reason being that this line competed directly with the ScanDutch consortium's fast and modern container ship fleet. To that end, both Companies ordered a single large vessel from the Ishikawajima shipyard in Japan, the first for Maersk Line and the second for Kawasaki. In the autumn of 1972, A.P. Møller's Head of Newbuilding, Sven Højer (appointed in 1967), along with other senior figures from the Company, had been invited guests on a presentation trip on board the EAC-owned ScanDutch container ship *Selandia* and it is likely that this experience helped to focus their minds further on the urgent need also to introduce dedicated container tonnage.[277]

While the new vessels were under construction in Japan, Kawasaki withdrew from the joint operation with Maersk Line as, for one reason or another, the Japanese Government apparently disapproved of their relationship. Consequently, from January 1973, Maersk Line was forced to continue alone, taking delivery of its first-ever container vessel, the *Svendborg Mærsk*, in January 1974. Unfortunately, as Maersk no longer had an operating partner between Europe and the Far East, it had little option but immediately to charter the ship out for operation in the Australia-Europe Container Service. (This was a consortium consisting of Hapag-Lloyd, Messageries Maritimes, Nedlloyd, Lloyd Triestino and OCL.) After four return trips, the *Svendborg Mærsk* was returned to her owner and laid up for six months – an inauspicious start to Maersk Line's involvement in container shipping.[278]

The *Svendborg Mærsk* was a 38,540gt vessel, powered by two 12-cylinder Sulzer diesels driving twin screws and providing a 26.5-knot service speed. Capable of carrying up to 1,815

A number of older Maersk Line general cargo ships continued in service after the first container ships were introduced. Here, the ***Trein Mærsk*** is seen with a good load of containers on deck in the latter 1970s. (Bruce Peter collection)

The **Leda Mærsk**, photographed at Hong Kong in the late 1970s. (Bruce Peter collection)

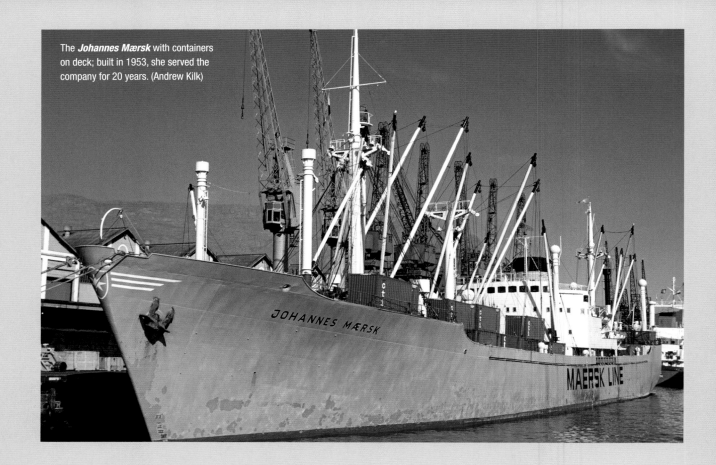

The **Johannes Mærsk** with containers on deck; built in 1953, she served the company for 20 years. (Andrew Kilk)

The small **Herta Mærsk**, ex **Romø Mærsk**, in Hong Kong; built in 1959, she was sold in 1978. (Bruce Peter collection)

The C-class cargo liner **Cecilie Mærsk** with a large cargo of containers on deck. (Bruce Peter collection)

TEU, she was typical of container ships of her era but, having two propellers, was atypical of Maersk Line's existing and subsequent liner fleets.[279] Indeed, after just over a decade, she was rebuilt in Japan with one B&W 12-cylinder diesel driving a single propeller. Although a one-off ship in a fleet otherwise consisting of standard classes, she was fast, efficient and also long-lived, being sold by Maersk Line only in 1999 and scrapped in 2002.[280]

Meanwhile, attention was focused upon the implementation of a radical and potentially risky plan to containerise fully Maersk Line's highly successful Panama Line service between US ports and the Far East. As we have already seen, the cross-Pacific service was Maersk Line's most profitable area of liner operation and the route already supported a variety of break-bulk tonnage, the most recent of which could carry containers on deck. Given that American and Japanese operators were moving increasingly to container ship operation, A.P. Møller's senior management reasoned that Maersk Line too would have to join the fray and to do so more efficiently than rivals. (The first pure container ship on the Pacific was the American Matson Line vessel *Hawaiian Citizen*, introduced in 1960.)[281]

In coming into container shipping slightly later than, for example, Seatrain Lines, United States

With the acquisition of the Japanese-built ***Svendborg Mærsk*** in 1974, Maersk Line first operated a fully-cellular container ship. (A.P. Møller-Maersk)

The **Svendborg Mærsk**, sailing slowly through a glassy sea. (A.P. Møller-Maersk)

Lines, American President Lines and others, let alone Denmark's East Asiatic Company, A.P. Møller's technical staff also had the opportunity to study which design aspects of existing vessels and port infrastructure had worked most effectively and where improvements could be made. Besides, Maersk Line's own experience with the Svendborg Mærsk enabled the Company to learn about the detailed planning and operation of ships of this type.

In 1973, A.P. Møller created a Container Ship Development Division and appointed in charge an imaginative young engineer, Jens J. Kappel, who had proven to be a creative thinker since joining A.P. Møller in 1965. Kappel was not a naval architect and, indeed, his background prior to joining A.P. Møller was only indirectly related to the shipping industry. A bright student, Kappel skipped a year at school and served his apprenticeship as a mechanic in the 1946-1950 period. Following that, he joined the Danish Air Force before enrolling to study mechanical engineering at the Technical University of Denmark in Copenhagen between 1957 and 1962. Thereafter, he worked with marine steam turbines for a subsidiary of Brown Boveri in Paris, moving next to the firm's headquarters in Switzerland until he returned to Denmark and found employment with A.P. Møller. There, he was initially involved in the development of large turbine-powered oil tankers before being switched to concentrate on container ship design. Maersk Line's first and second generations of container ships were realised under his leadership and that of his boss, Captain Troels Dilling, who was in overall charge of A.P. Møller's Technical Department.[282]

The A-class container ships were financed in part through the sale in 1975 of three 284,000gt R-class VLCC tankers to Texaco. The Rosa Mærsk, Roy Mærsk and Richard Mærsk were less than four years old – but A.P. Møller sold them when the market for such large tankers was near its peak. Subsequently, due to over-capacity and changing trading patterns following the re-opening of the Suez Canal, the bottom fell out of the large tanker market and many leading shipping lines in the oil trade – not least A.P. Møller – were forced to lay up expensive recently-delivered tonnage. Although Mærsk Mc-Kinney Møller was far from certain that the new container ships would be a success, according to Kappel, he was, at least thankful to have ships other than oil tankers on order.

The nine-ship A-class order was split between Blohm & Voss in Hamburg (six ships) and Flender Werft in Lübeck (three ships). Because the two builders were also rivals, they refused to

co-operate in sharing lines plans and so, although all of the A-class had similar characteristics in terms of overall dimensions, speed and capacity, they had different hull configurations, the Flender-built examples having pronounced knucklejoints in their bows.[283]

At Blohm & Voss, Kappel became very good friends with the Senior Naval Architect, Hans Langenberg, whose very specific technical knowledge of container ship planning and construction complemented Kappel's instinctive ideas about how the design of the new Maersk Line vessels should be approached. Blohm & Voss had recently delivered several container ships to Hapag-Lloyd which Langenberg and his colleagues had designed. (In contrast, A.P. Møller's Odense Staalskibsværft had no expertise whatsoever in designing and building such vessels and instead

Above: The steam turbine-powered container ship **Adrian Mærsk** when newly delivered.
(A.P. Møller-Maersk)

Right: The **Albert Mærsk** at the quay; the traditional labour-intensive loading and unloading of cargo liners could now be done with a couple of cranes.
(A.P. Møller-Maersk)

was focused on the building of large oil tankers.) During the ensuing decade, Langenberg and Kappel worked closely together to improve the efficiency of container ships and A.P. Møller undoubtedly benefited significantly from their good working relationship. They also published independently a number of papers for the technical journals on their research work and design innovations. Kappel argues that Maersk Line's success as a container ship operator was due to 'being late on the scene, but not too late' – meaning that it had the opportunity to learn from other container operators' mistakes and to build better and more efficient ships at a time when the world's economy appeared to be recovering from the recession of the early 1970s. Moreover, according to Kappel, Mærsk Mc-Kinney Møller 'had an excellent technical knowledge of stability, block co-efficient calculations and engine capacity. He liked people clearly to express their opinions and always accepted a good business argument.'[284]

In containerising Maersk Line's Far East-USA cross-Pacific routes outwith a consortium, Møller was taking a significant financial risk as Maersk Line would not only have to invest in a large fleet of new ships but also containers, trucks and shore infrastructure. Thus, he was very keen that the initiative should work as perfectly as possible and he took a keen personal interest in the project's development. Møller preferred single-screw vessels to twin-screw or triple-screw varieties as he felt that single-screw installations were more reliable with far fewer moving parts to break or overheat and distort. To achieve the necessary 26-knot service speed from such a ship would require steam turbine propulsion as, in the early 1970s, there were no single diesel engines capable of the necessary 36-40,000 hp output – 27,000 hp being about the maximum then achievable – although, within a decade, that situation changed. Kappel also studied the design drawings for Hapag-Lloyd's twin-screw *Tokyo Express*, which was powered by Stal-Laval

A stern-quarter view of the ***Adrian Mærsk*** undergoing builder's trials.
(A.P. Møller-Maersk)

The Blohm & Voss-built
Anders Mærsk, following
her first lengthening.
(A.P. Møller-Maersk)

turbines giving a 27-knot service speed. The fastest single-screw vessels then were British turbine-powered examples in the OCL and ACT consortia, whose turbines gave a 22-knot service speed. Møller reasoned that, as Maersk Line was not in a consortium, there would be no need for such large twin-screw vessels and that, instead, it would be more prudent to built nine smaller ships to maintain a schedule of frequent departures from each port. Nonetheless, through careful planning to optimise the hull volume and to pack the container cells as close together as possible, it was feasible to achieve a capacity of 1,600 TEU in vessels each measuring only around 27,000gt and with dimensions of 210.75 x 30.56 metres. (This compares very favourably with the 2,272 TEU capacity of EAC's 49,890gt *Selandia* and *Jutlandica*, described above.)[285] Maersk Line's intention was to maintain a fairly high service speed of around 24 knots and, therefore, so as to avoid burning an unacceptably large amount of fuel, it was important to reduce drag as much as possible. To achieve this aim, Hans Langenberg designed a hull configured with an unusually slender aftbody, the lines of which were very similar to those at the bow.

The A-class were fully automated, meaning that the boilers and turbine could be controlled directly from the bridge, and they were also fitted with IBM computers which were intended to speed up a number of onboard management jobs but which, in practice, were not trusted by the officers and crews. Nevertheless, the fact that they were specified at all showed that A.P. Møller was looking to the future and subsequently, with further development, such installations have become standard practice in container shipping.

The first A-class container ship, the *Adrian Mærsk*, was delivered from the Blohm & Voss shipyard in Hamburg in August 1975 and introduced on Maersk Line's service from the American Eastern Seaboard to the Far East that September. Thereafter, Blohm & Voss completed the *Albert Mærsk*, *Anna Mærsk*, *Arthur Mærsk*, *Axel Mærsk* and *Anders Mærsk*, while Flender Werft constructed the *Arnold Mærsk*, *Alva Mærsk* and *Arild Mærsk* – the last of the series, which was delivered in August 1976. Their great ability to maintain schedule ensured that Maersk Line could offer their customers guaranteed departure times, meaning that goods to be shipped could be delivered to the terminals closer to sailing time than hitherto and delivered 'just in time' at the other end.[286]

Following the introduction of the A-class, A.P. Møller's Container Ship Development Division was disbanded and Kappel was placed in overall charge of the Company's Newbuilding

Above: The **Arild Mærsk** after lengthening; A-class ships built by Flender had a knuckle-joint in the bow. Note too that, amongst the containers, a catamaran ferry has been loaded, as well as a consignment of earth-moving equipment. (A.P. Møller-Maersk)

Below: The **Arthur Mærsk** after lengthening. (Bruce Peter collection)

Above: A stern-quarter view of the **Arthur Mærsk** at Philadelphia. (Bruce Peter collection)

Below: The **Alva Mærsk** at Philadelphia. (Bruce Peter collection)

Department; he was, therefore, responsible for all of A.P. Møller's new ships until he was moved once again to the Oil and Gas Division in 1984.[287]

At first, Maersk Line's agents did not think that the Company could get enough containerised cargo to fill the new ships. However, in the late 1970s a lucrative contract was gained to ship electronic components from General Electric in the USA to Singapore for assembly and return to the USA. This was time-critical and depended on the high speed and punctuality of the nine A-class ships and on the security of container transport. It gave the new container service a welcome early boost and was a good example of how inter-modal container-based transport systems created new demands for transport, enabling the manufacture of high-value products and components to be outsourced, even half-way around the world. Indeed, such was the rate of growth in demand for Maersk Line's container service between the USA and Far East ports that, after only a very short time in service, it became necessary to lengthen the nine A-class

vessels. Kappel recalls that 'a lot of preparation and negotiation took place before the lengthening of the nine ships could take place at Hitachi in Japan. On a monthly basis, one A-class ship at a time was docked there and lengthened by one 40-foot bay. During the rebuilding programme, the *Svendborg Mærsk*, which had been a non-standard one-off and, therefore, difficult to schedule, became very useful as a replacement for each of the vessels being rebuilt.'[288] With new midbody sections fitted, the tonnage of the A-class ships rose to 29,902gt with an increase in capacity to 1,890 TEU. This was the first of a number of reconstructions of this class of container ship.[289]

The lengthening of the A-class coincided with a rare incident of bad luck for Maersk Line, resulting from an embarrassing navigational error. On the evening of 19 September 1977, the *Adrian Mærsk* sailed from Hong Kong under the command of one of the Company's most experienced senior Masters. Ahead, there was a French container ship which obscured the lighthouse on Lantao Island. As a result, the *Adrian Mærsk*, which was steaming at around 18 knots, ran aground and suffered very serious hull damage. During the following weeks, a variety of small craft and local work-parties using floating cranes grafted to offload the containers. Then, the Royal Navy was called in to blast away at the rock in order to free the bow section. Next, four powerful tugs managed to refloat the ship, which was patched up and towed to Japan for repair.[290]

Above: The **Mc-Kinney Mærsk** at sea. (A.P. Møller-Maersk)

Below: The **Marchen Mærsk**. (A.P. Møller-Maersk)

Notwithstanding the expansion of trans-Pacific container services, there remained a niche (albeit a declining one) for general cargo vessels on the Middle East-Far East and Middle East-USA routes well into the 1980s. Not all ports were equipped specifically to handle containers and so the C-class continued to be useful even after the A-class container ships had been introduced.

Indeed, A.P. Møller ordered a further series of four B&W diesel-powered, 21-knot combined general cargo and container ships, fitted with large electric cranes and equipped with side hatches for palette loading, which were delivered from Nakskov in 1974-75 for Maersk Line service between South East Asia and the Middle East; these were the 10,367gt *Marchen Mærsk*, *Margrethe Mærsk*, *Mathilde Mærsk* and *Mc-Kinney Mærsk*. In many respects, they represented a further development of the Nakskov-built EAC container-carrying cargo liners of the latter 1960s.[291] Further less successful deliveries were a series of six 13,706gt, 18.5-knot Sulzer-engined E-class multi-purpose ro-ro and container ships built at the Odense Lindø shipyard in 1979-80 for a service linking Japan with Hong Kong and Singapore. Named *Eleo Mærsk*, *Emma Mærsk*, *Estelle Mærsk*, *Emilie Mærsk*, *Evelyn Mærsk* and *Elizabeth Mærsk*, they were known as

Above: The lounge on one of Maersk Line's M-class vessels with 1980s colours and a portrait of H.M. The Queen on the bulkhead. (Nakskov Local History Collection)

Left: The dining saloon on an M-class ship. (Nakskov Local History Collection)

The **Elizabeth Mærsk**
during outfitting at the Lindø
shipyard, showing her large
ro-ro stern quarter ramp
lowered to the quay.
(A.P. Møller-Maersk)

Right: The newly-completed
Elizabeth Mærsk.
(A.P. Møller-Maersk)

Below: The **Elizabeth
Mærsk**, partially loaded with
containers.
(A.P. Møller-Maersk)

Opposite top: The **Charlotte
Mærsk** at San Francisco
before rebuilding as a
container ship.
(A.P. Møller-Maersk)

Opposite bottom: The
Christian Mærsk after
reconstruction.
(Thomas N. Olesen
collection)

'Caroliners,' but suffered many of the same problems as EAC's notorious LRV vessels, being too slow and unable to carry out one job properly. In 1982 the majority were disposed of to the United States Sealift Command.[292]

By the 1980s, however, Maersk saw that the future of liner shipping between the Middle East and the USA also lay in pure container ships and so in 1980-81 the seven C-class cargo liners were comprehensively rebuilt as such by Hitachi Zosen in Japan for further service on this prospering route. Each vessel was cut in two just ahead of the superstructure and fitted with a

new cellular forward section, slightly wider than the original hulls had been (29.7 metres versus 25 metres). After the conversion, each vessel could carry 1,222 containers, the design maximising capacity with a very small mooring deck forward and a breakwater, behind which the container stacks began. The wheelhouse was raised by one deck, allowing containers to be loaded four-deep on the hatch covers and twelve across amidships. Although, according to J.J. Kappel who oversaw these conversions, the superstructures remained less compact than would have been ideal and the engines were far from pristine after 12-14 years' continuous usage, Mærsk Mc-Kinney Møller liked the C-class ships and the conversion price of 12 million dollars per vessel was considerably less than it would have cost to build anew. Notwithstanding the wider hull dimensions, the ships lost only a half-knot in speed due to the rebuilding work.[293]

Next, between 1983 and 1985, four members of the A-class were subjected to a second rebuilding, also at Hitachi, during which they were further lengthened and converted from steam turbine to diesel propulsion. Since they had been conceived a decade previously, fuel costs had increased exponentially for steam turbine vessels, while focused development work by B&W had resulted in increasing efficiency and far higher power outputs from slow-speed marine diesels with larger cylinder bores than hitherto. A.P. Møller expected a fuel saving of up to 50 per cent as a result of this work.[294]

In order to enable this complicated rebuilding to take place with each ship only out of service for less than two months, it was decided to swap the aft sections of the hulls around with the ships being treated on a rolling basis. That way, work could take place to strip out the steam plants and install new diesel engines. The process began with the construction of a brand-new aft section for the *Arthur Mærsk*. The ship herself was then temporarily withdrawn from her regular schedule and brought to the shipyard, where she was cut in two and her bow section attached to the new stern portion, which of course already had a new diesel engine and a longer midbody. The superstructure was cut away from the old aft section and fitted to the new one. Then, once the rebuilt ship had returned to service, the old aft section was re-engined and extended in time for the arrival of the second ship to be treated, which was the *Anders Mærsk*. She too was cut amidships and the forward section attached to the lengthened aft section of what had originally

The *Clara Mærsk*, after rebuilding as a container ship, departs Vancouver. (Bruce Peter collection)

Left: The **Arthur Mærsk** in the process of being dismantled to be lengthened and rebuilt as a motor ship; her superstructure is being moved to a newly-built stern section. The existing stern thereafter formed part of the **Anders Mærsk**. (A.P. Møller-Maersk)

Right: A view into the aft section of the **Arthur Mærsk**, where the steam boilers and turbines are being dismantled and replaced by a diesel motor and the section became part of **Anders Mærsk**. (A.P. Møller-Maersk)

Left: The **Arnold Mærsk**, fitted with a ramp and garage aft of the superstructure to carry cars between the USA and the Middle East. (A.P. Møller-Maersk)

Right: A fine bow-quarter view of the **Axel Mærsk** as she appeared following her second lengthening and conversion to diesel propulsion.
(A.P. Møller-Maersk)

Below: The **Anna Mærsk**, following her second lengthening and re-engining as a motor ship.
(Bruce Peter collection)

Opposite: The **Anders Mærsk**, rebuilt as a motor ship. (A.P. Møller-Maersk)

been the *Arthur Mærsk*. The process was repeated for the *Anna Mærsk* and the *Axel Mærsk*, meaning that each vessel was taken out of use for only a very short time to be welded together with the aft section of the previous sister.[295]

While this project was approaching a conclusion, it was decided also to rebuild the *Adrian Mærsk*, *Albert Mærsk* and *Arnold Mærsk* for future use between the USA and Persian Gulf ports. Not only were these re-engined and lengthened, but they were also fitted with large garages abaft their superstructures to transport American-made cars to the increasingly oil-rich Arab countries. Of these three, the Flender-built *Arnold Mærsk* required to be dealt with separately, as she had a completely different hull construction from the vessels built by Blohm & Voss.

The A-class rebuilding programme was as follows:
Arthur Mærsk (fitted with newly-built aft section)
Anders Mærsk (fitted with aft section from *Arthur Mærsk*)
Anna Mærsk (fitted with aft section from *Anders Mærsk*)
Axel Mærsk (fitted with aft section from *Anna Mærsk*)
Adrian Mærsk (fitted with aft section from *Axel Mærsk* and a new garage)
Albert Mærsk fitted with aft section from *Adrian Mærsk* and a new garage)
Arnold Mærsk (fitted with new midbody and a new garage)
Alva Mærsk (fitted with new midbody)
Arild Mærsk (fitted with new midbody)
The original stern section from the *Albert Mærsk* was scrapped.

ANDERS MÆRSK
RØMØ

Above: The **Arthur Mærsk** is shown at sea after reconstruction as a motor ship. (Bruce Peter collection)

Below left: The **Lexa Mærsk** under construction at the Lindø shipyard; the Panamax L-class did not occupy much of the building dock, which was designed to accommodate supertankers. (A.P. Møller-Maersk)

Below right: The **Laura Mærsk** being floated out at Lindø. (A.P. Møller-Maersk)

At the end of the 1970s, Maersk Line's major routes consisted of the long-established trans-Pacific Panama Line plus a Far East to the Middle East service, dating from 1950, and a third from Europe to the Far East, opened in 1968. The Far East to Middle East route was scheduled to enable speedy trans-shipment of containers in Hong Kong to and from the Panama Line, thereby creating a cohesive US East Coast-Persian Gulf operation.[296]

Only three years after the A-class first entered service, in 1978 development work began on a second generation of Maersk Line container ships – the L-class, which were intended to operate between Europe and the Far East in competition with ScanDutch, OCL and several other powerful consortia. Although these were to be built at Odense Lindø rather than in West Germany, Hans Langenberg from Blohm & Voss was retained as a project consultant to design the hull and machinery layout. In A.P. Møller's Newbuilding Department, J.J. Kappel was greatly assisted by his close colleague, the naval architect Ole Christiansen, and by John Nepper Larsen from the Odense Lindø shipyard. This time, rather than being fitted with costly steam turbines, a single Burmeister & Wain 12-cylinder 2-stroke diesel was specified – the largest yet fitted to a single-screw ship. Capable of a 47,003 ihp output, it enabled a 24-knot speed to be maintained; this also demonstrates the rapid development of marine diesel technology during the 1970s.

As with the fractionally smaller A-class, the L-class were fast in relation to their length (when first delivered, the L-class measured 212.48 x 32.26 metres) and also significantly more capacious, each being able to carry 2,100 TEU in comparison with the A-class' maximum load of around 1,600. Yet, in order to maintain a high speed, their hulls still required to be very fine-lined. This brought forth the need for a very delicate balance to be struck between speed, stability and container capacity; although the L-class were slender in order to fit through the Panama

Canal's locks, containers needed to be stacked six-high on the hatch covers. With Langenberg's assistance and with the aid of a great deal of research and model testing, an extremely effective solution was achieved.[297]

The ***Lica Mærsk*** prior to lengthening.
(A.P. Møller-Maersk)

Accommodation on the A-class container ships was, as with the C-class cargo liners, very spacious – unnecessarily so, Kappel believed, observing that his boss, Captain Dilling, apparently could not get the officers' and crew areas big enough. Consequently, when it came to developing Maersk Line's second generations of container ships, the L- and M-classes, he simply drew a narrow rectangle on the hull to show where the superstructure would go, then took the plans directly to Mærsk Mc-Kinney Møller for approval before Dilling had a chance to intervene. According to Kappel, Møller, who was a sophisticated gentleman but a conservative in aesthetic matters, did not initially take to the appearance of the L-class, telling him that 'you've designed the world's most ugly ship,' to which Kappel replied 'yes, Mr Møller, but it's the world's most efficient' – a winning argument.[298] The new L-class vessels certainly were unprecedented in terms of appearance but possessed a very clean and functional aesthetic of their own.

On the L-class, the machinery space was some way forward of the superstructure better to balance the hull as Kappel and Langenberg were keen that the aftbody should be as slender as possible to reduce drag and cavitation (if the propeller were working in the slipstream of a broad stern configuration, serious shaking might ensue). Structurally, it was also desirable to locate the heavy engine closer to amidships. Containers could, of course, be stacked outboard of the engine compartment, which was T-shaped and surrounded by a complex, but effective, supporting structure. Viewed externally, the hulls of the L-class container ships had aft lines very similar to those at the bow, albeit finishing in a flat transom. Another important innovation pioneered by Kappel was a slimmer design of cell-guide, saving half a metre of space between each container stack and enabling the vessels to be five metres shorter than would otherwise have been the case for the same capacity.[299]

The first L-class to be completed was the 30,694gt, 2,100 TEU *Laura Mærsk*, delivered in November 1980. The sister ships *Leise Mærsk*, *Lexa Mærsk*, *Lica Mærsk* and *Leda Mærsk* were delivered over the course of the following two years. The *Luna Mærsk* and *Regina Mærsk*, completed in 1982 and 1983 respectively, were longer by 29 metres and with a 2,536 TEU capacity.[300] Furthermore, these were fitted with a new and significantly more fuel-efficient type of 12-cylinder B&W diesel which combusted fuel under higher pressure (105 bar as opposed to the hitherto usual 89). In addition, both bow and stern lateral-thrust propellers were installed to avoid the need for tugs when manoeuvring in port. Upon delivery, the *Regina Mærsk* was regarded as the Maersk Line flagship and she was named by the Danish Queen Mother, H.M. Queen Ingrid, in Copenhagen. (Over the years, Queen Ingrid named four different A.P. Møller-owned ships *Regina Mærsk*.) The *Luna Mærsk* and *Regina Mærsk* were followed by further examples that were longer still at 269.98 metres – the 43,431gt, 3,088 TEU *Laust Mærsk*, *Louis Mærsk*, *Lars Mærsk* and *Mc-Kinney Mærsk*, all delivered from Odense Staalskibsværft in 1983-85. Thereafter, the shorter early examples of the L-class were lengthened and thus became 269.7 metres long.

This large fleet was financed through a special Danish system of investment funds called 'Dansk Investeringsfond Kommanditselskaber,' or Difko, through which each vessel was financed by a different syndicate of investors then chartered for a 15-year period to Maersk Line with a purchase option offered at the end. During the 1980s, Difko funds were widely used to finance new tonnage in Denmark and this arrangement helped to furnish the Danish merchant fleet in general with state-of-the-art tonnage better able to take on foreign competition.[301]

The advent of the L-class enabled Maersk Line's network to be expanded through the displacement of the pioneering A-class from the Panama Line. Thereafter, Maersk Line's strategy for serving emerging markets through trans-shipment to and from smaller or older ships at centrally-located hub ports, such as Hong Kong, was perpetuated. In the mid-1980s additional hubs were established in Algeciras and Dubai. The former is located next to Gibraltar and, unusually for a container port, serves no immediate industrialised hinterland. As it is on an important global trade route at the junction of the Atlantic Ocean and the Mediterranean Sea, it enabled networks of Maersk Line feeder services to be set up in the Western Mediterranean and also links to East African ports. These gathered containers to be shipped onwards from Algeciras on Maersk Line's big long-haul container ships. Algeciras thereby provided the model for subsequent hub ports developed as the Company further expanded in the 1990s.[302]

In terms of the optimisation of container capacity, Kappel and Langenberg believed more could still be done further to refine the design of cell-guides so that even larger numbers of containers could be fitted into the hulls of Panamax-width vessels. They observed that existing cell-guide designs, which were fairly deep in section and with tapering corners to allow the crane operator to 'guide' the containers into the cells, caused delays as it was necessary to slow down movement to line the containers up before finally lowering them into the cells. The best results were observed in ships with cell-guides of varying height so that the crane operator could line the containers up against the taller guides before finally lowering them into the cells – a simpler procedure which cut the time to load each container and led to a significant overall reduction in turnarounds at each port of call. Kappel took the development a step further as he left out the tapering corners, instead relying only on the height difference for guidance, and developed a very narrow guide, measuring only about 30mm. Kappel made a mock-up of this proposal to demonstrate to the A.P. Møller directors and to Lloyd's classification officers that it would work

Right: The *Lica Mærsk* at the container terminal in Hong Kong.
(A.P. Møller-Maersk)

Opposite: The *Leise Mærsk*, showing her slender aft lines and the large amount of the hull's area given over to container stacks.
(A.P. Møller-Maersk)

The *Luna Mærsk* loading containers. (A.P. Møller-Mærsk)

and it was indeed adopted, but only once Kappel had moved from A.P. Møller's Container Division to his final job with the Oil and Gas Division in 1984.[303]

Most significantly, the so-called 'slim slim' guides also allowed eleven containers to be loaded abreast in the holds of a Panamax container ship, as opposed to ten on the existing L-class vessels. In general, the new guide system could increase the container-carrying capacity by up to ten per cent in a vessel of the same main dimensions. Furthermore, by having the resultant extra weight of containers in the hull, stability would improve, meaning that it would also be possible to stack containers higher on deck.

The first of a new class incorporating 'slim slim' guides, the 52,191gt *Marchen Mærsk*, was completed by Odense Staalskibsværft in April 1988, followed by the *Marit Mærsk, Margrethe Mærsk, Mette Mærsk, Mathilde Mærsk, Maren Mærsk, Majestic Mærsk, Marie Mærsk, Magleby Mærsk, Mc-Kinney Mærsk, Madison Mærsk* and *Mayview Mærsk*.[304] As with the previous L-class, the majority were financed by Difko investment syndicates but two were funded from profits earned by another subsidiary of the A.P. Møller Group, Dansk Supermarked A/S, which owned the Bilka, Føtex and Netto supermarket chains and Salling department stores. Thus, money earned through retail activities was redirected to pay for ships.[305]

Apart from the extra row of containers made possible by Kappel's 'slim slim' guides, the M-class were also slightly longer than any Panamax container ships hitherto constructed. The reason was that during the early stages of the building of the first of the class, senior staff at A.P. Møller spotted an anomaly in the Panama Canal's regulations governing vessel sizes able to pass through the locks. While freight ships could only be a maximum length of 950 feet, cruise ships of up to 965 feet were allowed. When challenged on this, the Panama Canal Authority admitted that this was illogical and that any new Maersk Line vessels could indeed be built to the longer length (the metric equivalent being 294.32 metres). At this point, the great advantage to A.P. Møller of building ships 'in house' at Odense Lindø became very apparent. As former Senior Naval Architect Kjell Harr explains, shipyards generally would not accept the need to lengthen a hull already under construction without imposing draconian penalties to compensate them for the delay. At Odense Lindø, in contrast, it was perfectly possible to optimise the M-class design by lengthening the hull even as the first vessel was taking shape in the building dock. As a result, at the last moment, the M-class gained extra capacity.[306]

Each member of the M-class could carry an unprecedented 4,437 TEU.[307] Furthermore, the M-class were the first container ships fitted with lashing bridges on deck to make the container stacks more accessible to the stevedores whose job it was to lock them together. In addition, a new semi-automatic container locking system was developed so that, rather than needing to crawl around on 14-metre-high container stacks to lash them, stevedores could instead insert twist-locks in the four bottom corner eyes on each container as it was being loaded. These rotated automatically into the 'locked' position under the container's weight as the eyes were placed over those on the container immediately below. They could just as easily be unlocked by using a metal pole to push up a handle, releasing the lock.[308]

Unlike the slender stern configurations of the A- and L-classes, the M-class was squared off at main deck level to maximise deck capacity. Their flat transom sterns narrowed quickly below so that a slim configuration was maintained at and below the waterline. Thanks to further developments in hydrodynamic design by the naval architects employed at Odense Lindø and by A.P. Møller's increasingly ambitious technical staff, led by Ole Høg, possible problems of increased drag and cavitation were avoided. Høg was a graduate in naval architecture of the Technical University of Denmark in Copenhagen. He had first been employed by A.P. Møller in the latter 1960s, being promoted to Head of the Technical Department towards the end of the 1980s. Apart from ship design, he was also responsible for technical matters pertaining to the operation of the Company's entire fleet.

The jump in capacity of the M-class over previous single-screw diesel container ships was matched by a jump in power, their 10-cylinder 2-stroke B&W diesels generating 53,600 bhp. The last examples of the class were more powerful still, being fitted with 12-cylinder engines yielding 66,480 bhp. This had the potential to give rise to pressure pulses which, as they worked aft, could transfer to the superstructure, possibly making life for the officers and crew very uncomfortable.

Top: The **Leise Mærsk** at Southampton.
(Bruce Peter collection)

Centre: The **Lexa Mærsk** after lengthening.
(A.P. Møller-Maersk)

Left: The **Laust Mærsk** was one of the L-class
vessels built to a length of 255.7 metres.
(Bruce Peter collection)

Top: A starboard side view of the **Laust Mærsk**, showing how similar the forward and aft hull lines are. (Bruce Peter collection)

Left: The **Laust Mærsk** at sea, well loaded with containers. (Bruce Peter collection)

Below: The **Lars Mærsk** leaves Southampton, heavily loaded with containers. (Mick Lindsay)

With the M-class, the size
limit of the Panama Canal
for container ships was
reached. Here, the **Marchen
Mæsk** passes through one
of the canal's locks.
(A.P. Møller-Maersk)

Furthermore, the velocity of the water passing the rudder might cause cavitation, damaging it and leading to the need for regular and costly drydockings for repair. (Repeated changes in water pressure from high to low create suction and, over time, this can cause underwater steelwork to appear to have been eaten away.) Extensive model tests were carried out in tanks in Hamburg and in The Netherlands to find the optimum hull shape while cavitation was avoided through the selection of a six-bladed propeller with skewed blades. As a result of this research work, the M-class performed very well in service – indeed, according to Kjell Harr, Odense-built container ships never suffered serious cavitational problems – but other builders and operators of similarly dimensioned vessels often were far less fortunate.[309]

The M-class were all fitted with a very innovative engine waste heat recovery system which used hot exhaust gases generated by the main engine to power a turbine, producing 3.5 megawatts over and above the main engine's 53,600 bhp output. This drove an electric auxiliary motor mounted on the propeller shaft, saving fuel and further adding to these vessels' operational efficiency (the motor could also be used as an electric generator, providing power for onboard services). While subsequent batches of Maersk Line container ships were not fitted with this system, development work continued further to improve its efficiency and it was reintroduced in enhanced form on all large new Maersk Line container ships constructed after the millennium,

The **Mayview Mærsk** being
manoeuvred by tugs at the
Lindø shipyard.
(A.P. Møller-Maersk)

commencing with the G- and E-classes. By then, a combination of increasing fuel costs and concerns about the environmental impact of shipping made waste heat recovery a very desirable shipboard technology – and one in which A.P. Møller was a pioneer.[310]

Unfortunately for the close relationship between J.J. Kappel and his employer, Lloyd's officials suggested that his innovative 'slim slim' cell-guide design should be patented. A.P. Møller, of course, claimed that the innovation was its intellectual property whereas Kappel, with the support of his professional organisation, the Ingenørforeningen (Society of Engineers), argued that the design was his alone and that he was, therefore, due royalty payments. While it appears that neither side particularly wanted a fight, an important issue of principle was at stake. The result of a lengthy and high-profile legal battle between A.P. Møller and Kappel was that Kappel won, but consequently he was forced to leave A.P. Møller for good.[311]

Even although his career with A.P. Møller came to a bitter and premature conclusion, his contribution to the Company's container shipping activities was significant. Firstly, his involvement with the development of the original series of A-class container ships and, secondly, the ingenious rebuilding programmes to expand capacity in both the A- and C-classes and then to re-engine and further lengthen the A-class, gave Maersk Line a substantial fleet of efficient ships for far less than the cost of building anew. Thirdly, the groundbreaking L- and M-classes set new standards for effectiveness and functionality and several of their design innovations have now become orthodox throughout the industry. Due largely to these innovative ship types, Maersk Line expanded rapidly as a container shipper.

The introduction of the M-class coincided with Maersk Line's opening of a new trans-Atlantic liner route between Europe and the USA meaning that, for the first time, its liner services completely encircled the globe. To feed the premier USA-Far East, Europe-USA and Europe-Far East routes, a number of secondary lines were also established, initially using chartered tonnage. These linked Northern European ports with the Middle East, Algeciras in Spain with West Africa, the US Eastern Seaboard with South American East Coast ports and the US Western Seaboard

The *Magleby Mærsk* nearing completion and ablaze with lights at the fitting out quay at the Lindø shipyard. (A.P. Møller-Maersk)

with South American West Coast ports. Next, in 1993, A.P. Møller bought the East Asiatic Company's container service between Europe and the Far East, served by five vessels with a total capacity of around 21,000 TEU, thereby greatly increasing Maersk Line's market share in this trade.[312] This, however, was only the beginning of an expansion programme which shortly would see Maersk Line achieve global dominance in the container business.

In 1990-1991, A.P. Møller's Newbuilding Department was re-designated Mærsk Ship Design, while still being located in Odense Staalskibsværft's offices at Lindø. The idea was that this organisation would act as a link between various shipbuilders around the world constructing vessels for the various A.P. Møller fleets (such as container vessels, oil-rig support ships, tankers, bulk carriers, tugs and car carriers) and the Company's Copenhagen headquarters. Distinct from the yard's own drawing office, Mærsk Ship Design oversaw design and construction processes, modified and approved designs and acted as an independent research and development department anticipating and incorporating the latest naval architecture and marine technology in A.P. Møller-owned vessels. Subsequently, it also took part in collaborative university-based research, working with the Technical University of Denmark and at the University of Southampton particularly to improve ships' fuel economy.[313] Being located within the Odense Lindø complex meant, however, that its drawing office could lend Mærsk Ship Design assistance as necessary.

Maersk Line's expansion coincided with a new and positive Danish political interest in shipping. While A.P. Møller's various shipping operations were an ongoing success story, the situation experienced by the Danish merchant fleet as a whole had been less bright since the 1973 Oil Crisis; its gradual subsequent decline reflected similar tonnage reductions in most North European countries. During the decade 1976-1986, the Danish merchant fleet shrank by a third and there was a similar drop in the numbers employed in the shipping industry (from around 17,000 to around 10,000, half of whom were ships' officers). To cut costs, many ships were re-registered under so-called 'flags of convenience,' mainly in Third World countries such as Panama, Liberia, Singapore and the Bahamas. During 1987 alone, the merchant fleet shrank further from 564 to only 510 ships, principally due to companies shifting tonnage to foreign-flag subsidiaries in order to reduce liability to taxation. If this trend continued to be allowed to develop,

The *Mc-Kinney Mærsk*.
(Bruce Peter collection)

by the end of 1988 it was estimated that there would be only around 300-350 Danish-flagged vessels left. Therefore, the Government decided to create a new Danish International Shipping Register (DIS) to compete with similar initiatives in other leading European maritime nations – most notably Norway. The Minister for Industry, Nils Wilhjelm, explained that as the international freight market was suffering from over-capacity and as freight rates were low, it was necessary to support the Danish Merchant Navy as it appeared that the situation would not ease in the short or medium term. Flagging out was occurring at an increasing rate in all the traditional European

The *Maren Mærsk* sets off from Lindø for her builder's trials, assisted by a flotilla of Svitzer tugs.
(A.P. Møller-Maersk)

maritime nations as it enabled lower cost Third World crews to be employed rather than seamen from the nation of ownership, who were paid comparatively high union-agreed rates.[314]

The proposed DIS Register would insist on high safety standards in terms of crew training and ship maintenance, and thus DIS-registered tonnage would be distinguished from poor quality vessels under Third World flags of convenience. Furthermore, it would be possible to hire crews from wherever was cheapest – so long as they were properly trained. The law enabling the creation of the DIS Register was passed in the Danish Parliament (Folketinget) in June 1988 and the Register became operative from 1 January 1990.[315]

Another influential initiative on the part of the Danish Government was 'Project Ship.' This was promoted by the Ministry for Industry which sought to involve various Danish suppliers in the development of an advanced and highly competitive cargo ship type further to boost the revival of the Danish merchant fleet. Not only would this have a low fuel consumption thanks to ongoing developments in engine technology and hull hydrodynamics, but also the incorporation of an unprecedented amount of advanced automation would enable the crew to be reduced. The prototype vessels exemplifying these developments were four 14,406gt refrigerated cargo ships for J. Lauritzen. These were known as the 'Family class' as they bore the names of leading Lauritzen family members – *Ditlev Lauritzen*, *Ivar Lauritzen*, *Knud Lauritzen* and *Jørgen Lauritzen*. They were designed and built by Danyard in Frederikshavn (who worked closely with the refrigeration consultants Sabroe) and delivered in 1990-91. Although not intended for liner service, their sophisticated design and computerised control systems had a profound impact on Danish merchant ships constructed thereafter – including Maersk Line's forthcoming classes of container vessels.[316]

In March 1991 the Ministry for Industry published a discussion document on how best to develop the merchant fleet; this was entitled 'Det blå Danmark' (which literally translates as 'The Blue Denmark'). For the first time, this analysed the potential economic contribution of the Danish maritime sector as a whole, viewing all aspects as parts of a holistic 'industrial complex.' These included research and development, shipbuilding, outfitting, parts supply, crew and officer training, human resources, plus all sectors of ship operation including liner agencies and other dependent businesses. It was estimated that, at that time, the Danish maritime industry was worth 45 billion kroner per annum and employed 35,000 people. In addition, Danish shipping companies had orders placed in Danish shipyards worth 16 billion kroner over the following three years and the shipping lines themselves were valued at 4.1 billion kroner. There was found to be a close relationship between Danish shipping lines and shipbuilders, particularly in the development of new and improved vessel types. Surrounding the core maritime complex was another large block of supply industries which depended on the maritime industry for part of their revenue, but were also involved in non-maritime activities; this was estimated to be worth a further 6.5 billion kroner.[317]

The political awakening regarding the importance of shipping and associated maritime industries to the Danish economy was important as subsequent Government policies actively encouraged the growth of the sector. From a situation of decline in the 1980s, the Danish merchant fleet expanded during the 1990s and onwards into the new millennium. Maersk Line was at the forefront of these positive developments.

Chapter 12

The post-Panamax era and the global economy

While the M-class was being designed, Maersk Line was contacted by American President Lines, one of its long-standing rivals in the cross-Pacific liner trade. APL wanted to sound Maersk out about the possibility of collaborating in the construction and operation of a potential new class of post-Panamax container ships (i.e. vessels wider than the Panama Canal's locks). These would link US West Coast ports with the Far East. On *terra firma* in America, the railroad industry was investing heavily in container facilities, meaning that it now arguably made more sense to trans-ship containers from coast to coast by train rather than on container ships of restricted size via the Panama Canal. Thus, the bulk of the trans-Pacific container trade from America was expected to shift in the 1990s to Californian ports. Since the mid-1970s, APL had been an innovator in inter-modal operations, combining forces in 1977 with the Burlington Northern Railroad to distribute containers by rail all over the United States. Until then, American railroads had considered container ship operators as additional ordinary freight customers, supplying them with standard flatbed wagons. Later, in the 1980s, double-stack wagons were developed by none other than the Sea-Land founder, Malcom P. McLean. In 1990, Maersk Line too adopted railroad vehicles of this type, forming an alliance with the Santa Fe Railroad, which even painted a locomotive in Maersk livery for publicity purposes.[318]

As Maersk Line was already committed to building the Panamax M-class for US East Coast-Far East service and, moreover, did not think that the market was quite big enough to sustain such substantially larger vessels as APL was proposing, it declined to become involved. Therefore, APL alone ordered a pioneering series of five C10-type post-Panamax container ships from two West German shipyards, Howaldtswerke Deutsche Werft (HDW) in Kiel and Bremer-Vulkan in Bremerhaven. The first of this class, the 61,926gt, 4,500 TEU *President Truman* was delivered from HDW in 1988. APL believed that the economic advantages inherent in such large vessels, each crewed by only 21, were self-evident. Indeed, post-Panamax container ships had the potential to reduce freight rates by as much as 30 per cent.[319] Economies of scale aside, such broad-hulled vessels had one obvious operational advantage: as the deck capacities of Panamax

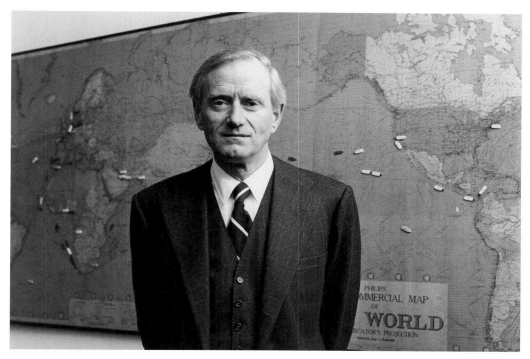

For half a century, Mærsk Mc-Kinney Møller oversaw the expansion of Mærsk Line into a global liner shipping giant. (A.P. Møller-Maersk)

container ships had grown, they had to carry more ballast water in order to compensate for the extra top weight so as to maintain stability – but this would not be a problem with a broader post-Panamax hull with a length-to-breadth ratio of approximately 7:1.[320]

APL's five C10 post-Panamax vessels were part of a $900 million investment by the Company, also involving improvements to terminals and new railroad cars to carry containers double-stacked. The thinking behind these projects was sound, but APL's timing was poor as no sooner were the ships and infrastructure in place than there was a global recession in the early 1990s which reduced the numbers of containers requiring to be transported. Moreover, the investment was funded mainly with borrowed money and this left APL with a serious debt burden from which it never escaped. In 1997, it was taken over by the Singaporean Neptune Orient Line and the combined Company was named APL (but never to be referred to as 'American President Lines').[321]

By 1994, the worst of the recession was over and so Maersk Line decided that it too should develop post-Panamax container ships capable of carrying 14 containers across the beam of their holds and 17 across on deck. Moreover, if Maersk chose to stick only with Panamax vessels, it would be bound sooner or later to lose market share to potentially cheaper competitors. Whereas Maersk had been a late adoptor of fully-cellular container ships in the mid-1970s, it was now an early and enthusiastic operator of post-Panamax vessels. With the benefit of hindsight, both strategies proved successful in the varying circumstances under which they were deployed. If containerising late allowed Maersk Line to learn from others' costly mistakes, the early adoption of post-Panamax vessels was crucial to remaining competitive in a commercial and mercantile world speeding up rapidly and becoming increasingly inter-connected. Maersk Line, of course, had an important role to play in furthering these processes.[322]

Maersk Line's first post-Panamax container ship, the **Regina Mærsk**, illuminated at dusk. (A.P. Møller-Maersk)

Moreover, the need for post-Panamax container ships reflected a changing world order and new patterns of industry and wealth distribution. The rapid growth of the Pacific Rim nations' economies and the subsequent emergence of China as a manufacturing powerhouse in the new millennium saw a rapid growth in traffic between Europe and the Far East and also in trans-Atlantic services, none of which involved passages via the Panama Canal. America's North Eastern industrial base meanwhile declined during the 1980s and '90s, while Southern and Western states grew on the back of oil and digital technologies. The container trades evolved to serve these expanding markets and, in the post-Panamax era, their operational patterns also changed. Back in the early 1970s, it was typical that container ships would make numerous short voyages between ports before sailing at maximum speed without stopping to the Far East, where further multiple calls were made. Once post-Panamax ships were introduced, there was a shift to so-called 'hub and spoke' networks in which the largest vessels, built to carry vast loads on long voyages, operated from equally commodious and highly automated centralised 'hub' ports. There, containers were brought from smaller terminals elsewhere by 'feeder' container ships.[323] (This reflected orthodoxy in the airline industry with the largest wide-bodied jetliners – such as Boeing 747s, MD11s and TriStars – operating long-haul flights from hub airports carrying passengers brought from provincial airports by smaller planes.)

Generally, post-Panamax container ships were deployed on East-West routes – across the Pacific from the US West Coast to the Far East and from Europe to the Far East via the Suez Canal – and the smaller vessels they displaced were redeployed to North-South secondary services.

As a result of the early-1990s recession, Maersk Line's senior management were anxious not to commission post-Panamax container vessels too big for the amount of freight requiring shipping. Consequently, Mærsk Ship Design's initial plan for a 288.9-metre long hull design was accepted but the design team was instructed also to prepare a shorter variation of the hull minus one 40-foot bay, reducing the length by 15 metres. Following a brief but severe slump, in the second half of the 1990s the world economy began to grow at ever greater rates and so, before the first post-Panamax Maersk Line vessels were built, there was a further change of strategy, two extra holds being added to give an overall length of 318.2 metres while the breadth was 42.8 metres.[324]

During the ensuing two decades, Maersk Line rode an unprecedented global economic boom,

The **Regina Mærsk** was the first of a long series of post-Panamax container ships built at Lindø.
(Flor van Otterdyk)

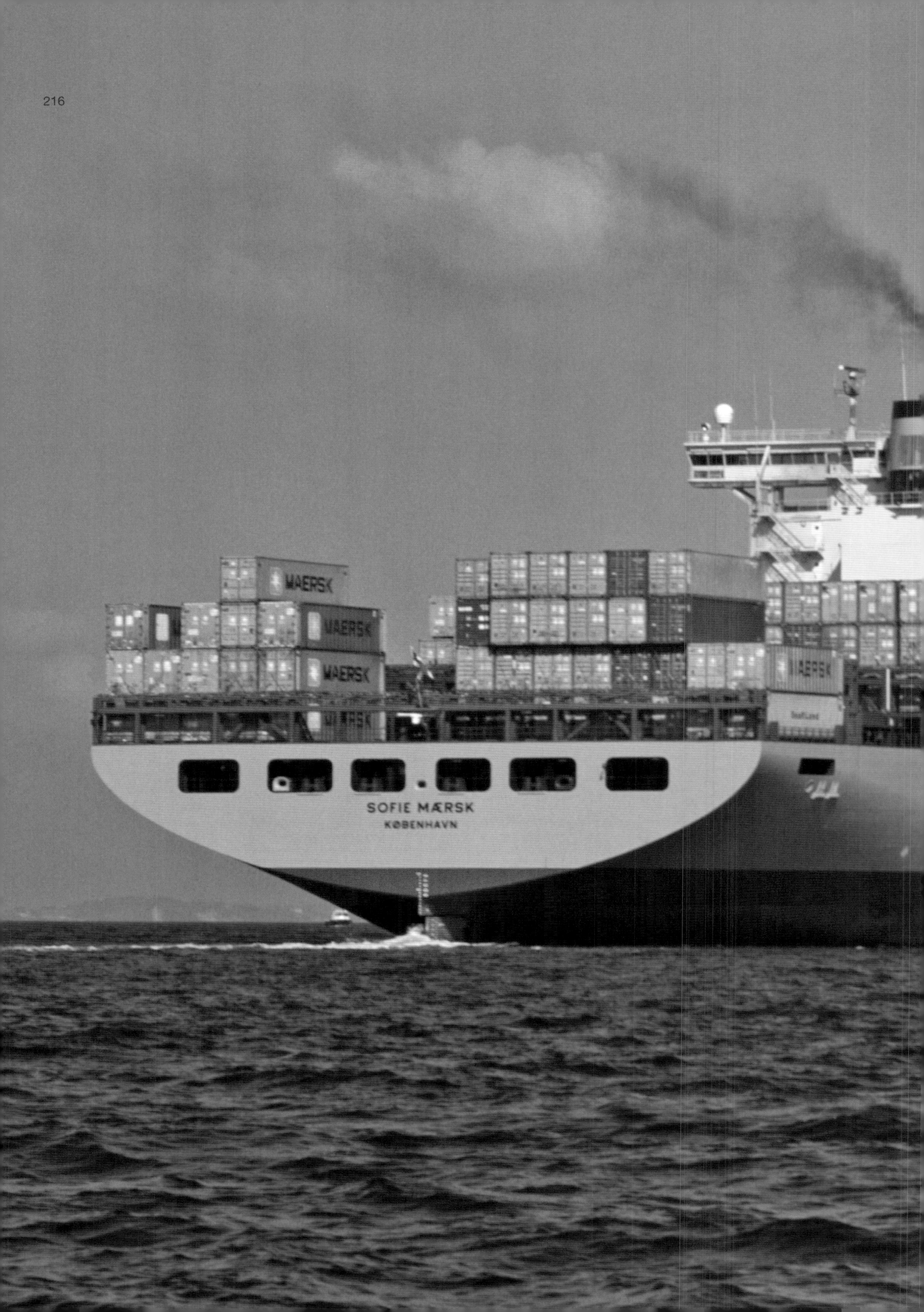
MAERSK
MAERSK
MAERSK
MAERSK
SOFIE MÆRSK
KØBENHAVN

The **Sofie Mærsk** in the Singapore Strait. (Bruce Peter collection)

The ***Sine Mærsk*** nearing completion at the Lindø shipyard.
(A.P. Møller-Maersk)

growing exponentially and becoming the world's biggest container ship operator while creating the most comprehensive 'hub and spoke' route network. To make the necessary investments, it helped that the Company was in a financially strong position – all of its subsidiaries evidently benefiting from the profits generated by the Maersk Oil North Sea drilling, extraction and oil-rig support businesses. Furthermore, the fact that A.P. Møller did not have substantial and powerful external shareholders demanding large dividends and the liquidation of assets to realise their value meant that a coherent long-term strategy could be developed.

Most importantly, the A.P. Møller Group was well managed and the Chairman and Managing Director, Mærsk Mc-Kinney Møller, set an excellent example of hard work, shrewdness and financial probity. Although by far Denmark's wealthiest man, he lived in a large suburban villa, even although he could easily have afforded a castle, and became famous for his immaculate manners and generous philanthropy. He was also famously scrupulous in personally responding to all correspondence and particularly adept at charming the most and least important people he encountered – world leaders and office cleaners equally being flattered by his encouraging words. Middle management, however, were given shorter shrift and expected to perform precisely to his exacting standards. Genteel and tough in equal measure, there can be little doubt that the growing personality cult surrounding Mærsk Mc-Kinney Møller created a positivist atmosphere which percolated down through the entire Group and partly accounted for Maersk Line's ongoing success.[325]

Maersk Line's post-Panamax K-class vessels measured 81,488gt and were powered by a 12-cylinder MAN-B&W diesel, enabling them to maintain a 25-knot service speed. Unlike the previous M-class, they were not fitted with waste heat recovery systems as Mærsk Mc-Kinney Møller found them to be too technically complicated and not quite reliable enough for his liking. As owner and patriarch, he was the final arbiter and, by the mid-1990s, he had accumulated nearly half-a-century of hands-on experience in the design, construction, management and operation of cargo liners and container ships. Indeed, technical staff referred to him as the 'top naval architect.' He often sought external advice from his close friend Robert Lockhart, who was Deputy Chief Ship

Surveyor at Lloyd's Register of Shipping in London until his retirement in 1982. Kjell Harr recalls that Lockhart too had an encyclopaedic knowledge of ship design and operation and, as he was well connected within the industry, he was able to pass on useful gossip about what rival operators might be planning. Not surprisingly for a former senior Lloyd's inspector, according to Harr, he was also rather conservative in his views and tended not to like radical change.[326]

While neither Møller nor Lockhart approved of complex and less than completely reliable shipboard systems, almost uniquely Møller thought that stabilisers were a very good idea on container ships and continued to insist that these be fitted long after other operators had abandoned them. There were sound reasons for this. Firstly, by reducing rolling motion, less strain was placed on the container locks and lashings and so the chance of losing containers overboard in stormy weather was diminished. This gave confidence to customers to entrust valuable goods to Maersk Line and also reduced the likelihood of having to pay compensation. Secondly, stabilisers allowed ships better to maintain schedule through stormy weather and also increased the comfort of their crews.[327]

Appropriately, the first of the new K-class was named *Regina Mærsk* by H.M. Queen Ingrid in February 1996. (In late 1995, the existing *Regina Mærsk* became *Leise Mærsk* to free up the royal name for the new post-Panamax flagship.) Five sisters – the *Knud Mærsk*, *Kate Mærsk*, *Karen Mærsk*, *Katrine Mærsk* and *Kirsten Mærsk* – followed her into service at approximately three-monthly intervals, the speed of their construction reflecting the efficiency and competence of the Odense Lindø shipyard.

Following hard on their heels came a further series of nine generally similar S-class post-Panamax container ships that were longer still at 346.9 metres. The S-class measured 91,560gt and these too had a capacity of 6,600 TEU. The first, named *Sovereign Mærsk*, was completed in September 1997 at Odense Lindø, where she was named by H.M. Queen Margrethe II.[328] Next came the *Susan Mærsk*, followed by the *Sally Mærsk*, *Sine Mærsk*, *Svendborg Mærsk*, *Sofie Mærsk*, *Svend Mærsk*, *Sorø Mærsk* and *Skagen Mærsk* – the last named being delivered in August 1999. The class were placed in service between Europe, South East Asia and the American West Coast. When the *Susan Mærsk* made her maiden call at Long Beach in California, she became the largest container ship to dock in an American port. A.P. Møller-Maersk's house magazine *Mærsk Post* reported:

> 'Under Captain Per Hermansen's command, the *Susan Mærsk* was welcomed by a flotilla of tugs with water cannon, yachts and helicopters carrying the media when she arrived with a record load of freight from the Far East. CNN and NBC Nightly News filmed her arrival, toured on board and interviewed Captain Hermansen and Chief Engineer Jørgen Blum…
>
> Last year imports across the Pacific to America grew by 20 per cent and American refrigerated exports grew by 10 per cent. The *Susan Mærsk* and her sisters each can carry 700 reefer containers, the biggest capacity for refrigerated cargo of any vessels in existence, which is good news for California's farmers.'[329]

Next, between November 1999 and November 2002, Odense Lindø delivered the broadly similar ten-strong C-class, commencing with the *Clifford Mærsk* and continuing with the *Cornelius Mærsk*, *A.P. Møller*, *Caroline Mærsk*, *Carsten Mærsk*, *Chastine Mærsk*, *Charlotte Mærsk*, *Cornelia Mærsk*, *Columbine Mærsk* and *Clementine Mærsk*.

Maersk Line, hitherto loyal to MAN-B&W when buying machinery for its biggest container vessels, this time split the engine order for the C-class between MAN-B&W and Wärtsilä-Sulzer types. As the emerging giant of the liner shipping world, its policy could be related to that of the larger airlines flying mixed Boeing and Airbus fleets so as to patronise both leading manufacturers, thus negotiating lower prices, reducing risk and encouraging research and development through comparative analysis. Simultaneously, a new 93,496gt, 8,272 TEU A-class was also being assembled in Odense and this type was slightly longer again at 352.6 metres, while maintaining the same 42.8 metre beam as the S- and C-classes. The *Anna Mærsk*, *Axel Mærsk*, *Arnold Mærsk*, *Arthur Mærsk*, *Adrian Mærsk* and *Albert Mærsk* were completed between

The K-class post-Panamax container ship **Knud Mærsk** at Dunkerque. (A.P. Møller-Maersk)

A stern-quarter view of the **Knud Mærsk**. (Flor van Otterdyk)

Modern liner shipping requires efficient port infrastructure, as illustrated by the **Johannes Mærsk** at
the container terminal in Algeciras. (Søren Lund Hviid)

The ***Carsten Mærsk*** arrives
at Århus in evening light.
(Søren Lund Hviid)

Above: The **Kate Mærsk**. (Flor van Otterdyk)

Below: The Lindø shipyard became very efficient at producing large container ships in quick succession. Here, the **Sovereign Mærsk** nears completion while the next vessel in the series, the **Susan Mærsk**, takes shape in the building dock. These ships were delivered only a few months apart. (A.P. Møller-Maersk)

The *Axel Mærsk* with Mount Rainer in the background. (A.P. Møller-Maersk)

The *Axel Mærsk* at sea, well loaded with containers. (A.P. Møller-Maersk)

Top and bottom: The *Lexa Mærsk*, one of the new generation of L-class container ships. (Robert Wisse)

Right: The **Laust Mærsk** in
lightly-loaded condition,
clearly showing the function
of the bulbous bow in
altering the wave form
ahead of the hull.
(Robert Wisse)

Below: With the expansion
of hub ports, such as
Algeciras, served by large
post-Panamax vessels,
Maersk Line developed
feeder services, using ships
such as the **Maersk Euro
Quarto**, one of a series built
by Ørskov in Frederikshavn.
(Bruce Peter collection)

May 2003 and August 2004. All of these were fitted with Wärtsilä-Sulzer 12-cylinder diesels.

Between deliveries of these vessels, Odense Staalskibsværft also constructed a new seven-ship L-class for use on secondary routes. These measured a mere 50,721gt and had a capacity of 4,400 TEU, 800 of which were refrigerated – indeed, at the time of their construction, the L-class were the world's largest reefer container ships. They were fitted with MAN-B&W 10-cylinder engines, giving a 24-knot speed.[330] The *Laura Mærsk*, *Laust Mærsk*, *Leda Mærsk*, *Lexa Mærsk*, *Lica Mærsk* and *Luna Mærsk* were all delivered between April and December 2001 with the *Lars Mærsk* being added in October 2004.

The nearly doubling in gross tonnage and increase in container capacity by a third in typical Maersk Line newbuildings commissioned since the 1990s for premier East-West routes were impressive but, within a decade, vessels twice their size would be joining the Maersk Line fleet. This rapid upscaling of container ships required a parallel increase in the size and capacity of the largest marine diesel engines. In order to deliver more horsepower to a single shaft with a propeller measuring no more than nine metres in diameter (due to the need to maintain a maximum loaded draft of no more than 13.5 metres) engines with larger bore cylinders needed to be developed. Already MAN-B&W had produced a 900 mm bore cylinder for the 12K90MC already fitted in the majority of post-Panamax Maersk Line container ships; this delivered 75,000 horsepower. Meanwhile, Wärtsilä-Sulzer developed an engine with 960 mm bore cylinders. A challenge in designing such wide cylinders was to achieve an even and efficient fuel combustion pattern and so the number of injectors also needed to be increased. Wärtsilä-Sulzer additionally improved

turbocharging and so the 11-cylinder RTA96C engine proved to be very effective indeed when first installed in the Japanese Nippon Yusen Kaisha container ship *NYK Antares*, built at Kure and delivered in 1997. Next, a 12-cylinder version was produced and this was fitted to the British-registered (but also Japanese-built) *P&O Nedlloyd Southampton*.[331] Wärtsilä-Sulzer was now neck-and-neck with MAN-B&W in creating engines with the necessary capacity to power the largest container ships of the new millennium.[332]

Chapter 13

Expansion by absorption

In 1991, Mærsk Mc-Kinney Møller, now aged 78, announced his successor as Managing Director of Dampskibsselskabet Svendborg and Dampskibsselskabet af 1912. Many assumed that his obvious replacement would be his most senior right-hand man, Ib Kruse. Having served since 1979 as one of only a few named 'skibsreder' ('shipowners') in the Company's senior management, Kruse had arguably been most responsible for Maersk Line's meteoric growth as a container shipper during the 1980s. By 1991, he was aged 59, however, and therefore considered too old for the top job (even although he was almost twenty years Møller's junior).

The younger alternative was Jess Søderberg. Unlike other senior A.P. Møller people of the older generation, whose backgrounds were as ships' officers or managers, Søderberg had a formal business education, graduating from Handelshøjskolen as a specialist in operations analysis. In 1970, he joined A.P. Møller as a new graduate and in 1975 he was sent to the United States as Accounts Director for its American operation, Maersk Inc. This was at the point when the A-class container ships and associated port infrastructure were being introduced and, during the next three years, the Company's American offices grew in number from three to 38 as container shipping proved highly successful.[333] In 1978, he became Accounts Director for the entire A.P. Møller organisation in Copenhagen and therefore one of Mærsk Mc-Kinney Møller's key advisers. In 1986 he too became a 'skibsreder,' the youngest by far in the Company's history. Having dedicated his entire business career to the A.P. Møller Group's successful expansion, in April 1991 he was invited by Mærsk Mc-Kinney Møller to become Managing Director from July 1993 – an offer he was delighted to accept.[334]

In the interim, there began a phase of consolidation in the container shipping market during which smaller and less competitive players either merged or were taken over by larger and more powerful operators. A.P. Møller's first such acquisitions were the liner services of the French Chargeurs Reunis and Franco-Belgian Services, including their rights in the Mediterranean-Far East Line; these were taken over in 1987. A subsequent candidate for absorption was the East Asiatic Company's liner division. This consisted of a long-established route from Europe to the Far East, plus four additional services between Asia and Australia as well as a fleet of seven container ships, the majority of which dated from the early 1970s. Notwithstanding an ageing fleet, EAC's liner shipping operations complemented well the existing Maersk Line network and provided extra capacity between Europe and the Far East.[335]

Next, in 1999, Safmarine (The South African Marine Corporation) and Sea-Land were taken over. Safmarine's liner services – comprising 40 ships and 60,000 containers – came on the market when the majority shareholder, the South African insurance company Old Mutual, decided that its parent company, Safren, should be sold. As nobody wanted to buy Safren as a single entity, Old Mutual split the company into its constituent parts – liner services, bulk and reefer shipping and air cargo – and sold each as a separate unit.[336]

A.P. Møller's senior management reasoned that Safmarine was a company with great potential. During South Africa's latter apartheid years, international sanctions had restricted South African trade but, this notwithstanding, during the mid-1970s Safmarine had introduced four large container ships to supply the home market with commodities; these replaced the Union-Castle/Safmarine passenger and mail service from Southampton to Cape Town from 1977 onwards. Once South

The *Munkebo Mærsk* (ex *Alsia*) in a hybrid of EAC hull livery and Maersk Line funnel. (Bruce Peter collection)

MAERSK LINE

MAERSK LINE · BRIGIT MAERSK

MAERSK COLOMBO · HAMBURG · MAERSK LINE

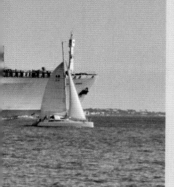

Left: The 57,079gt *Maersk Nanhai*, formerly the *Toyama* of EAC and Wilh. Wilhelmsen, in the Solent. (Bruce Peter collection)

Opposite centre: The *Brigit Mærsk*, formerly the *Svendborg Mærsk*, Maersk Line's pioneering container ship, is shown late in her career; she was scrapped in 2000. (Bruce Peter collection)

Opposite bottom: The chartered 37,398gt *Maersk Colombo* was launched as the *Hansa Australia* by Samsung in South Korea in 1993 for the German company Leonhardt & Blumberg. Maersk Line operated her until 1997. Chartering vessels such as this enables liner operators to reduce their exposure to market fluctuations. (Bruce Peter collection)

Below: The former Ben Line container ship *Benarty* (55,889gt, built in 1973) was acquired by EAC in 1992, then was taken over the following year by Maersk Line, becoming first the *Maersk Edinburgh* and, soon after, the *Edinburgh Maersk*, as shown here in the Solent. She was sold 1998. (Bruce Peter collection)

Bottom: The 52,682gt *Maersk Hamburg*, formerly the *Ortelius* of Compagnie Maritime Belge, was built by Boelwerf at Temse in Belgium in 1976 and is shown docking at Southampton. Maersk Line operated her for two years between 1993 and 1995 and she was scrapped in 2009. (Bruce Peter collection)

Africa was re-admitted to the world community following the release of Nelson Mandela in 1990 and the staging of elections in which all took part in 1994, this resource-rich country began to attract significant international investment. Besides, as Safmarine operated services from Europe and South America to Cape Town, Durban and other important ports in the African continent, its acquisition would further strengthen Maersk Line's emerging global route network. Therefore, A.P. Møller paid $290 million (1.7 billion kroner) for Safmarine.[337]

Three years later, in September 2002, A.P. Møller further strengthened Maersk Line's position in West Africa by taking over Torm Lines' services from US East Coast and Gulf ports plus connecting feeder services for 63 million kroner ($8.3 million). In West Africa, Torm Lines was the market leader, its vessels calling at the major ports of Dakar in Senegal, Abidjan in Ivory Coast, Tema in Ghana, Lagos and Port Harcourt in Nigeria and Douala in Cameroon. Cargo from smaller ports between Mauritania and Angola was trans-shipped via Dakar and Abidjan.

Torm had originally taken over the former Dansk-Fransk-operated Gulwa Line in 1979, employing Captain Henrik Schrum, who had lengthy experience of running liner services to Africa, to manage its Liner Department. At that time, numerous companies were involved in this trade but during the 1980s and 90s most of them disappeared. Thus, Torm Lines ended up being the only comprehensive direct service between the USA and West Africa.[338] It operated using mainly chartered tonnage, supplemented with a single owned multi-purpose vessel, the 13,651gt *Torm Agnete*, which it acquired in 1996. By the latter 1990s, its annual profit reached $8 million when five liners and four feeder vessels were employed, enabling a weekly departure in each direction. Eastbound, Torm Lines carried oil-well supplies to Nigeria and Angola, as well as general cargo. In the opposite direction, cocoa, coffee and timber were transported in large quantities from the Ivory Coast, Ghana and Cameroon to the US market.

Thereafter, Maersk Line began to undercut Torm by shipping containers from the USA to West Africa via its Algeciras hub. Torm Lines served lucrative niche markets, carrying high value commodities for as much as $7,000 per 40 foot container, while Maersk allegedly was prepared to ship for half that rate. This had a significant impact on Torm Lines' profitability and so there was little option other than to sell out to Maersk. Thus ended Torm's 75-year association with liner shipping and subsequently it concentrated on the tanker and bulk cargo markets.[339]

For A.P. Møller, the successful acquisition of Sea-Land was an altogether more ambitious

The former Ben Line container ship *London*, ex *London Maersk*, ex *Benalder*, under charter to Maersk Line in 1999; she was broken up in China in 2001.
(Bruce Peter collection)

Above: Maersk Line bought Safmarine's container shipping activities in 1999, although the subsidiary retained its existing name and visual identity. (A.P. Møller-Maersk)

Right: For West African coastal service, Torm Lines used the small feeder container vessel *Torm Africa* to collect goods for trans-shipment to and from the USA. The vessel was designed like a landing craft and could therefore load directly from beaches. (Jørn Bent Jensen)

Below: Torm Lines' chartered 13,688gt *Torm Birgitte*, photographed at Houston in Texas in 1999, operated between the USA and West African ports, a service taken over by Maersk Line in 2002. The vessel was built in Warnemünde 1987 as the *Borussia* and was operated by Torm, then Maersk, from 1994 until 2003. (Marc Piché)

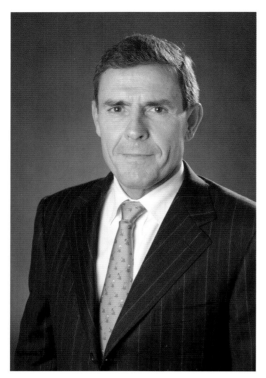

Under the leadership of Jess Søderberg, Maersk Line grew rapidly, to a large extent through the purchase of other liner operators. (A.P. Møller-Maersk)

undertaking. The company was the container shipping pioneer and it too had expanded throughout the 1960s and '70s with a large network of services, focused on United States ports. Furthermore, it was involved with the US Navy in the supply of stores and equipment to America's various military interventions around the world.

It will be recalled that Mærsk Mc-Kinney Møller was himself half-American and, fondly remembering American actions to defeat Germany in the Second World War, he had a long-standing admiration for the country – and also powerful business and political acquaintances there. During the 1960s, Maersk Line ships had helped deliver American supplies to Vietnam during the war. More recently, in 1991, when an Allied coalition of forces liberated Kuwait from Iraqi occupation, Maersk Line supplied two container ships free of charge to the United States Sealift Command to transport equipment and materials from the USA to Saudi Arabia. In America, this gesture was greatly appreciated and only added to the high esteem in which Møller was held. [340]

In 1986, Sea-Land was purchased by CSX, a major American railroad corporation. A decade later, CSX was keen to take over another freight railroad, Conrail, and so required to raise the $10.2 billion expected to be needed for a successful bid. In preparation for this, CSX announced in January 1999 that Sea-Land was to be split into three divisions – one concerning international liner routes, another controlling domestic coastal services (affected by the Jones Act) and a third operating port and associated infrastructure. This new corporate structure would allow Sea-Land's international liner routes to be sold off as a separate unit – and A.P. Møller was the expected purchaser.[341] Besides, since 1991, Maersk Line and Sea-land had co-operated on cross-Pacific services from the US West Coast to the Far East.

Sea-Land was suffering from competition from companies using newer, larger vessels which could achieve far superior economies of scale than most of its own fleet. In 1998, profits had declined by 78 per cent over the previous year, a situation which CSX's Board found unacceptable. Thus, in 1999 Sea-Land was sold to A.P. Møller for $800 million (5.6 billion kroner). Through this deal, Maersk Line added 70 vessels to its fleet, 200,000 containers, 16 port terminals and 25 routes radiating from the United States in all directions around the world. The combined Company was renamed Maersk-Sealand (note 'Sealand' without a hyphen). As A.P. Møller's Managing Director Jess Søderberg explained in *Mærsk Post*:

> 'Maersk Line has for several years had a close operational partnership with Sea-Land and the complete integration of the two lines under the name Maersk-Sealand is a natural development. In building on the best characteristics of the two organisations, we will be able to offer our over 100,000 customers a stand-alone service over the whole world. The acquisition of Sea-Land is one of A.P. Møller's biggest and most demanding investments ever. Maersk-Sealand will enter the new millennium as the no. 1 container operator with the resultant responsibilities that entails.'[342]

To ensure that the integration process went smoothly, the long-serving A.P. Møller director Ib Kruse was given responsibility for seeing it through. With EAC, Safmarine and Sea-Land integrated into the Maersk-Sealand fleet, the Company now possessed offices in over 100 countries, a grand total of 250 container ships and 600,000 containers – twice as many as the second largest operator, the Taiwanese Evergreen. None of its competitors had the strategic resources or the financial muscle to compete on anything like an equal footing. Moreover, while many leading container shippers recorded losses in the latter 1990s, Maersk-Sealand was reliably profitable.

The former Sea-Land-owned port facilities were merged with Maersk Line's own portfolio and a new subsidiary, APM Terminals, was established in 2001.[343] Two years thereafter, Maersk-Sealand's global activities were split into fifteen regional subsidiaries, each with its own Head of Operations, the idea being to decentralise and delegate at least some decision-making away from

Above: With the acquisition of Sea-Land, Maersk Line's name was altered to Maersk Sealand, as shown on the *Maersk Merlion*, a vessel originally built for EAC as the *Arosia*. (Zee-photo)

Below: In addition to the giant container ships operating long routes, Maersk Sealand also expanded its feeder network, run by smaller vessels, such as the *Cecilie Mærsk*, built at Lindø in 1994 and carrying up to 1,500 TEU. (Flor van Otterdyk)

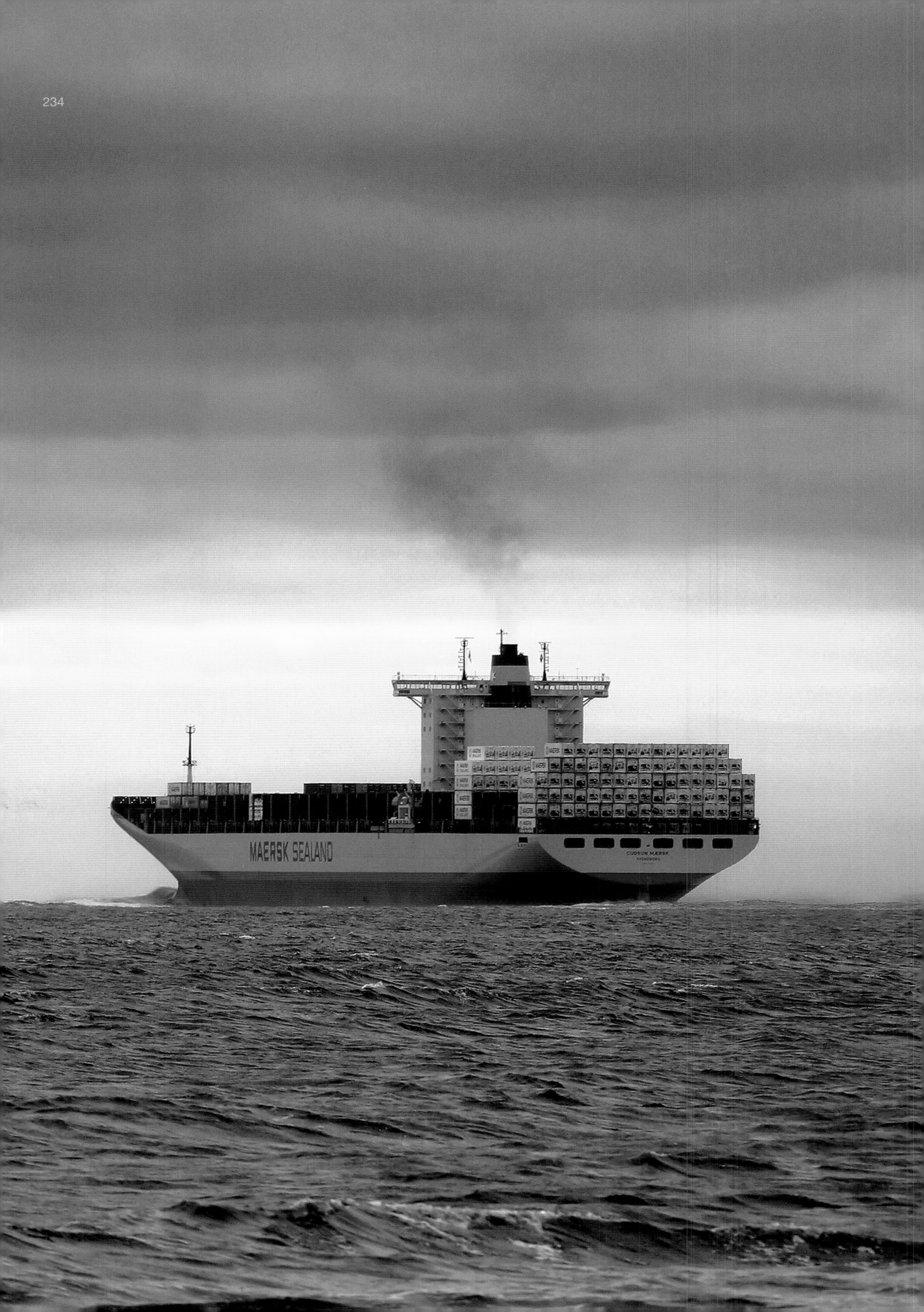
MAERSK SEALAND

Copenhagen, encouraging contact to be maintained with customers on regional and local levels.

In the following years, APM Terminals bought shares in container ports in Pipavav in India, Puerto Cabello in Venezuela, Rotterdam, Los Angeles, Shanghai and Quingdao in China, Luanda in Angola, Port Quasim in Pakistan and several other locations. At its original hub port, Tangier, a vast civil engineering project was undertaken to build a new terminal with 1,600 metres of quay and 16 cranes; this ambitious project was completed in 2007. In the United States, a similarly impressive new port facility was constructed at Portsmouth in Virginia – the third largest container port on the US East Coast after Newark and Charleston and capable of handling 1.2 million TEU per annum; this was opened only three months after the extension at Tangier.[344] The expansion of APM Terminals was important as, through the control of port facilities, it was easier to guarantee that services would keep to schedule and that customers would receive their goods on time.

In the wider context of global container ship operation in the latter 1990s, the old consortium model of the 1960s had been superseded by a number of 'global alliances.' Again, this was analogous to strategy within the airline industry, in which the largest airlines are members of groupings such as One World and Star Alliance, meaning that their networks are dovetailed and through-ticketing gives member airlines global reach. In container shipping, the major alliances were Global Alliance – consisting of APL (the former American President Lines and Neptune Orient Line), Mitsui-OSK and Orient Overseas Container Line (OOCL) – and Grand Alliance, whose members were P&O Nedlloyd, Hapag-Lloyd and Nippon Yusen Kaisha. Apart from Maersk-Sealand, the only other big container ship operators not to be alliance members were Evergreen and a similarly recently established, but rapidly developing, Swiss-Italian firm called Mediterranean Shipping Company (MSC).

As with Sea-Land, Maersk Line and Evergreen, this was largely the vision of one man, the Swiss-domiciled Italian shipowner Gianluigi Aponte. Aponte had bought his first cargo vessel in 1970 and began in the tramping trade around the Mediterranean and African coasts. Later on, he introduced liner routes from Southern Europe to Africa and to Asia, mainly employing second-hand ships to keep costs as low as possible. In 1984, the Europe-Africa service was the first to be containerised, mainly using converted general cargo vessels, and thereafter MSC's progress was rapid. Next, a trans-Atlantic line was developed and, in 1988, MSC inaugurated a hub container harbour at Freeport on Grand Bahama Island in the Caribbean. By the mid-1990s, MSC was commissioning purpose-built tonnage. In the 1995-2010 period, MSC had an average annual growth rate of 15 per cent against Maersk Line's 8 per cent. Come the millennium, MSC was the second biggest container ship operator, after Maersk-Sealand.[345]

In 2003, Mærsk Mc-Kinney Møller decided finally to retire as Chairman of the Boards of Dampskibsselskabet Svendborg and Dampskibsselskabet af 1912; he was aged 90 and had successfully led the Companies since his father's death in 1965. At this point, it was announced that they would be fused together to create a new single parent company, named A.P. Møller-Maersk A/S. The job of Chairman was given to Michael Pram Rasmussen, formerly of the insurance company Topdanmark.

Following the successful acquisitions of EAC, Safmarine and Sea-Land, there was a clear take-over momentum in A.P. Møller-Maersk's Copenhagen headquarters. Partly, this reflected a belief that, in the emerging global economy, it was important to gain as much market share as possible through acquisitions as well as organic growth. In addition, Managing Director Jess Søderberg possibly felt that he needed to demonstrate corporate machismo. During the summer of 2005, negotiations began to purchase P&O Nedlloyd – the world's third largest container shipping company, operating 160 vessels and 400,000 containers. It had been created in 1996 through the fusion of P&O's container services (the former OCL) and the Dutch Nedlloyd firm. Previously, in 2002, Søderberg had visited P&O's London headquarters to establish whether its Chairman Lord Sterling would be willing to sell P&O Nedlloyd. Sterling was positive – but, according to the business historian Niels Lunde, Mærsk Mc-Kinney Møller quickly vetoed any possibility of concluding a deal at that time. Apparently, Møller was strongly of the opinion that there was little to be gained from the acquisition of that particular rival operator.[346]

Between 1991 and 1996, P&O and Maersk Line had entered an agreement to share port facilities, but when it ended P&O introduced a new Europe-Far East route in direct competition with Maersk Line. Less than a decade later, in August 2005, A.P. Møller-Maersk struck a deal to acquire P&O Nedlloyd for 2.3 billion euro ($2.9 billion). In the end, this was achieved in three stages. Firstly, in April 2004, P&O sold to Royal Nedlloyd its 50 per cent stake in P&O Nedlloyd in return for 25 per cent of the listed company, renamed Royal P&O Nedlloyd, plus cash. Next, in June 2005, P&O sold its 25 per cent stake in Royal P&O Nedlloyd to A.P. Møller-Maersk. Finally, in August the same year, A.P. Møller-Maersk bought the remainder of Royal P&O Nedlloyd. The integration of the two companies' operations did not begin until February 2006, however, so as to enable P&O Nedlloyd to honour its existing conference agreements. (Until being taken over by A.P. Møller-Maersk, it was a member of Grand Alliance, a group of container shippers also including Hapag-Lloyd and Nippon Yusen Kaisha.)[347] It was planned that, following the integration of P&O Nedlloyd into Maersk-Sealand, the combined Company would revert once more to the original straightforward name of Maersk Line. (It could hardly have been called Maersk-Sealand-P&O Nedlloyd!)

Most of P&O Nedlloyd's route network was already duplicated by Maersk Line's existing services and so the acquisition only added capacity to existing services by eliminating a competitor, rather than giving much that was new. The purchase was a gamble as the container market was peaking and so the price was high, but A.P. Møller-Maersk's calculations must have

Having taken over P&O Nedlloyd, Maersk Sealand was changed back to Maersk Line. Here, the **Gunvor Mærsk** has the new title, but the **Maersk Djibouti** is yet to be repainted.
(A.P. Møller-Maersk)

shown that it would be faster and less expensive to acquire increased market share in this way than through organic growth. Besides, one of A.P. Møller-Maersk's senior directors at that time, Per Jørgensen, who was in Jess Søderberg's 'inner circle' of advisers, explained the acquisition simply: 'because we could.'[348] Thanks to its oil and gas revenues, A.P. Møller-Maersk was financially strong and so Maersk Line had a unique opportunity to become the world's largest container shipping company. Jess Søderberg and his colleagues must have reasoned that by being the biggest, it would also be the most profitable.

A.P. Møller-Maersk's senior management were well aware that the integration of Maersk-Sealand and P&O Nedlloyd to create a greatly enlarged Maersk Line would be a complicated task. In *Mærsk Post*, Søderberg observed:

> 'The route towards the integration of the two organisations will be full of challenges. Bringing together two large global businesses with a vast network of ships, logistical activities and offices is no small task. As well as detailed planning, we need to keep our focus on our customers, continuing to provide the high level of service they expect…'[349]

However, due to an unfortunate confluence of circumstances, this did not actually happen in practice. Immediately prior to the purchase of P&O Nedlloyd, Maersk-Sealand had 12 per cent of

the global container ship market while P&O Nedlloyd claimed nearly an 8 per cent market share; together, they would therefore control just below 20 per cent. P&O Nedlloyd was, however, a very different kind of shipping company from A.P. Møller-Maersk. Whereas the latter kept most of its shares with voting rights 'in house' and tended to invest for the long term, owning outright the majority of its assets, P&O Nedlloyd was rather more leveraged and a significant proportion of the fleet was chartered. Furthermore, many of P&O Nedlloyd's container ships were of a different type from standard Maersk Line vessels. P&O Nedlloyd had come to favour a hatch-free design which saved weight and freed up deadweight capacity but also exerted a lot of pressure on containers near the bottoms of the holds (on container ships with hatch covers, these constitute a new deck where the stacking principle begins again).[350] P&O Nedlloyd was, nevertheless, a very efficiently-run business with its own distinctive internal culture, processes and strategy.

Furthermore, P&O Nedlloyd used a different IT platform from Maersk-Sealand to track containers and so, in order to harmonise the two Companies, it was decided at the highest level that a new, rapidly-developed IT system should be introduced across the entire Maersk Line container operation at the earliest opportunity. Earlier, in August 2004, A.P. Møller-Maersk had sold its in-house IT division, Maersk Data, to IBM, giving the latter firm 30 per cent of the Danish computer services market. It will be remembered that Mærsk Mc-Kinney Møller's relationship with IBM stretched back to the Second World War when, living in New York, he became friends with the Chairman, Tom Watson. Thereafter, between 1970 and 1984, he served as an IBM director. In the early 1960s, IBM had pioneered data management systems for Sea-Land's container shipping activities and so it had considerable expertise in this area. Maersk Line's rate of growth was so rapid that A.P. Møller-Maersk's senior management believed that Maersk Data would be unable to keep pace without significant investment. Instead of enabling that investment, they argued that IT development was a non-core activity. As a consequence of the sale, A.P. Møller-Maersk perhaps had insufficient direct control of the development of the new IT system which instead took place at IBM and was also arguably introduced with undue haste while the incorporation of P&O Nedlloyd was simultaneously in progress.

Hitherto, Maersk-Sealand used a variety of IT systems for container booking, the calculation of freight rates and billing clients. These required a lot of manual labour, employed in numerous regional offices. The new IT system was intended to bring Maersk Line fully up-to-date in terms of efficient operation and the minimisation of paperwork and labour. Within the Company, there was some scepticism about whether it would actually be possible simultaneously to integrate P&O Nedlloyd while introducing new IT and training so many office workers in the new processes and routines required to make it operate smoothly.[351]

Regrettably, Maersk Line's new IT system did not work as well as had been expected – indeed, it proved inflexible and unreliable. In the spring of 2006, customers began to notice that all was

At first, the former P&O Nedlloyd ships were only given new names and funnel colours, but repainting of the hulls of those deemed worthy of retention followed later. Here, the 50,358gt *Maersk Madrid*, ex *Peninsular Bay*, passes through the Singapore Strait in 2010. (Bruce Peter)

not well. For a whole month, Maersk Line was unable to send out invoices and, when they were finally printed and dispatched, they contained errors.[352] Meanwhile, containers ordered by customers failed to arrive, or arrived late, or were incorrectly dispatched to the wrong port – all of which caused businesses relying on Maersk Line's services to lose income as many required their goods to arrive and leave 'just in time.' (It has been alleged that some containers arriving at the Algeciras hub terminal from the United States and bound for West Africa were either incorrectly returned whence they came or forwarded to the Far East.) As Maersk Line hitherto built its reputation upon absolute reliability, when that ceased to be the case, not surprisingly it quickly lost customers. By the end of 2006, its share of the container market fell to 16.8 per cent and by July 2007 it was down to 14 per cent after a fifth of its clients decided to take their business elsewhere. (This was estimated to correspond to around a million container shipments.)[353] In *Mærsk Post*, Jess Søderberg reported:

> 'The first six months of 2006 [A.P. Møller-Maersk] showed a profit of 1.2 billion dollars. This is, however, a decrease of more than a third compared with the same period last year. The disappointing result is due to an unsatisfactory loss in the container business even though many employees are making an extra effort for the business after the implementation of the new IT systems and the integration of P&O Nedlloyd…'[354]

In quoting A.P. Møller-Maersk's results, rather than those of Maersk Line specifically, Søderberg emphasised the positive: by the end of 2006, the latter business had lost 3.4 billion kroner, as opposed to the 7.6 billion earned in the previous year. In other words, Maersk Line's result had declined by no less than 11 billion kroner.[355] All of this happened during a sustained economic boom when, instead of losing patronage, Maersk Line should have been making significant gains to offset steeply rising fuel prices and other sharply increasing operational costs. Due to the problems associated with integrating P&O Nedlloyd, on 27 June 2006 A.P. Møller-Maersk announced to the Copenhagen Stock Exchange that its expected profit in 2006 would be 40 per cent below the previous year's figure, a predicted fall of 5 billion kroner. (This situation also shows how profits earned by A.P. Møller-Maersk's other businesses partially disguised Maersk Line's problems.)

At the same time, across the container shipping sector revenue declined by 6 per cent as the cost of fuel went up by a staggering 35 per cent.[356] This was offset by a 14 per cent increase in cargo volumes between Asia and Europe and an 11 per cent gain between Asia and the USA.[357] Such increases were necessary because, for an operation of Maersk Line's scale, a decline of just 1 per cent equates to a loss of 1 billion kroner.[358] In 2006, the average cost of shipping a 40-foot container between Europe and the Far East was $1,550.[359]

For A.P. Møller-Maersk's senior management, the consequences of the IT *débacle* were profound. Such a failure could not be tolerated and so in June 2007 the Chairman of the Board, Michael Pram Rasmussen, announced that the Managing Director Jess Søderberg would be replaced; he left on 1 December 2007. During the following year, other senior managers responsible for IT strategy and implementation were also given their marching orders.[360] Unlike EAC in the 1970s-90s period, A.P. Møller-Maersk demonstrated a low toleration of failure by those whose task it was to deliver satisfactory results.

During the period leading up to Maersk Line's IT problems, Søderberg allegedly had devoted much of his time to a management development programme involving an 'internal conversation' amongst senior managers to create, then 'roll out' a set of shared corporate values across the entire A.P. Møller-Maersk organisation. In the wider business world, the idea of developing shared corporate values was fashionable at that time – but arguably it was not an essential activity when there was so much else requiring detailed attention.[361] Yet, with hindsight, it appears that Jess Søderberg was as much a victim of an unfortunate combination of circumstances as he was the author of his own downfall. Had Maersk Line's new IT system functioned as expected, he would be remembered for having spent most of his life working to build A.P. Møller-Maersk into a global transport logistics giant. While Maersk Line's IT problems were most disappointing – and could have ruined a less fundamentally robust company – Søderberg's legacy of expansion still remains as a remarkable corporate achievement.

Chapter 14

The light blue giants

While A.P. Møller-Maersk's absorption of other container ship operators was under way, simultaneously a new generation of giant post-Panamax Maersk Line container ships was under construction at Odense Staalskibsværft. These vessels represented another important dimension to Maersk Line's ongoing expansion during the Søderberg era.

While the size of container ships had grown at an increasing rate, their basic construction had remained more or less the same since the East Asiatic Company's *Selandia* and *Jutlandia* were completed in the early 1970s. The holds of typical Odense Staalskibsværft-built Maersk Line post-Panamax vessels carried 14 containers across in the holds with 17 across on deck. In the mid-1990s, however, the South Korean Hyundai Group – which, like A.P. Møller-Maersk, controlled shipbuilding and container shipping interests – developed a new design with open spans across the entire width of their holds. In other words, they jettisoned the parallel box girders at upper deck level which strengthened the hulls of typical container ships built to Panamax and post-Panamax dimensions. Research carried out during the preceding decade had established that these were ineffective in reducing warping stresses and could only lessen their absolute magnitude.[362] As the holds were no longer split into three sections across the hull's width by these girders, they could carry 15 containers across. In terms of adding an extra row along the entire length of the hull, Hyundai's innovation in post-Panamax container ship design to an extent reflected that of J.J. Kappel in optimising the capacity of Panamax vessels in the latter 1980s through the adoption of his 'slim slim' cell-guide design.

Hyundai's innovation was made possible by new developments in steel technology. New types of very-high-tensile steel needed to be used to build hulls intended to allow for significantly larger deflections than hitherto considered acceptable. As before, the hulls derived much of their integrity from the bottom and side constructions, effectively creating a broad U-shaped structure. As the hull flexed when at sea, the sides moved longitudinally and so stresses were transferred to the upper part, converging around the hatch openings. Therefore, it was necessary to use high-tensile steel 36 for much of the hull's structure and even higher tensility steel 40 for the hatch coamings.[363]

Once again, A.P. Møller-Maersk became early adopters of this new approach to container ship hull design. In 2000, Mærsk Ship Design's naval architects and other senior technical people investigated whether a modified version of the S-class design could be built without hull girders. A.P. Møller-Maersk's senior management instead wanted a really big container ship capable of carrying 22 containers across the width of the holds; this would require an overall beam of 56 metres. At that time, the only ships of such wide dimension were oil tankers, but their hulls were fully enclosed, enabling a much more comprehensive torsional strength-giving structure to be incorporated than in open-decked container ships. Furthermore, to maintain a speed of at least 25 knots, it would be necessary to employ twin-screw propulsion and the cost of a second engine, shaft, propeller and associated control systems would add significantly to each ship's cost, limiting any yield to be achieved through greater economies of scale.[364] Therefore, the proposal was temporarily abandoned.

Meanwhile, the 97,933gt G-class, numbering six vessels, was under construction at Odense Staalskibsværft; these were a further development of previous Maersk Line post-Panamax designs but, following Hyundai's constructional innovation, their holds were single-span without separating girders. Therefore, each could carry 7,668 containers within similar 366.9 x 42.8 metre length and breadth dimensions to existing vessels. As their hulls were consequently designed to have greater flexibility, the container stacks, hatch covers and lashing bridges also moved around with deflections of up to 300 mm. Indeed, the hatch covers were designed to sit on the openings to the holds, providing stiff platforms for the

Opposite top: The *Gunvor Mærsk* nears completion at Lindø in September 2005. The forward holds are yet to have hatch covers installed and so one can clearly see that these fill the entire beam of the vessel. (A.P. Møller-Maersk)

Opposite bottom: The *Gudrun Mærsk* in the Dover Strait. (A.P. Møller-Maersk)

Danish-owned container ships connect all of the world's markets and have played an important role in globalisation, as demonstrated by the **Gunvor Mærsk** off Hong Kong. (A.P. Møller-Maersk)

container stacks on deck, unaffected by the bending of the hull beneath.[365] To prevent wear and tear being caused by the hatch covers rubbing on the coamings, reinforced rubber support pads were fitted to the underside of the hatch covers, allowing them to float over the coamings, reducing friction and the unwelcome possibility of the hull's topsides suffering steel cracks. These pads were a Maersk Line/ Odense Staalskibsværft innovation but are now widely employed.[366]

Furthermore, the G-class was fitted with a sophisticated so-called Integrated Computer System (ICS), developed by the engineering and information technology specialists ABB. This enabled most of the ship's key systems to be remotely monitored by thousands of sensors, feeding performance data back to a central computer which could be accessed by officers on the bridge, in the engine control room and even in their cabins. Consequently, the G-class had the potential to operate with a crew of only 13 although, in practice, 15 are employed to build in a better safety margin. Having already maximised the container capacity within given hull dimensions and having also done a great deal to optimise hull hydrodynamics, the development of software of this type represented an important new step in container ship design development.[367] (It will be remembered that the Danes first pioneered automation in the 1960s when Søren T. Lyngsø developed a remote engine control system, first installed on Torm and EAC cargo liners.)

With growing environmental concerns about 'climate change' and 'global warming' and increasing criticism of the international shipping industry's role in producing so-called 'greenhouse gases' – not to mention exponential increases in the cost of marine bunker oil – A.P. Møller-Maersk decided that it was time to re-visit waste heat recovery technology. The last instance of such a system being installed on Maersk Line container ships was the M-class of the latter 1980s. Since that time, a great many improvements had taken place, meaning that waste heat recovery systems were now more reliable and could regain up to 30 per cent of the energy contained in the exhaust gases which, on the G-class, corresponded to a remarkable 10 per cent fuel saving.[368] Waste gases produced by the main engine, a 93,000 bhp Wärtsilä-Sulzer 12-cylinder unit, were used to drive a turbine for electricity generation. This, in turn, powered an electric motor mounted on the propeller shaft to help achieve a speed of 25 knots.[369] Electronic engine control, meanwhile, minimised fuel consumption and it was expected that, when fully laden, the G-class would use only a litre of fuel to carry each container 35 kilometres at full speed. To spare further energy, A.P. Møller-Maersk and Odense Staalskibsværft technical staff devised a new water cooling system for refrigerated containers, saving up to 20 per cent of power use on each container carried.[370]

The first of the class of six G-class vessels, the *Gudrun Mærsk*, was completed in June 2005 with the remaining five – the *Grete Mærsk*, *Gunvor Mærsk*, *Gjertrud Mærsk*, *Gerd Mærsk* and *Georg Mærsk* – following at two-monthly intervals. Initially, they operated between South East Asia and Europe – but A.P. Møller-Maersk already had plans for a further series that would be more impressive still.

In 2003, A.P. Møller-Maersk decided to revive previously abandoned plans for a significantly larger container ship type, the design and construction of which would push naval architecture and marine engineering into previously uncharted territory. This decision was predicated on expected growth in China to average 12 per cent per annum from 2007 onwards. According to typically used models, growth of 3 per cent will see a 6 per cent increase in trade and a corresponding 9 per cent requirement for extra container capacity. (Conversely, if container capacity is increased by 9 per cent, then economic growth must not fall below 3 per cent, or container operators will incur losses).[371]

The eight-strong E-class would number among the largest merchant ships ever constructed. Vessels of superlatives, each would measure 170,794gt, with length and breadth dimensions of 398 metres by 56.4 metres. It was announced that they would each carry up to 11,000 TEU but, not long after their introduction, this figure increased to 14,770. In May 2010 one of the E-class, the *Ebba Mærsk*, set a world record by being loaded experimentally with 15,011 TEU at Maersk Line's Tangier Med container terminal to prove that this was possible. In January 2011 it was announced that a new official capacity limit of 15,550 TEU had been negotiated.

At the time the *Emma Mærsk* was delivered in August 2006, the only merchant ship of greater dimensions in existence was the Norwegian-owned floating oil storage tanker *Knock Nevis* (ex *Jahre Viking*, ex *Seawise Giant*) – but she was a stationary ship rather than one engaged in trade under her own power. Super-tankers such as the *Knock Nevis* have bluff hull forms, are structurally relatively simple, slow-moving and the result of incremental technological advances, developed over a long period of time.[372] In contrast, as we have seen, container ships have fine-lined hulls with complex internal structures and typically operate at relatively high speeds. Furthermore, to design and build the E-class, it was necessary to cope with a jump in size of around 90 per cent over the existing largest Maersk Line vessels. There was consequently a lengthy design phase, the initial feasibility study alone lasting half a year in order to make A.P. Møller-Maersk's senior management confident that the design could work in practice. Such a lengthy lead-in process was most unusual in the wider shipbuilding industry and again demonstrates the advantages to A.P. Møller-Maersk of owning a shipyard and design division.[373]

Odense Staalskibsværft's Executive Vice-President Peter Tang-Jensen took charge of the design of the E-class. A graduate of the Technical University of Denmark's School of Naval Architecture and of the Harvard Business School, he first joined A.P. Møller in 1985. Significant external advice was received from Preben Terndrup Pedersen, Professor in Strength of Maritime Structures at the Technical University of Denmark, and from senior naval architects at the American Bureau of Shipping, A.P. Møller-Maersk's favoured classification society. Terndrup Pedersen provides a commentary on the challenges inherent in designing the E-class:

> 'I became fascinated by large container ships because there are so many areas in need of further research. The structural design of such large vessels poses a number

The Lindø shipyard viewed from the air in August 2006 with the *Emma Mærsk* nearing completion at the outfitting quay while the *Estelle Mærsk* is ready for floating out as soon as the *Emma Mærsk* has gone. With the advent of the E-class, the building dock at Lindø was occupied almost to its maximum dimensions. (A.P. Møller-Maersk)

of technical challenges. The increase in their size has been so rapid that there has been little feedback from service experience. Therefore, these ultra-large steel structures have to be designed solely by direct calculations. When Maersk Line's E-class was on the drawing board, the classification societies had no rules covering such large ships. There were a number of unsolved challenges associated with the design for such large and fast ships. Firstly, all the important structural loads on ships vary with time. The most important loads are caused by wave-induced motions of the water around the ship and the resulting motions of the ship herself. When ships increase in size, and when materials with higher strength are used, the hull flexibility plays an important role in the response of the vessel. The hull girder's natural frequencies become so small that when calculating the wave-induced loads, it is not

Above: With the delivery of the **Emma Mærsk**, a new paradigm was set for container ships. Their dimensions were equivalent to those of the super tankers of the 1970s. (Ronald Ribbe)

Right: The **Emma Mærsk**'s mighty dimensions become clearly apparent when contrasted with the slightly older post-Panamax container ship berthed behind. (Søren Lund Hviid)

Left: The **Ebba Mærsk** approaching Århus with a tug in attendance and a Mols-Linien ferry to port. (Søren Lund Hviid)

Below: The **Ebba Mærsk** at Århus. (Søren Lund Hviid)

sufficient to consider the ship's hull as a rigid body. Thus, the effects of structural hull deformation become important. In consequence, for such ultra-large containerships, there are a number of hydro-elastic effects which must be considered.

Secondly, since container vessels have very open deck areas in order to facilitate easy loading and unloading of containers below deck the hull girders of these vessels have very low torsional rigidity. When the ships sail in oblique waves, the torsional loads may cause considerable deformations, or warping. The result will be deformations of the hatch openings and large stresses where the deck beams are attached to the side shell, as well as especially large stresses in front of the

The world's largest diesel engine, an impressive Wärtsilä-Sulzer unit, installed on the *Emma Mærsk*. Note that fuel is delivered hydraulically to the tops of the cylinders. (Søren Lund Hviid)

The 120-metre-long propeller shaft of the **Emma Mærsk**, capable of delivering over 100,000bhp to the propeller. (Søren Lund Hviid)

The bridge on the **Emma Mærsk** is 50 metres wide. Throughout, the vessel contains a very great deal of automation and sophisticated monitoring equipment. (Søren Lund Hviid)

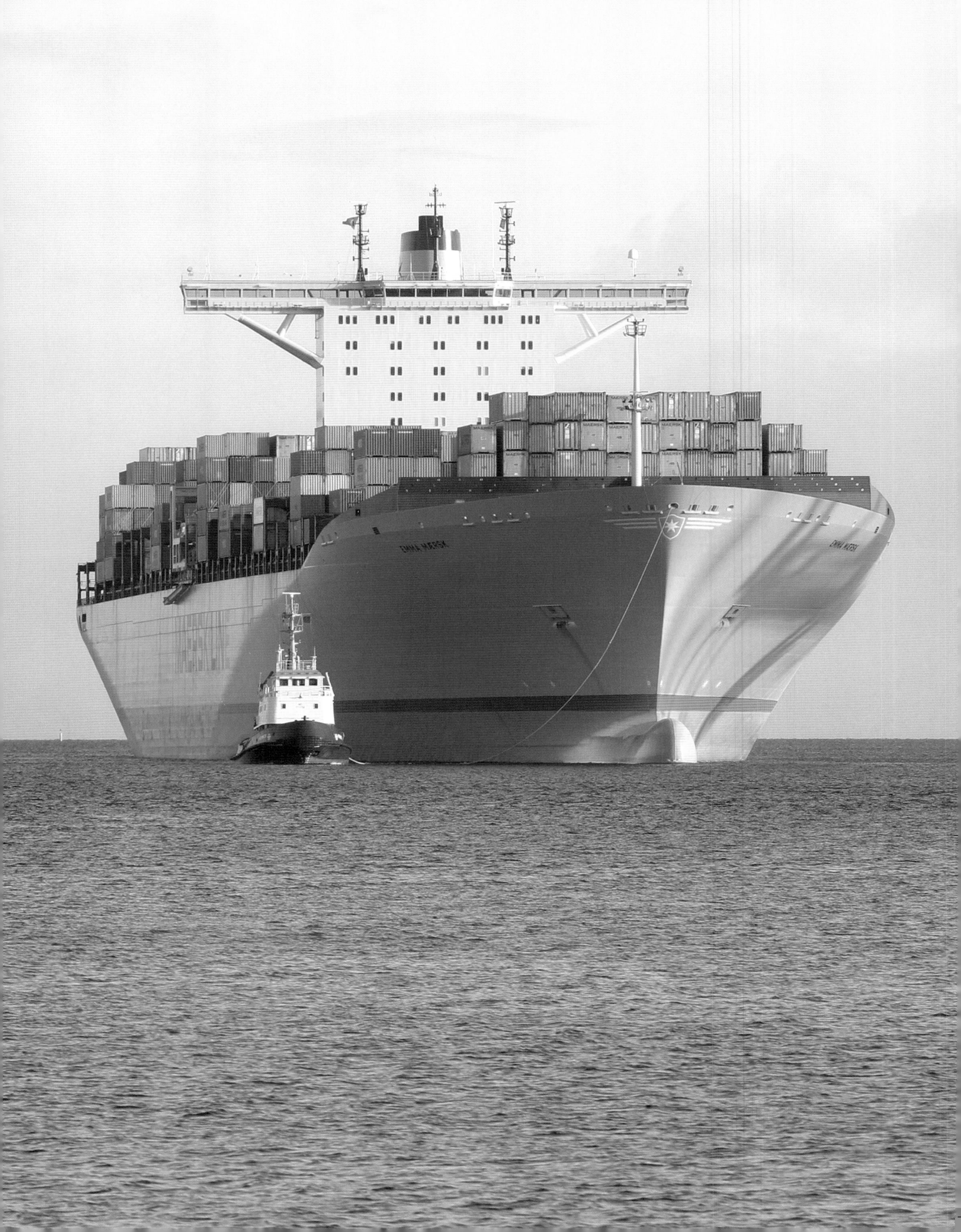

superstructure. On existing ships, fatigue cracks have often been found in these areas. No consistent mathematical procedures existed for predicting torsional stresses on flexible hulls.

A third serious wave-induced effect on the fatigue strength of flexible ship hulls is *springing*, or the continuous excitation of the lowest hull girder's natural frequencies due to the high-frequency components in the wave spectrum and due to non-linear excitation effects. On ultra-large container ships, springing can cause structural hull girder vibrations in moderate seas with stress magnitudes which can cause significant fatigue damage to the hull within only a couple of years of operation. Again, no reliable

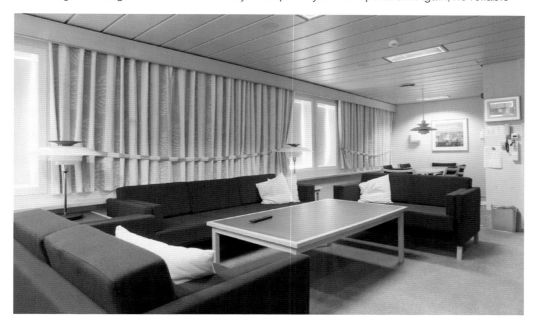

Opposite: The **Emma Mærsk** arriving at Århus. (Søren Lund Hviid)

Above: Like a gigantic steel sculpture, the **Emma Mærsk**'s superstructure towers above the hatches. (Søren Lund Hviid)

Left: A comfortably-appointed saloon on the **Emma Mærsk**. (Søren Lund Hviid)

procedure existed to predict these springing loads on large ships.

To reduce the resistance and to increase the deck area, the hull forms of large container ships are unique with excessive bow flare and stern overhang. The result is that in harsh weather conditions slamming loads can potentially threaten the integrity of the ship's hull. Slamming loads cause large local impact forces on the hull which may dent the plating and buckle internal frames. A second significant effect of slamming is transient vibration of the entire hull. This slam-induced hull girder vibration is called *whipping.* The combination of the still water loads, and the wave-induced loads on the hull and the hull girder vibration response to bow or stern slamming impact can induce bending moments and shear forces which may cause hull collapse.'[374]

The remedies to these problems were achieved by further developing the structural solutions used in earlier large Maersk Line vessels. To prevent torsional forces deflecting the hull beyond acceptable limits, it would be necessary to locate the superstructure amidships so as to provide the maximum strength to brace the hull – but this had implications for the placement of the engine room. One option was to locate this and the exhaust uptakes towards the stern while placing the main superstructure further forward. For operational reasons, this idea of reverting to two superstructures – as seen on Sea-Land's first generation of purpose-built container ships of the early 1960s – was rejected in favour of a midships engine room with the accommodation and navigation bridge above. Maersk Line at that time did not want the holds split into three sections as it felt this would not give an even distribution of cranes when loading and unloading, leading to one section of the ship being completed sooner than the others. Consequently, the longest propeller shaft ever designed – 120 metres – was needed to span the gap between the engine and the ship's stern. Matters of strength and integrity aside, a midships superstructure would give navigating officers a clear view ahead and all the crew would have a direct link by elevator to the engine room, many decks below.

For Peter Tang-Jensen's design team at Odense-Lindø, the project produced further severe challenges. Firstly, the question of how big a single-screw ship one could build was contingent upon recent developments in diesel engine and propeller technology – a problem that Tang-Jensen's colleague, Kjell Harr, was set to analyse.[375] Fortunately, in anticipation of a limited number of very large container ships being developed by various shipyards and operators, Wärtsilä-Sulzer had in the interim developed a new 14-cylinder engine based on its existing largest 12-cylinder design and generating a staggering 108,080 bhp (80,080 kW). With a cylinder bore of 96 cm, this was the largest diesel engine ever produced and Doosan in South Korea manufactured it under licence. To attain a top speed of 26 knots, the engine needed to be coupled to the biggest propeller yet made, weighing 130gt and able to absorb 90 mW of power. (This was cast in Mecklenburg in Germany and the manufacturer had to fell rows of trees along the avenue outside the factory in order to enable it to be transported past.) Such an untried combination risked giving rise to unexpected vibration problems which required analysis so that they could be designed out prior to construction commencing.[376]

A waste heat recovery system was again specified to generate electricity from hot exhaust gases to provide 8 megawatts of power, thus regaining ten per cent of the engine's output. This electricity is used partly to power additional electric motors attached to the propeller shaft, partly to feed onboard equipment and partly to power the refrigeration plants of the 1,000 reefer containers E-class vessels can carry. In addition, there are five MaK auxiliary engines, offering significant redundancy to maintain power supply to the refrigeration plants even in the event of a breakdown of the main engine. Additionally, a pair of lateral-thrust propellers was installed in the bow to ease manoeuvrability when in port, each giving 25 tons of thrust.

In terms of size, the only other container ships in existence comparable to the E-class are Mediterranean Shipping Company's subsequent class of no fewer than 26 owned and chartered 135,000gt, 14,000 TEU vessels built by Samsung and Daewoo in South Korea. These represent an alternative design approach with the engine room (containing a 12-cylinder, 98,280 bhp MAN-B&W diesel) and funnel placed aft of amidships and a separate forward-located superstructure and wheelhouse. With less onboard automation than Maersk Line's E-class, these vessels are, however, less efficient in terms of the manpower required for day-to-day operation as each carries a crew of 30 (being Liberian-registered, the wage cost is significantly lower than on Danish-flagged tonnage). On the other hand, the 'two island' design offers certain advantages in terms of strength, weight saving, rigidity and also ease of construction. As the hull beneath the superstructure on Maersk Line's E-class is made of very thick steel, it is heavy and the plates proved difficult to weld together. On MSC's design, these problems were avoided. Otherwise, the only real disadvantage for the E-class was the additional cost of a long propeller shaft.[377] So ubiquitous has the MSC design proven, however, that Maersk Line chartered several vessels of a similar type from the German Rickmers Reederei to supplement its existing fleet in Europe-Far East service.

For Odense Staalskibsværft's design staff, a further winning argument in favour of locating the superstructure amidships was that the building dock, which had been constructed in the 1960s to assemble oil tankers, was not deep enough to float out such large container ships easily unless the hull was in perfect balance when in light (ie unloaded) condition. Empty oil tankers weigh much less than container ships as their structural steelwork is lighter and is more evenly distributed throughout their hulls. Container ships, on the other hand, have a much greater empty weight in relation to their buoyancy and so, had the building dock at Odense been designed for their construction rather than tankers, it would have been deeper. With the engine and superstructure amidships, it would be possible to float out the E-class hulls undamaged, but with very little draft beneath the keel.[378]

Following a year of analysis carried out in conjunction with the American Bureau of Shipping to overcome potential structural and propulsive problems, construction of the first E-class vessel, the *Emma Mærsk*, commenced at the end of 2004, thereafter taking a year-and-a-half to complete. From bridge to keel, the E-class is 20 decks high – the height of one of the larger

In Denmark, interest in Maersk Line's giant container ships was considerable and so, whenever one was completed, large numbers of onlookers came to observe the departure from Lindø. Here, the *Elly Mærsk* passes through Odense Fjord on 27 August 2007, assisted by numerous tugs. (Thomas Nørgaard Olesen)

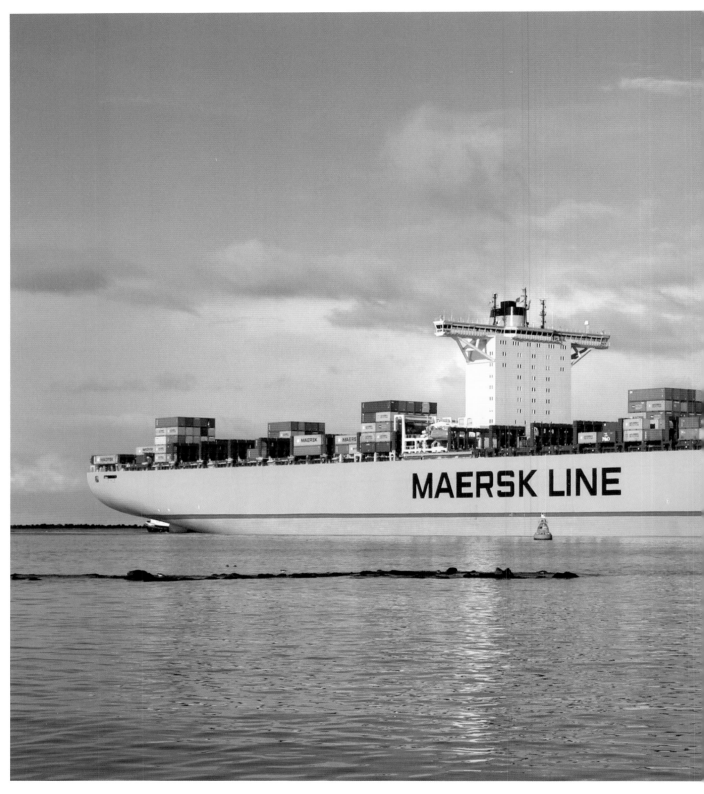

The newly-delivered **Eleonora Mærsk**'s immaculate blue hull and cream superstructure make a beautiful reflection. (Dick Muijs)

urban high-rise blocks of flats – and from wing to wing their navigation bridges are 56 metres wide. Yet, notwithstanding such great dimensions, they have the potential to be operated by a crew totalling just 13 (although accommodation is actually provided for up to 30 to ensure a reasonable safety margin and so that extra maintenance staff can travel, carrying out repairs *en route*). As with the earlier G-class, an ICS system is installed, consisting of 8,000 sensors connected to a central computer to monitor nearly every aspect of the ship's performance, enabling officers on the bridge, in the engine control room – and even via computers in their

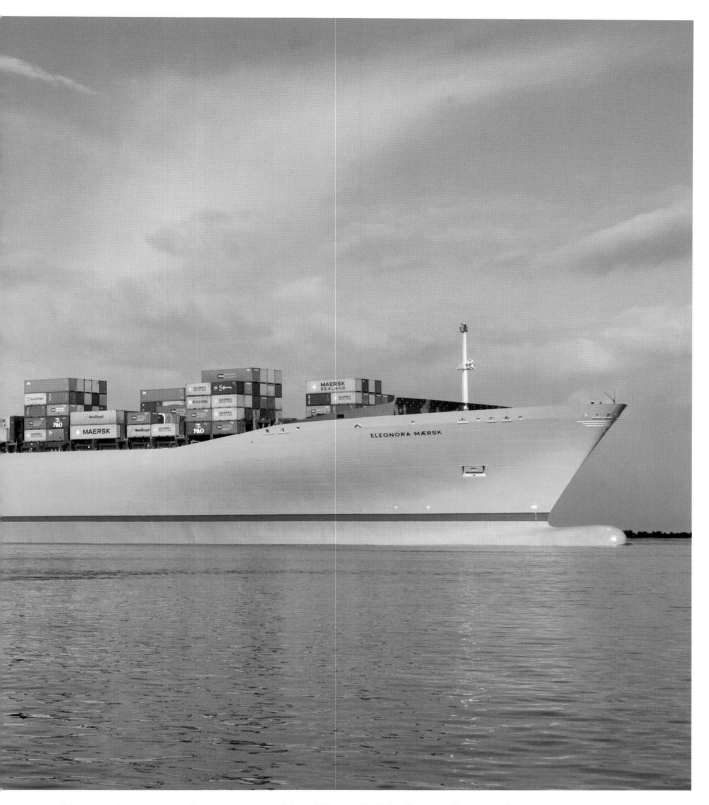

cabins – to keep a remote eye on everything. When off duty, the small crew enjoys very spacious and well-appointed accommodation including a cinema, a fitness room and a computer café.

The *Emma Mærsk* was delivered from Odense Staalskibsværft in August 2006, only slightly delayed by a fire caused by welding sparks severely damaging her superstructure. Fortunately, the superstructure of the next vessel in the series was already well advanced and so this was used instead on the *Emma Mærsk*, meaning that her completion was delayed by only seven weeks. Even her paint was state-of-the-art, her hull below the waterline being coated in an environmentally-friendly silicone finish, helping to reduce water resistance and reducing her fuel consumption by an expected 1,200 tons per annum.[379]

When the *Emma Mærsk* sailed from Odense Lindø on the evening of 16 August, an estimated 10,000 spectators turned out to watch her leave.[380] Three months later, she was followed by the *Estelle Mærsk*, with the *Eleonora Mærsk* being completed in January 2007 and the remainder of the class – consisting of the *Ebba Mærsk*, *Evelyn Mærsk*, *Edith Mærsk* and *Eugen Mærsk* – following at approximately three-monthly intervals. To have built such vast and complex vessels so quickly speaks volumes for Odense Staalskibsværft's efficiency.

Meanwhile, further orders for somewhat smaller new container ships for A.P. Møller-Maersk's British and Singaporean container ship-operating subsidiaries were placed. The Maersk Company Ltd, registered in London and managing the former P&O Nedlloyd fleet, was given a class of eight very speedy 29-knot B-class container ships, built by the Volkswerft GmbH in Stralsund, Germany. Measuring 48,853gt and with a capacity of only 4,504 TEU to offset the cost of their 68,640 kW 12-cylinder Wärtsilä-Sulzer engines, these vessels were obviously more costly to operate than the big G- and E-classes. They entered service in 2006-07 on the original Maersk Line route from the US East Coast via the Panama Canal to South East Asia. Their tremendous speed enabled them to make the voyage within only a week, addressing the 'just in time' needs of Maersk Line's highest-value customers. In a period of strong economic growth, there was felt to be a market for such vessels as enough clients were willing to pay a premium to have stock delivered speedily. (This also saved them the cost of storing extra inventory in case of shipping delays.) These vessels are distinguished by their rectilinear aft profiles, their hulls widening quickly from the waterline at the stern to provide extra buoyancy and counteract the tendency to submerge more deeply at high speed, increasing resistance and also fuel costs. (In January 2007, Maersk Line also announced a new 21-day non-stop express service from China to Europe, using slightly slower standard tonnage.)

To many observers, the B-class were the ultimate container ships but, alas, they quickly became victims of the sudden and deep 2008-2010 global recession. When Maersk Line introduced a policy of 'slow-steaming' to offset increased fuel costs for the majority of their fleet, several of the greedy B-series were taken out of service and temporarily laid up. Soon, only four of the type remained in Maersk Line service – the *Maersk Baltimore*, *Maersk Batam*, *Maersk Brownsville* and *Maersk Buffalo* – while the other four – *Maersk Beaumont*, *Maersk Bentonville*, *Maersk Boston* and *Maersk Brooklyn* – were chartered to other operators.

Below right: The towering mass of the **Ebba Mærsk**. (Zee-photo)

Opposite top: A long series of very large container ships was built in South Korea by Hyundai for a variety of shipping companies, including Rickmers of Hamburg, which chartered four examples to Maersk Line, including the 141,716gt **Maersk Elba**. With a length of 366 metres and 48 metres in width, she is 30 metres shorter and 8 metres narrower than the E-class. (Jens Grabbe)

Opposite bottom: The **Emma Mærsk**'s superstructure is so tall that her funnel has vanished between the container cranes. (Olaf Schmidt)

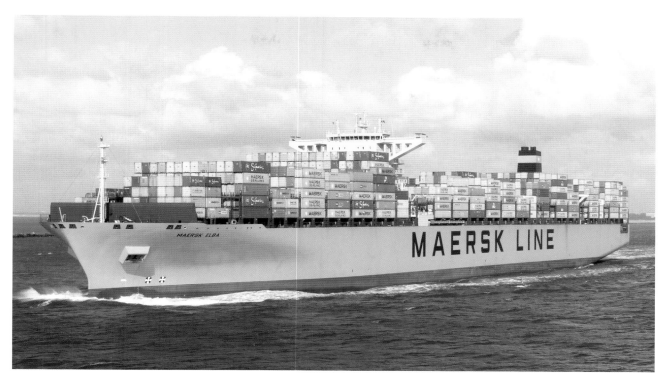

While these prestigious vessels were under construction, Maersk Line placed further orders with the Hanjin, Hyundai and Samsung shipyards in South Korea for even larger numbers of post-Panamax and intermediate-sized container ships for American, British and Singaporean subsidiaries. Hitherto, A.P. Møller-Maersk had built its largest container ships only at the Odense Staalskibsværft for two key reasons. Firstly, the yard had unique expertise accumulated over many years and had developed hull designs, structural solutions and onboard software which arguably had helped to give Maersk Line a commercial advantage and market leadership over its competitors. Secondly, Mærsk Mc-Kinney Møller strongly

The B-class, built by Volkswerft in Straslund, are among the world's fastest merchant ships, but the recession which began in August 2008 made them uneconomic. Here, the **Maersk Baltimore** is shown. (Frans Sanderse)

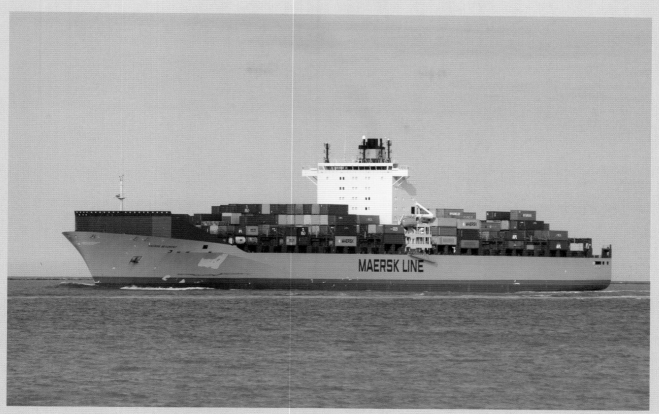

Above: The **Maersk Beaumont** which, like her sisters, can operate at over 30 knots; her wide stern configuration at the waterline prevents the hull from being sucked downwards when operating at high speed. (Olaf Schmidt)

Below: The **Maersk Baltimore**, operating under the shortened charter name **Baltimore**. (Jens Grabbe)

Above: The interiors of the Lindø-built container ships were outfitted with Danish designer furniture and lighting, as shown on the *Margrethe Mærsk*. (Søren Lund Hviid)

Below: Royal portraits survey the dining saloon on the *Margrethe Mærsk*. (Søren Lund Hviid)

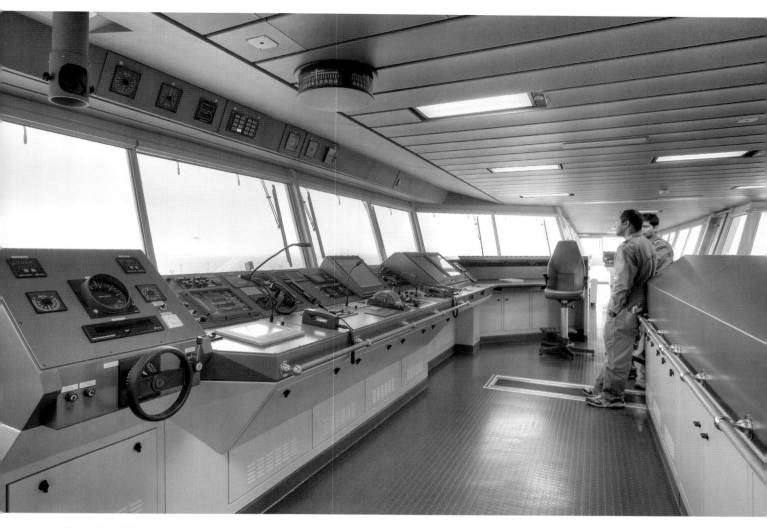

The bridge on the
Margrethe Mærsk.
(Søren Lund Hviid)

believed that Danish business should show loyalty to Denmark, even when this was the more costly option. Further high-profile examples of what might be termed 'benevolent capitalism' included financing the construction in Denmark of educational facilities, the restoration of historic artefacts such as the frigate *Jylland* and, most famously, the provision of a new opera house facing Copenhagen Harbour. Building large ships in Denmark and employing Danish seafarers could be viewed as part of this policy. Following Møller's retirement, A.P. Møller-Maersk inevitably has become more like a normal global conglomerate, its senior management seeking to find the most economically advantageous solutions to the Company's development so as to retain a pre-eminent position in tough markets.

With the growing importance of the South East Asian countries to Maersk Line's operations and the obvious further advantage of generally lower labour rates there, it was decided in 2009 that no more Maersk Line ships would be built in Denmark. The final container ships to be constructed at Odense Staalskibsværft were a new M-class, measuring 98,268gt and able to carry 9,038 TEU. As with other recent newbuildings from the yard, each of these was fitted with a 12-cylinder Wärtsilä-Sulzer diesel, generating 68,640 kW and giving a top speed of 25 knots. The *Margrethe Mærsk*, *Marchen Mærsk*, *Maren Mærsk*, *Mette Mærsk*, *Marit Mærsk* and *Mathilde Mærsk* were completed between March 2008 and March 2009. Thereafter, the yard built six Cape-size bulk carriers, eight ro-ro freight ferries and three frigates for the Danish Royal Navy. All the large building docks at Lindø were subsequently taken over by a ship repair company from Fredericia and renamed Fayard, refitting vessels of all kinds. The *Mathilde Mærsk* was, therefore, the final liner ever to be built in Denmark.[381] In 2005, Maersk Ship Design was moved to a new office in Copenhagen and thereafter was reorganised as Maersk Maritime Technology.

The **Maren Mærsk** is manoeuvred
out of Odense Fjord on 14 July 2008.
(Thomas Nørgaard Olesen)

The brand new **Maren Mærsk** at Århus at the commencement of her
career. After leaving Lindø, Århus was frequently used as the base
from which sea trials were conducted. (Thomas Nørgaard Olesen)

Chapter 15

Maersk Line today and tomorrow

By 2008, to a large extent thanks to former Managing Director Jess Søderberg's expansion strategy, A.P. Møller-Maersk had grown ten-fold in only a decade and was now a very large global company with an annual turnover of around 300 billion kroner, approximately 100,000 employees and billions of investment in various ongoing projects around the world. In light of the enormous changes, it was necessary to recruit a new Managing Director of exceptional ability who was already known and respected in business and finance arenas around the world. In a Danish context, there were only a small number of businesses of a scale and complexity even remotely comparable with A.P. Møller-Maersk – and one of these was the drinks conglomerate Carlsberg. Its Managing Director, Nils Smedegaard Andersen (born 1958), already had a thorough knowledge of operating a large corporate group and, as he had served since 2005 on A.P. Møller-Maersk's Board of Directors, he was also well acquainted with the Group's prime activities – transport, retailing and oil production. At Carlsberg, Andersen had gained a reputation for clear strategic thinking to eliminate waste and improve efficiency and for identifying what he termed 'must-win battles.' Having a background in brewing, a more directly consumer-orientated industry than the majority of A.P. Møller-Maersk's subsidiaries, he strongly believed that customers were most important and, therefore, the entire corporate structure should be orientated towards ensuring their satisfaction. Andersen also was known for his willingness to explain his thinking to journalists – something hitherto virtually unknown, indeed completely taboo, at A.P. Møller-Maersk.[382]

Andersen's appointment as A.P. Møller-Maersk's Managing Director on 5 November 2007 took place at a very challenging time between Maersk Line's IT *débacle* and the global economic crisis which followed in the autumn of 2008. Apart from the problematic new IT system, which caused a great deal of expensive and time-consuming manual work to correct mistakes, the Maersk Line organisation was found to be too big for the amount of containers requiring transporting (the fourth largest container shipping company, Hapag-Lloyd, moved 25 per cent more containers per worker than Maersk Line). As Maersk Line had grown so quickly, there had been insufficient time to rethink the Company's corporate structure which, Andersen argued, had become too centralised and bureaucratic; this negated possibilities for local decision-making and quick action. There was, therefore, considerable potential for cost savings.

In November 2007, Eivind Kolding was appointed Managing Director of Maersk Line with a mandate from Andersen to sort out the Company's problems. Born in 1959, Kolding was a lawyer by training. In 1996, he was appointed as Managing Director of Maersk Hong Kong and two years thereafter, he became the A.P. Møller Group's Chief Financial Officer. One month after becoming Managing Director of Maersk Line, Kolding sent a letter to this subordinate managers in which he pointed out that half of the containers being shipped were arriving at their destinations a day late and 20 per cent of invoices were incorrect. If this situation was not sorted out quickly, Maersk Line's reputation would be severely damaged, market share would be lost, routes closed down and there would be no money to invest in new tonnage.[383] Therefore, priority was given to addressing reliability issues, but a more fundamental transformation of Maersk Line's managerial and operational structures was also planned for implementation in the medium term.

For the 2007 financial year, Maersk Line made a 5 billion dollar pre-tax profit but, following the onset of the global economic crisis, A.P. Møller-Maersk's annual report for 2009 showed an overall loss of 2.1 billion kroner across all of the Group's activities. Maersk Line carried 14 per cent fewer containers and at freight rates on average 24 per cent lower than in the previous year.[384] Eivind Kolding observed that freight rates were so low that, in some instances, a loss of up to 1,000 dollars was being recorded on each container transported. At the same time, Maersk Line's Swiss- and French-owned rivals Mediterranean Shipping Company and CMA-CGM were continuing to grow quickly, heaping on further pressure. In addition, Asian-owned container operators on the cross-Pacific routes, such as APL (the former American President Lines, nowadays owned by Neptune Orient Line in Singapore), had lower crewing costs than Maersk Line. Meanwhile, global oil prices had dropped by 54 per cent, meaning that the Group's Oil and Gas Division was also negatively affected by what were described as extraordinary trading conditions.[385]

Since the mid-1970s, Maersk Line's volume of containers shipped had grown at roughly ten per cent per annum and, hitherto, the poorest year had been 1982 when only 4.6 per cent growth was recorded – but 2009 was the first when the market had actually contracted. In a continuation of Nils Smedegaard Andersen's strategy at Carlsberg, Maersk Line's aim was no longer primarily to be the world's largest container ship operator and therefore the most profitable, as had been Jess Søderberg's policy, but instead to become the most profitable and, consequently, remain the largest.

In the *Financial Times* in May 2008, Andersen announced that Maersk Line's key support services would be kept 'in house' as much as possible, rather than being franchised out to external providers – a situation which led to the Company's recent IT fiasco. The previous vertical integration of Maersk Line's operations – which had seen ships built at Odense Staalskibsværft carrying Maersk Line's own containers between A.P. Møller-Maersk-owned terminals – would also be dismantled and each subsidiary would instead be required to compete in more open internal and external markets, all the better to remain competitive. Therefore, Maersk Logistics and APM Terminals would henceforth be expected significantly to increase numbers of containers handled for operators other than Maersk Line if sufficiently lucrative deals could be struck and if there were enough space to do so.[386] In order to distance Maersk Logistics' brand from Maersk Line, it was subsequently renamed Damco.

Andersen observed that significant changes to A.P. Møller-Maersk's centralised corporate structure were required as he believed that more agile and reflexive management had the potential to save one billion dollars annually.[387] Prior to the Group's vast expansion during the Søderberg years, it had been managed much like any large family-owned shipping company with very few decisions by-passing the top management layer in Copenhagen. In future, however, operational decision-making would increasingly be handed over to the various constituent business units and junior management would be given clearer responsibilities and targets to be achieved. As Andersen explained: 'Headquarters concentrates on setting overall performance targets and supporting the business units… so we can spend more time on real business issues instead of getting caught up in internal paperwork.'[388]

Rather than cutting back on its route network, however, Maersk Line instead applied what might be termed 'lean management thinking' to reduce operational costs while increasing reliability. In the spring of 2008, Eivind Kolding introduced a three-year-long improvement strategy called 'StreamLINE' – one early result of which was the redundancy of 3,000 middle managers (accounting for nearly one-eighth of Maersk Line's total workforce).[389] This slashing of bureaucracy was highly controversial and, as shown in a recent book by the shipping journalist Lars Jensen entitled 'The Culture Shock at Maersk

As an initial response to the 2008 recession, Maersk Line put excess tonnage into lay-up. Five vessels were mothballed on the Firth of Clyde, including the **Maersk Maryland** and the **Maersk Maine**, which were berthed at Greenock. Built in 1991-2 by Hyundai, they were subsequently taken over by MSC and returned to service. (Bruce Peter)

Line,' considerable resistance was encountered from long-serving employees and some senior managers.[390] Yet, once StreamLINE was fully implemented, operational performance did indeed improve. Maersk Line was restructured as a container ship operator with land-based services given over to Maersk Logistics/Damco, a separate subsidiary of A.P. Møller-Maersk, whose task it was to ensure customer satisfaction and to adapt nimbly to the characteristics of each local market and client base.

Ten container ships (including several of the fuel-hungry B-class) were taken out of service and temporarily laid up, removing 42,000 TEU of container capacity from the Maersk Line network. 'StreamLINE' was a four-phase strategy: the first priority was called the 'Global Network Design Leap,' whereby the efficiency of ship utilisation was optimised to ensure that the most appropriate tonnage was used on each route and that loadings were high; this initiative apparently achieved an 11 per cent cost reduction.[391] The ensuing 'Sales Traction Leap,' 'Bunker Leap' and 'Yield Leap' respectively aimed to increase market share through better attention to customers' needs, save fuel costs and provide customers with more accurate prices and much simpler contracts. As Maersk Line's largest single overhead was its 35 billion kroner fuel bill, a slow-steaming initiative was introduced whereby each ship's speed was reduced by a couple of knots and, on key longer routes, an extra ship was added to maintain a regular schedule of departures. ('Slow steaming' is an intriguingly anachronistic expression, dating from previous economic downturns when a majority of ships were indeed steam-powered.)

By the time that A.P. Møller-Maersk's half-yearly report was published in August 2009, Nils Smedegaard Andersen could report to shareholders that, whereas one year previously Maersk Line's costs to ship a container were on average 200 dollars poorer than its nearest competitors, now they were 100 dollars better. Reliability had also improved, but Eivind Kolding believed that further improvements could be made:

> 'We are already the most reliable in the industry… But being ranked as leader with a schedule reliability performance of 70 per cent highlights the unsophisticated nature of the industry. In the future, we are aiming for a game-changing 95 per cent on-time delivery performance. Such a dramatic increase in reliability would allow our customers significantly to reduce their inventory buffer and would increase our lead over our competitors.'[392]

In future, South East Asia would become a most important hub for Maersk Line's activities – including the supply of seafarers. The inter-Asian container shipping market was growing quickly and Maersk was determined to be a significant player. To achieve this aim, in 2009 its Asian feeder subsidiary MCC Transport (Mercantile Cargo Consolidators) – at that time operating around 40 chartered vessels – became responsible for all regional container services in Asian waters; presently, its fleet is approximately sixty-strong. Originally purchased in 1993 with the East Asiatic Company's liner services, it is one of a number of wholly-owned sub-brands developed by Maersk Line in recent years to serve specific markets. Another is Seago Line, running feeder container ships in the Baltic, North Sea and Mediterranean areas. Early in 2014, the reintroduction of the Sealand brand for North American coastal services was announced.

To reduce exposure to market fluctuations – always a risk in liner shipping – Maersk Line henceforth would primarily concentrate on owning and operating large 'economy of scale' container ships deployed on primary routes between Europe, South East Asia and the USA. A greater proportion of chartered tonnage would maintain secondary routes and feeder services. Chartering vessels helps to reduce risk as their capital costs are spread amongst a number of owners and certain types of charter contract can be rescinded whenever there is a drop in trade. Already, a large proportion of the MCC Transport and Seago Line fleets consists of chartered tonnage.

As in the past, ongoing research and development would be needed to enable Mærsk's various ship-owning divisions to remain competitive. In line with Nils Smedegaard Andersen's policy of devolving management from the corporate centre

A.P. Mølller-Maersk's CEO, Nils Smedegaard Andersen, since December 2007 ultimately responsible for all of the Group's activities, including Maersk Line. (A.P. Møller-Maersk)

Eivind Kolding, CEO of Maersk Line until February 2012. (A.P. Møller-Maersk)

Søren Schou, the current CEO of Maersk Line. (A.P. Møller-Maersk)

to subsidiaries, day-to-day responsibility for the technical management of ships was given to each business unit. The hitherto extensive Technical Organization was thereby slimmed down to focus instead on advanced project work. Restyled as Maersk Maritime Technology, henceforth, it would concentrate on gathering and making use of know-how to optimize technical operations, to develop new solutions to enhance forthcoming generations of vessels and to devise significant modifications for existing ones. While it was pragmatic for mundane technical matters to be shifted to the divisions, it was nonetheless felt necessary to retain a central organisation of sufficient size and influence to attract the most talented and ambitious naval architects and research engineers to work there.

Bo Cerup-Simonsen was appointed as Vice President, Head of Maersk Maritime Technology in August 2008 at the precise moment when the shipping industry was plunged into recession. As with many of his predecessors and colleagues at A.P. Møller-Maersk, he was a graduate of the Technical University of Denmark, where he first was employed as an Associate Professor in Naval Architecture and Offshore Engineering. Subsequently, he worked in Oslo for the classification society Det Norske Veritas as its Head of Maritime Technology Consultancy. There, he was responsible for a large number of ship technology projects, latterly focusing increasingly on fuel efficiency in design and operation which would obviously also later become a key area for MMT. An important initiative in MMT, working in close collaboration with Maersk Line and Maersk Tankers, was further to develop Maersk's performance management system whereby the energy consumption and operating conditions of more than 800 Maersk Line and Maersk Tanker ships are constantly monitored, enabling shipboard and shore-based staff to keep an eye on the performance of the entire fleet and introducing an element of competition between crews to maximise energy efficiency while maintaining schedule. Such monitoring additionally generates a great deal of useful data which can be analysed and applied when designing new ships or converting existing ones.

Cerup-Simonsen sees innovation happening gradually in all areas of ship design, construction and operation. He describes Maersk Maritime Technology as having a strategic overview of emerging techniques and practices coupled with a deep knowledge of Maersk's ships and operations. Thus, Maersk benefits commercially from being able to apply the most advanced and appropriate ship technology solutions for its fleets and infrastructure. This can involve the development and procurement of better engines, propellers, pumps, pipes, anti-fouling paint, emission-cleaning technologies and new fuel types. Headquartered in Copenhagen's

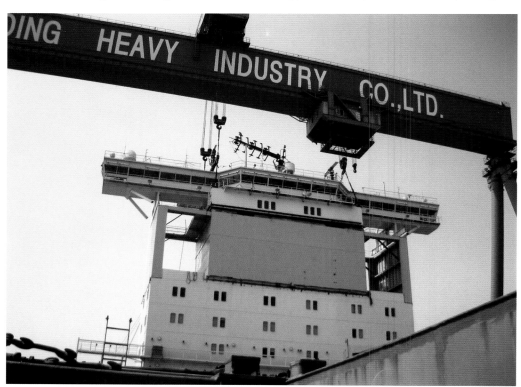

Raising the wheelhouse on an S-class container ship. (A.P. Møller-Maersk)

Christianshavn area, Maersk Maritime Technology has approximately 130 employees, many of whom are stationed in site offices at shipyards where they supervise newbuilding and conversion projects, as well as in subsidiary offices located in Singapore and Mumbai. Cerup-Simonsen points out that some synergies between Maersk's divisions can be identified and exploited; certain tankers and container ships use the same engine type, for example, and so data gleaned from Maersk Tankers has the potential to inform technical decisions affecting Maersk Line. The management of newbuilding projects is a particularly good example of how learning from one experience can assist subsequent projects for other divisions.[393]

Only months before the August 2008 downturn and Cerup-Simonsen's appointment to Maersk Maritime Technology, Maersk Line placed orders for two new series of container ships with South Korean shipyards. One class consists of sixteen 7,450 TEU vessels built by Daewoo (with *Maersk Lima*, registered in Singapore, as the lead ship). The other class is of twenty-two 4,500 TEU ships from Hyundai (with *Maersk Conakry*, likewise registered in Singapore, as the initial vessel). These new ships were designed with the maximum possible hull dimensions to fit harbours respectively on routes from South America to Asia and from West Africa to Asia. Thus, the classes were known as 'SAMMAX' (South America Max) and 'WAFMAX' (West Africa Max). Their construction for these trades shows Maersk Line's emerging focus beyond areas where there is already significant growth – such as the so-called BRIC-nations (Brazil, Russia, India and China) – to invest in up-to-date tonnage for emerging markets with untapped potential, such as Africa.

The SAMMAX and WAFMAX container ships were designed according to pre-recession speed and fuel economy parameters and, as contracts for their construction were signed in the summer of 2008, little could be done to optimise them for slow steaming at around 18 knots, as opposed to their intended 21 and 23 knot respective speeds. Nonetheless, the shape of the bulbous bow was reconfigured and under-rating of engines gave some fuel efficiency gains.[394]

Next, Maersk Line re-established its tradition of optimising the capacity of existing vessels through rebuilding work. The new enlargement programme, launched in 2011, was referred to in internal documents as 'Capacity Boost'. One of the first manifestations of 'Capacity Boost' was the 'Bridge Elevation Project,' whereby 16 Lindø-built post-Panamax container ships had their navigation bridges raised by three decks, making it possible to stack an extra 1,418 TEU on each

The ***Maersk Lima***, built by DSME at Geoje and delivered in the spring of 2011, has a capacity of 7,450 TEU. Named after the capital of Peru, her nomenclature signals Maersk Line's focus on South America as an important emerging market. (A.P. Møller-Maersk)

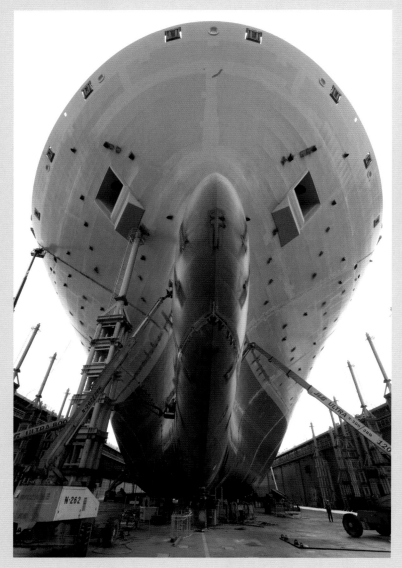

Left: The bow configuration of a Triple-E class container ship, shown during construction at the DSME shipyard at Okpo in South Korea. (Søren Lund Hviid)

Below left: The view from the bridge of the **Mærsk Mc-Kinney Møller** as she nears completion with sister ships **Majestic Mærsk** and **Mary Mærsk** under construction to the left. (Søren Lund Hviid)

Opposite: The hull and superstructure of a Triple-E class container ship at DSME in South Korea. (Søren Lund Hviid)

The *Mærsk Mc-Kinney Møller* passes beneath the Great Belt Bridge in August 2013 at the end of her successful maiden voyage to Europe. (Søren Lund Hviid)

ship's deck while still retaining a clear view ahead from the bridge. The rebuilding of these vessels took place in 2011-2012 at the Bei Hai shipyard in Quingdao, China. Altogether, the 'Bridge Elevation Project' increased the Maersk Line fleet's capacity by 20,000 TEU.

For its next major project for Maersk Line, Maersk Maritime Technology was able to work from scratch. As part of its ongoing fleet development programme, Maersk Line needed up to 20 new super-container ships for Asia-Europe service. These were to be known as the 'Triple-E class,' the three 'E's standing for Energy efficiency, Environmental performance and Economy of scale.

While Bo Cerup-Simonsen and his colleagues at Maersk Maritime Technology instigated technical aspects of the Triple-E project's development, from a business perspective Michael Heimann, Maersk Line's Senior Sales & Purchase Portfolio Manager, was also a significant figure. An economics graduate of Copenhagen University, from 2008 onwards Heimann bought and sold ships for Maersk Line before joining the Triple-E project in 2010. He observes that, when the recession began, some of Maersk Line's competitors were in a worse situation and so there was perhaps an opportunity to buy large container ships of recent construction on the second-hand market. One problem was that, as young vessels had been built when the market was at its peak, their book values were too high while another was that all had been designed for pre-2008 conditions, emphasising high speed. Instead of buying over-valued and only partially suitable vessels such as these, it would surely be better to build anew and with a particular focus on fuel economy. Because bunkers nowadays represent more than half the cost of running a ship, by investing more to increase its efficiency one could significantly reduce its operational cost.[395] Although various Asian shipyards market so-called Eco-designs, none was in the size category Maersk Line required and, besides, as the world's leading liner operator and with the reputation and resources to carry out research, it was decided instead to attempt to devise the most energy-efficient container ship achievable within sound commercial parameters.

Heimann used a 'Total Cost of Ownership' (TCO) model when carrying out financial evaluations. Typically, a large container ship has a 20-year write-down period. As experience demonstrated that it was difficult or impossible to bet on market conditions over such a lengthy timeframe, a more expensive ship type would need to pay back the additional investment involved during its first couple of years in operation. As Heimann points out, 'the real risk is that the future will be different from all predictions.'[396] Yet, four years after the pioneer E-class *Emma Mærsk* entered service, the type remained the most fuel-efficient in Maersk Line's fleet. In comparison, eight slightly smaller vessels built by Hyundai and chartered from Rickmers of the kind also operated by MSC and others were somewhat inferior in this regard.[397] Thus, as Heimann observes, 'getting the right ship for a particular trade is more important than getting the cheapest ship.' He uses the analogy of buying a domestic freezer, a type of household appliance rated A to D with regard to energy efficiency, the D-rated example initially being the cheapest but invariably the most expensive to run over a lifetime.[398] Each Triple-E class is rumoured to cost approximately 185 million dollars, whereas a standard mass-produced container ship of similar capacity built in South Korea typically costs between 140 and 160 million dollars.[399]

The design and procurement processes for the Triple-E class began in the spring of 2010 and, as they progressed, fundamental changes in design thinking and practice were instituted. Typically, standard merchant ships of the types built in South East Asia are designed primarily to enable shipyards to carry out effective low-cost volume production. Furthermore, their hulls are optimised for the maximum speed specified by the contract, which can be very different from the typical speed at which they operate in everyday service. For example, a container ship may normally sail at 18 knots, but would need the potential to go much faster if it became necessary to meet a time deadline for joining a convoy through the Suez Canal. Bo Cerup-Simonsen observes as a comparator that sports cars, geared for high speed, perform badly in average city traffic – and, equally, ships with hulls and machinery selected to achieve the maximum speed stated in contract documentation have similar problems.[400]

Instead of designing the Triple-E class with the least expensive manufacture and the top speed as governing parameters, it was decided to consider operational cost over the vessels' lifetime – including end-of-life recycling. Achieving this change was easier in theory than in practice because it involved challenging the long-established perspectives and processes of

Opposite top and bottom:
The ***Mærsk Mc-Kinney Møller*** arrives at Århus for the first time. (Bruce Peter)

the shipbuilding industry. Just like shipping itself, large-scale commercial shipbuilding is governed to maximize productivity and speed of throughput. Any new ideas likely to cause bottlenecks in the production process are strongly discouraged.

In 2011, the Technical University of Denmark published research investigating how container ship transport might be environmentally assessed and how the statistics revealed could be used

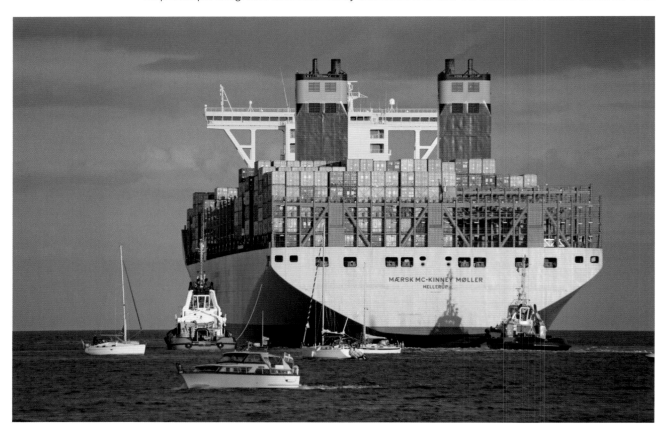

to target further research in the most efficacious way to make such vessels more efficient still. Professor Hans Otto Kristensen was one of the researchers who carried out initial investigations on behalf of the International Maritime Organisation (IMO), leading to the development of an 'Energy Efficiency Design Index.' This gives an overall figure for any large container ship's environmental performance in terms of carbon dioxide output. The findings suggested that, in some cases, this figure could be reduced by up to a quarter through carrying out a number of simple design changes, for example de-rating the main engine, increasing the hull length by 5 per cent, reducing the steel weight by 3 per cent through further structural optimisation and increasing the propeller's efficiency by 5 per cent.[401] Analysis for the Energy Efficiency Design Index was, however, based on ships' published maximum speeds as recorded during their pre-delivery sea trials. Through monitoring its fleet, Maersk Line has gathered a vast amount of data about container ship operation at typical service speeds that is unpublished and therefore unavailable to external researchers, such as Kristensen and his colleagues.

Bo Cerup-Simonsen observes that container ships typically operate at top speed for only a very small percentage of the time (see Figure 1). A fair amount of time is spent 'super slow steaming', for instance, when there is excess time available before the next port, when moving empty containers back to Asia or when navigating through crowded or constricted waters. For the vast majority of time, vessels nowadays operate at between 16 and 18 knots, but until the advent of the Triple-E class none was designed to be most effective in this speed range. As Cerup-Simonsen states, in the Triple-E design 'everything – hull form, engines, propellers – has been selected for the 99 per cent of the time when not sailing at the maximum speed.'[402]

In a diagram relating increasing speed on the X axis to hull resistance and required power on the Y axis, a shipyard will typically prefer a hull form with lowest resistance at the maximum speed when in unloaded (or only partially-loaded) sea trial condition, thereby making it easier to meet contract specifications using the smallest possible engine type (Curve A, Figure 2). Maersk Line, however, actually needed the lowest resistance in the range of most typical operational speed and hull drafts (Curve B). As can be seen, having a seldom-used high top speed could spoil a ship's performance at the condition in which it sepnds the greatest part of its time. Thus, Maersk Maritime Technology's staff worked with their commercial colleagues to develop a matrix for different load and speed conditions, also factoring in the cost of fuel. A difficult decision, however, was to decide what the top speed should be. As we have seen from EAC's unfortunate experience with its frustratingly ponderous LRV ships in the 1970s, betting on slowness can be catastrophic when engaged in the liner trades and so a 23-knot maximum speed was chosen. Bo Cerup-Simonsen states that all merchant ship design should be market-led and that it is Maersk Maritime Technology's job to inform commercial colleagues that 'we have identified twenty-five options and variable parameters for container ships – now we need to find the one that is best for your business.'[403]

Ship design is only one important component in achieving competitive advantage, however, as, once in service, vessels need to be filled and utilised effectively. To produce the ideal outcome from a business perspective, an optimal ship design requires to be complemented by efficient port infrastructure, officers trained to achieve best fuel economy and wider systems comprising

Opposite top: Crowds gather to admire the ***Mærsk Mc-Kinney Møller*** at Århus in August 2013. (Bruce Peter)

Opposite bottom: The ***Mærsk Mc-Kinney Møller*** leaving Århus. (Bruce Peter)

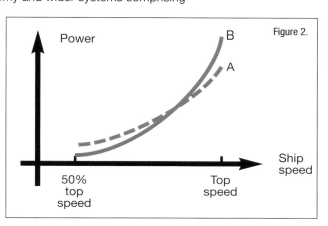

The second of the Triple-E class, the **Majestic Mærsk**, at Langelinie in Copenhagen for her naming ceremony. There, over the course of a week, around 50,000 people visited her. (Bruce Peter)

The ***Seago Istanbul***, formerly the ***Maersk Buffalo***, in the livery of Maersk's subsidiary, Seago Line. She and four of her B-class sisters operate between Northern Europe and Mediterranean ports. (Robert Wisse)

information technology, customer relations, freight forwarding and security. The environment in which the Triple-E class and other super-container ships operate is therefore highly integrated and specialised.

Closely linking technical and commercial research provided a new and, so far as can be ascertained, unprecedented paradigm for procuring a ship. Negotiations then began with various potential builders, the successful candidate being Daewoo Shipbuilding & Marine Engineering Co. (DSME) at Okpo in South Korea. Bo Cerup-Simonsen is generous in his praise for the shipyard and the high quality of its outputs, but he points out that, like many another, its culture is one of procuring raw materials and components at lowest cost, then assembling them as cheaply and quickly as possible. It is a 'well-oiled machine, optimised for production rather than innovation and so disturbing its systems caused several department managers initially to be resistant.'[403] Thus, there was a need to push hard for innovation and flexibility so that modifications could be incorporated into the Triple-E design even once construction of the first vessels had begun so that subsequent examples could incorporate changes in light of experience with the initial ones. Indeed, this requirement for ongoing development work throughout the project was written into the contract – even although the yard understandably would have preferred to build twenty absolutely identical ships.

Maersk Maritime Technology's Senior Lead Specialist in Naval Architecture, Troels Posborg, was a key specialist guiding the Triple-E class project. Prior to joining Maersk Ship Design at Odense Lindø in 1998, Posborg worked in Aalborg Værft's drawing office where, among other diverse projects, he assisted in designing the Carnival cruise ship *Holiday*, the New Zealand train ferry *Arahura*, 'Seajet' catamaran ferries for Mols-Linien plus so-called 'Standardflex' vessels for the Danish Royal Navy. At Maersk Ship Design, he was involved in designing all classes of Odense-built container ships, liquefied natural gas (LNG) tankers, oil supply vessels and roll-on, roll-off freight ferries.

The Triple-E class is a two-island design and this approach was driven by the need to maximise capacity, it being possible to fill the hull midbody with containers rather than this area being blocked by a superstructure, engine room and long propeller shaft tunnel. A further advantage is that the hull is strengthened by two subdivisions instead of only one and, with the engines at the stern, shorter propeller shafts are required, saving weight, space and maintenance costs. Operating at a lower service speed of between 18 and 20 knots to save fuel, the Triple-E class' hull volume is much greater than on the rather fine-lined E-class; indeed, its bow and stern configurations more closely resemble those of recent large cruise ships than any existing Maersk Line container vessels.

As a result of their beamier hull form and split superstructure, each Triple-E class carries 16 per cent more 20-foot containers than an E-class, amounting to 2,700 additional units, giving a published total capacity of 18,000 TEU. Yet, the two classes' hull dimensions are similar, the Triple-E measuring 399.2 x 59 metres while the E-class is 398 x 56.4 metres. Thanks to its slight extra width, the Triple-E class carries 23 rows of containers across its beam, whereas the E-class has only 22. Michael Heimann observes that bigger container ships usually need to be faster to offset longer loading times, but that another solution is to add more cranes at each terminal. The E-class uses four-to-five cranes at once, but the Triple-E needs six-to-seven to load within a similar timeframe and so port facilities owned both by APM Terminals and other operators needed to install additional cranes with sufficient reach to cover the Triple-E class hull.

To reduce bunker costs, it was necessary to find the most efficient means of propulsion and this involved the specification of the newest generation of ultra-long-stroke engines. The benefit of ultra-long-stroke units is that, when coupled to a very large propeller, the combined efficiency of the propulsion system is enhanced, resulting in a significant reduction in fuel consumption. Initially, the plan was to use a single, very large engine because the initial cost of single-line propulsion would be lower but it was found that, to make best use of its 60mW output, the propeller would need to be so big that it would most likely cause other problems and would only be fully effective when the hull was near maximum draft. As Bo Cerup-Simonsen observes, on vessels with a beam-to-draft ratio of 4:1, twin screw is the winning solution when relative costs are measured over a ship's lifetime. Erring on the side of caution, Maersk Line insisted on the installation of two 8-cylinder engines and so twin MAN Diesel 8S80ME-C9-2 units were specified for the first members of the Triple-E class. Shortly thereafter, however, an engine design upgrade meant that 7-cylinder units would be optimum and so the specification for later members of the class was changed accordingly. Maersk Line states that the Triple-E class uses 35 per cent less bunkers than is typical for container ships in the category transporting 13,000 TEU and above while the carbon dioxide produced per TEU shipped is 50 per cent lower than on other large container ships.[404] The Triple-E-class are the first purpose-built twin-screw container ships in Maersk Line's fleet since the *Svendborg Mærsk* of 1974, although many second-hand examples have been operated in the interim. A round voyage from Northern Europe to Asia will be completed in 70 days with 20 days as the shortest time from Hong Kong to Algeciras.

Working with the Environmental Protection Encouragement Agency, a German non-governmental organisation, Maersk Maritime Technology and Maersk Line developed a 'cradle-to-cradle' passport by which every steel plate and many of the fixtures and fittings on board the Triple-E class have a code describing their material composition and location. These codes relate to a systematic demolition plan, enabling the ships to be safely and efficiently recycled at the end of their projected 25-year lifespan. By that time, it is hoped that the ship recycling industry will have been transformed in terms of safety and reduced environmental impact. With regard to ship demolition, A.P. Møller-Maersk have already set industry-leading standards by investing in their own relatively safe and environmentally-sound demolition yard near Shanghai in China. Rather than adding to the severe pollution and human degradation brought about by breaking life-expired vessels on beaches in India, Pakistan or Bangladesh, old Maersk Line ships are systematically dismantled under controlled conditions in a modern, purpose-built facility – something no other shipping line has considered, let alone built and operated.

As we have seen, A.P. Møller-Maersk traditionally was a rather secretive company that built its largest, most prestigious ships 'in house' and therefore carrying out such a major project elsewhere brought forth issues of confidentiality. However, even when building vessels at Odense Lindø, there were many external suppliers of major items of equipment, as well as the classification societies, who were obliged to keep certain aspects of Maersk's designs and data secret. Bo Cerup-Simonsen explains that, while DSME owns the Triple-E design, specific innovations within it developed by Maersk Maritime Technology and external specialists – such as its new hull form, new propellers and new, highly advanced monitoring systems – are protected. Legalities aside, he adds that, as the design was developed specifically to fit a bigger system of port infrastructure, schedules, typical loadings and other parameters specific to Maersk Line's Asia-Europe trade, to compete effectively, other shipowners would be better to carry out their own research and to produce ships equally well tailored to their specific requirements.

In February 2011, Maersk Line held a press conference in London to announce the forthcoming placement of orders for the Triple-E class. That September, a further announcement was made, heralding a new timetable for Maersk Line's trunk Asia-Europe liner traffic. This would fuse together seven existing routes into one main service with departures every day from each port at a set time. The concept is called 'Daily Maersk' and the route, otherwise known as AE10, commences at Busan in South Korea, calling at Kwangyang, also in South Korea, Ningbo, Shanghai and Yantian in China, Tanjung Pelepas in Malaysia, Algeciras, Rotterdam, Bremerhaven, Gdansk, Århus and Gothenburg.[405] Consequently, Maersk Line customers will no longer have to plan their deliveries to coincide with sailing days but will instead be able to deliver goods for shipping whenever most convenient for them. In theory, a container can be delivered to a Daily Maersk port and it will be shipped from there within 24 hours. Daily Maersk has a shipping time of 34 days from Shanghai to Rotterdam and Maersk Line will pay compensation to customers for containers delivered behind schedule.[406]

Substantial resources are required to operate Daily Maersk, no fewer than seventy large container ships being needed at any one time to enable the specified intensity of departures. In the early-1970s when the ScanDutch container service was launched, the consortium used only seven or eight vessels, each with a capacity of around 2,000 containers and this was considered impressive. Daily Maersk uses some of the same harbours that ScanDutch once did, but with ten times as many ships, each on average six times as big as the old ScanDutch vessels. Therefore, Daily Maersk has a total capacity that is sixty times as big as ScanDutch. This situation clearly demonstrates the meaning of 'globalisation' in practice – and it could only have happened thanks to containerisation.

The Daily Maersk announcement happened concurrently with the placing of orders with DSME for the first batch of Triple-E class vessels and was accompanied by an attention-grabbing press campaign, designed by the Mensch advertising agency.[407] This campaign made extensive use of new media with film clips posted on YouTube, for example. Thus, Maersk Line's public relations changed rapidly in character from a traditional position of absolute secrecy to one of far greater openness and a desire for positive engagement with the public at large. With the advent of the Triple-E class, Maersk Line engaged in a further marketing blitz, using inter-active websites and social media to inform the general public of the vessels' advantages and characteristics. Maersk Line's Facebook page gained over a million 'likes' and a special Triple-E class website 'worldslargestship.com,' featuring computer animations and speeded-up films of the first vessel's construction. In addition, a special model was commissioned from Lego, thus enabling admirers to build and operate their own miniature version at home.

Maersk Line's CEO Eivind Kolding resigned in February 2012 for a new appointment as Head of Den Danske Bank, his replacement being a close colleague, Søren Schou, who had worked for Maersk since 1983.[408] His promotion did not, however, result in immediate strategic changes. Only three months thereafter, the Company's patriarch Mærsk Mc-Kinney Møller died aged 98 on 16 April 2012. His reputation was immense, his business career exceptional and his contributions to Danish public life prominent, albeit occasionally controversial. His passing led to discussions about how his life and work should be commemorated. What better way to honour such a great shipowner than to name to the first of the Triple-E class in his memory?

By June 2013, the *Mærsk Mc-Kinney Møller* was completed and during sea trials reached a speed of over 23 knots, thus demonstrating that, although designed for slow steaming, she could sail quite quickly when required. Most gratifying was that when running at 18 knots, her fuel economy was as projected and there was neither vibration nor cavitation. Meticulous research and extensive co-operation between Maersk Maritime Technology, Maersk Line, DSME and MAN

Diesel appeared to have paid off. Any small problems could easily be fixed but, as the design fundamentals lived up to expectations, on 2 July, she was handed over to Maersk Line to begin her maiden voyage to Europe. As this progressed, her Captain posted blog reports to inform the general public of her steady progress. In European ports, meanwhile, Maersk Line was preparing a series of press events to ensure maximum publicity for the new 'wonder ship.' On the sunny summer evening of 25 August, she made her maiden Danish call at Århus, where tens of thousands of people lined the waterfront all around the bay to gaze in awe as her massive blue hull was manoeuvred gingerly towards the berth.

Already, the second of the class, *Majestic Mærsk*, was *en route* from South Korea and, for a week in late-September, she visited Langelinie in Copenhagen where over 49,500 people visited her. The city's squares were decorated with Maersk Line banners and, when HRH Crown Princess Mary performed the naming ceremony, thousands of Maersk blue balloons were released. On the quay, meanwhile, there was a big public exhibition about Maersk Line's activities.

In Helsingør, meanwhile, the construction of a new Danish national maritime museum, Museet for Søfart, was nearing completion. Located in and around the old shipyard drydock where many of the vessels described earlier in this book were completed or overhauled, its design by the up-and-coming Copenhagen-based architects, Bjarke Ingels Group (BIG), is strikingly futuristic. The museum was financed by eleven foundations, one of the major sponsors being A.P. Møller-Maersk's majority owner, A.P. Møller og Hustru Chastine Mc-Kinney Møllers Fond til almene Formaal. The museum's galleries contain fashionable thematic displays and, fittingly, the last of these relates the story of containerisation to globalisation. In the centre, there is a 20-foot Maersk Line shipping container and, adjacent to this, a vast and superbly detailed 8.5-metre-long model of the *Mærsk Mc-Kinney Møller*. The model's underwater hull form, however, allegedly does not accurately replicate the prototype, the precise shape of which is supposed to remain as a secret for the time being.

While the *Mærsk Mc-Kinney Møller* and the *Majestic Mærsk* were wowing great crowds in Århus and Copenhagen, in cinemas around the world the film *Captain Philips* – made with Maersk Line's co-operation – was also drawing large audiences and receiving critical acclaim. Directed by Paul Greengrass, it is a claustrophobic thriller, telling the story of the 2009 hijacking by pirates off the Somali coast of the 14,120gt *Maersk Alabama*. She is one of the smaller, older and less glamorous members of Maersk Line's vast fleet, operating on a feeder service between Salalah in Oman and Mombasa in Kenya. Built in 1998 in Taiwan as the Danish-flagged *Alva Mærsk*, since 2004 she has been run by an American Maersk Line subsidiary called Waterman Shipping. Maersk purchased this firm some years previously as part of its take-over of Sea-Land (described above). Sailing regularly through pirate-infested waters along the Somali coast, the *Maersk Alabama* was the subject of several attempted hijackings. In April 2009, four particularly brazen and well-armed teenage Somalis succeeded in boarding her and, having encountered resistance from her twenty-strong crew, they took hostage her captain, Richard Philips (played in the film by Tom Hanks), then escaped at gunpoint with him in the *Maersk Alabama*'s fast rescue boat. After four days, an American naval patrol consisting of a frigate and a destroyer arrived on the scene. Following a tense stand-off and inconclusive negotiations, three pirates were shot dead by US Navy SEALS, the fourth was arrested and the eponymous Captain Philips was rescued.

Ingeniously scripted, convincingly acted, spectacularly filmed and tautly edited though it is, *Captain Philips* only occasionally alludes to the wider economic, cultural and political frameworks in which both the *Maersk Alabama* and the Somali pirates operate. Being aimed primarily at a 'multiplex' audience, it focuses mainly on the very real bravery of her Captain and crew in the face of extreme adversity and on the professional conduct of their military rescuers. The pirates are young would-be gangsters, recruited by a large, well-resourced criminal organisation ashore, running a lucrative international extortion racket. It demands large pay-outs from seized vessels' insurers for their release and the safe return of their crews.

The Somali coastal villages from which the pirates come traditionally were fishing communities but foreign factory trawlers over-fished the seas in the vicinity and so, unable to make an honest living, some of the fishermen turned instead to piracy. Yet, the complex international ownership structure of the *Maersk Alabama* goes without comment, meaning that American audiences would not necessarily realise that the ship was ultimately controlled from Copenhagen, one minor and mundane unit operating a branch service for the vast global transportation conglomerate that is Maersk Line.

As with many another contemporary merchantman, the *Maersk Alabama* is managed from wealthy Western nations but cross-trades between a prosperous Gulf State, Oman, and a rapidly developing African nation, Kenya. In sharp contrast Somalia, whose coast she skirts, is an impoverished failure, battered by external market forces and internally riven by religious and tribal warfare. There, a parallel 'black economy,' dealing in extortion and terrorism, threatens not only regional stability but also the ability of shipping companies such as Maersk Line to trade unmolested, unless protected by Western military deployments. *Captain Philips*, therefore, also contains a depressing sub-narrative, throwing into sharp focus the problem of a very unequal world, divided between nations with the economic, technological and educational resources to protect and advance their interests and of others, such as Somalia, that have practically disintegrated.

In the meantime, the increasing strength of the environmental movement has led many to question the wisdom of shipping consumer goods around the world; many feel that this activity causes unnecessary pollution and that, for the sake of the planet, people should consume less and source their requirements locally. Human ecology also plays a part in such debates – there being a fear that Third World labour is being unfairly exploited in Asian 'sweatshops,' that the whole infrastructure of modern liner shipping is somehow alienating as vessels dock only briefly at automated out-of-town ports and, furthermore, that the ships are operated by 'skeleton' crews across 'empty' oceans. The largest container ships are, therefore, criticised as symbols of what some view as being the unacceptable face of globalisation, abetting the decimation of natural resources, alienating people, polluting the planet and being complicit in the maintenance of established wealth and power hierarchies.

There is, however, an alternative viewpoint. Recently, researchers in Copenhagen Business School carried out an investigation into the effects of Maersk Line's expansion into developing countries in South East Asia – such as Vietnam. They concluded that Maersk Line was playing a very important active role in Third World development and has a proud track record in, as they put it:

> 'Integrating global production processes, not only by moving goods from A to B and co-ordinating multiple modes of transport, but also co-ordinating and integrating increasingly atomised production processes on a global scale… A.P. Møller-Maersk assist developing countries in establishing container transport infrastructure… providing cheaper and faster access to international markets, thus potentially making [their products] more attractive to buyers… Furthermore, A.P. Møller-Maersk's container business may play an important and possibly growing role in integrating developing countries into global value chains… by creating economies of scale, by delivering operational efficiency and by optimising and improving supply chains.'[410]

They observed that Maersk Logistics' so-called 'vendor management services' help forge links with partner firms around the globe and even assist them to reach the required levels of quality and punctuality. While A.P. Møller-Maersk is a global company, its representatives in each market have intimate local knowledge and so they can assist business development at both micro and macro levels. Maersk Line's clients range from established multi-nationals to small firms run by single entrepreneurs and it is able to bring the two types together for mutual benefit.[411]

In a Danish context, A.P. Møller-Maersk is unique not only in terms of size but also political, economic and cultural influence. Its clout, therefore, also makes it controversial. Were it to be headquartered in a big and populous country, such as the United States of America, it would be only one of many businesses of such a scale. During his lifetime, Mærsk Mc-Kinney Møller often spoke of the difficulties (as well as the benefits) of running an expansive business from such a small and often inward-looking country as Denmark. For example, his personal diplomacy to win influence amongst the governing classes in less democratic developing countries was often interpreted in Denmark's liberal press as being diametrically opposed to the will of the Danish people – yet, for A.P. Møller-Maersk to be a successful business, it was a necessity to cultivate good trade relations in such emerging markets.

Following its purchase of Sea-Land, A.P. Møller-Maersk became responsible for much of the logistical support for the US Military in fields of war around the world; this became politically controversial during the Iraq War, which many Danes considered illegal (even though their Government actively supported America's intervention to depose Saddam Hussein).[412] Of course, A.P. Møller-Maersk exists principally to make money, yet these observations highlight how the Company inevitably has a paradoxical relationship with Denmark and with the Danish people. Many Danes are very gratified by its great achievements and feel pride when glimpsing Maersk Line's big light blue container ships on the world's sea lanes. They also enjoy considerable indirect social benefits enabled through taxation of the profits A.P. Møller-Maersk generates. Yet, some also have suspicions about aspects of what it actually represents culturally and ideologically. In all likelihood, when most go shopping, they will never even pause to consider the complex but hidden infrastructures of transport, distribution, finance, design and engineering making possible our contemporary experience of a consumer society.

Raising the flags on a Maersk Line container ship; today, the company employs seafarers and shore staff from all over the world. (Hanne Hansen)

Conclusion

Denmark's leading status in liner shipping is a remarkable story of technical innovation and visionary business strategies. Burmeister & Wain's development of a reliable marine diesel engine and its early adoption by leading Danish shipping companies gave a decisive advantage in terms of fuel economy and cargo capacity over coal-fired steamships. During the inter-war era economic downturns appear to have helped Danish lines to achieve greater market share by reducing numbers of less competitive rivals.

The story of Danish liner shipping is also one of visionary individuals and productive relationships between financiers, shipowners, shipbuilders and freight customers. Shipping entrepreneurs – such as Carl Frederik Tietgen, Hans Niels Andersen and, in particular, the remarkable 'father and son' dynasty of A.P. and Mærsk Mc-Kinney Møller – demonstrated ingenuity, vision and financial perspicacity in creating great shipping and industrial enterprises. It appears also that Denmark's liberal business culture better enabled talented people to advance from humble backgrounds, or without having the connections which might have been expected in equivalent British contexts. One cannot imagine in Britain a comparable situation to Jens J. Kappel's rise to become Head of A.P. Møller's Container Ship Development Division when he had no naval architectural qualifications, but merely an innate sense of how such vessels worked and how they could be made to work even better.

Furthermore, A.P. Møller-Maersk's ownership structure has protected it from needing to accede to institutional investors' short-term profit motives. Instead, ongoing design development with a view to the future has been encouraged – a strategy that has paid dividends in the longer term. Although the East Asiatic Company was similarly organised, arrogant management and poor decision-making brought about its rapid decline and its exit from liner shipping.

A view looking upwards at the vast expanse of steel forming the topside of the **Emma Mærsk**; presently, she is one of many Maersk Line super container ships providing a daily service between Europe and the Far East. (Søren Lund Hviid)

The development of Danish-owned container shipping was the key advance ensuring the country's continued success in liner shipping during the last half-century. The East Asiatic Company's initial diesel container ships were slightly more efficient than the steam turbine-powered examples used by competing operators. Maersk Line's late entry into the container business enabled lessons to be learned from others' experiences and vessels to be designed and built that were more efficient still. The fact that Maersk Line ships frequently use A.P. Møller-Maersk-owned hub port facilities has given the Company the possibility of developing integrated systems of a scale and with a global reach that none of its competitors can match.

With the world's population expected shortly to reach 7 billion people – and an expanding Asian and African middle class keen to enjoy the consumerist lifestyle most Westerners have long taken for granted – liner shipping will surely continue to have an important role in global development. The issue is how goods might be transported more sustainably and this will require further sophisticated engineering research. Throughout this narrative, a central theme has been to acknowledge and celebrate the work of Danish naval architects and engineers in increasing the operational efficiency of cargo liners and container ships. This is an ongoing process at the Technical University of Denmark, MAN Diesel (formerly B&W), A.P. Møller-Maersk and in the Danish maritime cluster as a whole. These may increase initial building costs, but it has been shown time and again that such expenditure is quickly offset by the benefits of reduced costs throughout a ship's service life. Certainly, the *Selandia* demonstrated this in 1912, while the Triple-E class shows similar advantages in the present era.

Research of this kind is merely one facet of Denmark's forward-thinking maritime industry as equal attention is paid to the training and up-skilling of those employed at sea and ashore. For example, Maersk Training is a significant division of the A.P. Møller-Maersk Group, offering a broad range of courses in shipping industry skills and practices, mainly delivered in a purpose-built training centre in Svendborg.[413] The Copenhagen Business School, meanwhile, has developed a special Executive Master of Business Accounting in Shipping and Logistics, known as the 'Blue MBA', for those seeking careers in ship management.[414]

During recent decades, there has been an explosion in container traffic between Europe, the Far East and the USA. In light of this, one may wonder whether there are limits to how large growth elsewhere can be in the future. New markets and supply chains are, of course, constantly emerging and these will bring about new areas of expansion in container shipping capacity. In September 2011, Professor Anil K. Gupta of the University of Maryland observed that trade between Africa and Asia, which was worth 304 billion dollars in 2010, will expand five-fold during the next decade. Due to the outsourcing of manufacturing from Europe and the USA, there is now an increasing Asian demand for the raw materials of industry from Africa. Gupta argues that resultant economic growth in Africa brought about by increasing exports to Asia should result in higher standards of living there – at least for some.[415] Notwithstanding the recent financial crisis that has negatively affected Europe and the USA, there is strong growth elsewhere in the world and so liner companies, including Maersk Line, are shifting their focus to capitalise on these emergent opportunities.

Notes

1. In 1919, A.P. Møller and Hans Isbrandtsen established a joint company called the Isbrandtsen-Moller Company (ISMOLCO) in New York with the intention of eventually establishing liner services.
2. Dag Bakka Jr, Linjer Rundt Jorden, Seagull, Bergen, 2008, p9.
3. Peter Mathias, The First Industrial Nation: An Economic History of Britain 1700-1914, Methuen, London, 1969, p312.
4. Ove Hornby, 'With Constant Care…' A.P. Møller: Shipowner 1876-1965, Schultz, Copenhagen, 1988, pp13-17.
5. Søren Thorsøe, Peter Simonsen, Søren Krogh-Andersen, Frederik Frederichsen and Henrik Vaupel, DFDS 1866-1991: Ship Development through 125 Years – from Paddle Steamer to Ro/Ro Ship, World Ship Society and DFDS, Copenhagen, 1991, pp20-33.
6. Ove Hornby, 'With Constant Care…' A.P. Møller: Shipowner 1876-1965, Schultz, Copenhagen, 1988, p140.
7. See http://investor.maersk.com for details of how the ownership of A.P. Møller-Maersk's shares is structured.
8. Ove Hornby, 'With Constant Care…' A.P. Møller: Shipowner 1876-1965, Schultz, Copenhagen, 1988, pp154-155.
9. Kåre Lauring, Containertrafik gennem 50 år, Handels- og Søfartsmuseet på Kronborg, 2008, p90.
10. Ole Mikkelsen, 'Skibet er ladet med julegaver,' Berlingske Tidende, 14 November 2006.
11. Professor Dr-Ing Dr-Ing E.h. J. S. Meurer, 'The Rise of the Diesel Engine – An Outline of Early Developments,' special supplement to The Motor Ship, April 1970, p9.
12. Professor Dr-Ing Dr-Ing E.h. J. S. Meurer, 'The Rise of the Diesel Engine – An Outline of Early Developments,' special supplement to The Motor Ship, April 1970, pp2-3.
13. Rudolph Diesel, 'Theory and Design of an Economical Heat Engine to replace Steam Engines and Today's Internal Combustion Engines,' Spon, London & New York, 1894, p80.
14. Professor Dr-Ing Dr-Ing E.h. J. S. Meurer, 'The Rise of the Diesel Engine – An Outline of Early Developments,' special supplement to The Motor Ship, April 1970, pp3-4.
15. Jack A. Somer, and Helmut Behling, From The Mountains To The Seas: The Sulzer Diesel Engine, Wärtsilä NSD, Winterthur, 1998, p16.
16. John Guthrie, A History of Marine Engineering, Hutchison, London, 1971, p203.
17. Professor Dr-Ing Dr-Ing E.h. J. S. Meurer, 'The Rise of the Diesel Engine – An Outline of Early Developments,' special supplement to The Motor Ship, April 1970, p5.
18. A.P. Chalkley, 'Rudolf Diesel: A detailed biography and an historical survey of the origin and development of the diesel engine,' December 1937, pp314-317.
19. A. P. Chalkley, Diesel Engines for Land and Marine Work, Constable, London, 1912.
20. J. Berring M.Sc., M.I.Mar. E., 'Burmeister & Wain – Pioneers of Low-Speed Marine Diesel Engines,' special supplement to The Motor Ship, April 1970, pp10-13.
21. Johannes Lehmann, Burmeister & Wain Gennem Hundrede Aar, Burmeister & Wain, Copenhagen, 1943, pp121-124.
22. Johannes Lehmann, Burmeister & Wain Gennem Hundrede Aar, Burmeister & Wain, Copenhagen, 1943, p144.
23. Ole Sørensen, B&W-dieselmotorens historie 1898-2008, MAN Diesel/Diesel House, Copenhagen, 2008, p21.
24. Ole Sørensen, B&W-dieselmotorens historie 1898-2008, MAN Diesel/Diesel House, Copenhagen, 2008, p36.
25. Søren Ellemose, Kompagniet: H.N. Andersens ØK 1884-2007, Jyllands-Postens Forlag, 2007, p75.
26. The Selandia actually measured 4,964gt.
27. Søren Ellemose, Kompagniet: H.N. Andersens ØK 1884-2007, Jyllands-Postens Forlag, 2007, pp14-21.
28. Søren Ellemose, Kompagniet: H.N. Andersens ØK 1884-2007, Jyllands-Postens Forlag, 2007, pp22-24.
29. See Ole Lange, Stormogulen C.F. Tietgen: En finansmand, hans imperium og hans tid 1829-1901, Gyldendal, Copenhagen, 2006 for a detailed description of Tietgen's life and work.
30. Søren Thorsøe, Peter Simonsen, Søren Krogh-Andersen, Frederik Frederichsen and Henrik Vaupel, DFDS 1866-1991: Ship Development through 125 Years – from Paddle Steamer to Ro/Ro Ship, World Ship Society and DFDS, Copenhagen, 1991, pp25-26.
31. Søren Thorsøe, Peter Simonsen, Søren Krogh-Andersen, and Frederik Frederichsen, Skandinavien-Amerika Linien: DFDS' passager- og fragtfart på Amerika, World Ship Society, Copenhagen, 2001, pp15-16.
32. Søren Thorsøe, Peter Simonsen, Søren Krogh-Andersen, Frederik Frederichsen and Henrik Vaupel, DFDS 1866-1991: Ship Development through 125 Years – from Paddle Steamer to Ro/Ro Ship, World Ship Society and DFDS, Copenhagen, 1991, pp27-29.
33. Søren Thorsøe, Peter Simonsen, Søren Krogh-Andersen, Frederik Frederichsen and Henrik Vaupel, DFDS 1866-1991: Ship Development through 125 Years – from Paddle

34. The most comprehensive account of the sinking of the Norge is provided by Per Kristian Sebak, Titanic's Predecessor: The S/S Norge Disaster of 1904, Seaward Publishing, Laksevaag, 2004.
35. Søren Ellemose, Kompagniet: H.N. Andersens ØK 1884-2007, Jyllands-Postens Forlag, 2007, pp61-65.
36. Ove Hornby, 'With Constant Care…' A.P. Møller: Shipowner 1876-1965, Schultz, Copenhagen, 1988, p15.
37. 'The Diesel Motor Ship Selandia,' The Shipping World, February 1912, pp209-212.
38. Ole Sørensen, B&W-dieselmotorens historie 1898-2008, MAN Diesel/Diesel House, Copenhagen, 2008, p41. The number was subsequently increased to 14, following complaints of under-manning from her Chief Engineer, K.F. Holm.
39. Ole Sørensen, B&W-dieselmotorens historie 1898-2008, MAN Diesel/Diesel House, Copenhagen, 2008, p41.
40. 'The Selandia's 25 Years' Service,' The Motor Ship, February 1937, p395.
41. Erik Schacke, the Danish Consul, in a letter to The Scotsman, 28 November 1938, p11.
42. Ole Sørensen, B&W-dieselmotorens historie 1898-2008, MAN Diesel/Diesel House, Copenhagen, 2008, p45.
43. 'The Selandia's 25 Years' Service,' The Motor Ship, February 1937, p395.
44. Ole Sørensen, B&W-dieselmotorens historie 1898-2008, MAN Diesel/Diesel House, Copenhagen, 2008, p43.
45. John Guthrie, A History of Marine Engineering, Hutchison, London, 1971, pp211-212.
46. 'The Selandia's 25 Years' Service,' The Motor Ship, February 1937, p394.
47. 'The Motor Ship Jutlandia,' The Shipping World, 29 May 1912, pp541-543.
48. See Alan S. Mallett and Andrew M. Bell, The Pirrie-Kylsant Motorships 1915-1932, Mallett and Bell Publications, Coltishall, 1984 for a detailed description of Harland & Wolff-built B&W-engined motor ships.
49. Ole Sørensen, B&W-dieselmotorens historie 1898-2008, MAN Diesel/Diesel House, Copenhagen, 2008, p46.
50. Ole Stig Johannesen, ØK's skibe – The EAC Fleet, Forlaget Nautilus, Frederiksværk, 2003, p96.
51. 'The Selandia's 25 Years' Service,' The Motor Ship, February 1937, p395.
52. 'The Selandia's 25 Years' Service,' The Motor Ship, February 1937, p395.
53. Ove Hornby, 'With Constant Care…' A.P. Møller: Shipowner 1876-1965, Schultz, Copenhagen, 1988, pp28-29.
54. Dansk-Russisk was taken over by DFDS after the First World War. See Søren Thorsøe, Peter Simonsen, Søren Krogh-Andersen, Frederik Frederichsen, and Henrik Vaupel, DFDS 1866-1991: Ship Development through 125 Years – from Paddle Steamer to Ro/Ro Ship, World Ship Society and DFDS, Copenhagen, 1991, p38.
55. Ove Hornby, 'With Constant Care…' A.P. Møller: Shipowner 1876-1965, Schultz, Copenhagen, 1988, pp32-33.
56. Ove Hornby, 'With Constant Care…' A.P. Møller: Shipowner 1876-1965, Schultz, Copenhagen, 1988, pp30-34.
57. Thomas Larsen and Finn Mortensen, Mærsk Mc-Kinney Møller: En personligt portræt af Danmarks største erhvervsmand, Gyldendal Business, Copenhagen, 2008, pp268-269.
58. Ove Hornby, 'With Constant Care…' A.P. Møller: Shipowner 1876-1965, Schultz, Copenhagen, 1988, p57.
59. Anders Monrad Møller, Henrik Dethlefsen and Hans Christian Johansen, Dansk Søfarts Historie 7 1870-1920: Sejl og Damp, Gyldendal, Copenhagen, 2000, pp225-228.
60. Søren Ellemose, Kompagniet: H.N. Andersens ØK 1884-2007, Jyllands-Postens Forlag, 2007, pp82-83.
61. Poul Graae, Hundrede år på havene: DFDS 1866-1966, DFDS, Copenhagen, 1966, pp136-138.
62. Poul Graae, Hundrede år på havene: DFDS 1866-1966, DFDS, Copenhagen, 1966, p138.
63. Poul Graae, Hundrede år på havene: DFDS 1866-1966, DFDS, Copenhagen, 1966, pp138-139.
64. Poul Graae, Hundrede år på havene: DFDS 1866-1966, DFDS, Copenhagen, 1966, p139.
65. Anders Monrad Møller, Henrik Dethlefsen and Hans Christian Johansen, Dansk Søfarts Historie 7 1870-1920: Sejl og Damp, Gyldendal, Copenhagen, 2000, p123.
66. Anders Monrad Møller, Henrik Dethlefsen and Hans Christian Johansen, Dansk Søfarts Historie 7 1870-1920: Sejl og Damp, Gyldendal, Copenhagen, 2000, pp188-189.
67. Ove Hornby, 'With Constant Care…' A.P. Møller: Shipowner 1876-1965, Schultz, Copenhagen, 1988, pp65-66.

68. Anders Monrad Møller, Henrik Dethlefsen and Hans Christian Johansen, Dansk Søfarts Historie 7 1870-1920: Sejl og Damp, Gyldendal, Copenhagen, 2000, pp229-231.

69. Ove Hornby, 'With Constant Care…' A.P. Møller: Shipowner 1876-1965, Schultz, Copenhagen, 1988, p67.

70. Søren Ellemose, Kompagniet: H.N. Andersens ØK 1884-2007, Jyllands-Postens Forlag, 2007, p84.

71. Søren Thorsøe, Peter Simonsen, Søren Krogh-Andersen, Frederik Frederichsen, and Henrik Vaupel, DFDS 1866-1991: Ship Development through 125 Years – from Paddle Steamer to Ro/Ro Ship, World Ship Society and DFDS, Copenhagen, 1991, p36.

72. Poul Graae, Hundrede år på havene: DFDS 1866-1966, DFDS, Copenhagen, 1966, pp162-170.

73. Brian J. Cudahy, How Container Ships Changed the World, Fordham University Press, New York, 2006, p2.

74. Eric Jennings, Cargoes: A Century Story of the Far Eastern Freight Conference, Meridian Communications, Singapore, 1980, p43.

75. Søren Thorsøe, Peter Simonsen, Søren Krogh-Andersen, Frederik Frederichsen, and Henrik Vaupel, DFDS 1866-1991: Ship Development through 125 Years – from Paddle Steamer to Ro/Ro Ship, World Ship Society and DFDS, Copenhagen, 1991, p39.

76. Ove Hornby, 'With Constant Care…' A.P. Møller: Shipowner 1876-1965, Schultz, Copenhagen, 1988, p84.

77. Ole Stig Johannesen, ØK's skibe – The EAC Fleet, Forlaget Nautilus, Frederiksværk, 2003, pp132-172.

78. Ove Hornby, 'With Constant Care…' A.P. Møller: Shipowner 1876-1965, Schultz, Copenhagen, 1988, p84.

79. Søren Thorsøe, Peter Simonsen, Søren Krogh-Andersen, Frederik Frederichsen, and Henrik Vaupel, DFDS 1866-1991: Ship Development through 125 Years – from Paddle Steamer to Ro/Ro Ship, World Ship Society, DFDS, Copenhagen, 1991, p35.

80. Ove Hornby, 'With Constant Care…' A.P. Møller: Shipowner 1876-1965, Schultz, Copenhagen, 1988, pp80-81.

81. See Per Koch, Nakskov Skibsværfts Historie: Episoder under teater, Per Kochs Forlag, Nakskov, 2005 for a detailed history of Nakskov Skibsværft.

82. Ole Stig Johannesen, ØK's skibe – The EAC Fleet, Forlaget Nautilus, Frederiksværk, 2003, p14.

83. Søren Ellemose, Kompagniet: H.N. Andersens ØK 1884-2007, Jyllands-Postens Forlag, 2007, p116.

84. Ove Hornby, 'With Constant Care…' A.P. Møller: Shipowner 1876-1965, Schultz, Copenhagen, 1988, p96.

85. John Guthrie, A History of Marine Engineering, Hutchison, London, 1971, p211.

86. Frank A. Rasmussen, Bendt Vedsted Rønne and Hans Christian Johansen, Dansk Søfarts Historie, Volume 6: 1920-1960: Damp og Diesel, Gyldendal, 2000, p176.

87. Ove Hornby, 'With Constant Care…' A.P. Møller: Shipowner 1876-1965, Schultz, Copenhagen, 1988, p97.

88. Ole Stig Johannesen, Mærskbådene: Rederiernes skibe gennem de første 50 år, Editions Maritimes, Roskilde, 2006, pp73-75, p78 and pp89-90.

89. Frank A. Rasmussen, Bendt Vedsted Rønne and Hans Christian Johansen, Dansk Søfarts Historie, Volume 6: 1920-1960: Damp og Diesel, Gyldendal, 2000, pp175-176.

90. Ole Sørensen, B&W-dieselmotorens historie 1898-2008, MAN Diesel/Diesel House, Copenhagen, 2008, pp60-61.

91. Ole Sørensen, B&W-dieselmotorens historie 1898-2008, MAN Diesel/Diesel House, Copenhagen, 2008, p61.

92. 'Dr H.H. Blache,' The Motor Ship, October 1934, p254.

93. J. Berring M.Sc., M.I.Mar. E., 'Burmeister & Wain – Pioneers of Low-Speed Marine Diesel Engines,' special supplement to The Motor Ship, April 1970, p12.

94. J. Berring M.Sc., M.I.Mar. E., 'Burmeister & Wain – Pioneers of Low-Speed Marine Diesel Engines,' special supplement to The Motor Ship, April 1970, p12.

95. Ole Stig Johannesen, ØK's skibe – The EAC Fleet, Forlaget Nautilus, Frederiksværk, 2003, pp145-149, p151, pp156-158.

96. Ole Sørensen, B&W-dieselmotorens historie 1898-2008, MAN Diesel/Diesel House, Copenhagen, 2008, p57.

97. 'The Motor Ship Amerika,' The Motor Ship, February 1930, pp433-434.

98. 'The East Asiatic Co.'s Californian Service,' The Motor Ship, April 1931, p35.

99. 'The Motor Ship Amerika,' The Motor Ship, February 1930, p436.

100. See Alan S. Mallett and Andrew M. Bell, The Pirrie-Kylsant Motorships 1915-1932, Mallett and Bell Publications, Coltishall, 1984 for a comprehensive description of these and other similar vessels.

101. 'The Motor Ship Amerika,' The Motor Ship, February 1930, p438.

102. 'The Motor Ship Amerika,' The Motor Ship, February 1930, p442.

103. Søren Thorsøe, Peter Simonsen, Søren Krogh-Andersen and Frederik Frederichsen, Skandinavien-Amerika Linien: DFDS' passager- og fragtfart på Amerika, World Ship Society, Copenhagen, 2001, pp253-260.

104. Ove Hornby, 'With Constant Care…' A.P. Møller: Shipowner 1876-1965, Schultz, Copenhagen, 1988, pp106-107.

105. Ove Hornby, 'With Constant Care…' A.P. Møller: Shipowner 1876-1965, Schultz, Copenhagen, 1988, p109.

106. Jan Cortzen, Myten Møller, Børsens Forlag, Copenhagen, 2009, p51.

107. Ove Hornby, 'With Constant Care…' A.P. Møller: Shipowner 1876-1965, Schultz, Copenhagen, 1988, p110.

108. Information from Henning Morgen of A.P. Møller-Maersk.

109. Ove Hornby, 'With Constant Care…' A.P. Møller: Shipowner 1876-1965, Schultz, Copenhagen, 1988, pp113-114.

110. 'A 15-knot Cargo Liner, Mr A.P. Møller's single-screw, double-acting, two-engine-cycled M.S. Nora Maersk, built for Japan-New York service, The Motor Ship, October 1934, pp235-236.

111. Ove Hornby, 'With Constant Care…' A.P. Møller: Shipowner 1876-1965, Schultz, Copenhagen, 1988, pp116-117.

112. Ove Hornby, 'With Constant Care…' A.P. Møller: Shipowner 1876-1965, Schultz, Copenhagen, 1988, pp150-154.

113. See John K. Galbraith, The Great Crash 1929, Penguin, London, 1954 for a detailed description of the circumstances leading to and consequences of the Wall Street Crash.

114. Ian Johnston, Ships for a Nation: John Brown & Company Clydebank 1847-1971, Dunbartonshire Libraries & Museums, Clydebank, 2000, pp189-196.

115. Ole Sørensen, B&W-dieselmotorens historie 1898-2008, MAN Diesel/Diesel House, Copenhagen, 2008, p76.

116. Frank A. Rasmussen, Bendt Vedsted Rønne, and Hans Christian Johansen, Dansk Søfarts Historie, Volume 6: 1920-1960: Damp og Diesel, Gyldendal, 2000, pp88-93.

117. 'Psychology in Depression in Shipbuilding,' The Motor Ship, May 1931, Editorial page.

118. 'Scandinavia and Motor Shipping,' The Motor Ship, February 1937, p401.

119. 'Scandinavia and Motor Shipping,' The Motor Ship, February 1937, p401

120. Frank A. Rasmussen, Bendt Vedsted Rønne, and Hans Christian Johansen, Dansk Søfarts Historie, Volume 6: 1920-1960: Damp og Diesel, Gyldendal, 2000, pp178-179.

121. Frank A. Rasmussen, Bendt Vedsted Rønne and Hans Christian Johansen, Dansk Søfarts Historie, Volume 6: 1920-1960: Damp og Diesel, Gyldendal, 2000, pp183-190.

122. Søren Ellemose, Kompagniet: H.N. Andersens ØK 1884-2007, Jyllands-Postens Forlag, 2007, pp121-122.

123. Søren Thorsøe, Peter Simonsen, Søren Krogh-Andersen and Frederik Frederichsen, Skandinavien-Amerika Linien: DFDS' passager- og fragtfart på Amerika, World Ship Society, Copenhagen, 2001, pp218-226.

124. Poul Graae, Hundrede år på havene, DFDS, Copenhagen, 1966, p210.

125. 'Plight of Shipping Industry' (letter from 'Economist'), The Scotsman, 24 November 1938, p13.

126. 'Plight of the Shipping Industry' (letter from Erik Schacke, Royal Danish Consul), The Scotsman, 25 November 1938, p13.

127. Nick Tolerton, Reefer Ships: The Ocean Princesses, Willson Scott, Christchurch, 2008, pp9-12.

128. Ole Lange, Logbog For Lauritzen 1884-1995, Handelshøjskolens Forlag, Copenhagen, 1995, pp131-138.

129. Ole Lange, Logbog For Lauritzen 1884-1995, Handelshøjskolens Forlag, Copenhagen, 1995, pp134-135.

130. Ole Lange, Logbog For Lauritzen 1884-1995, Handelshøjskolens Forlag, Copenhagen, 1995, p137.

131. Bent Mikkelsen, Danske Rederier Volume 7: The Lauritzen Fleet 1884-1945, Forlaget Betty Nordgas, Ringkøbing, 2009, p38.

132. Ole Lange, Logbog For Lauritzen 1884-1995, Handelshøjskolens Forlag, Copenhagen, 1995, pp138-142.

133. Ole Lange, Logbog For Lauritzen 1884-1995, Handelshøjskolens Forlag, Copenhagen, 1995, p144.

134. Nick Tolerton, Reefer Ships: The Ocean Princesses, Willson Scott, Christchurch, 2008, p109 and p114.

135. 'New Burmeister and Wain Engine: Two-stroke Single-Acting Units with Poppet Exhaust Valves in the Fruit-carrying Ships Asta and Dora, The Motor Ship, October 1934, pp246-249.

136. 'Fruit Ships at Cape Town,' The Motor Ship, December 1934, p410.

137. Ole Stig Johannesen, The Torm Ships: The Torm Fleet Through 120 Years, Editions Maritimes, Roskilde, 2009, p8.

138. Ole Stig Johannesen, The Torm Ships: The Torm Fleet Through 120 Years, Editions Maritimes, Roskilde, 2009, pp86-103.

139. Søren Thorsøe, Peter Simonsen, Søren Krogh-Andersen, Frederik Frederichsen and Henrik Vaupel, DFDS 1866-1991: Ship Development through 125 Years – from Paddle Steamer to Ro/Ro Ship, World Ship Society, DFDS, Copenhagen, 1991, pp354-359.

140. Ole Stig Johannesen, Mærskbådene: Rederiernes skibe gennem de første 50 år, Editions Maritimes, Roskilde, 2006, p125.

141. Ole Stig Johannesen, J. Lauritzen: Skibene i årene 1888-1952, Editions Maritimes, Roskilde, 2012, p25.

142. Ole Stig Johannesen, J. Lauritzen: Skibene i årene 1888-1952, Editions Maritimes, Roskilde, 2012, pp170, 174, 121 and 184.

143. Ole Stig Johannesen, J. Lauritzen: Skibene i årene 1888-1952, Editions Maritimes, Roskilde, 2012, p28.

144. Ole Stig Johannesen, The Torm Ships: The Torm Fleet Through 120 Years, Editions Maritimes, Roskilde, 2009, pp12-13.

145. Ole Stig Johannesen, Mærskbådene: Rederiernes skibe gennem de første 50 år, Editions Maritimes, Roskilde, 2006, p134.

146. Ole Stig Johannesen, ØK's skibe – The EAC Fleet, Forlaget Nautilus, Frederiksværk, 2003, pp169-172.

147. Brian J. Cudahy, How Container Ships Changed the World, Fordham University Press, New York, 2006, pp3-5.

148. Ove Hornby, 'With Constant Care…' A.P. Møller: Shipowner 1876-1965, Schultz, Copenhagen, 1988, pp161-162.

149. Søren Thorsøe, Peter Simonsen, Søren Krogh-Andersen, Frederik Frederichsen, and Henrik Vaupel, DFDS 1866-1991: Ship Development through 125 Years – from Paddle Steamer to Ro/Ro Ship, World Ship Society and DFDS, Copenhagen, 1991, pp42-43.

150. Frank A. Rasmussen, Bendt Vedsted Rønne and Hans Christian Johansen, Dansk Søfarts Historie, Volume 6: 1920-1960: Damp og Diesel, Gyldendal, 2000, p96.

151. 'Virket I USA: interview med Thorkil Høst, president for Moller Steamship Co. Inc., 1947-1967, Mærsk Post, 1976 (særnummer).

152. See Jan Cortzen Myten Møller, Børsens Forlag, 2009, pp39-79 for a detailed description of A.P. Møller's shipping affairs under Isbrandtsen management in New York.

153. Ove Hornby, 'With Constant Care…' A.P. Møller: Shipowner 1876-1965, Schultz, Copenhagen, 1988, pp177-180.

154. See L.A. Sawyer and W.H. Mitchell, The Liberty Ships: The History of the 'Emergency' Type Cargo Ships Constructed in the United States During World War Two, Lloyd's of London Press, London, 1985 for a detailed account of the Liberty ships' design and operation. See also Peter Elphick, Liberty: The Ships that Won the War, Chatham Publishing, Chatham, 2001.

155. 'Virket I USA: interview med Thorkil Høst, president for Moller Steamship Co. Inc., 1947-1967, Mærsk Post, 1976 (særnummer).

156. 'Virket I USA: interview med Thorkil Høst, president for Moller Steamship Co. Inc., 1947-1967, Mærsk Post, 1976 (særnummer).

157. Jan Cortzen, Myten Møller, Børsens Forlag, Copenhagen, 2009, p76.

158. Ove Hornby, 'With Constant Care…' A.P. Møller: Shipowner 1876-1965, Schultz, Copenhagen, 1988, pp251-253.

159. Jan Cortzen, Myten Møller, Børsens Forlag, Copenhagen, 2009, p79.

160. Frank A. Rasmussen, Bendt Vedsted Rønne and Hans Christian Johansen, Dansk Søfarts Historie, Volume 6: 1920-1960: Damp og Diesel, Gyldendal, 2000, pp94-111 and pp201-211.

161. This had first been established in 1942, but the plate-rolling plant did not open until 1949.

162. Søren Thorsøe, Peter Simonsen, Søren Krogh-Andersen, Frederik Frederichsen, and Henrik Vaupel, DFDS 1866-1991: Ship Development through 125 Years – from Paddle Steamer to Ro/Ro Ship, World Ship Society and DFDS, Copenhagen, 1991, p44.

163. Ole Stig Johannesen, Mærskbådene: Rederiernes skibe gennem de første 50 år, Editions Maritimes, Roskilde, 2006, pp153-173.

164. Ove Hornby, 'With Constant Care…' A.P. Møller: Shipowner 1876-1965, Schultz, Copenhagen, 1988, pp184-189.

165. Ove Hornby, 'With Constant Care…' A.P. Møller: Shipowner 1876-1965, Schultz, Copenhagen, 1988, pp187-188.

166. Ole Stig Johannesen, Mærskbådene: Rederiernes skibe gennem de første 50 år, Editions Maritimes, Roskilde, 2006, p201 and pp206-208.

167. Ole Stig Johannesen, Mærskbådene: Rederiernes skibe gennem de første 50 år, Editions Maritimes, Roskilde, 2006, pp234-235, p237, p244 and p246. See also Ole Stig Johannesen, Mærskbådene II: Skibene i årene 1955-1975, Editions Maritimes, Roskilde, 2007, pp26-30, pp33-46, p48, p55 and p63.

168. Poul Westphall, Aktieselskabet Det Østasiatiske Kompagni – The East Asiatic Company Ltd, Det Østasiatiske Kompagni, Copenhagen, 1972, pp126-129 and pp144-155.

169. Ole Stig Johannesen, ØK's skibe – The EAC Fleet, Forlaget Nautilus, Frederiksværk, 2003, pp163-164.

170. Ole Sørensen, B&W-dieselmotorens historie 1898-2008, MAN Diesel/Diesel House, Copenhagen, 2008, pp92-93.

171. 'Extensive Tests of Supercharged Engine – Trials of the MS Songkhla, owned by the East Asiatic Co. 35 per cent increase in output from supercharged 8,750 bhp engine,' The Motor Ship, May 1953, pp 55-59.

172. 'Extensive Tests of Supercharged Engine – Trials of the MS Songkhla, owned by the East Asiatic Co. 35 per cent increase in output from supercharged 8,750 bhp engine,' The Motor Ship, May 1953, p55.

173. J. Berring M.Sc., M.I.Mare. E., 'Burmeister & Wain – Pioneers of Low-Speed Marine Diesel Engines,' special supplement to The Motor Ship, April 1970, p12.

174. Bruce Peter, Knud E. Hansen A/S: Ship Design through Seven Decades, Forlaget Nautilus, Frederiksværk, 2007, pp19-25.

175. Ambrose Greenway, Cargo Liners: An Illustrated History, Seaforth Publishing, Barnsley, 2009, p98 and pp103-104.

176. Ole Stig Johannesen, Skoubådene – skibene fra rederiet Ove Skou, Forlaget Nautilus, Frederiksværk, 2004, pp9-11.

177. Ole Stig Johannesen, Skoubådene – skibene fra rederiet Ove Skou, Forlaget Nautilus, Frederiksværk, 2004, pp37-40.

178. Ole Stig Johannesen, Skoubådene – skibene fra rederiet Ove Skou, Forlaget Nautilus, Frederiksværk, 2004, p69, pp91-103, pp108-123, pp127-130 and pp140-143.

179. Interview with Hans Henrik Petersen, formerly of Helsingør Skibsværft, by Bruce Peter by telephone on 15 January 2009.

180. Ole Stig Johannesen, The Torm Ships: The Torm Fleet Through 120 Years, Editions Maritimes, Roskilde, 2009, pp114-118 and pp120-128.

181. Ole Stig Johannesen, Dansk-Fransk – skibene fra A/S Det Dansk-Fransk Dampskibsselskab, Editions Maritimes, Roskilde, 2005, pp121-129.

182. Ole Stig Johannesen, Dansk-Fransk – skibene fra A/S Det Dansk-Fransk Dampskibsselskab, Editions Maritimes, Roskilde, 2005, pp9-10.

183. Ole Stig Johannesen, Dansk-Fransk – skibene fra A/S Det Dansk-Fransk Dampskibsselskab, Editions Maritimes, Roskilde, 2005, pp13-14.

184. Ole Stig Johannesen, Dansk-Fransk – skibene fra A/S Det Dansk-Fransk Dampskibsselskab, Editions Maritimes, Roskilde, 2005, p14.

185. Ole Stig Johannesen, Dansk-Fransk – skibene fra A/S Det Dansk-Fransk Dampskibsselskab, Editions Maritimes, Roskilde, 2005, pp15-16.

186. Søren Thorsøe, Peter Simonsen and Frederik Frederichsen, The Dannebrog Fleet 1883-1993, Dannebrog Rederi A/S, Rungsted, 1993, p10.

187. Søren Thorsøe, Peter Simonsen, Søren Krogh-Andersen, Frederik Frederichsen and Henrik Vaupel, DFDS 1866-1991: Ship Development through 125 Years – from Paddle Steamer to Ro/Ro Ship, World Ship Society and DFDS, Copenhagen, 1991, pp385-386 and pp391-395.

188. Søren Thorsøe, Peter Simonsen, Søren Krogh-Andersen, Frederik Frederichsen and Henrik Vaupel, DFDS 1866-1991: Ship Development through 125 Years – from Paddle Steamer to Ro/Ro Ship, World Ship Society and DFDS, Copenhagen, 1991, p48. See also Dag Bakka Jr, Linjer Rundt Jorden, Seagull, Bergen, 2008, p64, p70 and p212.

189. Søren Thorsøe, Peter Simonsen and Frederik Frederichsen, The Dannebrog Fleet 1883-1993, Dannebrog Rederi A/S, Rungsted, 1993, pp10-11.

190. Bent Mikkelsen, Bent, Danske Rederier Volume 7: The Lauritzen Fleet 1884-1945, Forlaget Betty Nordgas, Ringkøbing, 2009, p243.

191. Dag Bakka Jr, Linjer Rundt Jorden, Seagull, Bergen, 2008, p160.

192. Dag Bakka Jr, Linjer Rundt Jorden, Seagull, Bergen, 2008, pp89-90.

193. Ole Stig Johannesen, The Torm Ships: The Torm Fleet Through 120 Years, Editions Maritimes, Roskilde, 2009, pp14-15.

194. Ambrose Greenway, Cargo Liners: An Illustrated History, Seaforth Publishing, Barnsley, 2009, pp109-110.

195. Interviews with Henrik Ditlev-Jørgensen, former member of the East Asiatic Company's Newbuilding Department 1969-1983, by Bruce Peter by telephone on 6 and 9 January 2009.

196. Ole Stig Johannesen, ØK's skibe – The EAC Fleet, Forlaget Nautilus, Frederiksværk, 2003, pp212-216, p219 and p225.

197. Ole Stig Johannesen, ØK's skibe – The EAC Fleet, Forlaget Nautilus, Frederiksværk, 2003, pp222-223 and pp227-229.

198. Ole Stig Johannesen, ØK's skibe – The EAC Fleet, Forlaget Nautilus, Frederiksværk, 2003, p228.

199. Interview with Henrik Ditlev-Jørgensen, former member of the East Asiatic Company's Newbuilding Department 1969-1983, by Bruce Peter by telephone on 6 January 2009.

200. Ole Stig Johannesen, The Torm Ships: The Torm Fleet Through 120 Years, Editions Maritimes, Roskilde, 2009, pp131-134.

201. Ole Stig Johannesen, Mærskbådene II: Skibene i årene 1955-1975, Editions Maritimes, Roskilde, 2007, pp49-50 and pp52-53.

202. Ole Stig Johannesen, ØK's skibe – The EAC Fleet, Forlaget Nautilus, Frederiksværk, 2003, pp229-237.

203. Interview with Henrik Ditlev-Jørgensen, former member of the East Asiatic Company's Newbuilding Department 1969-1983, by Bruce Peter by telephone on 9 January 2009.

204. 'Falstria – an 18,300 ton d.w. cellular container ship for the East Asiatic Co., The Motor Ship, November 1971, pp330-331. Regarding the control of torsionional forces, Preben Terndrup Pedersen of the Technical University of Denmark observes that it was subsequently found that longitudinal box girders were ineffective in reducing warping stresses but could lessen their absolute magnitude.

205. 'Atrevida – East Asiatic Co's 10,880/ 14,200gt 21 ½-knot Cargo Liner, The Motor Ship, May 1968, p61.

206 Ole Stig Johannesen, ØK's skibe – The EAC Fleet, Forlaget Nautilus, Frederiksværk, 2003, pp229-237.

207. Interview with Henrik Ditlev-Jørgensen, former member of the East Asiatic Company's Newbuilding Department 1969-1983, by Bruce Peter by telephone on 6 January 2009.

208. Thomas Larsen and Finn Mortensen, Mærsk Mc-Kinney Møller: et personligt portræt af Danmarks største erhvervsmand, Gyldendal Business, Copenhagen, 2008, pp105-106.

209. Ove Hornby, 'With Constant Care…' A.P. Møller: Shipowner 1876-1965, Schultz, Copenhagen, 1988, pp201-208.

210. Ove Hornby, 'With Constant Care…' A.P. Møller: Shipowner 1876-1965, Schultz, Copenhagen, 1988, p206.

211. Ole Stig Johannesen, Mærskbådene II: Skibene i årene 1955-1975, Editions

Maritimes, Roskilde, 2007, pp87-88, pp91-92 and pp103-104.

212. Ove Hornby, 'With Constant Care…' A.P. Møller: Shipowner 1876-1965, Schultz, Copenhagen, 1988, pp203-206.

213. Ove Hornby, 'With Constant Care…' A.P. Møller: Shipowner 1876-1965, Schultz, Copenhagen, 1988, pp207-208.

214. Ove Hornby, 'With Constant Care…' A.P. Møller: Shipowner 1876-1965, Schultz, Copenhagen, 1988, pp237-240.

215. Thomas Larsen and Finn Mortensen, Mærsk Mc-Kinney Møller: En personligt portræt af Danmarks største erhvervsmand, Gyldendal Business, Copenhagen, 2008, pp278-279.

216. Interview with Erik Heirung by Bruce Peter at his home in Oslo on 29 May 2013.

217. Interview with Erik Heirung by Bruce Peter at his home in Oslo on 29 May 2013.

218. Interview with Erik Heirung by Bruce Peter at his home in Oslo on 29 May 2013.

219. Ole Stig Johannesen, Mærskbådene II: Skibene i årene 1955-1975, Editions Maritimes, Roskilde, 2007, pp133-137, pp140-144, pp146-151 and pp157-159.

220. Brian J. Cudahy, How Container Ships Changed the World, Fordham University Press, New York, 2006, pp20-29.

221. Brian J. Cudahy, How Container Ships Changed the World, Fordham University Press, New York, 2006, pp30-41.

222. Ewan Corlett, The Ship: The Revolution in Merchant Shipping, National Maritime Museum, London, 1981, p4.

223. Søren Thorsøe, Peter Simonsen, Søren Krogh-Andersen, Frederik Frederichsen, and Henrik Vaupel, DFDS 1866-1991: Ship Development through 125 Years – from Paddle Steamer to Ro/Ro Ship, World Ship Society and DFDS, Copenhagen, 1991, pp411-412, pp414-415 and pp418-419.

224. '£11 Million Programme for a series of eight 20-knot cargo liners,' The Motor Ship, September 1966, pp260-261.

225. Bent Mikkelsen, Bent, Danske Rederier Volume 8: The Lauritzen Fleet 1945-2009, Forlaget Betty Nordgas, Ringkøbing, 2009, pp242-244.

226. Kåre Lauring, Containertrafik gennem 50 år, Handesls- og Søfartsmuseet på Kronborg, 2008, p29.

227. Brian J. Cudahy, How Container Ships Changed the World, Fordham University Press, New York, 2006, pp86-87.

228. Poul Westphall, Aktieselskabet Det Østasiatiske Kompagni – The East Asiatic Company Ltd, Det Østasiatiske Kompagni, Copenhagen, 1972, p12.

229. Brian J. Cudahy, How Container Ships Changed the World, Fordham University Press, New York, 2006, p105.

230. Søren Thorsøe, Peter Simonsen, Søren Krogh-Andersen, Frederik Frederichsen, and Henrik Vaupel, DFDS 1866-1991: Ship Development through 125 Years – from Paddle Steamer to Ro/Ro Ship, World Ship Society and DFDS, Copenhagen, 1991, pp411-412, pp414-415 and pp418-419.

231. Brian J. Cudahy, How Container Ships Changed the World, Fordham University Press, New York, 2006, p103.

232. Kåre Lauring, Containertrafik gennem 50 år, Handesls- og Søfartsmuseet på Kronborg, 2008, p42.

233. Poul Westphall, Aktieselskabet Det Østasiatiske Kompagni – The East Asiatic Company Ltd, Det Østasiatiske Kompagni, Copenhagen, 1972, p12.

234. Dag Bakka Jr, Linjer Rundt Jorden, Seagull, Bergen, 2008, p84 and p140. See also Eric Jennings, Cargoes: A Century Story of the Far Eastern Freight Conference, Meridian Communications, Singapore, 1980, pp59-63.

235. Ole Stig Johannesen, ØK's skibe – The EAC Fleet, Forlaget Nautilus, Frederiksværk, 2003, pp18-20.

236. Interview with Henrik Ditlev-Jørgensen, former member of the East Asiatic Company's Newbuilding Department 1969-1983, by Bruce Peter by telephone on 6 January 2009.

237. 'Falstria – an 18,300gt d.w. cellular container ship for the East Asiatic Co., The Motor Ship, November 1971, p331.

238. Interview with Henrik Ditlev-Jørgensen, former member of the East Asiatic Company's Newbuilding Department 1969-1983, by Bruce Peter by telephone on 6 January 2009.

239. 'Falstria – an 18,300gt d.w. cellular container ship for the East Asiatic Co., The Motor Ship, November 1971, p330.

240. 'Falstria – an 18,300gt d.w. cellular container ship for the East Asiatic Co., The Motor Ship, November 1971, pp330-331.

241. Poul Westphall, Aktieselskabet Det Østasiatiske Kompagni – The East Asiatic Company Ltd, Det Østasiatiske Kompagni, Copenhagen, 1972, p196.

242. Thorsten Rinman, Rederiet: Johnson Line under 100 år, Rinman & Lindén, Gothenburg, 1990, p156.

243. David Howarth and Stephen Howarth, The Story of P&O, Weidenfeld & Nicolson, London, 1986, pp172-173.

244. Interview with Henrik Ditlev-Jørgensen, former member of the East Asiatic Company's Newbuilding Department 1969-1983, by Bruce Peter by telephone on 9 January 2009.

245. L. Sinclair, and A. Emerson, 'The Design Development of Propellers for High-powered Merchant Vessels,' Shipbuilding and Shipping Record, February 1968, pp161-166.

246. Interview with Henrik Ditlev-Jørgensen, former member of the East Asiatic Company's Newbuilding Department 1969-1983, by Bruce Peter by telephone on 9

January 2009.

247. Interview with Henrik Ditlev-Jørgensen, former member of the East Asiatic Company's Newbuilding Department 1969-1983, by Bruce Peter by telephone on 9 January 2009.

248. 'The 84,600-bhp triple-screw container ship Elbe Maru,' The Motor Ship, June 1972, pp105-111.

249. 'Recent Motor Ships of Interest: Toyama,' The Motor Ship, March 1973, p533.

250. 'First ScandDutch-consortium Far East triple-screw container ship completed: The Öresundsvarvet-built Nihon of 50,000 gross tons, powered by three Götaverken 850/1700 VGS-U engines totalling 75,000 bhp,' The Motor Ship, July 1972, pp167-169.

251. Interview with Henrik Ditlev-Jørgensen, former member of the East Asiatic Company's Newbuilding Department 1969-1983, by Bruce Peter by telephone on 9 January 2009.

252. 'Selandia: 60 years on – a 75,000 bhp container ship,' The Motor Ship, October 1972, pp298-299.

253. Ole Sørensen, B&W-dieselmotorens historie 1898-2008, MAN Diesel/Diesel House, Copenhagen, 2008, p116.

254. Interview with Henrik Ditlev-Jørgensen, former member of the East Asiatic Company's Newbuilding Department 1969-1983, by Bruce Peter by telephone on 6 January 2009.

255. Eric Jennings, Cargoes: A Century Story of the Far Eastern Freight Conference, Meridian Communications, Singapore, 1980, p61.

256. Interviews with Henrik Ditlev-Jørgensen, former member of the East Asiatic Company's Newbuilding Department 1969-1983, by Bruce Peter by telephone on 6 and 9 January 2009.

257. Kåre Lauring, Containertrafik gennem 50 år, Handesls- og Søfartsmuseet på Kronborg, 2008, p50.

258. Interview with Finn Wollesen Pedersen, Managing Director of Knud E. Hansen A/S by Bruce Peter at the Shippax Conference in Bastia on 17 May 2008.

259. Ole Sørensen, B&W-dieselmotorens historie 1898-2008, MAN Diesel/Diesel House, Copenhagen, 2008, pp141-142.

260. Ole Sørensen, B&W-dieselmotorens historie 1898-2008, MAN Diesel/Diesel House, Copenhagen, 2008, pp146-147.

261. Søren Ellemose, Kompagniet: H.N. Andersens ØK 1884-2007, Jyllands-Postens Forlag, 2007, p192.

262. Interview with Niels Otto Knudsen, former Chief Naval Architect, Nakskov Skibsværft, by Bruce Peter by telephone on 29 January 2011.

263. Interview with Niels Otto Knudsen, former Chief Naval Architect, Nakskov Skibsværft, by Bruce Peter by telephone on 29 January 2011. See also the appendix in Per Koch, Nakskov Skibsværfts Historie: Episoder under teater, Per Kochs Forlag, Nakskov, 2005.

264. Kåre Lauring, Containertrafik gennem 50 år, Handesls- og Søfartsmuseet på Kronborg, 2008, p52.

265. Kåre Lauring, Containertrafik gennem 50 år, Handesls- og Søfartsmuseet på Kronborg, 2008.

266. Søren Ellemose, Kompagniet: H.N. Andersens ØK 1884-2007, Jyllands-Postens Forlag, 2007, pp191-192.

267. Søren Ellemose, Kompagniet: H.N. Andersens ØK 1884-2007, Jyllands-Postens Forlag, 2007, pp194-253.

268. Kåre Lauring, Containertrafik gennem 50 år, Handesls- og Søfartsmuseet på Kronborg, 2008, p57.

269. Kåre Lauring, Containertrafik gennem 50 år, Handesls- og Søfartsmuseet på Kronborg, 2008, p57.

270. Ole Stig Johannesen, ØK's skibe – The EAC Fleet, Forlaget Nautilus, Frederiksværk, 2003, pp20-21.

271. Ole Stig Johannesen, ØK's skibe – The EAC Fleet, Forlaget Nautilus, Frederiksværk, 2003, pp20-21.

272. Kåre Lauring, Containertrafik gennem 50 år, Handesls- og Søfartsmuseet på Kronborg, 2008, pp70-71.

273. See Chresten A. Bjerrum, ØK i uvejr: Da ØK's aktiekapital sank i Stillehavet, Forlaget Børsen, Copenhagen, 1993.

274. Kåre Lauring, Containertrafik gennem 50 år, Handesls- og Søfartsmuseet på Kronborg, 2008, p72.

275. Ole Stig Johannesen, ØK's skibe – The EAC Fleet, Forlaget Nautilus, Frederiksværk, 2003, pp241-242.

276. Ole Stig Johannesen, Mærskbådene II: Skibene i årene 1955-1975, Editions Maritimes, Roskilde, 2007, p10.

277. Interviews with Henrik Ditlev-Jørgensen, former member of the East Asiatic Company's Newbuilding Department 1969-1983, by Bruce Peter by telephone on 6 and 9 January 2009.

278. Ole Stig Johannesen, Mærskbådene II: Skibene i årene 1955-1975, Editions Maritimes, Roskilde, 2007, p16.

279. 'Månedens Skib: Svendborg Mærsk,' Søfart, No. 3, 1974, pp18-21.

280. Interview with Carsten Melchiors, Danish Maritime Fund, by Bruce Peter by telephone on 29 January 2011.

281. Brian J. Cudahy, How Container Ships Changed the World, Fordham University Press, New York, 2006, p69.

282. Interview with Jens J. Kappel, former Head of Newbuilding, Maersk Line, by Bruce

Peter on 28 April 2008.

283. Several former crew members have told the author that the Flender-built examples were of far inferior quality to those from Blohm & Voss.

284. Interview with Jens J. Kappel, former Head of Newbuilding, Maersk Line, by Bruce Peter on 28 April 2008.

285. 'TS *Adrian Maersk*: Das erste von sechs Vollcontainerschiffen für A.P. Moeller, Kopenhagen,' Schiff & Hafen, Vol. 11, 1975, pp 979-984.

286. 'Månedens Skib: *Adrian Mærsk*,' Søfart, No. 6, 1975, pp14-15. See also Ole Stig Johannesen, Mærskbådene II: Skibene i årene 1955-1975, Editions Maritimes, Roskilde, 2007, pp196-201, pp205-207 and pp210-215 and Ole Stig Johannesen, Mærskflåden: Skibene i årene 1976-1990, Editions Maritimes, Roskilde, 2010, pp23-24, pp26-28 and pp30-31.

287. Interview with Jens J. Kappel, former Head of Newbuilding, Maersk Line, by Bruce Peter on 28 April 2008.

288. Interview with Jens J. Kappel, former Head of Newbuilding, Maersk Line, by Bruce Peter on 28 April 2008.

289. Ole Stig Johannesen, Mærskbådene II: Skibene i årene 1955-1975, Editions Maritimes, Roskilde, 2007, pp196-201.

290. Interview with Per Jørgensen, Director and Skibsreder, A.P. Møller-Maersk, by Bruce Peter on 17 February 2008.

291. Ole Stig Johannesen, Mærskbådene II: Skibene i årene 1955-1975, Editions Maritimes, Roskilde, 2007, pp192-194 and p202.

292. Ole Stig Johannesen, Mærskflåden: Skibene i årene 1976-1990, Editions Maritimes, Roskilde, 2010, pp44-51.

293. Interview with Jens J. Kappel, former Head of Newbuilding, Maersk Line, by Bruce Peter on 28 April 2008.

294. Interview with Jens J. Kappel, former Head of Newbuilding, Maersk Line, by Bruce Peter on 28 April 2008.

295. Interview with Per Jørgensen, Director and Skibsreder, A.P. Møller-Maersk, by Bruce Peter on 17 February 2008. See also Ole Stig Johannesen, Mærskbådene II: Skibene i årene 1955-1975, Editions Maritimes, Roskilde, 2007, pp200-201.

296. Ole Stig Johannesen, Mærskbådene II: Skibene i årene 1955-1975, Editions Maritimes, Roskilde, 2007, p196.

297. Interview with Kjell Harr, formerly of Odense Staalskibsværft, by Bruce Peter by telephone on 12 January 2011.

298. Interview with Jens J. Kappel, former Head of Newbuilding, Maersk Line, by Bruce Peter on 28 April 2008.

299. Interview with Jens J. Kappel, former Head of Newbuilding, Maersk Line, by Bruce Peter on 28 April 2008.

300. Ole Stig Johannesen, Mærskflåden: Skibene i årene 1976-1990, Editions Maritimes, Roskilde, 2010, pp52-56, p61, pp63-64 and pp76-77.

301. Ole Stig Johannesen, Mærskflåden: Skibene i årene 1976-1990, Editions Maritimes, Roskilde, 2010, p89.

302. Antoine Fremont, 'Global Maritime Networks: The case of Maersk,' No. 15, 2007, p435.

303. Interview with Jens J. Kappel, former Head of Newbuilding, Maersk Line, by Bruce Peter on 28 April 2008.

304. Ole Stig Johannesen, Mærskflåden: Skibene i årene 1976-1990, Editions Maritimes, Roskilde, 2010, pp99-104, p106 and pp109-114.

305. Hans Jeppesen, Svend Aage Andersen and Hans Christian Johansen, Dansk Søfarts Historie 7 1960-2000: Containere & koncentration, Gyldendal, Copenhagen, 2000, p147.

306. Interview with Kjell Harr, formerly of Odense Staalskibsværft, by Bruce Peter by telephone on 12 January 2011.

307. Interview with Kjell Harr, formerly of Odense Staalskibsværft, by Bruce Peter by telephone on 12 January 2011.

308. Interview with Kjell Harr, formerly of Odense Staalskibsværft, by Bruce Peter by telephone on 12 January 2011. See also Ole Stig Johannesen, Mærskflåden: Skibene i årene 1976-1990, Editions Maritimes, Roskilde, 2010, p101.

309. Interview with Kjell Harr, formerly of Odense Staalskibsværft, by Bruce Peter by telephone on 12 January 2011.

310. Interview with Kjell Harr, formerly of Odense Staalskibsværft, by Bruce Peter by telephone on 12 January 2011. See also Ole Stig Johannesen, Mærskflåden: Skibene i årene 1976-1990, Editions Maritimes, Roskilde, 2010, p106.

311. Interview with Jens J. Kappel, former Head of Newbuilding, Maersk Line, by Bruce Peter on 28 April 2008.

312. Hans Jeppesen, Svend Aage Andersen and Hans Christian Johansen, Dansk Søfarts Historie 7 1960-2000: Containere & koncentration, Gyldendal, Copenhagen, 2000, p147.

313. 'Optimising the Ship's Design,' Mærsk Post, No 1, March 2006.

314. Hans Jeppesen, Svend Aage Andersen and Hans Christian Johansen, Dansk Søfarts Historie 7 1960-2000: Containere & koncentration, Gyldendal, Copenhagen, 2000, pp117-119.

315. Hans Jeppesen, Svend Aage Andersen and Hans Christian Johansen, Dansk Søfarts Historie 7 1960-2000: Containere & koncentration, Gyldendal, Copenhagen, 2000, pp118-121.

316. Ole Lange, Logbog For Lauritzen 1884-1995, Handelshøjskolens Forlag, Copenhagen, 1995, pp335-336. See also Bent Mikkelsen, Danske Rederier Volume 8:

The Lauritzen Fleet 1884-1945, Forlaget Betty Nordgas, Ringkøbing, 2009, pp240-241.

317. Hans Jeppesen, Svend Aage Andersen and Hans Christian Johansen, Dansk Søfarts Historie 7 1960-2000: Containere & koncentration, Gyldendal, Copenhagen, 2000, pp121-122.

318. Brian J. Cudahy, How Container Ships Changed the World, Fordham University Press, New York, 2006, pp163-165.

319. Brian J. Cudahy, How Container Ships Changed the World, Fordham University Press, New York, 2006, p211.

320. Interview with Kjell Harr, formerly of Odense Staalskibsværft, by Bruce Peter by telephone on 12 January 2011.

321. Brian J. Cudahy, How Container Ships Changed the World, Fordham University Press, New York, 2006, pp211-214.

322. Everett Rodgers' 'Diffusion of Innovations' theory is illustrated by a bell-curve diagram. At the front of the curve are a small number of innovators and in the centre are early adoptors and late adoptors of new trends (who form the majority of any given population). At the rear are conservative rejectionists, who are difficult to persuade to try anything new. Rodgers suggests that it is early adoptors who usually enjoy the greatest success, learning and improving upon the work of innovators, then selling their ideas on to late adoptors. See Everett Rodgers, Diffusion of Innovations, Glencoe, New York, 1962.

323. Antoine Fremont, 'Global Maritime Networks: The case of Maersk,' Journal of Transport Geography, No. 15, 2007, pp431.

324. Interview with Kjell Harr, formerly of Odense Staalskibsværft, by Bruce Peter by telephone on 12 January 2011.

325. See Thomas Larsen and Finn Mortensen, Mærsk Mc-Kinney Møller: et personligt portræt af Danmarks største erhvervsmand, Gyldendal Business, Copenhagen, 2008 and Jan Cortzen, Myten Møller, Børsens Forlag, Copenhagen, 1993 and 2009 for detailed accounts of Mærsk Mc-Kinney Møller's life and business career.

326. Interview with Kjell Harr, formerly of Odense Staalskibsværft, by Bruce Peter by telephone on 12 January 2011.

327. Interview with Kjell Harr, formerly of Odense Staalskibsværft, by Bruce Peter by telephone on 12 January 2011.

328. '*Sovereign Mærsk*,' Mærsk Post, No 3, September 1997, p3.

329. '*Susan Mærsk* sætter ny rekord,' Mærsk Post, No 3, September 1999, p14.

330. 'Den nye L-type,' Mærsk Post, No 1, March 2002, pp12-13.

331. Jack A. Somer, and Helmut Behling, From The Mountains To The Seas: The Sulzer Diesel Engine, Wärtsilä NSD, Winterthur, 1998, pp143-147.

332. Jack A. Somer, and Helmut Behling, From The Mountains To The Seas: The Sulzer Diesel Engine, Wärtsilä NSD, Winterthur, 1998, pp146-147.

333. Thomas Larsen and Finn Mortensen, Mærsk Mc-Kinney Møller: et personligt portræt af Danmarks største erhvervsmand, Gyldendal Business, Copenhagen, 2008, pp200-201.

334. Thomas Larsen and Finn Mortensen, Mærsk Mc-Kinney Møller: En personligt portræt af Danmarks største erhervsmand, Gyldendal Business, Copenhagen, 2008, pp195-202.

335 Ole Stig Johannesen, ØK's skibe – The EAC Fleet, Forlaget Nautilus, Frederiksværk, 2003, p21.

336. 'Den sydafrikanske forbindelse,' Mærsk Post, No 3, September 1999, p22.

337. 'Den sydafrikanske forbindelse,' Mærsk Post, No 3, September 1999, p22.

338. Information courtesy of Michael Brauner Clausen, formerly of Torm Lines and Danmarks Rederiforeningen, sent to the author in an email dated 19 January 2014.

339. Information courtesy of Michael Brauner Clausen, formerly of Torm Lines and Danmarks Rederiforeningen, sent to the author in an email dated 19 January 2014.

340. Thomas Larsen and Finn Mortensen, Mærsk Mc-Kinney Møller: En personligt portræt af Danmarks største erhervsmand, Gyldendal Business, Copenhagen, 2008, pp167-174.

341. Brian J. Cudahy, How Container Ships Changed the World, Fordham University Press, New York, 2006, pp187-189.

342. Foreword by Jess Søderberg, Mærsk Post, No 3, September 1999, p2.

343. Kåre Lauring, Containertrafik gennem 50 år, Handesls- og Søfartsmuseet på Kronborg, 2008, pp81-82.

344. 'Containerterminaler over hele verden,' Mærsk Post, No 2, June 2002, pp6-7.

345. See A.M. Shipper and J.M. Janse, Mediterranean Shipping Company SA: Over 30 Years of Success, Shipper and Janse, Antwerp, 2003 for a detailed analysis of the Company's history and development.

346. Niels Lunde, Hr. Møllers nye mand: Nils Smedegaards revolution på Esplanaden – og på Carlsberg, Jyllands-Postens Forlag, Copenhagen, 2008, pp141-142.

347. Niels Lunde, Hr. Mollers Nye Mand: Nils Smedegaards revolution på Esplanaden – og på Carlsberg, Jyllands-Postens Forlag, Copenhagen, 2008, pp.141-142.

348. Interview with Per Jørgensen, Director and Skibsreder, A.P. Møller-Maersk, by Bruce Peter on 17 February 2008.

349. 'Forenede kræfter,' Mærsk Post, No 4, December 2005, p5.

350. See Bram Oosterwijk and Wim de Regt, Back on Course: Royal Nedlloyd – Three Decades, P&O Nedlloyd, Rotterdam, 2004 for a detailed description of P&O and Nedlloyd container ship design development.

351. Søren Ellemose, Hr. Møller: Årets gang i A.P. Møller-Maersk, Documentas, Hellerup, 2008, p90.

352. Søren Ellemose, Hr. Møller: Årets gang i A.P. Møller-Maersk, Documentas,

Hellerup, 2008, p90.

353. Søren Domino, 'Konkurrenter sejler Mærsk agterud,' Berlingske Tidende, 24 July 2006.

354. Foreword by Jess Søderberg, Mærsk Post, No 3, September 2006, p2.

355. Søren Ellemose, Hr. Møller: Årets gang i A.P. Møller-Maersk, Documentas, Hellerup, 2008, p89.

356. Søren Domino, 'Konkurrenter sejler Mærsk agterud,' Berlingske Tidende, 24 July 2006.

357. Birgitte Erhardtsen and Vibeke Vestergaard, 'Topposter: det er godt nok pinligt,' Berlingske Tidende, 1 December 2006. See also Søren Domino, 'Flere bølgedale end normalt for Mærsk,' Berlingske Tidende, 1 December 2006.

358. Aktieugebrev No. 6, 2006, cited in Kåre Lauring, Containertrafik gennem 50 år, Handesls- og Søfartsmuseet på Kronborg, 2008, p86.

359. Berlingske Tidende, 23 July 2006, cited in Kåre Lauring, Containertrafik gennem 50 år, Handesls- og Søfartsmuseet på Kronborg, 2008, p86.

360. 'Endnu en Mærsk-boss i kulden,' Berlingske Tidende, 7 January 2009.

361. Niels Lunde, Hr. Møllers nye mand: Nils Smedegaards revolution på Esplanaden – og på Carlsberg, Jyllands-Postens Forlag, Copenhagen, 2008 pp158-163.

362. 'A Beam Model for the Torsional-Bending Response of Ship Hulls,' The Royal Institution of Naval Architects Transactions Vol. 125, pp 171-182, 1983.

363. Interview with Kjell Harr, formerly of Odense Staalskibsværft, by Bruce Peter by telephone on 12 January 2011.

364. Interview with Kjell Harr, formerly of Odense Staalskibsværft, by Bruce Peter by telephone on 12 January 2011.

365. 'Beyond Class: Making the Emma Maersk,' Surveyor: A Quarterly Magazine from ABS, American Bureau of Shipping, Winter 2008, pp2-7.

366. Interview with Kjell Harr, formerly of Odense Staalskibsværft, by Bruce Peter by telephone on 12 January 2011.

367. Interview with Kjell Harr, formerly of Odense Staalskibsværft, by Bruce Peter by telephone on 12 January 2011.

368. 'To miljøvenlige damer,' Mærsk Post, No 3, September 2005, pp4-5.

369. Interview with Kjell Harr, formerly of Odense Staalskibsværft, by Bruce Peter by telephone on 12 January 2011.

370. 'To miljøvenlige damer,' Mærsk Post, No 3, September 2005, p5.

371. Aktieugebrev No 24, 2006, cited in Kåre Lauring, Containertrafik gennem 50 år, Handesls- og Søfartsmuseet på Kronborg, 2008, p87.

372. 'Beyond Class: Making the Emma Maersk,' Surveyor: A Quarterly Magazine from ABS, American Bureau of Shipping, Winter 2008, p3.

373. Interview with Kjell Harr, formerly of Odense Staalskibsværft, by Bruce Peter by telephone on 12 January 2011.

374. Email message from Preben Terndrup Pedersen to Bruce Peter, 14 March 2011.

375. Interview with Kjell Harr, formerly of Odense Staalskibsværft, by Bruce Peter by telephone on 12 January 2011.

376. 'Beyond Class: Making the Emma Maersk,' Surveyor: A Quarterly Magazine from ABS, American Bureau of Shipping, Winter 2008, p2.

377. Interview with Kjell Harr, formerly of Odense Staalskibsværft, by Bruce Peter by telephone on 12 January 2011.

378. Interview with Kjell Harr, formerly of Odense Staalskibsværft, by Bruce Peter by telephone on 12 January 2011.

379. 'The world is enthusiastic about Emma Mærsk,' Mærsk Post, No 3, September 2006, p16.

380. 'The world is enthusiastic about Emma Mærsk,' Mærsk Post, No 3, September 2006, p16.

381. 'Sidste containerskib fra Lindø?,' Søfart, 6 March 2009, p147.

382. See Niels Lunde, Hr. Møllers nye mand: Nils Smedegaards revolution på Esplanaden – og på Carlsberg, Jyllands-Postens Forlag, Copenhagen, 2008 for a detailed description of Andersen's background and business career.

383. Jørgen Andresen, 'FT: Store omvæltninger I Maersk Line,' Børsen, 4 December 2007 and 'Maersk-chef: 50 pct af containerlaster forsinket,' Børsen, 10 December 2007.

384. Søren Ellemose, Esplanaden: APM i krise og forandring: Årets gang i A.P. Møller-Maersk, Forlaget Documentas, Hellerup, 2009, p23.

385. Søren Ellemose, Esplanaden: APM i krise og forandring: Årets gang I A.P. Møller-Maersk, Forlaget Documentas, Hellerup, 2009, p23.

386. Robert Wright, 'Maersk halts size and integration strategies,' Financial Times, 26 May 2008.

387. Thomas Grøndorf, 'Changing our corporate mindset,' Mærsk Post, No 2, June 2009, p6.

388. Thomas Grøndorf, 'Changing our corporate mindset,' Mærsk Post, No 2, June 2009, p6.

389. Søren Ellemose, Esplanaden: APM i krise og forandring: Årets gang i A.P. Møller-Maersk, Forlaget Documentas, Hellerup, 2009, p25.

390. See Lars Jensen, The Culture Shock at Maersk Line, Vespucci Maritime Publishing, Copenhagen, 2014.

391. Michael Storgaard, 'A StreamLINE snapshot,' Mærsk Post, No 2, 2009, p22.

392. Philip Lee and John Churchill, 'We will change the game,' Mærsk Post, No 2, 2010, pp14-15.

393. Interview with Bo Cerup-Simonsen, Vice President, Maersk Maritime Technology, by Bruce Peter on 26 November 2013.

394. Interview with Bo Cerup-Simonsen, Vice President, Maersk Maritime Technology, by Bruce Peter on 26 November 2013.

395. Interview with Michael Heimann, Senior Sale & Purchase Portfolio Manager, Maersk Line, by Bruce Peter on 26 November 2013.

396. Interview with Michael Heimann, Senior Sale & Purchase Portfolio Manager, Maersk Line, by Bruce Peter on 26 November 2013.

397. The Hyundai type measures 366m x 49m whereas the E-class measures 398m x 56 m.

398. Interview with Michael Heimann, Senior Sale & Purchase Portfolio Manager, Maersk Line, by Bruce Peter on 26 November 2013.

399. 'Big, Bigger, Biggest,' Lloyd's List, 30 August 2013, p1.

400. Interview with Bo Cerup-Simonsen, Vice President, Maersk Maritime Technology, by Bruce Peter on 26 November 2013.

401. PdF of academic paper on 'Modern Environmental Assessment of Container Ship Transport,' supplied by Hans Otto Holmgaard Kristensen, Department of Mechanical Engineering, Denmark's Technical University, 2010. This was presented at the Society of Naval Architects and Marine Engineers' 2010 Annual Meeting in Seattle.

402. Interview with Bo Cerup-Simonsen, Vice President, Maersk Maritime Technology, by Bruce Peter on 26 November 2013.

403. Interview with Bo Cerup-Simonsen, Vice President, Maersk Maritime Technology, by Bruce Peter on 26 November 2013.

404. Interview with Bo Cerup-Simonsen, Vice President, Maersk Maritime Technology, by Bruce Peter on 26 November 2013.

405. Interview with Bo Cerup-Simonsen, Vice President, Maersk Maritime Technology, by Bruce Peter on 26 November 2013.

406. www.maritimedanmark.dk/?Id=11841, 15 September 2011.

407. Børsen, 14 September 2011, p48.

408. Børsen, 14 September 2011, p48.

409. Kolding's tenure at Den Danske Bank was also very short, lasting a mere 18 months that were marred by controversy. As a lawyer by training and a shipping manager by profession, he perhaps lacked the credibility of a career banker and so the Board of Directors dismissed him.

410. Majbritt Greve, Michael Wendelboe Hansen and Henrik Schaumburg-Müller, Container Shipping and Economic Development: A Case Study of A.P. Møller-Maersk in South East Asia, Copenhagen Business School Press, Copenhagen, 2007, pp65-66.

411. Majbritt Greve, Michael Wendelboe Hansen and Henrik Schaumburg-Müller, Container Shipping and Economic Development: A Case Study of A.P. Møller-Maersk in South East Asia, Copenhagen Business School Press, Copenhagen, 2007, pp66-67.

412. In the past, Maersk Line had supplied the US Military during the Korean War, the Vietnam War and the Gulf War.

413. http://maersktraining.com/maritime

414. http://www.cbs.dk/en/Continuing-Education/Master-Programmes/MBA-Uddannelser/Executive-MBA-in-Shipping-Logistics-The-Blue-MBA

415. www.bloomberg.com, 15 September 2011.

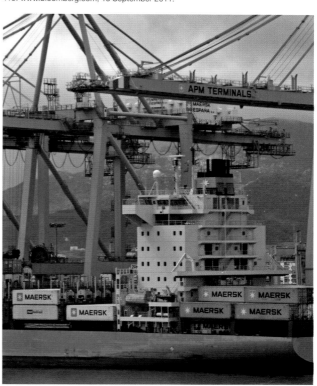

Bibliography

Interviews

Interview with Flemming Bredmose, formerly of Helsingør Skibsværft, by Bruce Peter by telephone on 8 January 2011.
Interview with Michael Brauner Clausen, formerly of Torm Lines, by Bruce Peter on 11 February 2011.
Interview with Bo Cerup-Simonsen, Vice President, Maersk Maritime Technology, by Bruce Peter on 26 November 2013.
Interviews with Henrik Ditlev-Jørgensen, former member of the East Asiatic Company's Newbuilding Department 1969-1983, by Bruce Peter by telephone on 6 and 9 January 2009.
Interview with Kjell Harr, formerly of Odense Staalskibsværft, by Bruce Peter by telephone on 12 January 2011.
Interview with Michael Heimann, Senior Sales & Purchase Portfolio Manager, Maersk Line, by Bruce Peter on 26 November 2013.
Interview with Per Jørgensen, Director and Skibsreder, A.P. Møller-Maersk, by Bruce Peter on 17 February 2008.
Interview with Jens J. Kappel, former Head of Newbuilding, Maersk Line, by Bruce Peter on 28 April 2008.
Interview with Niels Otto Knudsen, former Chief Naval Architect, Nakskov Skibsværft, by Bruce Peter by telephone on 29 January 2011.
Interview with Carsten Melchiors, Danish Maritime Fund, by Bruce Peter by telephone on 29 January 2011.
Interview with Finn Wollesen Pedersen, Managing Director of Knud E. Hansen A/S, by Bruce Peter at the Shippax Conference in Bastia on 17 May 2008.
Interview with Hens Henrik Petersen, formerly of Helsingør Skibsværft, by Bruce Peter by telephone on 15 January 2011.
Interview with Troels Posborg, Senior Lead Specialist Naval Architecture, Maersk Maritime Technology, by Bruce Peter on 26 November 2013.
Interview with Peter Povelsen, MAN Diesel, by Bruce Peter by telephone on 1 February 2011.

Books

Authored or edited works:
Bakka Jr, Dag, Linjer Rundt Jorden, Seagull, Bergen, 2008.
Bjerrum, Chresten A., ØK i Uvejr: Da ØK's aktiekapital sank I Stillehavet, Forlaget Børsen, Copenhagen, 1993.
Brooks, Mary R., Sea Change in Liner Shipping, Regulation and Managerial Decision-making in a Global Industry, Pergamon, Oxford, 2000.
Chalkley, A.P., Diesel Engines for Land and Marine Work, Constable, London, 1912.
Corlett, Ewan, The Ship: The Revolution in Merchant Shipping, National Maritime Museum, London, 1981.
Cortzen, Jan, Myten Møller, Børsens Forlag, Copenhagen, 1993 and 2009.
Cudahy, Brian J., How Container Ships Changed the World, Fordham University Press, New York, 2006.
Diesel, Rudolph, 'Theory and Design of an Economical Heat Engine to replace Steam Engines and Today's Internal Combustion Engines', Spon, London & New York, 1894.
Donovan, Arthur and Bonney, Joseph, The Box That Changed The World. Fifty years of container shipping – an illustrated history, Commonwealth Business Media, East Windsor, New Jersey, 2006.
Ellemose, Søren, Århundredets Stjerne, Jyllands-Postens Forlag, 2004.
Ellemose, Søren, Kompagniet: H.N. Andersens ØK 1884-2007, Jyllands-Postens Forlag, 2007.
Ellemose, Søren, Hr. Møller: Årets gang i A.P. Møller-Maersk, Documentas, Hellerup, 2008.
Ellemose, Søren, Esplanaden: APM i krise og forandring: Årets gang I A.P. Møller-Maersk, Forlaget Documentas, Hellerup, 2009.
Elphick, Peter, Liberty: The Ships that Won the War, Chatham Publishing, Chatham, 2001.
Eriksen, Erik, Værftet bag de 1000 skibe: Burmeister & Wain Skibsværft 1843-1993, Burmeister & Wain, Copenhagen, 1993.
Galbraith, John K., The Great Crash 1929, Penguin, London, 1954.
Gibson, Andrew and Donovan, Arthur, The Abandoned Ocean: A History of United States Maritime Policy, University of South Carolina Press, Columbia, 2000.
Graae, Poul, Hundrede år på havene, DFDS, Copenhagen, 1966.
Greenway, Ambrose, Cargo Liners: An Illustrated History, Seaforth Publishing, Barnsley, 2009.
Greve, Majbritt, Hansen, Michael Wendelboe and Schaumburg-Müller, Henrik, Container Shipping and Economic Development: A Case Study of A.P. Møller-Maersk in South East Asia, Copenhagen Business School Press, Copenhagen, 2007.
Guthrie, John, A History of Marine Engineering, Hutchison, London, 1971.
Holck, Jørgen and Simonsen, Jørgen D., Frit hav: Dansk skibsfart i 100 år, Danmarks Rederiforening, Copenhagen, 1984.
Hornby, Ove, 'With Constant Care…' A.P. Møller: Shipowner 1876-1965, Schultz, Copenhagen, 1988.
Howarth, David and Howarth, Stephen, The Story of P&O, Weidenfeld & Nicolson, London, 1986.
Hviid, Søren Lund (ed), Dansk Illustreret Skibsliste 2009, Sea Press, Århus, 2008.
Højbo, Flemming, Det Sidste Kompagni: ØKs storhed og fald, Schultz, Copenhagen, 1993.
Jennings, Eric, Cargoes: A Century Story of the Far Eastern Freight Conference, Meridian Communications, Singapore, 1980.
Jensen, Lars, The Culture Shock at Maersk Line, Vespucci Maritime Publishing, Copenhagen, 2014.
Jeppesen, Hans, Andersen, Svend Aage and Johansen, Hans Christian, Dansk Søfarts Historie 7 1960-2000: Containere & koncentration, Gyldendal, Copenhagen, 2000.
Johannesen, Ole Stig, ØK's skibe – The EAC Fleet, Forlaget Nautilus, Frederiksværk, 2003.

Johannesen, Ole Stig, Skoubådene – skibene fra rederiet Ove Skou, Forlaget Nautilus, Frederiksværk, 2004.

Johannesen, Ole Stig, Dansk-Fransk – skibene fra A/S Det Dansk-Franks Dampskibselskab, Editions Maritimes, Roskilde, 2005.

Johannesen, Ole Stig, Mærskbådene: Rederiernes skibe gennem de første 50 år, Editions Maritimes, Roskilde, 2006.

Johannesen, Ole Stig, Mærskbådene II: Skibene i årene 1955-1975, Editions Maritimes, Roskilde, 2007.

Johannesen, Ole Stig, The Torm Ships: The Torm Fleet Through 120 Years, Editions Maritimes, Roskilde, 2009.

Johannesen, Ole Stig, Mærskflåden: Skibene i årene 1976-1990, Editions Maritimes, Roskilde, 2010.

Johnston, Ian, Ships for a Nation: John Brown & Company Clydebank 1847-1971, Dunbartonshire Libraries & Museums, Clydebank, 2000.

Jørgensen, Bent, Helsingør byggede skibe I 100 år: Nybygninger fra Helsingør 1883-1983 og træk af skibenes og værftets historie, private publication, Helsingør, 2003.

Koch, Per, Nakskov Skibsværfts Historie: Episoder under teater, Per Kochs Forlag, Nakskov, 2005.

Kolltveit, Bård, Fra Verdens Ende mot de syv hav: Anders Wilhelmsen & Co 1939-1989, Anders Wilhelmsen & Co, Oslo, 1989.

Kolltveit, Bård, Wilh. Wilhelmsen: History and Fleet List 1861-1994, World Ship Society, Kendal, 1994.

Lange, Ole, C.F. Tietgen, Gyldendals Stereoserie, Copenhagen, 1977.

Lange, Ole, Den hvide elefant: H.N. Andersens eventyr og ØK 1852-1914, Handelshøjskolens Forlag, Copenhagen, 1986.

Lange, Ole, Jorden er ikke store: H.N. Andersen, ØK og storpolitikken 1914-1937, Handelshøjskolens Forlag, Copenhagen, 1988.

Lange, Ole, Logbog For Lauritzen 1884-1995, Handelshøjskolens Forlag, Copenhagen, 1995.

Lange, Ole, Stormogulen C.F. Tietgen: En finansmand, hans imperium og hans tid 1829-1901, Gyldendal, Copenhagen, 2006.

Larsen, Thomas and Mortensen, Finn, Mærsk Mc-Kinney Møller: En personligt portræt af Danmarks største erhvervsmand, Gyldendal Business, Copenhagen, 2008.

Lauring, Kåre, Containertrafik gennem 50 år, Handesls- og Søfartsmuseet på Kronborg, 2008.

Larsson, Berit, Svenska varor på svenska kölar: Staten, industrialiseringen och linjesjöfartens framväxt I Sverige 1890-1925, Ekonomiska Historiska Institutionen, Handelshögskolan vif Göteborgs Universitet, 2000.

Lautrop, Simon, Lindø Værftet L208, Picto, Copenhagen, 2008.

Levinson, Marc, The Box: How the shipping container made the world smaller and the world economy bigger, Princeton University Press, Princeton and Oxford, 2006.

Liisberg, Bergin, Danmarks Søfart og Søhandel, vol. II, Nyt Nordisk Forlag, Copenhagen, 1919.

Mathias, Peter, The First Industrial Nation: An Economic History of Britain 1700-1914, Methuen, London, 1969.

Mallett, Alan S. and Bell, Andrew M., The Pirrie-Kylsant Motorships 1915-1932, Mallett and Bell Publications, Coltishall, 1984.

Mikkelsen, Bent, Danske Rederier Volume 4: Mercandia, Forlaget Betty Nordgas, Ringkøbing, 2007.

Mikkelsen, Bent, Danske Rederier Volumes 7-8: The Lauritzen Fleet 1884-1945, Forlaget Betty Nordgas, Ringkøbing, 2009.

Møller, Anders Monrad, Dethlefsen, Henrik and Johansen, Hans Christian, Dansk Søfarts Historie 7 1870-1920: Sejl og Damp, Gyldendal, Copenhagen, 2000.

Pedersen, Bjørn and Hawks, F.W., Norwegian America Line 1910-1995, World Ship Society, Kendal, 1995.

Peter, Bruce, Knud E. Hansen A/S: Ship Design through Seven Decades, Forlaget Nautilus, Frederiksværk, 2007.

Rasmussen, Frank A., Vedsted Rønne, Bendt, and Johansen, Hans Christian, Dansk Søfarts Historie, Volume 6: 1920-1960: Damp og Diesel, Gyldendal, 2000.

Rinman, Thorsten, Rederiet: Johnston Line under 100 år, Rinman & Lindén, Gothenburg, 1990.

Rodgers, Everett, Diffusion of Innovations, Glencoe, New York, 1962.

Roland, Alex, Bolster, W. Jeffery and Keyssar, Alexander, The Way of the Ship: America's Maritime History Re-envisioned 1600-2000, John Wiley & Sons Inc, Hoboken, New Jersey, 2008.

Sawyer, L.A. and Mitchell, W.H, The Liberty Ships: The History of the 'Emergency' Type Cargo Ships Constructed in the United States During World War Two, Lloyd's of London Press, London, 1985.

Schovelin, Jul, Det Forenede Dampskibs Selskab Aktieselskab - 40 Aars Udvikling, Dansk Reproduktions Anstalt, Copenhagen, 1926.

Shipper, A.M. and Janse, J.M., Mediterranean Shipping Company SA: Over 30 Years of Success, Shipper and Janse, Antwerp, 2003.

Stopford, Martin, Marine Economics, Routledge, Abingdon, 2009.

Thorsøe, Søren, Simonsen, Peter, Krogh-Andersen, Søren, Frederichsen, Frederik and Vaupel, Henrik, DFDS 1866-1991: Ship Development through 125 Years – from Paddle Steamer to Ro/Ro Ship, World Ship Society and DFDS, Copenhagen, 1991.

Thorsøe, Søren, Simonsen, Peter, Krogh-Andersen, Søren and Vaupel, Henrik, DFDS 1991-2006: Skibsudvikling forsætter, World Ship Society and DFDS, Copenhagen, 2006.

Thorsøe, Søren, Simonsen, Peter, Krogh-Andersen, Søren and Frederichsen, Frederik, Skandinavien-Amerika Linien: DFDS' passager- og fragtfart på Amerika, World Ship Society, Copenhagen, 2001.

Thorsøe, Søren, Simonsen, Peter and Frederichsen, Frederik, The Dannebrog Fleet 1883-1993, Dannebrog Rederi A/S, Rungsted, 1993.

Tolerton, Nick, Reefer Ships: The Ocean Princesses, Willson Scott, Christchurch, 2008.

Witthöft, Hans Jürgen, Container: Eine Kiste macht Revolution, Koehler, Hamburg, 2000.

Official Publications

Aktieselskab Det Østasiatiske Kompagni – The East Asiatic Company Ltd, Det Østasiatiske Kompagni, Copenhagen, 1957.

Burmeister & Wain Ships, Burmeister & Wain, Copenhagen, 1961.

Dansk Skibsfart 92, Danmarks Rederiforening, Copenhagen, 1993.

Dansk Skibsfart 90, Danmarks Rederiforening, Copenhagen, 1991.

Det Forenede Dampskibs-Selskab: Fem Aars Genopbygning, DFDS, Copenhagen, 1950.

Fred. Olsen Lines: A Brief History and List of Vessels 1848-1968, Fred. Olsen & Co, Oslo, 1968.

From Lake And River To Distant Oceans: Broströms 1865-1965, Broströms, Gothenburg, 1965.

Andreasen, Andreas, Fyrre år med dieselmotorer I Frederikshavn, MAN Diesel & Turbo, Frederikshavn, 2010.

Graae, Poul, Hundrede år på havene: DFDS 1866-1966, DFDS, Copenhagen, 1966.

Larsen, Kai Rømmelmayer, B&W-firetaktsmotorens historie 1910-2010, MAN Diesel & Turbo, Copenhagen, 2010.

Lehmann, Johannes, Burmeister & Wain Gennem Hundrede Aar, Burmeister & Wain, Copenhagen, 1943.

Oosterwijk, Bram and de Regt, Wim, Back on Course: Royal Nedlloyd – Three Decades, P&O Nedlloyd, Rotterdam, 2004.

Somer, Jack A. and Behling, Helmut, From The Mountains To The Seas: The Sulzer Diesel Engine, Wärtsilä NSD, Winterthur, 1998.

Sørensen, Ole, B&W-dieselmotorens historie 1898-2008, MAN Diesel/Diesel House, Copenhagen, 2008.

Westphall, Poul, Aktieselskab Det Østasiatiske Kompagni – The East Asiatic Company Ltd, Det Østasiatiske Kompagni, Copenhagen, 1972.

Periodicals

DNV Container Ship Update
'The Silver Lining', No. 2, Det Norske Veritas, 2010.

Hansa
'Neue Containerschiffe von Blohm + Voss', No 23, 1973, p 2135.

Journal of Transport Geography
Fremont, Antoine, 'Global Maritime Networks: The case of Maersk', No. 15, 2007, pp431-442.

Lloyd's List
'Big, Bigger, Biggest,' 30 August 2013, p1.

Mærsk Post
'Virket I USA: interview med Thorkil Høst, president for Moller Steamship Co. Inc., 1947-1967', 1976 (særnummer).
'Sovereign Mærsk', No 3, September 1997.
Foreword by Jess Søderberg, No 3, September 1999.
'Den sydafrikanske forbindelse', No 3, September 1999.
'Susan Mærsk sætter ny rekord', No 3, September 1999.
Maersk Sealand i Stillehavet, No 2, June 2001.
'Fra damp til diesel', No 2, June 2001.
'Den nye L-type', No 1, March 2002.
'Containerterminaler over hele verden', No 2, June 2002.
'Containeren før og nu', No 1, March 2004.
'APM Terminals på vej frem i Afrika', No 1, March 2004.
'APM Terminals har travlt', No 3, September 2004.
'To miljøvenlige damer', No 3, September 2005.
'Maersk Central America and Caribbean Ltd', No 3, September 2005.
'Historien on A.P. Møller-Maersk i Afrika', No 3, September 2005.
Foreword by Jess Søderberg, No 4, December 2005.

'Forenede kræfter', No 4, December 2005.
'Maersk Inc. gruppen', No 4, December 2005.
'Optimising the Ship's Design', No 1, March 2006.
'The world is enthusiastic about Emma Mærsk', No 3, September 2006.
Foreword by Jess Søderberg, No 3, September 2006.
Grøndorf, Thomas, 'Changing our corporate mindset', No 2, June 2009.
Axholm, Anne, 'Full focus on handling the financial crisis', No 2, June 2009.
Lund, Jan, 'Targeting the world's largest container market', No 2, June 2009.
Storgaard, Michael, 'A StreamLINE snapshot', No 2, June 2009.
Lee, Philip and Churchill, John, 'We will change the game', No 2, 2010, pp14-15.

The Motor Ship
'The First Long-stroke Diesel-engined Ship: The Leise Maersk, a 4,400-ton single-screw vessel', October 1921, pp230-232.
'The Motor Ship Amerika', February 1930, pp433-438.
'The Gertrude Mærsk: A 14 ½-knot Danish Compressionless-engined Cargo Ship', July 1930, p212.
'The East Asiatic Co.'s Californian Service', April 1931, p35.
'Psychology in Depression in Shipbuilding', May 1931, Editorial page.
'A 15-knot Cargo Liner, Mr A.P. Møller's single-screw, double-acting, two-engine-cycled M.S. Nora Maersk, built for Japan-New York service', October 1934, pp234-236.
'Selandia: The First Twenty Years', February 1932, pp382-383.
'Propelling Machinery and the Efficiency of Shipping', February 1932, pp429-430.
'The First Ocean-going Motor Ship', February 1932, p432.
'A 16-16 ½-knot Cargo and Passenger Liner', February 1932, pp433-439.
'The Largest Danish-Built Ship: The 13½-knot M.S. India. East Asiatic Co.'s 23rd Motor Ship', February 1933, pp502-506.
'New Burmeister and Wain Engine: Two-stroke Single-Acting Units with Poppet Exhaust Valves in the Fruit-carrying Ships Asta and Dora', October 1934, pp246-249.
'Dr H.H. Blache', October 1934, p254.
'Fruit Ships at Cape Town', The Motor Ship, December 1934, p410.
'Motor Shipbuilding in 1934', January 1935, p344.
'M.S. Canada's 20,000-mile Maiden Voyage, December 1935, pp340-341.
'The Selandia's 25 Years' Service', February 1937, pp394-396.
'Scandinavia and Motor Shipping', February 1937, pp401-402.
'The Influence of the Diesel Engine, Scandinavian Shipowners and Shipbuilders' Views', February 1937, p406.
'Motor Shipbuilding in Scandinavia', February 1937, pp408-409.
Chalkley, A.P., 'Rudolf Diesel: A detailed biography and an historical survey of the origin and development of the diesel engine', December 1937, pp314-317.
'Extensive Tests of Supercharged Engine – Trials of the MS Sonkhla, owned by the East Asiatic Co. 35% increase in output from supercharged 8,750 bhp engine', May 1953, pp 55-59.
'MS Bonanza – A 9,530-ton, 17-knot Ship', October 1953, pp304-305.

'£11 Million Programme for a series of eight 20-knot cargo liners', September 1966, pp260-261.

No Watchkeeping Engineers Required on New Cargo Liner: the East Asiatic Co.'s *Andorra*, June 1964, pp98-102.

'The Bridge-controlled, 15,000 bhp 12,765-ton d.w. Cargo Liner *Ancona*, July 1965, pp159-163.

'A £10 Million Series of Danish Cargo Liners', February 1966, p503.

'Which way to automate – Danish cargo liner series points the way', April 1967, pp22-24.

'*Atrevida* – East Asiatic Co's 10,880/14,200 ton 21.5 Knot Cargo Liner', May 1968, pp81-85.

'A Comparison of Container Ships on Order', July 1968, p159.

'ScanStar commences its container ship service to the N.W. Pacific', August 1971, pp209-212.

'First East Asiatic container ship for ScanStar service', October 1971, p304.

'*Falstria* – an 18,300-ton d.w. cellular container ship for the East Asiatic Co., November 1971, pp330-333.

Professor Dr-Ing E.h. J. S. Meurer, 'The Rise of the Diesel Engine – An Outline of Early Developments', special supplement to The Motor Ship, April 1970, pp2-8.

Bille, Torben, 'The East Asiatic Company's Motor Ships of More Than 50 Years Ago', April 1970, pp8-9.

J. Berring M.Sc., M.I.Mar. E., 'Burmeister & Wain – Pioneers of Low-Speed Marine Diesel Engines', special supplement to The Motor Ship, April 1970, pp10-13.

'*California* – The First of a Long Line of Motor Ships for DFDS', September 1970, pp303-304.

'The 84,600-bhp triple-screw container ship *Elbe Maru*', June 1972, pp105-111.

'First ScandDutch-consortium Far East triple-screw container ship completed: The Öresundsvarvet-built *Nihon* of 50,000 gross tons, powered by three Götaverken 850/1700 VGS-U engines totalling 75,000 bhp', July 1972, pp167-169.

'*Selandia*: 60 years on – a 75,000 bhp container ship', October 1972, pp298-302.

'Recent Motor Ships of Interest: *Toyama*', March 1973, p533.

Research in Maritime History

No 23, 2002, Broeze, Frank (ed), 'The Globalisation of the Oceans: Containerisation from the 1950s to the Present', International Maritime Economic History Association, St John's, Newfoundland, 2002.

The Royal Institution of Naval Architects Transactions

'A Beam Model for the Torsional-Bending Response of Ship Hulls', Vol. 125, pp 171-182, 1983.

Schiff & Hafen

' TS *Adrian Maersk*: Das erste von sechs Vollcontainerschiffen für A.P. Moeller, Kopenhagen', Vol. 11, 1975, pp 979-984.

Shipbuilding and Shipping Record

'*Cecilie* and *Cornelia Mærsk*: first two of seven 23-knot cargo liners for A.P. Møller', January 1968, pp18-20.

Sinclair, L. and Emerson, A., 'The Design Development of Propellers for High-powered Merchant Vessels', February 1968, pp161-166.

'*Atrevida*: further developments with Danish East Asiatic's 'A' class', May 1968, pp689-691.

'Odense Steel's Lindøyard today…', May 1968, p688.

'First Europe-US West Coast container service opened with self-loading/discharging *Axel Johnson*', June 1969, pp871-873.

'Scanservice: an eight-lane oceanway between Europe & the Far East', May 1970, p16.

'Line of choice: ScanAustral: Ship integration system gives advantages of total cost concept', May 1970, p17.

'Burmeister & Wain looks for shipyard stability', May 1 1970, p29.

The Shipping World

'The Diesel Motor Ship *Selandia*', February 1912, pp209-212.

'Naval and Engineering Notes: The Motor Ship *Selandia* in the Thames', March 1912, p252.

'From the Shipping Centres Glasgow: The trials of the Clyde's first large oil-engined vessel', May 1912, p491.

'The Motor Ship *Jutlandia*', 29 May 1912, p541-543.

Surveyor: A Quarterly Magazine from American Bureau of Shipping

'Beyond Class: Making the *Emma Maersk*', Winter 2008, pp2-7.

Søfart

'Månedens Skib: *Svendborg Mærsk*', No. 3, 1974, pp18-21.

Jens T. Clausen 'Køleskibsfarten – en specialitet på mange felter', No 3, 1975, pp17-18.

'Månedens Skib: *Adrian Mærsk*', No. 6, 1975, pp14-15.

Newspapers

Berlingske Tiden

Domino, Søren, 'Konkurrenter sejler Mærsk agterud', 24 July 2006.

Mikkelsen, Ole, 'Skibet er ladet med julegaver', 14 November 2006.

Erhardtsen, Birgitte and Vestergaard, Vibeke, 'Topposter: det er godt nok pinligt', 1 December 2006.

Domino, Søren, 'Flere bølgedale end normalt for Mærsk', 1 December 2006.

'Endnu en Mærsk-boss i kulden', 7 January 2009.

Børsen

Andresen, Jørgen, 'FT: Store omvæltninger i Maersk Line', 4 December 2007.

'Maersk kunne have tjent 18 mia ekstra', 6 December 2007.

'Maersk-chef: 50 pct af containerlaster forsinket', 10 December 2007.

'Dyrekilde, Birgitte, 'Kampen i Maersk Line hårdere end ventet', 7 January 2008.

Financial Times

Wright, Robert, 'Maersk halts size and integration strategies', 26 May 2008.

Wright, Robert, 'Maersk container line loses $555m', 12 May 2009.

The Scotsman
'Plight of Shipping Industry' (letter from 'Economist'), 24 November 1938, p13.
'Plight of the Shipping Industry' (letter from Erik Schacke, Royal Danish Consul), 25 November 1938, p13.

Søfart
Brandt-Jensen, Erik R., *Emma Mærsk*, No 36, 2006.
Brandt-Jensen, Erik R., *Margrethe Mærsk*, No. 14, 2008.
Brandt-Jensen, Erik R., 'Sidste containerskib fra Lindø?', 6 March 2009, p147.

Tradewinds
Berrill, Paul, 'Danish Raptor Devours Tiny Torm Lines', 13 September 2002.

Other Documents

Text recounting a voyage from Denmark to Australia and back on the East Asiatic Company's Selandia of 1912, written by former cook's assistant Høeg Povelsen and supplied by his son Poul Povelsen.

PdF of academic paper on 'Modern Environmental Assessment of Container Ship Transport', supplied by Hans Otto Holmgaard Kristensen, Department of Mechanical Engineering, Denmark's Technical University, 2010.

Email message from Preben Terndrup Pedersen to Bruce Peter, 14 March 2011.

Websites

www.worldslargestship.com
www.maerskline.com/triple-e
www.transportnyhederne.dk/?ld=41049 'Maersk Line bestiller 10 'Triple-E' megaskibe', 21 February 2011.
www.maritimedanmark.dk/?ld=10166, 22 February 2011.

Acknowledgements

The author wishes to express his special thanks to Pia Barnholdt Kristoffersen of Nautilus Forlag for publishing this book, to Hans Otto Kristensen and Preben Terndrup Pedersen for checking the manuscript for technical accuracy, to René Taudal Poulsen for checking the manuscript for accuracy pertaining to business history, to Henrik Ditlev-Jørgensen for checking the manuscript in relation to the history of EAC, to Henning Morgen for checking the manuscript in relation to the history of A.P. Møller and Maersk Line, to David Parsons for copyediting the manuscript, to John Peter for preparing the majority of the illustrations and to Ian Smith of Camrose Media for designing the book and laying it out.

The author also extends his thanks to the following contributors of information and additional illustrations: Samuel Barber, Jonathan Boonzaier, Erik R. Brandt-Jensen, Flemming Bredmose, David Buri, Bo Cerup-Simonsen, Michael Clausen, Anthony Cooke, Niels Fisker-Andersen, Ann Glen, Ambrose Greenway, Hanne Hansen, Kjell Harr, Michael Heimann, Christopher Howell, Søren Lund Hviid, Henriette Gavnholdt Jakobsen (Museet for Søfart), Per Jensen, Trevor Jones, Per Jørgensen, Jens J. Kappel, Andrew Kilk, Niels Otto Knudsen, Mick Lindsay, Carsten Melchiors, Hans Henrik Petersen, Troels Posborg, Christian Høeg Povelsen, Peter Povelsen, Russell Priest, Ian Schiffman, Søren Thorsoe and Robert Wisse.

The newly-completed Hong Kong-registered SAAMAX container ship *Maersk Londrina* is seen through tropical heat in the Singapore Strait in 2012. (Bruce Peter)

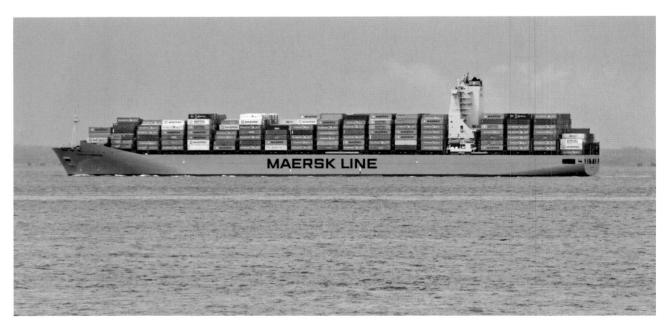

The ***Mærsk Mc-Kinney Møller*** off Århus in 2013. (Bruce Peter)

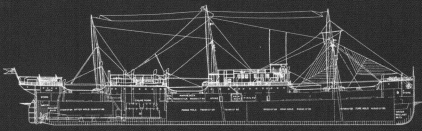

Selandia 1912, 112.7 m (370 ft)

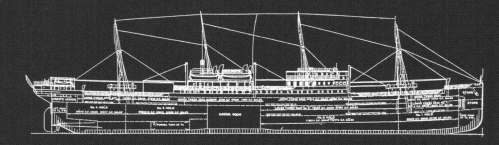

Alsia 1929, 129.54 m (425 ft)

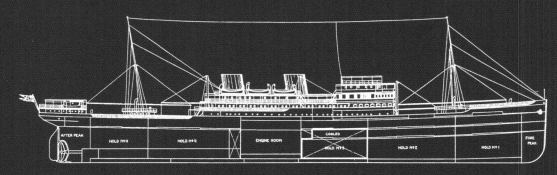

Amerika 1930, 141.73 m (465 ft)

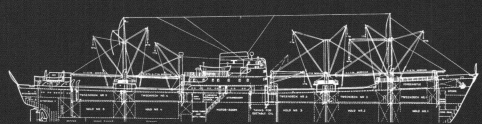

Freya Torm 1953, 129.23 m (424 ft)

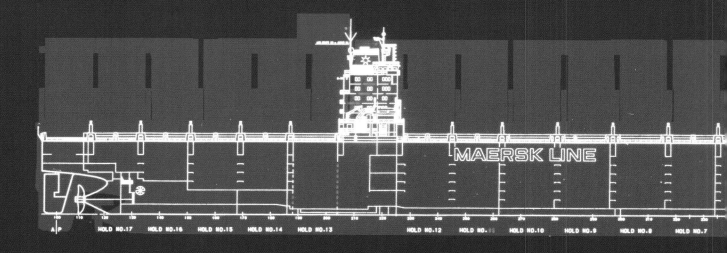

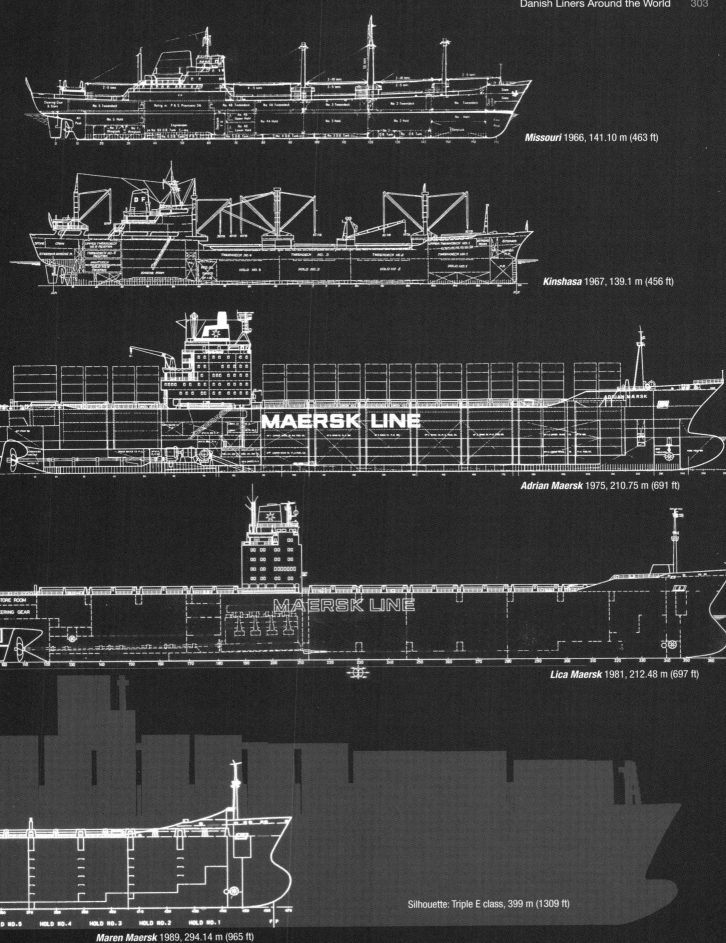

Missouri 1966, 141.10 m (463 ft)

Kinshasa 1967, 139.1 m (456 ft)

MAERSK LINE

Adrian Maersk 1975, 210.75 m (691 ft)

MAERSK LINE

STORE ROOM
STEERING GEAR

Lica Maersk 1981, 212.48 m (697 ft)

Silhouette: Triple E class, 399 m (1309 ft)

HOLD NO.5   HOLD NO.4   HOLD NO.3   HOLD NO.2   HOLD NO.1

Maren Maersk 1989, 294.14 m (965 ft)

Right: The superstructure of
the **Evelyn Mærsk** at
Malaga in 2011.
(Bruce Peter)

Below: The Rickmers-owned
Maersk Eindhoven at
Hamburg in 2011.
(Bruce Peter)